RACE
TO THE TOP OF THE
WORLD

RACE

TO THE TOP OF THE

WORLD

**RICHARD BYRD AND THE FIRST
FLIGHT TO THE NORTH POLE**

SHELDON BART

REGNERY
HISTORY

Cataloging-in-Publication data on file with the Library of Congress

ISBN 978-1-62157-082-0

Published in the United States by
Regnery History
An imprint of Regnery Publishing, Inc.
One Massachusetts Avenue NW
Washington, DC 20001
www.RegneryHistory.com

Manufactured in the United States of America

10 9 8 7 6 5 4 3 2 1

Books are available in quantity for promotional or premium use. Write to
Director of Special Sales, Regnery Publishing, Inc., One Massachusetts
Avenue NW, Washington, DC 20001, for information on discounts and
terms, or call (202) 216-0600.

Distributed to the trade by
Perseus Distribution
250 West 57th Street
New York, NY 10107

NOV ʔ 5 2013

For Tom Thorne

CONTENTS

For the rise of man is endless;
Every goal is only a tavern for his marching soul,
Only a camp for the night
In man's eternal flight.
Yes, some time he will pass the earthly bars,
Laugh and reach out his hand among the stars.

EDWIN MARKHAM
"To the Top of the World, An Ode in honor of
Commander Byrd, who—with Floyd Bennett—discovered
the North Pole from the air: May 9, 1926"

IDOLS

Have you noticed how economical the
human race is with its idols?

It sets them up, enjoys them, then falls upon them
and devours them until there is nothing left.

Even the complete consumption of the idol, if it is
another human being, is not the end. There are then
hundreds of years' worth of argument and analysis
to be worked through.

IDRIES SHAH
Caravan of Dreams

CAST OF CHARACTERS

Richard E. Byrd (1888–1957): A sharp, photogenic naval officer who carried the fire at the beginning of aerospace. He mastered aviation technology in its infancy and moved it several important steps forward through his own creativity and resourcefulness. He was not a coward, not an alcoholic, and not disliked by his men. There is no foundation whatsoever to the raging controversy over his North Pole flight and no substantial evidence that he was afraid to fly or afraid of anything other than going broke trying to make ends meet at the ends of the earth.

Floyd Bennett (1890–1928): The quintessential quiet man—upright, fearless, and taciturn. The greatest pilot and most beloved figure of early aviation, he had known extreme poverty as a child, and the stigma of the poorhouse had left an indelible mark on his soul.

Roald Amundsen (1872–1928): Norway's greatest explorer, a huge wintry-faced man who beat Robert Falcon Scott to the South Pole in 1911. Stoic, mysterious, a master of polar travel, and a victim of financial mismanagement always one step ahead of a subpoena, he and Byrd began as rivals and ended as good friends.

Robert Peary (1856–1920): So indomitable on the ice that he could have been played by Charlton Heston. Peary saw the potential of aviation and would have exploited it had he not been fatally misdiagnosed.

Donald B. MacMillan (1874–1970): Peary's heir and America's foremost polar explorer until eclipsed by Byrd. MacMillan was the classic rugged individualist—tough, crusty, and cantankerous. He always made the right decisions in matters of life and death but was otherwise a loose cannon.

Eugene F. McDonald (1888–1958): Imagine Humphrey Bogart playing George Steinbrenner. McDonald looked like the former and behaved like the latter at his most tyrannical. After inventing the installment plan for auto buyers, McDonald founded Zenith Radio. He was buddy-buddy with MacMillan and embarked as second in command of MacMillan's most ambitious expedition.

Lincoln Ellsworth (1880–1951): A fabulously wealthy and outwardly timid gentleman, Ellsworth abandoned Park Avenue for the polar frontier. Like his hero, Wyatt Earp, Ellsworth had a core of steel, and he was determined to make his mark as an explorer. He joined forces with Amundsen and competed with Byrd. But he always played by the Marquess of Queensberry rules.

George O. "Rex" Noville (1890–1963): Byrd, Bennett, and Noville were once called "The Three Musketeers of the Air." Noville was the Aramis of the trio, a celebrated womanizer. He was also an aviator and a fuel engineer who figured out how to warm up aircraft engines in the freezing cold.

Marie Byrd (1889–1974): Sweet, shy, gracious, Marie was her husband Richard's childhood sweetheart and a silent partner in his exploration career. An old friend described her as "a brave and smiling woman … with all of a woman's love and anxiety and her need to do something actively to help."

Rollin Arthur Harris (1863–1918): The man who started the ball rolling. A researcher with the U.S. Coast and Geodetic Survey, Harris "proved" the existence of an uncharted continent in the Arctic Ocean. His monograph launched an international race to find and claim the "lost Atlantis of the north."

Robert "Bob" Bartlett (1875–1946): The greatest Arctic mariner of the first half of the twentieth century. His life was like a John Ford movie, but unfortunately he looked nothing like John Wayne. An authentic hero miscast as comic relief.

Fitzhugh Green (1888–1947): Surely the Navy's first undercover publicist, Green, a lieutenant commander, described his job as "writing and conniving." He was good at both. An old friend of Byrd's from the Naval Academy, he sledged across the Arctic and blazed a literary trail in New York.

Bernt Balchen (1899–1973): A talented aviator, lovable, ambitious, and enigmatic. Balchen became world famous as a result of his association with Byrd but turned on Byrd after a number of later reversals. Perhaps he owed Byrd too much.

George Hubert (eventually Sir Hubert) Wilkins (1888–1958): An explorer who looked like one. Big, burly, and bearded, Wilkins, an Australian, was backed in the Arctic derby by the city of Detroit.

Albert H. Bumstead (1875–1940): A cartographer with the National Geographic Society, he created a huge navigation aid the size of small jar. He called it a "sun compass."

Bert Acosta (1895–1954): One of the leading fliers of the hard-drinking, barnstorming era. Acosta looked like Clark Gable, tall and macho, and easily glided from bottle to throttle. He pinch-hit for Floyd Bennett on Byrd's transatlantic flight, but the booze took its toll in a critical inning.

Clarence Chamberlin (1893–1976): Acosta's match in the cockpit but his opposite in temperament. Chamberlin was low-key, laid-back, and self-effacing. Quite possibly the only aviator in history to navigate across the Atlantic Ocean by means of the New York Times.

Anthony H. G. Fokker (1890–1939): A loud, boyish, self-promoting airplane manufacturer known for building high-performance aircraft and pulling lowbrow pranks. His favorite dish was ice cream.

Rodman Wanamaker (1863–1928): The opposite of Anthony Fokker. A genteel department store magnate who took seriously his role as a corporate citizen. Classical musicians performed in his store. If Wanamaker could have stomached Fokker, Byrd would have beaten Lindbergh to Paris.

Noel Davis (1891–1927): His classmates at the Naval Academy could envision him as president of the United States. One of the favorites in the transatlantic race until a fatal crash.

Charles A. Lindbergh (1902–1974): The dark horse in the transatlantic race, Lindy was lucky in numerous ways. Barring a court order, for example, Chamberlin would have been first across the Atlantic.

PART 1

THE
TRANSPOLAR
FLIGHT

1

ONE MILLION SQUARE MILES

*Captain Bartlett explains it with
his finger on the polar map.*

*"You see that white space? That's unexplored territory.
There's more than a million square miles of it. We want
to wipe that white space out"—he swept his hand across
the bit of blank space. "We want to brush it away."*

<small>Interview with Captain Bob Bartlett, polar explorer[1]</small>

Just after midnight, during the first hour of May 9, 1926, a Sunday, two navy aviators swathed in furs, their pockets lined with good-luck charms, conferred on a makeshift runway on the coast of Spitsbergen, a glacial island some seven hundred miles north of Norway and one thousand miles above the Arctic Circle. Spring at 78° 55' north latitude is a season of constant daylight. The runway, nothing more than a wide, clear track in the snow, was consequently visible without artificial illumination. It had been shoveled out and smoothed down on a hill overlooking a colony of Norwegian coal miners, the most northerly community of human beings on the planet at that time. A large, blue airplane, a Fokker trimotor, one of the most advanced aircraft of its day, stood at the head of the runway, facing downhill toward the shore and, beyond it, the pack ice on the edge of the Polar Sea. The power plants installed in the nose of the airplane and under both wings were air-cooled, radial engines, a recent innovation. A new and creative technique had been used to warm up the engines so they could be easily started: the mouth of a funnel-like device had been placed over the cowling of each of the three motors. The engine covering was made of canvas and connected to a flue that trailed down to the ground; the flue conducted heat from a gasoline-burning stove. The engine oil had been heated by placing cans of the lubricant in a ring around a bonfire. The snow immediately in front of the plane had been sprayed with water, which froze rapidly enough to ice down the head of the track for a fast start. This was the second time in half a day that the preflight preparations were completed, and many of the men working on the plane under zero-degree conditions had had to be treated for frostbite. An attempted takeoff the previous afternoon had been aborted when the plane failed to lift off the snow. Two out of three trial flights leading up to the aborted takeoff had also terminated at the end of the runway, the plane swerving into a snow bank due to faulty landing gear.

The sun, which had never set, and the moon appeared simultaneously on opposite sides of the blue horizon. The sun gleamed over the snow and over the varnished wooden wing almost as brightly as it would at midday; the moon was a pale and ghostly oval. Neither Lieutenant Commander Richard E. Byrd nor Chief Machinist Mate Floyd Bennett had slept for thirty-six hours. Byrd and Bennett had flown together over the Arctic the previous year as members of a Naval Unit attached to an expedition sponsored by the National Geographic Society. On this occasion they were officially on extended leave. Byrd had organized the present expedition privately, acquiring the plane, a ship to transport it north—the SS *Chantier*, now anchored in the bay offshore—and the services of fifty men who had volunteered to crew the ship and work on the plane. In the process, he had put himself enormously in debt.

Richard Byrd didn't look like an explorer. He didn't fit the popular stereotype—he wasn't big, brawny, or bulletproof. A handsome man, slightly built, with sensitive, delicate features, he looked more like a college professor than a polar traveler, a professor, say, of comparative literature or of Romance languages. When he was out of his furs and in civilian clothes, his appearance and his polite, gentlemanly manner seemed more befitting a thinking man—a man of vision— than a man of action. He was, in fact, both, and it was his ability to balance the intellectual and energetic aspects of polar exploration that brought him within striking distance of an elusive goal.

About seven hundred miles across the Polar Sea, on an ice field or an open lead of water, was a mathematical point that had galvanized the human spirit, 90° north latitude—the North Pole. Beyond that point lay an area half the size of the United States that no human being had ever seen. Byrd was thirty-eight years old, and for the past three years he had been grappling with the problem of adapting a rapidly developing but still new and uncertain technology—aircraft— for use in surveying this unknown and otherwise inaccessible region. He had approached the problem from all sides—theory and practice, navigation and logistics, organization and finances. But he was not alone in striving for a solution. Nearby, an immense gray nose poked out of the long sides of a hastily erected hangar like the tip of a gigantic hotdog. A 325-foot dirigible was poised to transport another expedition toward the pole, an expedition led by the most celebrated explorer in the world, Roald Amundsen. Some twenty-one hundred miles across the Polar Sea, George Hubert Wilkins of Australia was preparing to take off in another experimental airplane from Point Barrow, Alaska.

As always, the issue in exploration was not only to discover what was out there and get back safely (something no one had succeeded in doing since an aerial survey of the Arctic was first attempted almost thirty years earlier) but to get there *first*. Byrd and Bennett bent their hooded, fur-rimmed faces close together, exchanged a few words, and then crunched wordlessly across the snow to the Fokker's cabin door. They had resolved to "give her the gun" and either get airborne this time or smash-up trying.

The outcome would be reported in detail by an international press corps that had converged on Spitsbergen. Their dispatches were relayed to newsrooms in the United States and in Western Europe by radio operators aboard the *Chantier* or at the commercial station down the coast at King's Bay. For weeks now, millions of readers had been following the progress of the expeditions. The vicarious involvement of an attentive and enthusiastic public in the events unfolding in the Arctic had been anticipated (and to some extent engineered) by professionals in the business of exploiting such things. The marketplace, in turn, made exploration over the top of the world feasible. The leaders of the three competing expeditions had signed exclusive contracts with film producers, lecture bureaus, newspaper syndicates, and literary agencies. The contracts generated the revenue that enabled the explorers to meet their mounting expenses.

The prospective fight over the Polar Sea therefore took place in a dynamic and complex world. If successful, it would have a dazzling array of consequences. For one thing, it entailed the possibility of a major geographic discovery. Certainly, it would augment scientific knowledge and demonstrate the possibilities of aviation. It would also be a personal triumph. And in an age of mass media, it would amplify the possibilities of the expedition leader beyond his own imaginings. The flight would open the Pandora's box of a consumer society, releasing its most volatile forces—attention and sensation. The resulting exposure might immortalize the explorer or obliterate him. Or both.

Thirty-five years later, on April 12 and May 5, 1961, millions of television viewers, including many who were young when Byrd hopped off for the pole, watched booster rockets ignite and streak across the sky. On those dates, Yuri A. Gagarin and Alan B. Shepard Jr. became, respectively, the first humans to fly in space. Like the first manned space flights, the first polar flights occurred at a unique juncture in history, when a new technology was adapted to exploration. It was a moment of heroism and national pride, a time when the limitations of the past seemed to have finally been transcended and a far-off future appeared to move almost as close to the present as tomorrow, or the day after. In short, it was an event that marked the onset of an exciting new era, and as much as it was a beginning, it was also a culmination.

Context is everything. The original meaning of the word is "to weave together." Nothing exists or can be understood in isolation. Time and setting are woven together with people and their possibilities.

After all, everyone dreams, some more expansively than others. But the difference between successful individuals living out their wildest dreams and those who are merely living is often a thread that arises independently of the individual and over which one has little or no control: a certain pattern or alignment in the world at large, a favorable set of circumstances, a fitting context. Richard Byrd was a talented leader and manager, and he had vision, energy, and determination. He united himself with the loom of his times, and the context explains him as much as any of his personal characteristics.

His story, then, starts far in advance of his moment of fame and before the birth of aviation. It begins with an intriguing problem that captured the imagination of the world into which he was born.

By the end of the nineteenth century, after hundreds of years of death and suffering in the northern lands, Anglo-European explorers understood that a specialized technology existed for traversing them. This, of course, was the technology developed by the people native to those regions. Some of the most storied names in Arctic lore were tragic figures ignorant of that technology or inadequately trained in its use. Sir John Franklin, the classic example, disappeared with all hands on a voyage in search of the Northwest Passage in the 1840s. Forty years later, Lieutenant Adolphus W. Greely lost nineteen men—seventeen to starvation—in an ill-conceived American assault on the eastern Arctic. (Both parties may have been driven to cannibalism.)

During the Belle Époque, an era of thick Arctic sea ice and cooler global temperatures, a new generation of explorers learned from the mistakes of their predecessors and correctly attuned themselves to the polar environment. They sailed as close to the edge of the Arctic Ocean as the cakes of drifting ice would allow. Then, outfitted in garments made of seal, polar bear, and caribou skin, they drove onward in sledges hauled by dog teams. Like the Inuit, or Eskimos, they ate the meat of the animals whose skins they wore and slept in relative comfort in snow houses the Inuit taught them to make. In this way, the lands ringing the Polar Sea more or less on the eightieth parallel—Axel Heiberg Island, Ellesmere Island, northern Greenland, Franz Josef Land, the New Siberian Islands—were finally surveyed and their contours properly represented on world maps.

But there were limitations to Inuit technology. The surface of the Polar Sea is not smooth and motionless like a frozen lake on which skaters loop and glide. It is rough, fractured, and dynamic. It consists predominantly of fields of ice that are so extensive that if you were on a schooner coming abeam of one and you climbed up the mast to the crow's nest, you would still be unable to see the end of it (or even the middle). Due to the winds, tides, currents, and the rotation of the earth, these enormous ice fields are always in motion. When they inevitably collide, the force of impact reshapes the surface of the Polar Sea. The edges of the colliding fields press upward. The horizon is transformed into a sweeping badlands of ice—heaps, mounds, and piles the size of buildings.

These heaps and mounds are called pressure ridges, and explorers had to surmount them or hew a path through the jumbles with a pickaxe. They were required to portage their life support system—their sledges—over the steepest and most jagged ridges, each sledge loaded with rifle, ammunition, Primus stove, and about five hundred pounds of food and fuel. Their rate of travel could be reduced to a hundred yards per hour or, in a particularly rough stretch, as little as four hundred yards per day. This sort of work naturally wore out men, wore out dogs, and wore out sledges.

The drifting, colliding ice fields cause narrow leads, lanes, and channels of seawater to suddenly open up in one place (sometimes underfoot) and close in another. The impetus to proceed was unusually difficult to sustain under the physical and psychological conditions that prevailed at the high latitudes. With the notable exception of heroic and mighty obsessives like Peary, who were determined to force their way to the North Pole, few men made much headway at all over the Polar Sea. About a million square miles remained at the top of the world—an area the size of the United States east of the Mississippi River—that no one, neither European nor Inuk, had substantially penetrated. The unexplored region encompassed almost the entire Polar Sea. It ranged from the North Pole to Alaska and Siberia and was the largest blank space on the map at the turn of the twentieth century.

Human beings appear to abhor a vacuum as much as nature does. In July 1893, the *National Geographic Magazine* published an article titled "An Undiscovered Island Off the Northern Coast of Alaska." The scuttlebutt of the whaling industry, the reader was told, was that an uncharted island existed somewhere northeast of Point Barrow, Alaska. In the 1870s, the article continued, an American whaler, Captain John Keenan of Troy, New York, was fogbound in the Beaufort Sea, the body of water north of northern Alaska and the Yukon Territory. When the fog lifted, Keenan reported sighting land in the unexplored area due north. Keenan could not investigate; his business was to find whales, not land, and whales kept to the south of his position.

Several Inuit traditions added to the speculation. These were tales of hunters caught on breakaway ice floes in the Polar Sea who were carried off to a strange land in the north from which they eventually returned after many hardships. The author concluded by suggesting "the desirability of calling this very little-known land *Keenan Island*."[2] Captain Keenan, it should be noted, wasn't interviewed for the article. Nevertheless, the imprimatur of the National Geographic Society endowed the mythical "Keenan Land" with a certain amount of reality. This foreshadowed what was to come.

In April 1904, an obscure researcher at the U.S. Coast and Geodetic Survey presented a paper before the Philosophical Society of Washington. Rollin A. Harris, a forty-one-year-old mathematician with a Ph.D. from Cornell, specialized in the investigation of tides and currents. He reviewed some incontrovertible facts about a partially understood subject—the Polar Sea—and arrived at a fantastic conclusion. By Harris's day, it was established that the smooth flow of Pacific water entering the polar basin through the Bering Strait breaks up in the area north of Point Barrow and Wrangel Island. The action is similar to what would happen if you stuck your finger in a faucet of running water; due to the obstruction, the flow would divide in half. Harris hypothesized the presence of a major obstruction in the Polar Sea, "a large tract of land," which he believed was almost as big as Greenland. His conclusions were endorsed by the Coast and Geodetic Survey, and his paper, "Some Indications of Land in the Vicinity of the North Pole," was published in *National Geographic* in June 1904.

Two years later, on June 24, 1906, Robert E. Peary, on his seventh and penultimate Arctic expedition, stood on the heights above Cape Colgate on the northwest edge of Ellesmere Island. He had pushed to 87°6′ N earlier that season (within 175 miles of the pole) and now, having retreated back to the ice foot on the verge of dry land, contented himself with exploring the shore of the Polar Sea. He raised his binoculars. "North stretched the well-known ragged surface of the polar pack," he recorded in his diary, "and northwest it was with a thrill that my glasses revealed the faint white summits of a distant land which my Eskimos claimed to have seen as we came along from the last camp."[3] Four days later, the party reached Cape Thomas Hubbard, the northern tip of Axel Heiberg Island. Peary scaled a cliff of loose rocks. "[W]ith the glasses," he noted, "I could make out apparently a little more distinctly, the snow-clad summits of the distant land in the northwest, above the ice horizon."[4] His entry of June 28 would be widely quoted over the next two decades. The passage continues:

> My heart leaped the intervening miles of ice as I looked longingly at this land, and in fancy I trod its shores and climbed its summits, even though I knew that that pleasure could be only for another in another season.

Polar explorers invariably ingratiated themselves with their sponsors, heads of state, or influential observers whose goodwill it was essential to maintain by naming places in their honor. Axel Heiberg was the principal supporter of the Norwegian explorer Otto Sverdrup. The first earl of Ellesmere served as vice president of the Royal Geographical Society when Sir Edward A. Inglefield sailed north in search of the missing Sir John Franklin. Inglefield surveyed and named new territory in the course of his voyage. The members of the "Peary Arctic Club," the money-men who contributed to the admiral's expeditions, were rewarded with capes and fjords all along the northern coasts of Greenland and Ellesmere Island. Thomas H. Hubbard, for example, a lawyer, railroad executive, and president of the Peary Club, had donated fifty thousand dollars toward the construction of Peary's expedition vessel, the *Roosevelt*. The investment banker James C. Colgate, grandson of the soap manufacturer, had made an equivalent contribution. Peary named the "distant land" he believed he had discovered Crocker Land in honor of another backer, George Crocker. In the terminology of the muckraking journalists of his era, Crocker was an "octopus" with tentacles in chemicals, real estate, railroads, banking, and utilities.

Before Peary returned to the Arctic for the last time in 1908, he was directed by President Theodore Roosevelt to compile data on the rise and fall of the tides at various locations along the shore of the Polar Sea. "It is believed that such observations," said the president, "will throw light on the Coast Survey theory of the existence of a considerable land mass in the unknown area of the Arctic Ocean."[5] Peary took his research responsibilities seriously, assigning his subordinates the monotonous task of compiling hourly readings—around the clock—of the rise and fall of the tides at five promontories along the ice foot of northern Greenland and Ellesmere Island. These observations were made before and after the dash to the pole, and covered more than three hundred days of tide watching.

The controversial Dr. Frederick A. Cook mounted a North Pole expedition (1907–1909) at roughly the same time as Peary's venture. Cook sledged north from Cape Thomas Hubbard, some twenty degrees of longitude west of Peary's trail. En route, he reportedly sighted land far to the northwest, which he named "Bradley Land" after his financial angel—the gambler and casino owner John R. Bradley. Cook allegedly attained the pole on April 21, 1908, a claim that was subsequently discredited. Peary had trudged north from Ellesmere Island. He submitted his navigational records to the

National Geographic Society for confirmation, and these records, at the request of the society, were examined by the Coast and Geodetic Survey. Astronomers at the survey corroborated Peary's claim that he had planted the American flag at 90° north on April 6, 1909. Rollin Harris, meanwhile, analyzed the voluminous tidal data. Arguably, those numbers had the greater impact on history.

Harris put the Peary numbers together with soundings made by Fridtjof Nansen and other explorers at various points around the rim of the Arctic Basin, constructing a model of the ebb and flow of a vast tidal wave. He was able to show that the overall ebb and flow was basically out of whack with the periodicity one would expect to find in an *uninterrupted* sea. He overlooked the topography of the floor of the polar basin and other factors, but nevertheless believed he had evidence of his obstruction. He concluded that there was land in the Polar Sea, some "half a million square miles" of land, which would have made it the second-largest island in the world.[6] He published his conclusions in a monograph in 1911 and from that point on became the authority cited by explorers, journalists, and government officials speculating on what might be found in the unexplored region. Keenan/Crocker/Bradley Land was now referred to in geographical circles as Harris Land. The belief in this lost world was one thread in the developing pattern. Another was a new and evolving technology that would transcend by leaps and bounds the limitations of conventional polar exploration.

The aerial investigation of the Polar Sea was actually underway before there was such a thing as aviation. The Swedish engineer Salomon August Andrée and two companions boarded the round, wooden gondola of a hydrogen-filled balloon on Danes Island, off the northwest coast of Spitsbergen, in July of 1897. A stiff wind was blowing out of the south. The balloon ascended to six hundred feet, descended slightly and floated off over the pack ice in the direction of the North Pole. It never returned. The remains of the party were finally found on White Island, the easternmost island in the Svalbard archipelago, in 1930.

Andrée and his companions had flown almost halfway to the pole when they came down on the ice northeast of their starting point. They had packed survival gear, including a small boat, in compartments in the gondola and made their way over the floes and across leads of open water to White Island. Two more decades would pass before it was determined that the first aerial explorers of the Polar Sea had died of trichinosis. They had shot a bear for food. The meat was infected and insufficiently cooked when they ate it.

The second visionary to attempt to fly over the Polar Sea at least lived to tell the tale. Walter Wellman, a vigorous American journalist, very much in the mold of Teddy Roosevelt, had ambitions of being the Henry M. Stanley of the North Pole. In 1905, Wellman secured the support of Victor F. Lawson, the owner of the *Chicago Record-Herald* and the *Chicago Daily News*, and spent a quarter of a million dollars of Lawson's money on the construction of a pocket-sized dirigible. The 185-foot-long *America* was a football-shaped balloon inflated with hydrogen and steered from a 115-foot control car suspended beneath the gas bag. An internal-combustion engine propelled the ship.

The *America* embarked from Danes Island, the same launch pad Andrée had used, in September 1907. Wellman and his crew ran into a blizzard and came down safely on a glacier three hours after liftoff. He added a second engine and tried again in August 1909, taking off from the same base. This time he lost his ballast shortly after the launch. The ship ascended like a rocket. One of the crewmembers panicked, opened the gas valve to check the ascent—a little too abruptly—and the dirigible came down on the Greenland Sea.

Meanwhile, the first powered heavier-than-air craft had been successfully test-flown near Kitty Hawk, North Carolina, on December 17, 1903. The Wright brothers had made four flights that day. The fourth and final test was the longest; it lasted fifty-nine seconds and covered a distance of 852 feet. The average airspeed of the four trials was thirty-one miles an hour. Within a dozen years, airplanes were flying at speeds in excess of one hundred miles per hour. The most advanced models achieved a range of over one thousand miles and were able to stay in the air all day. Airplanes had crossed the English Channel, the Alps, and the Mediterranean Sea. They had flown in stages across the continental United States, routinely landed on and took off from the surface of the sea, and had been adapted for use in battle. No one was more cognizant of these developments than explorers who had experienced first-hand the limitations of dog and sledge in the rough ice wilderness of the Polar Sea. Or the young men who fancied themselves following in their footsteps.

⇥ 2 ⇤

CROCKER/
BRADLEY/HARRIS
LAND

POLAR NEWS

*"Scientists figure that there might be another Country,
undiscovered up there." Wouldn't it be great if we could
just find another Nation. That would give us another
entry in the next war. And just think of the loans
we could make them.*

WILL ROGERS[1]

R ichard Byrd came into the world between Peary's first
(1886) and second (1891) Arctic expeditions. He was born
in 1888, the year Nansen accomplished the first crossing
of the Greenland ice cap. He was thirteen when Scott first voyaged
to Antarctica. At about that time he decided that he wanted to be the
first man to reach the North Pole. He jotted the notion down in a
little notebook he carried with him and confided it to a special friend,
a girl named Marie.[2] He was fifteen when the Wright brothers got off

the ground and a twenty-one-year-old midshipman at the U.S. Naval Academy when Cook and Peary jousted over which one of them had actually arrived at 90° north. Byrd was in the middle of his senior year when Scott and Amundsen competed for priority at the South Pole. In 1913, during winter fleet maneuvers off Guantanamo, Cuba, he had his first ride in an airplane, an early-model flying boat. It was a rickety contraption, a wooden framework with two sets of wings and an engine. The propeller was the pusher-type, mounted aft. The pilot and the passenger actually sat on the lower wing, their feet dangling over the wing and resting on a float.

Lieutenant Alfred A. Cunningham, the first Marine Corps aviator, had the controls. He had been flying for less than a year. Byrd, an ensign, had met Cunningham on the beach and was invited for a spin. The overwhelming sensations on a first flight are astonishment and fear. Picking up speed, the machine seems to leap into the air of its own volition. It ascends a couple of thousand feet as quickly as a man climbs two flights of steps. You suddenly find yourself suspended in the middle of an immense bowl of horizon, cruising serenely, the world yawning alive beneath the wings.

The unaccustomed mind finds it all so inexplicable and dreamlike. Perched on the edge of the flying machine, the wind in his face and almost nothing under his feet but a half-mile of air, Byrd looked down for the first time on the breadth and roll of the ocean and the infinite rows of waves advancing on the foamy shore. The swaying trees, the hills, the battleship in the harbor, the sprawl of the coast—everything was so miniscule and at the same time his perspective had enlarged. "I remember how much I was impressed with the different appearance of the ship from the altitude," Byrd said. "I knew then that I was going into aviation some day."[3]

He was twenty-four years old. Whether he instantly united his new love of flight with his old ambition to reach the North Pole remains uncertain. But the continuing polar quest and the rapid progress of aviation were about to generate some unusual opportunities. Byrd was the right age and in the right profession to position himself to take full advantage of them.

The moment in time when aviation first converged with the campaign to penetrate the unexplored regions of the Arctic can be pinpointed with a fair degree of precision. A remarkable series of meetings were held in New York in December 1916 to coordinate the use of airplanes in what was expected to be the final phase of that campaign. The participants included the most celebrated polar explorers in the world: Admiral Peary, Roald Amundsen, and Captain Robert A. Bartlett. The indomitable Peary, age sixty at this time, had been an early champion of aviation. He was president of the Aerial League of America, one of the first national associations of aviation enthusiasts. He had also presided over a committee that produced the first aviation map of the United States—a chart showing natural and manmade landmarks as they would be seen from the air. Peary advocated an "aerial coast patrol," a squadron of planes that would be assigned to patrol the east and west coasts of the country to warn of the approach of an enemy armada. Some years earlier, he had predicted that the exploration of the Arctic and Antarctic would be completed by aircraft. "In the very near future," he had said at the 1912 annual dinner of the Explorers Club, "the biting air above both poles will be stirred by whirring aeroplane propellers, and when that time comes the inner polar regions will quickly yield their last secrets."[4]

Amundsen, forty-four, had seen the future in March 1913 when he flew as a passenger in a seaplane over San Francisco Bay. He took flight training a year later and reportedly received the first pilot's license issued in his native Norway. Amundsen had a history of "firsts." He was the first mariner to negotiate the Northwest Passage

(1903–1906). During that voyage, he became the first person to demonstrate that magnetic north, the spot a compass points to in the northern hemisphere, is not stationary but moves over time. Its position had initially been discovered in 1831, and Amundsen showed that the location had changed. On December 14, 1911, he achieved his most spectacular "first," arriving at the geographical South Pole, one month before a British party led by Robert Falcon Scott.

Captain Bob Bartlett had commanded the SS *Roosevelt* on Peary's 1905–1906 and 1908–1909 expeditions. He blazed a trail over the pressure ridges to within 150 miles of the North Pole in 1909; Peary continued on from this point accompanied by Matthew Henson and four Inuit from northern Greenland. Bartlett's next adventure was one of the great disaster sagas of Arctic exploration.

The Norse-Canadian explorer Vilhjalmur Stefansson had conferred with Rollin Harris and had fallen under the spell of his Arctic land mass theory. In 1913, Stefansson hastily outfitted three ships to search for new land in the unexplored area north of Alaska. Bartlett was engaged as captain of the flagship, the *Karluk*, an old wooden sailing vessel. The *Karluk* was not built to withstand the pressure of the pack ice, which eventually closed in, immobilizing the vessel in the waters off Point Barrow. Stefansson abandoned ship, taking five of the thirty people onboard, under the pretext of organizing a hunting party. In fact, he made his way to Alaska and embarked on a five-year program of geographical reconnaissance. Eventually he discovered three small islands in the Canadian Arctic archipelago and welcomed acclaim as a great explorer.

Meanwhile, the *Karluk* drifted westward with the Arctic pack. Bartlett removed the ship's provisions to the sea ice and evacuated the remaining passengers and crew (including an Inuit family) before the *Karluk* cracked in the grip of the ice and sank. He kept up the spirits of the survivors through a severe winter; when the months of darkness finally lifted, he led an exodus to the nearest point of land, Wrangel

Island, an uninhabited sprawl of tundra, rocks, and ice. Like Shackleton in the *Endurance* drama—being played out in the Antarctic Circle at roughly the same time—Bartlett then set out to get help, traversing two hundred miles of pressure ice and open leads *on foot* to Siberia. In the end, he brought his people home. He was forty-one at the time of the Peary-Amundsen conferences.

Amundsen had arrived in New York at the end of November 1916 to shop around for a plane to take north. He had devised a plan based on an innovation introduced by his mentor, Fridtjof Nansen. So long as the Arctic pack drifts in the direction of the North Pole, Nansen had reasoned, why fight it? Why not harness that current for exploration? In the 1890s, Nansen built the *Fram*, a ship capable of withstanding the grip of the ice, and deliberately allowed it to become frozen into the polar pack. Nansen brought sledges and dogs with him. When, after drifting for several years, the *Fram* finally approached the vicinity of the pole, Nansen and a companion tried to complete the journey by sledge, reaching 86°16′ N, a new record. Amundsen intended to replicate the Nansen drift, get as close as possible to the pole, but cover the last hundred miles or so by airplane. Peary and Bartlett decided to organize a project to work with him.

In that fabled era of gracious living, it wasn't possible to make a public announcement of such weighty plans without a lavish ceremony. Accordingly, on the evening of December 19, Peary, Bartlett, and Amundsen repaired to a lavish penthouse across the street from Bryant Park. The occasion was a white-tie dinner of the Hunter's Fraternity of America, an organization Peary had joined a year earlier. Peary and Amundsen were the guests of honor. Their host was Colonel Abraham Archibald ("A. A.") Anderson, the president of the fraternity and a successful portrait artist. The penthouse was the size of a floor of a midtown department store. It encompassed both Anderson's studio and living space, and was extravagantly decorated with trophies representing his principal obsessions in life: objets d'art and big game.

The discoverer of the North Pole sat on the uptown side of the enormous room, under an electric north star. The man who first set foot at the South Pole was seated on the downtown side, under an electric southern cross. They were lean, large, imposing men, Peary and Amundsen, the same physical type. Both had receding hairlines and big noses. In black cutaways, they looked like eagles with folded wings: the Norwegian, prematurely white, bronzed, weathered; the New Englander, a redhead in his youth, now as gray as old snow. Peary wore a handlebar mustache; his face was deeply lined, the result of prolonged exposure to the Arctic wind, and his narrow eyes, after years of scanning a sun-glazed white horizon, had a perpetual Arctic squint. What Peary was, Amundsen was in the process of becoming. Bartlett, an ordinary-looking man, would have seemed (and felt) slightly out of place.

At length, Anderson called upon Peary to speak. Seventeen years earlier, Peary's feet had frozen on the ice, and most of his toes had been amputated. When he rose, still powerful and erect, his whole form seemed to embody his personal motto: *Inveniam viam aut faciam* ("I shall find a way or make one"). He told Anderson and the assembled grandees that *both* Amundsen *and* Bartlett were going to mount drift voyages across the Polar Sea. Amundsen would enter the Arctic pack from the European side by Nansen's route through the Barents and Kara Seas. Bartlett would approach from the Alaskan end and proceed through the Bering Strait. The expeditions would carry airplanes and coordinate the work of completing, in Peary's words, "the geographical reconnaissance of the entire north polar ocean."[5]

Peary felt that he was too old to learn to fly. "I envy Amundsen and Bartlett their youth," he said.[6] He hoped that the operation would be so successful and resonate so favorably with the American public and political class that a new initiative would be mounted in Antarctica, a National Antarctic Expedition under his command. He was almost a quarter of a century ahead of his time; a project of that nature would be mounted in 1939 under the leadership of a national hero whose accomplishments would equal, if not eclipse, the majestic feats of the titans of the dog-and-sledge era.

In 1916, however, Richard Byrd considered himself a twenty-eight-year-old failure. A board of medical examiners found him unfit for duty in January of that year. Byrd had broken his right ankle doing gymnastics at the Naval Academy and had aggravated the injury during a shipboard assignment following graduation. The fracture had never properly healed, and Byrd was unable to stand a four-hour watch "without much discomfort, pain, swelling of joint, and a grating sensation at times."[7] The examiners recommended that Ensign Byrd be summoned before a retirement board, which convened in March.

Byrd was duly placed on the retired list and advanced to lieutenant, j.g. (In the military, officers retire at the next higher grade.) But with war raging in Europe, the navy was loath to lose an officer of Byrd's intellectual and administrative abilities. He was offered—and accepted—the assignment of mobilizing the Rhode Island naval militia. In this way, although officially retired, he managed to remain on the active list. Byrd was immersed in these duties on December 19 when Peary, Amundsen, and Bartlett dined with the Hunter's Fraternity.

For an ambitious, adventurous, and energetic young man eager to soar with the Pearys and the Amundsens, the Rhode Island assignment was utter misery. The navy considered him a "cripple," and Byrd thought of himself in those terms in his darker moments, but he was never crippled in spirit. He would not allow himself to be relegated to a sedentary existence. He carried on with his customary devotion to duty and restlessly awaited his moment, meanwhile wondering if it was ever destined to arrive.

What happened next was uncanny and for that reason compelling. It doesn't fit with the Western mindset, the notion that our destiny unfolds in a straight line or is always in our own hands. In similar circumstances, the Inuit might invoke a folklore figure, "old Torngak," the evil spirit of the north. When hunters set out in search of game and ran instead into a snow squall, or if the sea ice offshore suddenly broke up, trapping a hunter on a drifting floe, the Inuit would pass it off as old Torngak up to his mischievous tricks. Perhaps old Torngak had simply cast his evil eye on those relentless people from the south who sought to penetrate the secrets of the Polar Sea.

Roald Amundsen had bought his first airplane in 1914, but when the European nations began to mobilize for war, he folded his expedition plans and donated the plane to his country's defense forces. When after three years of stalemate on the western front the United States intervened to decide the issue, Amundsen's colleagues in America filed their plans away for the duration, too. Byrd meanwhile seized the opportunity to get out from behind a desk. He went back before the navy medical board in 1917 to plead for flight training. The board could hardly dismiss a young officer with a bad foot who had found a way to fight sitting down and fervently wanted to serve his country. Byrd won his wings and specialized in navigation. His first assignment after learning to fly at the Naval Air Station at Pensacola, Florida, had been to teach navigation during the next training cycle. He was interested in refining the techniques of aerial navigation and developing new kinds of instruments that would make long-range pioneering flights feasible. He envisioned himself ferrying heavy bombers over the ocean to the front. The navy, however, put him in charge of erecting and operating a seaplane base in Nova Scotia and patrolling for enemy submarines. He was in Halifax when the Armistice was signed, working on long-range navigation in his spare time.

The Great War accelerated the development of aviation. In the aftermath of Sarajevo, the single-engine biplane, the kind of plane Amundsen had briefly owned, was used almost exclusively for reconnaissance operations. The fuselage and wings of these contraptions were put together like a kite—a skeletal framework of wood or metal covered with fabric. The outline of the sleek modern airplane emerged from efforts to employ this clunky, first-generation flying machine as a tactical weapon and enhance its performance. All-metal planes with a single cantilever wing (without external struts or bracing) were produced in Germany in 1917. The multi-engine plane was put in service as a bomber by the Germans and the English. Aircraft engines themselves advanced both in size and capacity, from small, rotary models (cylinders in a circle) delivering eighty, ninety, or one hundred horsepower to America's large, V-shaped, twelve-cylinder, four hundred horsepower Liberty motor. Within six months of the Armistice, navy seaplanes were flown in stages across the Atlantic Ocean, and British fliers accomplished a non-stop hop from Newfoundland to Ireland. The navy aviators navigated with instruments developed or adapted by Richard Byrd.

Peary and Bartlett adjusted their polar plans to keep pace with the evolution of the airplane. In December 1918, one month after the Armistice, they announced a full-scale campaign to conquer the Polar Sea through the concentration of overwhelming force.[8] As in 1908–1909, they would sail as far north as possible and establish a base at Cape Columbia on the northern shore of Ellesmere Island, Peary's jumping-off point for the sledge journey to the North Pole. A four-engine seaplane would hop off from the base and fly straight over the pole, all the way across the Polar Sea to northern Siberia. A second branch of the expedition would have embarked from England or Norway and established a base at Cape Cheyluskin in the Russian Arctic. The fuel tanks of the multi-engine plane would be topped off again, and the plane would fly from Cheyluskin to Wrangel Island, the island north of Siberia where Bartlett had led the *Karluk* passengers and crew; a third base would be established here. The three bases—Cape Columbia, Cape Cheyluskin, and Wrangel Island—would effectively triangulate the entire unexplored area. The expedition would map and survey Keenan/Crocker/Bradley/Harris Land from the air and on the ground using small scout planes and dog and sledge parties.

When Theodore Roosevelt died in early January 1919, the project was named in his honor: the Roosevelt Memorial Arctic Expedition. Any land discovered in the Polar Sea by the Peary armada would henceforth be known as "Roosevelt Land."[9] The project was expected to take two to three years and cost at least a quarter of a million dollars. An ambitious plan, it required the prestige, energy, and active leadership of a towering figure like Admiral Robert E. Peary to make it happen. Late in 1917, however, Peary had come down with pernicious anemia, a disease of the stomach that usually afflicts older people. The stomach fails to produce a substance that enables the body to absorb vitamin B12; the result is a vitamin deficiency. In those days, however, pernicious anemia was mistakenly diagnosed as a blood disease. The treatment was a series of transfusions with predictable consequences: there were periods of remission, but Peary progressively declined over the next two years. By the summer of 1919, he didn't even have enough energy for a walk in the woods. He died on February 20, 1920. Six years later, medical researchers discovered that pernicious anemia could be successfully treated by having the patient eat large amounts of liver.

"I admit," Bob Bartlett wrote in his memoirs, "that sometimes when I got enthusiastic about the Eskimos or a little bit sore about the Cook-Peary business, I used to come out with language that wasn't exactly refined. And when I got to describing the muck and gurry of a seal hunt I had to push the English tongue pretty hard to get the colors somewhere near the real picture; and once in a while I used to talk loud, sometimes when everybody else was piping down. You see, a man's lungs get a bit powerful after bawling orders to windward against a gale. I shall always be more at home on a quarterdeck."[10] He was a great mariner, a master of ice navigation, and an authentic hero; his misfortune was that he lacked the *appearance* of greatness. On his own, he didn't have the stature to raise a quarter of a million dollars. He was a blocky, blunt-faced, rough-hewn seaman who spoke with the curious English-Irish accent common to the Newfoundland fishing community where he was born and bred. His eyes were too small, his jaw too large, his ears too big. He was also a bit of a character.

Peary had introduced Bartlett to his patrons in New York society, but society, for all its pretensions, inevitably consisted of superficialists who judged on the basis of appearances: money, pedigree, polish. Bartlett was quickly consigned to the ranks of supporting players, never a leading man. The smart set routinely cast him as comic relief, old "Captain Bob," who could always be relied on to entertain the guests at an evening soirée with a salty yarn. As his chances of sailing north once more as captain of a ship and master of his fate looked increasingly remote, Bartlett started hitting the bottle heavily and fell into a prolonged funk.

Roald Amundsen was initially able to finance his expedition himself. Like many of his countrymen, Amundsen took advantage of Norway's neutrality, invested in shipping, and made a fortune during the war years. He used the proceeds to construct and outfit the *Maud*, a three-masted schooner specially designed to "ride out" the perils of the pack ice. *Maud* had a rounded bottom shaped like a watermelon cut lengthwise in half. An ordinary vessel (such as the *Karluk*) caught between converging ice fields would eventually be crushed by the grinding ice. The *Maud*, instead of shattering, would pop up out of its clutches the way a round, wet bar of soap slips out of your hand.

Amundsen didn't even wait for the war to end. He weighed anchor in July of 1918, four months before the Armistice, and followed the Nansen route east along northern Russia and Siberia. Two years later, the *Maud* reached Nome, Alaska. Amundsen set off again, broke a propeller in the Chukchi Sea, and was forced to winter in among the native people of northeastern Siberia. He put into Seattle for a complete overhaul in the summer of 1921 and, for the time being, settled for having become the first mariner to negotiate both the Northwest and Northeast Passages.

With the *Maud* in dry dock, Amundsen returned to Norway to raise money for the next phase of the polar operation. He returned to Seattle in June 1922 with two American airplanes and two Norwegian pilots. One of the aircraft was a small biplane to be carried aboard the *Maud* when she resumed her drift voyage. The other was an American version of the all-metal monoplanes that had been developed in Germany during the First World War. These planes, designed by Hugo Junkers and introduced to the market by the entrepreneur John M. Larsen, were reputed to have long-distance capability. A Junkers-Larsen (JL) monoplane had recently broken an aviation endurance record, logging the equivalent of 2,200 air miles in a twenty-six-hour flight over New York.

The advent of the JL had inspired Amundsen to revise his plans. Rather than accompany the *Maud* on the next leg of her drift, he now planned to take the monoplane and one of his pilots to Point Barrow, Alaska. He would fly from there over the North Pole to a group of islands in the North Atlantic then known as Spitsbergen. Keenan/Crocker/Bradley/Harris/Roosevelt Land would be claimed in the name of Haakon VII, king of Norway.

Due to heavy ice and severe storms, the steamer Amundsen had chartered for himself, his pilot, and the disassembled monoplane only got as far as Wainwright, a north Alaskan coastal town one hundred miles southwest of Point Barrow. One could just as well fly in a straight line from Wainwright over the Pole to the Spitsbergen islands. Amundsen waited out the winter of 1922–1923 there. By spring, the JL was assembled and ready for takeoff.

The initial test flights, however, went poorly. The aircraft had been jury-rigged with skis in place of wheels, and one ski "crumpled like a piece of cardboard" on the first landing.[11] Worse, the JL failed to replicate its performance in the endurance flight. The airplane's fuel consumption and fuel capacity proved insufficient for the transpolar flight; it couldn't get off the ground with half the amount of fuel needed to reach Spitsbergen.

The *Maud* meanwhile had easily insinuated herself into the Arctic pack. The crew assembled the biplane and took her up for two flights. The aircraft crashed on the second hop, but no one was hurt.

Richard Byrd had been one of a cadre of naval aviators who had worked to create a Bureau of Aeronautics within the Navy Department. In November 1923, the bureau dispatched him to the navy's Great Lakes training facility to organize a reserve aviation unit. His duties included acquiring planes, flight-testing them, appointing flight instructors, and taking the instructors and their students up for check rides. At Great Lakes, he learned that Amundsen had ordered two late-model, all-metal, twin-engine flying boats and had begun organizing a new effort to find land in the Polar Sea. The heavy ice on the north coast of Alaska had convinced the Norwegian to switch directions. In the spring of 1924 he would attempt to fly from Spitsbergen over the North Pole to Point Barrow. The warm Gulf Stream waters flowing through the North Atlantic break up the pack ice and make Spitsbergen readily accessible by sea. Amundsen had invited the U.S. Navy to nominate a pilot for one his planes.

Byrd was one of thirty naval aviators who responded to a call for volunteers. In the end, however, the manufacturer refused to deliver Amundsen's planes because he couldn't pay for them. Amundsen blamed his financial advisor, a man he would later refer to as a "criminal optimist," and declared bankruptcy in September 1924.

Eight years after the quest for the transpolar flight was first trumpeted in New York, Peary was dead, Bartlett was despondent, and Amundsen was bankrupt.

But all the fanfare, false starts, and misadventures, particularly Amundsen's, had focused the attention of the industrialized world on polar aviation. Visionaries saw the Arctic Circle in a new light. Air travel was the wave of the future, they reasoned. The fast track between east and west, between, say, London and Tokyo, was an air route over the Polar Sea. The lost Arctic continent would be the hub of a new crossroads of international commerce. The geopolitical order would shift. Such speculation endowed Keenan/Crocker/Bradley/Harris/Roosevelt Land with strategic importance.

A British expedition brought a small biplane to Spitsbergen in 1924 and reached 80°15′ N, an aerial record. An Italian aviator, meanwhile, reconnoitered the North Atlantic in preparation for a polar mission, while the French, Germans, and Russians announced plans for transpolar flights. The "Soviet North Pole Flight" was conceived as an instrument of the class struggle. The Bolsheviks threatened to deploy "a specially designed airplane with four engines and powerful wireless equipment."[12] As soon as the pole was reached, the following message would be transmitted: "Workers of the entire world: Arise, the red flag of revolution floats at the top of the world."

On November 20, 1923, President Calvin Coolidge had authorized the transpolar flight of a navy dirigible, the *Shenandoah*. Fourteen years before the *Hindenburg* disaster, airships were expected to play an important part in military reconnaissance and a major role in commercial aviation. The *Shenandoah* was 680 feet long, three times the size of the airship that William Wellman launched at Dane's Island in 1907. A slender, silver thing, she was shaped like a torpedo or cigar, or a combination of the two. Lifting force was provided by twenty huge and bulging gas bags arrayed in compartments along the walls of the warehouse-like interior. For safety's sake they were inflated with helium instead of combustible hydrogen. The ship was propelled by five engines each suspended in a gondola beneath the outer envelope.

Shenandoah's home base was Lakehurst, New Jersey, fifty miles south of Newark, where the navy erected a hangar and a mooring mast. The mooring mast functioned as both launch pad and departure gate. It looked like a miniature Eiffel Tower, a 165-foot structure made of steel girders. When the weather was good, the airship was maneuvered from her hangar over to the mast by a ground crew of scores of sailors hauling guide ropes suspended from the dirigible. She was moored to the mast by a cable that extended from the top of the tower through a hook in her nose. There she would be left to bob in the wind, like a wind sock on an airfield. Passengers and crew would ascend an elevator to the tower and board the ship through the nose.

The navy planned to send *Shenandoah* from Lakehurst to the west coast. She would fly up the coast to Nome, Alaska, where a tender would be waiting for her. This ship would be fitted with a mooring mast and would be *Shenandoah*'s Alaskan base. The airship would then fly over the North Pole and annex Harris Land for the United States. Another tender also equipped with a mooring mast would be standing by at Spitsbergen. The mission was scheduled for June 1924 and placed under the command of Rear Admiral William A. Moffett, chief of the Bureau of Aeronautics.

William Moffett was Richard Byrd's mentor. Byrd was recalled to Washington from Great Lakes in January 1924 to assist in the preparations for the flight and to accompany Moffett across the Polar Sea. The Evil Spirit of the North, however, was about to unleash some fresh devilry. In the middle of January, the navy saw an opportunity to subject the mooring mast system to a severe weather test. A violent storm sweeping out of the southeast was heading north; sixty-mile-an-hour winds were expected. *Shenandoah* was left out on her mast to see how the system would weather the storm.

The gale struck on the afternoon of January 16, a Wednesday, inundating the New York–New Jersey metropolitan area with a torrential downpour and winds in excess of seventy miles per hour. Trees were uprooted on Staten Island. Power lines were blown down in Jersey City. Plate-glass windows were shattered in midtown Manhattan; pedestrians were blown off the sidewalks and into the path of passing cars. Out in Lakehurst, at 7:30 that evening, an unusually strong gust of wind—about seventy-five miles per hour—broadsided *Shenandoah*. The impact made the airship twist and spin, and as she rolled over the connection between her hull and nose cap was severed. The nose cap remained attached to the mast, and the rest of *Shenandoah* blew away over suburban New Jersey. A skeleton crew onboard quickly got the ship under control. The torso and stern of *Shenandoah* rode out the storm for the rest of the night and returned to Lakehurst in the morning.

The navy maintained that *Shenandoah*'s performance during the breakaway flight demonstrated her airworthiness. The breakaway flight, however, had occurred at the worst possible time. The dimensions of one of the greatest scandals in American political history were slowly emerging from an investigation conducted by the U.S. Senate. During the administration of the late President Warren G. Harding, a Republican, the Department of the Interior had assumed control of certain oil fields in California and Wyoming that had been reserved for the use of the navy. The oil fields had then been leased to private drillers in exchange for hundreds of thousands of dollars in bribes. The Senate Democrats were leading a full-scale inquiry into the scandal, which became known as "Teapot Dome," after the site of the Wyoming oil field.

Harding died early in August 1923 and was succeeded by Coolidge, the vice president. Coolidge himself was innocent of any wrongdoing, but 1924 was an election year, and the scandal jeopardized his chances of winning a full term. Meanwhile, the secretary of the navy, Edwin Denby, had been exposed as a stooge elevated by Harding; Denby had acquiesced in the transfer of the oil fields to the Interior Department. Three days after the breakaway flight of the *Shenandoah*, the naval committee of the House of Representatives held a hearing on the feasibility of the transpolar flight. Denby testified on behalf of *Shenandoah*, but he had lost his credibility. Key Democrats in the House and Senate denounced the proposed flight as a suicide mission. Senator Clarence C. Dill of Washington suggested that Keenan/Crocker/Bradley/Harris/Roosevelt Land should be called "Coolidge Land" because it was "cold and silent."[13] Dill and a number of Senate colleagues wanted to cut off funds for the mission or launch a full-fledged investigation.

Coolidge knew better than to buck an angry Congress over an Arctic expedition. The transpolar flight was indefinitely suspended.

⫷ 3 ⫸

ANOTHER
DOOR OPENS

I have been dreaming all winter of a trans-polar flight.

RICHARD E. BYRD[1]

When a door shuts, it is said, few people "realize that it is at that time that they might instead be looking at another door opening or preparing to open one."[2] Dick Byrd was one of the few who always seemed to be aware of the other door. His friends sensed this. He had energy and drive, a first-rate intellect, a wiry, athletic physique, and tons of personality. His personality drew people to him as friends, followers, and supporters all his life. He was a loyal friend, someone who could be relied on to listen and lend moral support or guarantee a loan. People believed in him and expected great things from him. At the same time, there was something faraway about him, some farther horizon to which he often tended to elevate his gaze.

He was a bit of a dreamer, but with both feet firmly on the ground.

Byrd was an unusually handsome man with that straight-arrow bearing that members of his profession call a "fine military air." A lifeguard at a beach frequented by the explorer in the early 1920s put it this way: "He is the nearest approach to a Greek-god-on-earth that I have ever seen. Many others have said the same thing."[3] He had black hair, wavy and close-cropped, a broad forehead, blue eyes, a cleft chin and the fine features of a movie star, a romantic lead. He was between five feet eight and five feet nine inches tall and weighed in the 150s. When he became famous, casual observers often evinced surprise that he was a much slighter man than they had imagined. He would lecture and attend functions in navy blues or whites with a breastful of decorations, looking splendid in uniform. But at the height of his fame, he could ride the New York City subways in a business suit and no one would recognize him. Byrd himself bowed to the popular stereotype of an explorer and expedition leader and gave as his vital statistics five feet ten inches and 165 pounds, but he might have been figuring his height and weight with the addition of furs and mukluks.

He hailed from a distinguished Southern family at a time when pedigree mattered infinitely more in American life than it does now. His ancestors were prominent members of the political class as far back as the seventeenth century. Byrd's own level of class-consciousness remains a matter of opinion. "Though he mingled with us with that easy grace and tact that makes him at home in every situation," said the lifeguard who knew him slightly in 1922, "yet there was always that indefinable something that caused even the dullest of us to sense...the fact that he was a true aristocrat and one of God's noblemen.... He was among us, but not of us." However, a New Zealander who met the explorer at the end of the same decade recalled, "Upon meeting him for the first time one is confident that there are no social or other barriers to break down, for one clasps the hand of a man to whose nature distinctions of class and creed are foreign."[4]

For the most part, those of Byrd's friends and associates who left any written records behind, as well as those still living, considered him a "regular guy." He wasn't materially rich; the family fortune had not survived the Civil War. But he was heir to a tradition of achievement, and he knew how the world worked. He had a wealth of connections. He spoke with a mild Virginia accent and did not limp noticeably. So long as he wasn't required to stand watch for hours on end, the bad ankle didn't bother him. His official status at the time of the *Shenandoah* flap, however, continued to be that of a retired officer on active duty.

On January 20, 1924, Byrd celebrated the ninth anniversary of his marriage to the former Marie Ames of Boston, Massachusetts, his childhood sweetheart. On the twentieth of every month he sent her one dozen deep red short-stemmed roses. The Byrds resided in a lovely four-story, red-brick townhouse on Brimmer Street on Boston's Beacon Hill. They had two children, Richard, four; Evelyn Bolling, two; and were expecting a third. Katharine Ames Byrd was born on March 24, 1924. Dick commuted to work in Washington. Despite the enforced absences, which only lengthened over the years, he was, and remained, a devoted family man. The townhouse came alive whenever he returned home. He would bound up the steps and through the front door and say, as the children ran to greet him, "Hello there, chickens, how's your copperocity?"[5] He delighted in making up his own words and his own stories.

At night, he would sit on the edge of Dickie and Bolling's bed, and later on Katherine's when she was old enough, and regale them with tales of a creature he called a "whiffle wolf." It was part dragon and part dinosaur and had wings like a bat. The whiffle wolf came at night to children's windows; good little boys and girls could ride on its back, but the naughty ones had better watch out, because the whiffle wolf would breathe his dragon's breath on them. Sometimes Byrd made up stories about miserly villains who lived in castles in the woods, and he would insert himself into the narrative as the hero who rescued the damsels in distress.

At least once a day when he was home, he liked to take the family out for a walk on the esplanade overlooking the Charles River, the children running to keep up with him. After the walk, the Byrds would assemble around the dining room table behind big stacks of chips and play poker. The family poker game was one of Dick's favorite pastimes. "When it is possible I always walk by the water when the sun is setting," he once said. "That is one of the most attractive scenes that has figured in my life. Another is to watch my children playing when the whole family is present. Another one is an airplane in flight."[6] Asked what his happiest moments were, he referred to a time when he was on an island retreat with his family, writing essays on philosophy. "Outside of that," he said, "was after I learned to fly, when I flew most of the daylight hours. Next comes the period I spent on the ocean with my shipmates."

In Washington, Byrd worked in the Old Executive Office Building on Pennsylvania Avenue at Seventeenth Street. Still one of the most impressive buildings in the District of Columbia, this regal, extravagant structure occupies the entire block west of the White House. It fairly overflows with windows and columns, and looks like it's made up entirely of entrances. In the 1920s, it housed three major departments of the executive branch: State, War, and Navy. While in town, Byrd stayed at the Powhatan, a hotel that stood at the intersection of Pennsylvania Avenue, H Street, and Eighteenth Street, one block from OEOB. The location was perfect, and the hotel was small and quiet, and appealed to his introspective side. There was a cafeteria on H Street near the Powhatan where Byrd often ate and where he struck up an acquaintanceship with H. R. W. Miles, the president of the Columbia Polytechnic Institute for the Blind, which was located at 1808 H Street. Miles himself was blind. When Byrd brought his tray over to Miles's table and sat down to eat, he would always greet him with a cheery "Hello, old sport!"[7] That—the personable, efferverscent side—was the aspect of himself that Byrd was most comfortable displaying in public.

The navy capitalized on every facet of Byrd's personality: his intelligence, organizational skills, and charm. One of his post-*Shenandoah* duties was to write a navy manual on aerial navigation. From April through November 1924, he was sent to Boston, New York, and Chicago to form reserve aviation units. By the end of the year, his working hours were spent on Capitol Hill, a mile and a quarter from the Navy Department. Byrd was no stranger to Congress, having previously lobbied for the creation of the Bureau of Aeronautics. Although he was assigned to the bureau, his principal duty was to lobby for whatever legislation was of interest to the navy as a whole. The admirals had deployed Byrd's polish, personality, and salesmanship skills where they felt they would do the most good, but he detested the role. "I am working up at the Capitol on all Navy legislation," he wrote to a fellow aviator, "and I don't like it any more than I ever did."[8] He was too adventurous and imaginative to relinquish his dreams. When, in February 1924, he learned that the *Shenandoah* mission had been suspended, he immediately went up to the Hill and pushed for a resolution in support of the flight. By then it was clear that momentum for the transpolar flight had waned and that neither Congress, the navy, nor the White House had any intention of reinstating the mission.

Byrd turned thirty-six in October 1924. The closing of the door on the navy's proposed transpolar flight was the turning point of his life. Instead of agonizing over *Shenandoah*, he looked to the possibility of organizing his own expedition.

The plan Byrd devised was entirely characteristic of him. He wasn't going to try to fly from Point Barrow to Spitsbergen or from Spitsbergen to Point Barrow. His conception was much more cautious and conservative. But on its own terms, it was also elegant and highly inventive. He proposed to retrace the route Peary had taken to the pole, but from the air. Peary had sailed to Etah in northern Greenland,

and from there he had established a base at Cape Columbia on the north shore of Ellesmere Island. The sledge journey to the pole had proceeded in stages from Cape Columbia. Byrd proposed to sail to Etah, as Peary had done, in a privately chartered ship, but he would bring with him a small, collapsed dirigible. He would inflate the airship at Etah, fly to Cape Columbia, put down fuel and supplies, and return to Etah for more provisions. Cape Columbia would be the staging point for a flight to the pole. On reaching the pole, Byrd would turn west and sweep across the unexplored area before starting for home. Like most of his contemporaries, he took the Harris theory as gospel and believed that there was land in the Polar Sea. He wanted to claim that land for the United States.

The *Shenandoah*, technically speaking, was a rigid airship, a dirigible with an internal framework. Non-rigid airships have no skeletal structure. They resemble the balloons in the Macy's Thanksgiving Day parade. The pressure of the gas with which they are inflated causes the envelope to fill out; when the gas is released, the bag collapses. Both rigids and non-rigids were used in the First World War—the British called the latter "limps." The U.S. Navy built a series of non-rigids in 1917 and designated them "B-class" airships. This gave rise to the term "B-limp," which in turn yielded the neologism *blimp*.

What Byrd had in mind was a TC-class airship, a blimp about two hundred feet long, less than one-third the size of *Shenandoah*. He would build a wood and canvas hangar at Etah and inflate the ship with hydrogen. A TC-class blimp was propelled by two engines and had a range of 2,500 to 3,000 miles, but Byrd thought he could boost this figure by 25 percent by installing hydrogen carburetors in the propulsion system. This was a deft touch: fuel is weight. As an airship consumes fuel, it gets lighter and rises. The flight crew has to release hydrogen to maintain altitude. The hydrogen carburetor would enable the released gas to be used as additional fuel, expanding the ship's range by five hundred or six hundred miles. If all went according to plan, Byrd would be able to swoop out toward the Siberian and Beaufort Seas before returning to Cape Columbia. He would cover more of the unexplored area than either Amundsen or *Shenandoah* would have done on a straight flight path from Point Barrow to Spitsbergen or the reverse.

The beauty of the plan was that it was eminently doable. By the end of February, 1925, Byrd had enlisted a major ally: Captain Bob Bartlett. "I have never given up the idea of flying across the Pole," he wrote to Bartlett on the twenty-fourth. Neither had Bartlett. They had met at the Navy Department over a year earlier. Bob Bartlett had been an enthusiastic and vocal advocate of *Shenandoah*'s northern adventure, and one of the members of a panel that had convened in December of 1923 to plan the mission. In the aftermath of the break-away flight, he had appeared before the House Naval Affairs Committee and testified along with Secretary Denby and Admiral Moffett in support of the expedition. He had apparently addressed the lawmakers in the same quarterdeck tone with which he bawled orders to windward against a gale: "Hell's bells! What are we going to do with the *Shenandoah* if we don't fly to the Pole? By heaven, I want to see the Stars and Stripes carried to the north. Don't read American history! Make it!"[9]

The cancellation of the flight was another in the series of rejections and reversals that had been Bartlett's lot since the Roosevelt expedition plans were first announced at the end of 1918. He was forty-nine years old now and paunchy, living on handouts and bathtub gin. The Byrd-Bartlett alliance made perfect sense. Bartlett needed a project, and, in turn, his formidable credentials in Arctic exploration made up for the field experience that Byrd lacked. Bartlett gave the enterprise credibility; he also knew all the ins and outs of expeditioning. He was able to steer Byrd to a shipbroker in New York who leased vessels utilized in the Newfoundland sealing trade, the industry in which Bartlett had acquired his sea legs. A steamer built to negotiate the

Arctic pack ice could be chartered in Manhattan for $5,000 per month. Byrd, for his part, contributed vision, dynamism and the U.S. Navy.

As might be expected, Admiral Moffett of the Bureau of Aeronautics signed off on the plan, as did Rear Admiral Edward W. Eberle, chief of Naval Operations, and the new secretary of the navy, Curtis D. Wilbur. (Edwin Denby had resigned from the cabinet on March 10, 1924, a casualty of the Teapot Dome scandal.) The plan was attractive to the navy basically because, in the person of Richard Byrd, it enabled the navy to do what it had wanted to do in the first place. Repackaged as a private expedition, the mission could proceed without congressional oversight and approval. A five-million-dollar airship wouldn't have to be put at risk. And, of course, if Byrd and Bartlett succeeded, the navy, or at least its proxy, would win the race for the transpolar flight. For these reasons, the department assisted the expedition by donating the use of navy equipment. This included the underpinnings of an airship: the control car, motors and engine fittings. The navy also agreed to furnish hydrogen cylinders, the receptacles in which the gas was stored and transported.

The Goodyear Tire and Rubber Company had, through a subsidiary, gone into the business of manufacturing airships. If Goodyear could be persuaded to provide the envelope—the gas bag—below cost, Byrd figured he could mount the expedition for $60,000. Bartlett had leaned on the old circle of Peary benefactors for $10,000. Byrd now had to raise the balance of the money. To do so, he proceeded in the most practical way: he went where the money was.

Like all technological revolutions, the development of the internal combustion engine and its numerous ramifications had produced an enormous amount of change in American life and, in the process, enormous wealth. By the 1920s, much of the latter was concentrated in the holdings of two formidable families: the Fords and the Rockefellers. John D. Rockefeller Jr. headed the list of the twenty-five Americans paying the largest amount of money in federal income tax in 1925; Henry and Edsel Ford were numbers two and three. The Fords made motors, automobiles, tractors, and trucks. The Rockefellers, among other things, refined the oil that motor vehicles consumed as fuel. In both families, power was slowly being transferred from the aging patriarch to the son and heir.

The Ford Motor Company manufactured the Liberty motor, the breakthrough aircraft engine that had been developed during the World War. As a result, Edsel Ford had established a business and personal relationship with Admiral Moffett. Ford trusted Moffett. Moffett wrote a letter of introduction to Henry Ford on Byrd's behalf, and Byrd was subsequently granted an interview with Edsel on Friday, the twentieth of March, 1925. Byrd was also able to leverage his connections and wrangle a letter of introduction to Edsel Ford from Major Oscar Solbert, a military aide to President Coolidge.

In an unpretentious office at the Ford company's Highland Park plant in Detroit, Michigan, Byrd found himself shaking hands with a slight, dark-haired, angular-looking man in his early 30s. Edsel Ford wasn't born to great wealth. During his boyhood, his father had worked days for the Detroit Edison Company and sat up nights tinkering on a horseless carriage. Edsel and the Ford Motor Company had grown up together. Earnest and unassuming, he listened to Byrd's presentation and asked questions.

Edsel was captivated by Byrd's personality and enthusiasm. But there was another reason why he was a receptive listener. Edsel was ten when the Wright Brothers had soared at Kitty Hawk. As a teenager he had gotten together with one of his father's employees and built an airplane—a small monoplane with a metal framework. The wings were covered with silk, the landing gear was a set of bicycle wheels, and the motor a Model T engine bored full of holes to make it weigh less. The craft had flown a short distance and crashed into a fence, but Edsel had never lost his interest in flight. He believed that a relatively inexpensive, efficient, and mass-produced airplane would be highly marketable and envisioned producing an aviation equivalent of the Model T automobile. Ford engineers were currently experimenting with aircraft design as a result of Edsel's initiative. In the meantime, the company had embarked upon a campaign to (quite literally) prepare the ground for the public acceptance of private aviation. The Fords built an airfield in Dearborn, Michigan, and were planning to erect a 200-foot mooring mast in Detroit so that celebrated airships such as the *Shenandoah* could visit the city. They invested heavily in (and would eventually acquire) the Stout Metal Airplane Company, makers of all-metal, single-engine monoplanes, and the Aircraft Development Corporation, a new company planning to manufacture metal dirigibles. Within weeks of Byrd's visit to Detroit, the Fords inaugurated America's first regularly-scheduled commercial aviation service, by subsidizing an aerial freight run between their Dearborn and Chicago plants.

On March 20, Byrd had easily demonstrated his grasp of the technical issues involved in flying over the Polar Sea and had emphasized the possibility of claiming Harris Land in the name of the United States. Another of his selling points was that the polar project would help promote aviation. Edsel was intrigued and pledged to contribute $15,000.

Unlike Edsel Ford, John D. Rockefeller Jr. was not involved in the management of the Standard Oil Company and the other Rockefeller industries. He was responsible for managing the family fortune, some five hundred million dollars, and the family philanthropies. Byrd's entrée to the princely throne was facilitated by a man named Raymond B. Fosdick. The epitome of a dynamic young lawyer, Fosdick was a protégé of Woodrow Wilson, his mentor at Princeton University. When, as president, Wilson brought the United States into the World

War, Fosdick was appointed chairman of the Commission on Training Camp Activities of the War and Navy Departments. One of Byrd's first duty assignments as a retired officer was a stint as Fosdick's secretary. After the war, Fosdick was due to be installed as undersecretary of the League of Nations. When the Senate failed to ratify the League covenant, Fosdick, a New Yorker, resigned, went home, and founded a law firm. His first client was John D. Rockefeller Jr.

Fosdick arranged an audience for Byrd at the Standard Oil Building on lower Broadway in New York, the citadel of the Rockefeller empire. As it happened, Rockefeller was unable to attend the meeting, but the petition of the young naval officer from Washington would not be ignored. Like all good fundraisers, Byrd knew that peers must solicit money from peers. He had therefore prevailed on Edsel Ford to write Rockefeller on his behalf. John D. Rockefeller Jr. lacked the vision and imagination of an Edsel Ford. He was a shy, cautious, dutiful man of middle age of whom it was said, "He never thought of humorous things himself, but he enjoyed humorous incidents or remarks by other people."[10] Responding according to his inclinations, Rockefeller, fifty, deferred to Ford, thirty-one. "Sorry not to have seen Commander Byrd. Was out of town when he called," he dashed off to Ford in a telegram on March 24. "I know but little about his project but if you fully approve it and would like to have me do so I will be glad to join you in the enterprise and duplicate your contribution."[11]

Ford responded in the affirmative, and Byrd had half his projected budget.

"I have been dreaming all winter of a trans-polar flight. I wonder if it will materialize," Byrd had written in his diary on January 1, 1925. By the end of March, he had a plan, the approval of the Navy Department, the support of Bob Bartlett, and thirty thousand dollars.

But resourceful old Torngak, the evil spirit of the north, was still determined to protect the secrets of the Polar Sea. In previous outings, he had hurled disease, mechanical failure, financial mismanagement, politics, and a natural disaster in the path of the most intrepid explorers to sail from the southern lands. Now, with equal cunning, he contrived to place a particularly thorny obstacle before Dick Byrd.

His name was Donald Baxter MacMillan.

⫸ 4 ⫷

PEARY MAN

*What a shame it is that personalities
must creep into exploration.*

FITZHUGH GREEN[1]

onald B. MacMillan was born in 1874, the same year as
Shackleton. Like the hero of the *Endurance* saga, he was a
major figure of the "heroic age" of polar exploration. Both
MacMillan and Shackleton debuted as supporting players in the expeditions of legendary figures, Robert Peary and Robert Falcon Scott,
respectively. But here the similarity ends. While Scott and Shackleton
became rivals, MacMillan was perceived as Peary's heir. MacMillan
emphasized field research and proved a transitional figure in the evolution of modern, scientific exploration; his expeditions were sponsored by major research institutions and distinguished museums. His
career lasted more than twice as long as Shackleton's, he wrote numerous books and magazine articles, lectured widely, and, but for the fact
that he did not die on the ice or collect hair-raising experiences, his
name might be as well-known today as it was in the 1920s.

MacMillan was built like a Marine drill instructor—small, square-
jawed, commanding. Even in midlife, he was strong, athletic, and had
tremendous physical presence. Part of his mystique was that he had

lived the life of a Horatio Alger character; as an Arctic explorer he had pulled himself up by his mukluk thongs. He was the son of a New England sea captain in the fishing trade. His father had sailed north of the Arctic Circle time and again, bringing back tales of icebound harbors and curious mementos. As a child, MacMillan's playthings included articles of clothing made by the native people of Greenland— fur boots and mittens, warm and feathery-light. When he was nine, his father was lost at sea. MacMillan's mother took in laundry to support the family. Apparently she never thought of herself as a widow. Every day she would walk to the top of a hill overlooking the waves and sit there watching for a sail.

As a boy, MacMillan assumed that his father was still in the Arctic. He longed to go north himself because in his mind that was where his father was.

His mother died three years after her husband's disappearance. MacMillan went to live with an older sister, worked at all sorts of odd jobs, and eventually managed to put himself through Bowdoin College. His ambition was to be a doctor. He began teaching at the high school level to save up for medical school. During these years, he opened a summer camp for boys on an island in the Casco Bay area and taught sailing and coastal navigation. One night, responding to cries for help, MacMillan rescued five vacationers clinging to the rail of a capsized sailboat. A few nights later, he saved three people clinging to an overturned rowboat—eight lives in one week. He received a certificate for this feat from the Humane Society of Massachusetts and was written up in the newspapers.

Between Arctic expeditions, Robert Peary, also a Bowdoin man, summered on Eagle Island in Casco Bay, within sight of MacMillan's cottage. The celebrated lifesaving episode brought MacMillan within Peary's orbit. Peary read about MacMillan and wrote to commend him. MacMillan wrote back, expressing an interest in polar exploration; he still harbored his youthful desire to go north.

At some point, Peary arrived at MacMillan's nautical camp and looked down his mustache at the smaller man, sizing him up. Young MacMillan had a receding hairline, a manly face, and considerable charm. He was handsome, bright, outgoing and charismatic. He was the right size too. "Small, wiry men have a great advantage over large ones," Peary believed.[2] Big men eat more, require more provisions and larger igloos, and are clumsier and less agile, a major disadvantage in crossing young, thin ice. Peary asked MacMillan to teach his son, Robert Jr., to swim, sail, and shoot. Eventually, Peary invited him to join his last expedition. Both Peary and Amundsen believed in recruiting inexperienced people; novices were not likely to challenge the authority of an experienced leader.

MacMillan's early career in Arctic exploration intersected with two of the key developments in the quest for land in the Polar Sea. Donald MacMillan was one of the workhorses Peary assigned to monitor the rise and fall of the tides in compliance with President Roosevelt's directive of 1908. In the darkness of the Arctic autumn of that year, MacMillan and a few Inuit assistants were sent out along the north coast of Ellesmere Island to Cape Columbia, some ninety miles from the anchorage of the expedition vessel. They drove a tide staff into the ice on the sloping shore of the cape. The zero position on the scale of the staff was then aligned with an improvised benchmark in the gravel bed exposed at low tide—an iron pipe hammered through the middle of a biscuit tin. MacMillan carved out a well hole around the staff and, over this, his assistants built a snow house. He spent the next month sitting in the igloo on a sledge draped with furs, watching by the light of an oil lamp, as the water surrounding the staff rose and fell. He compiled hourly readings. These figures, supplemented by data collected by Peary men at additional locations, were subsequently turned over to Rollin Harris of the Coast and Geodetic Survey and would become the empirical foundation of the theory of the undiscovered continent.

In 1913, MacMillan led an expedition launched by the American Museum of Natural History in an attempt to reach Crocker Land, the mountainous vistas Peary reported having spotted from Cape Colgate and Cape Thomas Hubbard in 1906. Starting at Etah, the MacMillan party crossed Ellesmere and Axel Heiberg Islands by dog sledge. They turned north for Cape Thomas Hubbard and mushed out from that point over the rough white surface of the Polar Sea. Penetrating some one hundred miles into the drifting icefields, the explorers at last saw what appeared to be solid ground: "Hills, valleys, snow-capped peaks extending through at least one hundred and twenty degrees of the horizon," MacMillan wrote.[3] It was exactly what Peary had seen, but MacMillan understood that it was a mirage.

Recent studies of mirage phenomena clarify the mechanisms that produce such distortions.

One of the controlling factors is temperature inversion.[4] Normally, temperature decreases with altitude; the inversion occurs when the configuration is reversed and the air at the higher altitude is slightly warmer than the layer below. Under these conditions, the atmosphere acts like a lens, blurring and distorting the horizon. This situation exists in the Polar Basin. Beneath the drifting icefields, relatively warmer Atlantic and Pacific water continually intermingles with frigid Arctic water. Therefore, more heat is radiated up from the surface of the Polar Sea than is received by it. This produces the inversion, the blurring lens.

Slight changes in temperature and wind direction or velocity may make the mirage vanish or alter its shape like an image in a kaleidoscope. MacMillan realized he wasn't looking at a real landscape when he started to see the distant "snow-capped peaks" change shape before his eyes. He pushed fifty miles further due northwest of Cape Thomas Hubbard, satisfied himself that he had cleared up the matter of Crocker Land and sledged back to Etah. The ship that had been chartered to take his party north in 1913 had been wrecked off the coast of Labrador. The expedition had transferred to a second vessel that had deposited them at Etah and returned south. Over the next few years, two relief ships had attempted to reach Etah to retrieve the team but were unable to press through the pack ice in Melville Bay. MacMillan continued to mount extensive surveys of Ellesmere Island and northern Greenland during each of the succeeding summers. Finally, the American Museum of Natural History dispatched a Newfoundland sealing steamer with Bob Bartlett at the helm, and Captain Bob rammed his way northwards to the rescue.

Having been cut off from the world like a latter-day Rip Van Winkle, MacMillan was astonished to learn that a Great War was raging in Europe and the United States was poised to intervene in the struggle. He was almost equally amazed when Bartlett described recent advances in aviation. The possibilities boggled his mind. "I know that an explorer with an airplane could accomplish more work in one day than he could do in twenty with a dog team," he told a reporter on arriving in New York. "We could accomplish more in one year than we did in the four I have just spent in the north."[5]

MacMillan enlisted in the Naval Reserves in 1918 and served stateside with the aviation service. He was a forty-four-year-old ensign. His principal duty was to fly as an observer in various types of aircraft and evaluate them. After his discharge, he raised money from his numerous supporters and built a 60-ton, 88-foot Arctic schooner of his own design. The *Bowdoin*, named for MacMillan's alma mater, had a spoon-shaped bow, like Amundsen's *Maud*, and was made of Maine white oak reinforced up to the waterline with Australian ironwood and cement. MacMillan embarked in July of 1921 for southwest Baffin Island, and here he began to overtake Bartlett as America's leading Arctic explorer. He returned to Etah in 1923 under the auspices of the Carnegie Institution and the National Geographic Society.

Two years later, MacMillan connected for the third time in his career with the quest for land in the Polar Sea and, for the first time, with aerial exploration. It all started innocently enough. On January 19, 1925, MacMillan announced plans for his next expedition. He was going to attempt to prove that the Vikings discovered America. MacMillan based his project on an historical riddle: sometime before the first millennium, Erik the Red sailed west from Iceland and discovered new territory. He gave it a marketable name, "Greenland," and soon induced a large number of his countrymen to return with him as colonists. Settlements were established all along Greenland's southern coast. But when Danish explorers arrived in Greenland several hundred years later, the Norse colony had vanished without a trace.

Ice cores extracted from the polar regions in recent decades have revealed dramatic fluctuations in global climate. The Greenland colony coincided with a period of global warming and was likely abandoned when decreasing temperatures discouraged agricultural activity. Lacking the benefit of modern research findings, MacMillan attributed the decline of the colony to disease. He believed that bubonic plague had been imported from Europe to Greenland. He was also convinced that before the colony expired voyages were made to America. He was aware of some curious ruins on certain islands off the coast of northern Labrador. They were about three feet high and appeared to be the rectangular foundations of ancient stone houses. MacMillan intended to compare these sites to the Viking ruins that abound in southern Greenland. In the correspondence of these structures, he felt, "probably lies the first chapter of American history."[6]

On February 7th, MacMillan reenrolled in the Naval Reserve and was commissioned "Lieutenant Commander (Technicist-Aviation)." The commission obviously required some pull, and additional leverage was provided by Eugene F. McDonald Jr., President of the Zenith Radio Corporation. McDonald, a pioneer broadcaster, a promotional genius, and a supersalesman, had co-sponsored MacMillan's previous expedition, and he and MacMillan had become fast friends. Both men wanted to add an extra dimension to the archeological program announced for 1925. MacMillan's commission was the first step of a master plan. McDonald then wrote to Secretary Wilbur on February 28 proposing that MacMillan be recalled to active duty for the purpose of mounting an Arctic expedition and that the navy contribute an airplane, a pilot, and a mechanic to the venture.

"MacMillan," McDonald deftly reminded the Secretary, "owns his own ship, his expedition is financed, but his work can be greatly broadened in scope by the use of an amphibion [sic] plane with which he can explore the interior of Baffin Land, the interior of Axel Heiberg Land, the interior of Ellesmere Land and the interior of Northern Greenland where exists the great Greenland Ice Cap which is yearly pouring out an avalanche of icebergs. These interiors, except for small sections, have never, so far as the records show, been seen by the human eye. Enormous lakes may be mapped, mineral deposits may be found, unknown shores will be delineated."[7]

MacMillan would carry the plane north in the schooner *Bowdoin*. If the channel between Greenland and Ellesmere Island was navigable, he would smash his way through the ice, as Bob Bartlett had done on the Peary expeditions, and establish a base close to the shore of the Polar Sea from which the airplane could survey "a small section of the unexplored area." Thinking within the conceptual framework of his era, McDonald acknowledged that full-scale exploration of the Polar Sea would probably be accomplished by a top-of-the-line navy dirigible. But "this proposed expedition of this summer with the one plane which we are asking of you," he said, winding up his pitch," is merely the first step to do for the United States what will be done by foreign governments if we do not move rapidly."

The McDonald letter was forwarded for review from the office of the secretary of the navy to the Office of Naval Operations.

From there it was forwarded to the Bureau of Aeronautics, where it came before the eyes of Richard Byrd.

Organizing an expedition is something of a juggling act; the leader is usually required to keep several balls in the air at the same time. While pushing his project through the Navy Department and soliciting contributions from Rockefeller and Ford, Byrd also dealt with the National Geographic Society and the Goodyear Tire and Rubber Company. He had every reason to expect considerable support from the former and substantial allowances from the latter. The National Geographic Society had a history of extolling navy explorers, including Robert Peary and the leader of a mid-nineteenth-century American expedition to Antarctica, Charles Wilkes. "It is a matter of pride to the members of the National Geographic Society," proclaimed Gilbert Grosvenor, president of the organization, "that the monuments to Peary and Wilkes in the Arlington National Cemetery were placed there by their society."[8] Grosvenor himself had been a member of the board convened by Admiral Moffett to plan the proposed transpolar flight of the *Shenandoah*. Goodyear, for its part, was an enthusiastic proponent of the dirigible. Paul W. Litchfield, vice president of the company (he would become president in 1926 and chairman of the board four years later), believed the dirigible had a future in commercial aviation and Goodyear had a future in manufacturing them. Byrd had met with Litchfield at the Goodyear plant in Akron, Ohio, on Tuesday, March 10. He could spend no more than $15,000 for the airship envelope and for the next two weeks waited impatiently to find out if the company was willing to deliver at that price. Meanwhile, Byrd went to see Gilbert Grosvenor at the National Geographic Society based in Washington, D.C., some six blocks from the Old Executive Office Building. Admiral Moffett accompanied Byrd when Byrd made his presentation.

At Grosvenor's request, Byrd forwarded on Monday, March 16, a detailed prospectus on the expedition. Three days later, Grosvenor wrote a cordial letter to Moffett rejecting the Byrd proposal. "All the staff of the National Geographic Society have been exceedingly impressed by the unusual personality and force of Commander Byrd," he said. But, "After full consideration of the matter, I do not think that we have sufficient time before the summer season to prepare adequately for the many obstacles that must be successfully overcome if this arctic expedition is to achieve the purposes desired." Three weeks later, Grosvenor issued his statement about Peary, Wilkes, and the Arlington monuments.

Byrd had counted on $40,000 from the Geographic Society and had the distinct impression that he would have acquired it if the negotiations with Goodyear had been wrapped up in advance of his meeting with Grosvenor. On March 24, Litchfield finally sent a telegram announcing that Goodyear saw "no possibility of meeting the 15,000 dollar limitation." There were innumerable expenses that Byrd hadn't anticipated: hydrogen for a test flight ($2,600-3,000); a crew for a test flight ($600-800); gas and air valves ($1,500); and so on. The total cost of assembling, testing, and transporting the gas bag would be between $38,000 and $40,000, exactly the amount of National Geographic largesse Byrd felt the company's foot-dragging had ultimately cost him.

In any event, Byrd had been having misgivings about airships prior to the Goodyear decision. Lieutenant Commander Zachary Lansdowne, captain of the *Shenandoah*, was a friend of Byrd's. One of Lansdowne's officers, Lieutenant Charles E. Bauch, happened to be among the few dirigible men in America who had actually flown in an airship equipped with a hydrogen carburetor, the device Byrd planned to install to boost the range of a TC-class blimp. Byrd was consulting with Bauch through the mail. On March 20, the day of Byrd's meeting with Edsel Ford, Bauch wrote bluntly: "Do not depend too much on a hydrogen carburetor for extra mileage." He also passed along Lansdowne's conviction that "nothing under the size of Shenandoah should attempt this flight." (Lansdowne's input was a bit self-serving; he was privately attempting to revive the *Shenandoah* transpolar flight, albeit on a reduced itinerary.)

Barely a year earlier, a gigantic French dirigible, the *Dixmude*, was lost in a thunderstorm over the Mediterranean on a flight from Marseilles to Algiers. The *Dixmude* was inflated with hydrogen and in all likelihood was struck by lightning. Hydrogen gas is highly flammable—but relatively cheap. Byrd would have been forced to use hydrogen in his blimp because helium was prohibitively expensive. The reason he intended to transport the blimp by ship to Etah, rather than fly to Greenland, was to avoid running into a storm over the North Atlantic and going up in smoke like the *Dixmude*. He was willing to take a 50-50 chance on survival, but it now began to seem to him that his chances with a small airship were only one in three.

The Goodyear estimate settled the issue, and Byrd immediately revised his plans. He had already raised with Bartlett the possibility of landing a seaplane in the Arctic pack in July and August. Bartlett had assured him that the leads cracking open in the Polar Sea during the summer would be wide enough to facilitate water landings. Byrd now solicited independent confirmation of that assessment from two other Arctic explorers, Vilhjalmur Stefansson and Commander Fitzhugh Green. Green, a naval officer on shore duty in New York, had been assigned as an ensign to MacMillan's Crocker Land Expedition. He was the physicist and seismographer of the team. Both he and Stefansson had lately reinvented themselves as writers. Stefansson had published an influential book, *The Northward Course of Empire*, in which he proclaimed the lands of tundra and permafrost to be endowed with vast mineral wealth and foresaw the development of major population centers in Arctic Canada and Siberia. Green had written a novel about a navy dirigible that flies over the Polar Sea and finds Harris Land, and had also penned a number of popular articles on the future of transpolar aviation. "Let the Arctic traffic begin to flow," he reasoned, "and, like Chicago, Alaska must spring to wealth."

Both of these visionaries concurred with Bartlett's optimistic pronouncement on polar landings. Green particularly understood the aviator's point of view and was able to get into the specifics of the operation. He and Byrd had met at the Naval Academy and were good friends. "Trash ice will not bother you. From two thousand feet you can distinguish a landing safely," he said. "What do you think of the practicability of getting up to Etah by July 1st, making Cape Columbia from there by aircraft, and establishing there a cache of food, fuel etc.?" Byrd asked. Green endorsed the outlines of the plan "My one objection," he advised, "would be the rather hazardous situation you would be in if you had to walk back from Columbia. Musk ox would be pretty far to the westward of your march and seals require some training in Eskimo hunting methods."

On Thursday, March 26, Byrd had typed up a formal proposal outlining his Cape Columbia plan for the navy hierarchy.[9] He wrote to Fitz Green the same day and received Green's reply on Friday, the twenty-seventh. In the United States towards the third decade of the twentieth century, the mail was swift and official business was conducted on Saturdays. On the twenty-eighth, MacMillan and McDonald arrived at the Navy Department for a meeting with Admiral Moffett.[10] Secretary Wilbur had turned down McDonald's request for a navy plane and personnel, but neither he nor MacMillan were disposed to take no for an answer. Byrd was one of a number of officers who attended the meeting. During the conference, Byrd did something he would not do for the rest of his career: he divulged in broad daylight the outline of a project that was still on the drawing board.

Dick Byrd had entered the Naval Academy in 1908, when baseball's paragon Christy Mathewson went 37-11 with a 1.43 ERA. That same year, a Tennessee sportswriter named Grantland Rice published a poem ("Alumnus Football") that included the immortal lines:

> "When the One Great Scorer comes to write against your
> name—
> He marks—not that you won or lost—but how you played
> the game"

Rice became established in New York in 1911, and a polished version of the poem appeared in his column in the fall of that year. It reappeared more or less annually after he was syndicated in 1915. Rice's couplet rapidly became an American idiom. It was part of the language that Byrd and his contemporaries used. In Byrd's case—he had been a student athlete—it influenced the way he interacted with the world. In his pitch letter to Paul Litchfield of Goodyear, he wrote:

> …we could so arrange the publicity that we could give you the credit in case of success and you would not get the discredit in case of failure. I would of course play the game with you in every way and consider it a matter of honor to do so.[11]

And, referring to the possible hazards of the expedition, in his letter to Grosvenor of the National Geographic Society:

> I would play the game safe in every way.[12]

Byrd never thought of himself in Matthewsonian terms. He never claimed to be a paragon of virtue. He thought his wife, Marie, was a perfect human being, but since he wasn't, he allowed himself a certain leeway in his adherence to a moral code. He smoked and drank, and was as ambitious and aggressive as any "enterprising young man" who sought to advance himself in a robust era of progress and prosperity. In his own estimation, he was often too exacting and moody. Nevertheless, as a rule he conducted his personal and professional relationships with courtesy and rectitude.

There were practical reasons for leveling with MacMillan. The Byrd-Bartlett and MacMillan expeditions would be able to go to one another's assistance in case of emergencies. (Byrd would have this type of arrangement the following year with the Putnam Arctic Expedition of 1926.) Byrd and MacMillan were both Masons, as were polar explorers Elisha Kent Kane, Adolphus Greely, and Robert Peary. Masons are enjoined to support one another. Byrd had been raised to the third degree at Federal Lodge in Washington and may or may not have known that MacMillan had followed Peary into the brotherhood. If he did not, he might at least have expected the older, more experienced man to be generous with his advice.

But these considerations were secondary. The real reason Byrd was open with MacMillan had to do with honor and integrity. There was only one make and model of amphibious aircraft in use in the United States in 1925, and so far only one of these planes had rolled off the assembly line. Byrd and MacMillan were essentially competing for the same equipment. Byrd knew it, MacMillan didn't, and Byrd didn't want to do anything behind someone else's back. That wasn't how he wanted to play the game.

In the end, he confided his plans to MacMillan because, he told an old friend, "it was the gentlemanly thing to do."[13]

MacMillan still believed there was land in the Polar Sea but far to the west of the reputed position of Crocker Land. He based this belief on his observations of the surface he had crossed in 1914. "Our eight days' travel out from Cape Thomas Hubbard was over ice which had not been subjected to great pressure," he wrote, "evidence that it was protected by some great body of land to the west against the tremendous fields of ice driven on by the Arctic current … across the Pole and down the eastern shore of Greenland." He now proposed to conduct a modest aerial survey of a location—the area north of Etah—where he didn't think land was likely to be found, because on a small ship like the *Bowdoin* he couldn't carry a large plane with sufficient range to reach the place where he was sure land existed.

The essence of Byrd's plan was to advance a refueling depot as a means of extending the range of small aircraft. No one who had flown or attempted to fly in the Arctic had established a cache en route. It was a leap of imagination that sprang from the mind of an original thinker and made it possible for Byrd to envision flying in stages from Etah to the North Pole in an aircraft he might be able to afford. That same leap of imagination solved MacMillan's problem.

MacMillan had turned fifty four months prior to the meeting in the Bureau of Aeronautics. He had lost all but the hair on the sides of his head by now and put on a few more pounds than he had carried on the Crocker Land adventure. He was nonetheless in fine trim and had about him the unmistakable bearing of an outdoorsman. A reporter who interviewed him in this period was apparently riveted by MacMillan's physical condition. "He has the air of a man born to the sea. He is," the newsman wrote, "well set up, and stands wide on his legs, as seamen have a way of doing."[14] Another writer portrayed him as having "the eyes of a seaman, far-away gray eyes accustomed to long distances and great difficulties."[15]

MacMillan was almost killed the first time he paddled a kayak out on a walrus hunt. He had served a lengthy apprenticeship in the north and emerged as a sympathetic interpreter of Inuit ways.

He was in the middle of compiling a dictionary of Inuktitut, the Inuit language. He had the privateer's disdain for the organization man and the self-made man's resentment of privilege. As he listened to the crisp, well-bred Annapolis graduate outline his plans, he understood that the same principles could be applied to a westerly flight. If his gray eyes had seemed particularly "far-away," it was because he had begun to envision a small plane flying in stages from Etah to an area a few hundred miles west of Ellesmere and Axel Heiberg Islands.

5

THREE-WAY RACE

Life is a ball in the hands of fate.

ROALD AMUNDSEN[1]

Roald Amundsen's recovery from bankruptcy had been dramatic. He had arrived in New York in October of 1924 to begin a lecture tour of the United States. He didn't like lecturing; "I distaste it," he would say, in his fractured English.[2] But it was the only way he could earn enough money to begin paying his debts. He sat in his room at the Waldorf Astoria one morning, calculating exactly how much he owed and how much income he might generate over time as a writer and lecturer, and figured that he should break even at the age of 110. He had just turned fifty-two.

At that very moment, incredibly enough, the telephone rang, and the caller happened to be the wandering son of one of the richest men in America. At forty-four, Lincoln Ellsworth had recently returned from a modest geological expedition to the Andes, which he had financed himself. He was tall, blond and fit, and worked out with professional wrestlers. His ambition was to be an Arctic explorer.

Desolate landscapes are uniquely appealing to solitary people. Ellsworth was a loner. His mother had died when he was eight, and his father, a workaholic, had neglected him. James Ellsworth, a cold and driven man, devoted himself to building a financial empire. Lincoln, meanwhile, found solace in the outdoors. He was born in 1880, four years after the Battle of the Little Big Horn and one year before the Gunfight at the O.K. Corral. Like many imaginative boys of his and succeeding generations, he was enchanted by the tales and images of the Wild West. He daydreamed of life on the frontier and as a young adult had followed his bent to the farthest horizons available. At twenty-three, he joined a work crew blazing a right-of-way through the wilderness of British Columbia for the Grand Trunk Pacific Railway. Ellsworth lived and hunted with the Native Canadians of the Peace River country of northern Alberta. He took part in the last wild buffalo round-up in the Bitterroot Mountains of Montana in 1910 and prospected for gold in the Klondike. In Alaska, he became aware of the Arctic frontier and a realm "beyond even the outermost edge of discovery," the unexplored region of the Polar Sea.

Ellsworth managed to acquire an erratic formal education and was trained as a civil engineer. He eventually settled in New York and spent most of his time at the American Museum of Natural History, where preparations for the Crocker Land Expedition were rapidly maturing. Ellsworth made the requisite connections and was considered for a role in the undertaking, but apparently he and MacMillan didn't hit it off. Ellsworth then tried to go north with Vilhjalmur Stefansson. He sought to induce his father to buy the ill-fated *Karluk* for Stefansson's expedition to the western Arctic. With James Ellsworth backing the project, Lincoln could assure himself of a berth on the ship. Fortunately for him, his father refused. In 1914, Ellsworth conferred with Admiral Peary on the use of airplanes in polar exploration. He learned to fly in France during the First World War as an overaged cadet in the French air corps.

Lincoln had come down with malaria in South America in 1924 and had returned to New York for treatment. When he read in the *Herald Tribune* that Roald Amundsen had checked into the Waldorf Astoria, he picked up the phone, called the hotel, and asked the switchboard operator for Amundsen's room. The Norwegian came on the line. Ellsworth introduced himself. He explained that he was interested in Arctic exploration and mentioned that he had access to some money. Amundsen told him to come over at once. He was always one step ahead of his creditors. A summons was slipped under the door of his suite while he and Ellsworth were becoming acquainted.

An Amundsen-Ellsworth polar flight was announced at the Waldorf on November 14, 1924. Amundsen had managed to charm $85,000 out of tight-fisted James Ellsworth, and perhaps as much as an additional $15,000 had been raised from a circle of prominent New Yorkers. He bought the European-made aircraft he had previously been unable to pay for and sailed from New York on February 3, 1925, to accept delivery of the seaplanes. Lincoln Ellsworth followed suit a few weeks later. Ellsworth was en route to Oslo to join Amundsen on the weekend when Richard Byrd met Donald MacMillan. Coverage of Amundsen's latest adventure had been splashed across the papers over the winter; neither Byrd nor MacMillan could have avoided knowing that the Norwegian was poised to challenge the Polar Sea by the end of May. That ratcheted the pressure up a notch on each of them to finalize their own plans and get underway while Harris Land remained undiscovered.

The most serious problem of flying in an uninhabited frontier was providing for emergencies. In case of structural or mechanical failure or adverse weather conditions in the High Arctic, who would mount a search-and-rescue mission? Expedition leaders needed to have a plan in place. Byrd's solution was to take two planes: one to be held in reserve as back-up for the other. He had been candid with MacMillan, perhaps too much so, advising him that the single plane he and McDonald requested from the navy was hardly sufficient.

MacMillan quickly conceded the point. He changed his request from one to two planes and began throwing his weight around town to ensure that he got them. On Saturday evening, March 28, MacMillan was the guest of honor at a dinner party hosted by Congressman Fred A. Britten of Chicago, a ranking member of the House Naval Affairs Committee. (He would become chairman of the committee in 1928.) The Britten dinner was probably orchestrated by Gene McDonald, who had accompanied MacMillan to Washington. On Monday the thirtieth, MacMillan had an audience with President Coolidge. MacMillan and McDonald seem to have been early practitioners of sound-byte politics. The explorer reminded the president that the Danes had established themselves in all of Greenland. Denmark, MacMillan suggested, posed a clear and present danger to an American presence in the Arctic. The future of aviation pointed to northern air routes. America needed to find and claim new land in the Polar Sea to establish the bases that would enable it to compete in a twentieth-century economy. Those remarks were widely quoted in the press. "Mr. MacMillan," said the *New York Times*, "informed the president that he would set out on another Arctic expedition in June and hoped to plant the American flag on land he believed he would discover near the Pole."[3] On Monday evening, MacMillan gave a private lecture in a ballroom of the Mayflower Hotel. It was attended by about forty-five people, including one-third of the cabinet—Curtis D. Wilbur, secretary of the navy; Herbert Hoover, secretary of commerce; James J. Davis, secretary of labor—former Congressman Everett Sanders, the president's personal secretary, and John Coolidge, the president's son, a college student home for spring break.

Byrd was aghast at these developments. He had gotten his project through the navy hierarchy, but Secretary Wilbur felt it necessary to get the president's approval. Wilbur was going to raise the issue at the cabinet meeting scheduled for Tuesday, March 31. Byrd feared that "economical and cautious Cal will decide against me."[4] He wrote to Bob Bartlett on Monday the thirtieth to keep him posted on how the situation was shaping up in Washington. He was, as he sat down to write, evidently feeling like a pitcher who had walked the bases loaded with two outs. Astonishing, how the world had turned over in the blink of an eye. "McMillan [sic] arrived Saturday," he said, "and when he found what our plans were he immediately changed his plans and adopted ours. It is most unfortunate, because it does not seem practical for two expeditions to attempt to accomplish the same thing in the same place."

Captain Bob's reply, written April 1, would not have lifted Byrd's spirits. "MacMillan came to N.Y. yesterday morning," he reported, "and saw the Newfoundland sealing steamer agents about chartering the same ship that I was telling you about. He had in the office with him a Mr. MacDonald [sic], the president of a radio concern."

MacMillan had shown motion pictures of his previous voyage to Etah at the invitation-only lecture the night before the cabinet meeting. Outmaneuvered in Washington and outflanked in New York, Dick Byrd reacted with characteristic chivalry. He submitted a memorandum to Secretary Wilbur on Wednesday, April 1, offering to withdraw "should my request for the assignment of aircraft to me for Polar exploration prevent the assignment of a plane or planes to Mr. Donald McMillan [sic] and so interfere with his proposed expedition.…" Byrd's mentors in the navy, however, were not about to let him fade into the background.

Rear Admirals Edward Eberle and William Moffett were, like Byrd, Southerners. Eberle was born in Denton, Texas, and Moffett in Charleston, South Carolina. Both had graduated from Annapolis well before the end of the nineteenth century. The officer corps in this period was a small, insular brotherhood, and it remained so throughout the early careers of Richard Byrd, Fitzhugh Green, and their contemporaries.[5] Midshipmen were removed from ordinary life for long periods of training and indoctrinated with the virtues of their calling. They lived a kind of monastic existence, first at the Naval Academy, then at sea, and they identified primarily with the service. Richard Byrd represented the future of the service. He was the master of a new technology, one that would sustain the brotherhood in a new age. Secretary Wilbur was also a product of the Naval Academy; he graduated in 1888, the year Byrd was born. Both Wilbur and the assistant secretary, Theodore Douglas Robinson, were favorably inclined towards Byrd. (Robinson was not an Annapolis man, but he was a member of another insular brotherhood, the Roosevelt family.)

Over the next couple of days, Moffett, Eberle, Robinson, and Wilbur resisted the pressure brought to bear by Britten and McDonald, and by Saturday, April 4, a compromise was reached: the Byrd and MacMillan expeditions would be combined into a single operation which MacMillan would command. MacMillan would not be recalled to active duty. Navy regulations authorized the activation of a reserve officer "only in connection with the instruction, training, and drilling of the Naval Reserve Force."[6] Not even Gene McDonald could construe an Arctic expedition as instruction, training, and drilling.

McDonald was back in Washington on the fourth to protect his interests, and he and Byrd got together on that date to work out the remaining details.

Byrd, MacMillan, McDonald. Three dynamic personalities were involved in the organization and management of the prospective expedition, and, unfortunately for Byrd, the other two were allies and already men of considerable accomplishments. McDonald, thirty-nine, was the tallest of the three and had the biggest ego. He believed he had the psychic power to divine winning business strategies. In 1945, at the peak of his career, he reminisced about his youth with a reporter who came to profile him for *Fortune* magazine. He recalled winning a string of Saturday-night crap games in Buffalo, New York, where he had briefly lived and worked on his way up. "I had no system," he said, "except believing I could do it." And then he added: "I seldom gamble but I can win any game of chance." He was described in the magazine as having "colossal self-assurance."

McDonald's signature on business correspondence was one inch high and three and a half inches across. He was equally striking in the flesh—elegantly attired, dark, suave, and forceful-looking. In the 1940s, when Humphrey Bogart became popular, people who came in contact with McDonald began to say he resembled the actor. Their facial lines were similar, both projected a latent sense of menace, and, like Bogart, McDonald was able to suggest, with a curl of his lip, that the consequences of disappointing him would not be agreeable. But there was something beyond mere physical resemblance that made the comparison seem so apt. It was a certain quality that defined the very essence of Eugene McDonald: he simply carried himself like a star.

McDonald had started out as a car salesman. He found his way to bustling Chicago before the First World War, invented the practice of buying and selling cars on the installment plan, and made a fortune. He enlisted in the navy in 1917, served stateside in Naval Intelligence, and emerged as a lieutenant commander in the reserves. Looking around for a new business opportunity in the years immediately following the Armistice, he discovered radio and decided to play a hunch. The radio industry at the beginning of the 1920s was in exactly the same position as the personal computer industry at the beginning of the 1980s. The first regular commercial broadcasts were made late in 1920 by independent stations in Pittsburgh and Detroit. In 1921, McDonald met two young men who called themselves the "Chicago Radio Laboratory." They were operating a mail-order business, basically from a kitchen table, building and selling radio sets. They also had an amateur radio station. There was no such thing as a radio network then, no *Jack Benny Program*, no *Burns and Allen Show*; nevertheless, McDonald saw dollar signs and possibilities, and offered to be the money man in the enterprise. In 1923, the Chicago Radio Laboratory formally became the Zenith Radio Corporation. McDonald became company president.

MacMillan and McDonald were introduced by a mutual friend at a dinner given in MacMillan's honor when the explorer arrived in Chicago during his 1923 lecture tour. McDonald, the marketing whiz, had an inspiration. He prevailed on MacMillan to take some of Zenith's experimental short-wave equipment with him on his next expedition. MacMillan was intrigued by the idea. McDonald had built Chicago's premier radio station, WJAZ, and had become a broadcaster as well as a manufacturer. On Wednesday evenings during the winter of 1923–24, he hosted a weekly program devoted to transmitting news and messages to the MacMillan party in northern Greenland. The shows attracted a large audience. Zenith rapidly launched a new advertising campaign emphasizing the brand's role in an Arctic expedition commanded by a famous explorer.

McDonald sought to help MacMillan expand the scope of his 1925 venture because MacMillan helped promote Zenith. Whatever he did was (or could be) associated in the public mind with Zenith Radio. The more newsworthy the expedition, the more people would pay attention to it. The more people, the more potential Zenith customers.

That was one reason; there was another. In June of 1923, McDonald had accompanied MacMillan on the first leg of the *Bowdoin*'s Arctic voyage. He had sailed as far as Labrador then went back to Chicago to do the radio broadcasts. He had liked what he had seen of the north and was going to participate as a full-fledged member of the expedition this time around. Due to his inflated sense of self, that expedition would have to be as spectacular as possible. When McDonald sat down with Byrd in Washington, he held power of attorney for MacMillan and proceeded to negotiate a one-sided agreement. He brought a bullying, board-room swagger to the proceedings. He insisted that MacMillan have the prerogative of naming his own second in command. It was understood that the slot was not going to be filled by Lieutenant Commander Richard Byrd, but by Lieutenant Commander Eugene McDonald. Byrd would be in charge of a unit of Naval aviators assigned to the expedition, but in the overall command structure, he would be subordinate to an imperious broadcaster.

The aviators would not follow Byrd's original flight path and wing straight to the North Pole, then veer west and south over the unexplored area of the Polar Sea. McDonald ordained that the primary mission of the navy unit would be to fly west out of Cape Thomas Hubbard and pick up the search for Harris Land where MacMillan had left off with dog and sledge in 1914. Afterward, they would follow the rest of the MacMillan agenda, which included aerial surveys of the Greenland ice cap and the interior of Axel Heiberg Island, Ellesmere Island, Baffin Island, and northern Labrador; the examination of Norse ruins in southern Greenland; and a journey to the archeological sites MacMillan had discovered off the Labrador coast.

From the search for land in the Polar Sea to Viking ruins and the vaunted "first chapter in American history," the expedition as conceived by MacMillan and McDonald had begun to sound like a

vaudeville bill with a headline attraction and a bunch of smash supporting acts. How the entire program was supposed to be accomplished in the space of one brief Arctic summer was a moot point the
impresarios never seemed to have stopped to consider.

McDonald did not invite discussion.

"I have the impression quite strongly," Byrd wrote to Fitzhugh
Green, "that I am up against an extremely selfish outfit that drives an
extremely hard bargain. I am afraid I am going to be up against it,
because McDonald does not seem to be able to give at all when a point
arises, and I rather imagine McMillan [sic] is the same type." Byrd
was even required to sign a nondisclosure provision that prohibited
him from divulging any information about the expedition without the
written permission of Donald MacMillan.

"I can not give a talk in my own home if I want to," he told Green.

Roald Amundsen was not the only European entry in the race for
the transpolar flight in 1925. Aerial ventures that were supposed to
have been launched from Rome, Paris, Berlin, and Moscow had so
far failed to get off the ground, but a private expedition was being
organized in Liverpool at the same time that the MacMillan extrava-
ganza was taking shape in Washington. The leader was a husky, boyish twenty-three-year-old Icelandic British Canadian named Grettir
Algarsson. Algarsson had high cheekbones, fair, wavy hair, and gray
eyes, and was an officer in the British merchant service. He was born
in Vancouver, British Columbia. His parents, the Algarssons, were
from Iceland, but Grettir had been adopted and raised by a Scottish
family, the Davidsons.

In 1925, he was living in Liverpool and working for the Blue Fun-
nel Line. Algarsson liked to sketch ships, planes, and mechanical
contrivances, and he had devised a plan that could only have been
formulated by a young man who was both wildly imaginative and

strapped for cash. He wanted to fly from Spitsbergen to the North Pole, but was unable to raise enough money for aircraft capable of reaching the Pole and returning to base. He therefore proposed to buy a plane that at least had sufficient range for the first leg. He would take off from Spitsbergen, crash-land at the Pole, and sledge back. This led to the intervention of a friend—a fellow Icelander—who had no faith in airplanes but offered to put up the money for a small airship to carry Algarsson to his goal *and* bring him safely back to King's Bay.

That put Algarsson in the running. He contracted for a blimp one-seventh the size of the dirigible Byrd had originally intended to use and bought a fifty-one-year-old steamer to transport the expedition to the Arctic. He also arranged for the vessel to be helmed by one of the men who had followed Ernest Shackleton to the ends of the earth and become a hero in his own right, the legendary Frank Worsley. Worsley had captained the *Endurance* on Ernest Shackleton's greatest adventure, and, after *Endurance* succumbed to the ice, he had navigated the lifeboat, the *James Caird*, on the extraordinary, 700-mile journey to the Island of South Georgia. Frank Worsley gave Algarsson the kind of instant credibility that Bob Bartlett had brought to Byrd's erstwhile North Pole project. By mid-April, Algarsson's steamer had arrived in Liverpool for refitting, and a pilot had been recruited to fly Algarsson to the Pole, a Lieutenant Humphrey Humphries of the RAF.

Algarsson had attempted to sail to the Arctic the previous year but had run into foul weather and bad luck. During a turbulent night in the North Sea, his little ship struck some floating wreckage and nearly foundered. He was considered a dark horse in the polar derby. Amundsen was the heavy favorite. The Norwegian had purchased two huge, all-metal flying boats made in Italy by Dornier, a German manufacturer. Flying boats are seaplanes with a watertight fuselage that floats in the water like the hull of a surface ship. Amundsen's planes—the Dornier *Wal,* German for whale—had one of the most unique designs in the history of aeronautics. They measured fifty-five feet long (eight feet shorter than a DC-3) and looked like a whale with a single high wing (like a modern Cessna). On top of the wing, over the center of the fuselage were two Rolls Royce engines, one *behind* the other. The pilot sat forward of the engines in an open cockpit about where the spout would be on a real whale. Passengers were carried in an enclosed and heated cabin in the belly of the plane.

A Norwegian naval vessel had been procured to transport the explorers and their aircraft to Spitsbergen. Amundsen and Ellsworth took off from King's Bay on May 21, a month before either Algarsson and Worsley or MacMillan and Byrd were prepared to weigh anchor. Amundsen captained one of the flying boats, Ellsworth the other. Each was accompanied by a two-man crew: a pilot and a mechanic. They hopped off the water at 5:15 p.m. on a clear and beautiful day, not far from where Andrée ascended in his balloon almost three decades earlier. The newspapers had played up the three-way race all spring; Amundsen's departure made headlines around the world. In the ensuing days and weeks, however, he and Ellsworth neither returned to Spitsbergen nor arrived in Alaska. The disappearance of the explorers would become an even bigger story.

The rapidity with which major expeditions were organized in the 1920s is altogether remarkable. When Byrd and McDonald signed their names to the agreement of April 4, they had nothing in place other than the intention of embarking in June. Three days later, McDonald, who was still in Washington, negotiated a deal with Grosvenor.[7] The MacMillan-navy enterprise would embark under the auspices of the National Geographic Society. MacMillan would write an article for the *National Geographic Magazine,* and the Society would have an option on all other reports and commentaries to emerge from the expedition, and exclusive rights to the photographs. Two representatives of the Society would accompany the expedition. In exchange for these considerations, the Society contributed $40,000.

On April 18, Byrd and MacMillan signed an agreement giving MacMillan "book rights" and "priority" in the matter of "lectures, newspaper and magazine articles."[8] Byrd, meanwhile, had been keeping his benefactors, Edsel Ford and John D. Rockefeller Jr., informed about the joint undertaking with MacMillan. Byrd felt uneasy about asking Ford and Rockefeller to deliver on the funds they had pledged since he was no longer on his own and the nature of the outing had changed so drastically from the proposal he had outlined in March. He merely requested that the Ford and Rockefeller donations be made available to him in the future "in case there [was] still left next year much to do for science." He now devoted his full attention to equipping and staffing the unit that would journey to the Arctic under his command.

The airplanes assigned to the expedition by the navy actually belonged to the army, and they did not in fact exist. They had been ordered from the manufacturer and were in production. In July of 1924, the U.S. Army Air Corps had placed an order for ten revolutionary new amphibians designed by Grover Loening, a brilliant engineer who was born in the same year as Richard Byrd. An amphibian is a flying boat with retractable wheels—an airplane that can take off and land both at sea and on dry ground. The Loening Amphibian was the only aircraft of this type on an American ramp in the spring of 1925; it was also, in its own way, equally as eccentric as Amundsen's Dornier Whales. Loening's ships were biplanes with two cockpits, one behind the other. (He would have preferred to build a monoplane, but biplanes were more marketable in the twenties when people erroneously assumed that two wings were better than one.) The framework was made of wood and was completely covered with watertight metal sheeting. A long prow protruded out from under the propeller like the bill of a duck or a Ubangi lip. This part of the air-craft—the lower fuselage—was designed to float on water. Overall, the ship looked like a small biplane cemented on top of a large kayak. The landing gear could be raised and lowered by pushing a button on the instrument panel or operating a hand crank. When the mechanism was engaged, the wheels would move like the flapping arms of an athlete doing jumping jacks: they would rotate upwards and fold into an indentation on either side of the lower prow, or rotate downwards for a landing on a dirt field.

The first Loening Amphibian was delivered to the army in January of 1925. The navy subsequently contracted for the planes but had to wait in line behind the army. Loening was a New Yorker. His planes were manufactured in a small plant on the East River at 31st Street, next door to a furniture factory. When a plane was assembled, it would be rolled out onto the docks and lifted by crane into the river for flight testing. The rest of the planes ordered by the army had to be built before the navy aircraft could be put into production.

Byrd led a navy assault on the army production schedule. He went up to the Capitol and argued persuasively that since the army intended to employ the Loenings in low-profile operations such as coast artil-lery spotting, American prestige and American aviation would be infinitely enhanced if the planes were assigned to the navy for its heroic quest for land in the Polar Sea. Secretary Wilbur essentially conveyed the same message to President Coolidge. In the end, the army was forced to relinquish to the navy the next three Amphibians that rolled out of the Loening plant.

Arctic flying was considered exceptionally hazardous. The death of Robert Scott and the privations of polar explorers from Greely to Shackleton established a certain atmosphere in the first quarter of the twentieth century that has almost completely dissipated. There was, in this period, a graveyard feeling associated with the polar regions, a sense of walking among the ghosts of disasters past. The perils of pioneer aviation amplified these feelings. No one had ever flown an airplane in the high latitudes without mishap. Like the sound barrier at a later stage of aviation history, the Polar Sea seemed to impose a kind of limit to powered flight. To attempt to transcend it was to take one's life in one's hands. For this reason, Coolidge insisted that the personnel assigned to the MacMillan expedition must be volunteers. Forty-three sailors and marines applied to join the navy contingent. MacMillan recommended that every applicant five foot eight or taller should be eliminated. "Big men are like big dogs," he said, "they wear out too quickly."[9] This may be taken as another allusion to Arctic dangers, from the point of view of a dog-and-sledge man. MacMillan, a bachelor, did not want any married men either. "I want men who are not hampered by families and who will not spend their leisure time contemplating the plight of their dependents. We must," he said, "have contented men."

Byrd chose people on the basis of competence, selecting two renowned navy pilots and three well-regarded pilot-mechanics. He also took an aerologist, an aviation weather specialist. The aerologist was a navy man with the rank of "Aerographer." His job was to set up a weather station in the Arctic and make forecasts on the spot. In addition to this, the aerologist had a special duty to perform that perhaps can best be understood with reference to the prevailing atmosphere of the times. The Department of the Navy was expected to take every precaution to ensure the safety of its aviators. Suppose a pilot made a forced landing in the bleak ice world of the Polar Sea and his ship was smashed and his radio rendered inoperative, how would he call for help? To reckon with such emergencies, the Department employed the most reliable, fail-safe technology at its disposal: it assigned ten U.S. Navy carrier pigeons to the expedition. The pigeons were based in the District of Columbia and were said to be capable of flying 500 miles a day to return home. They were fed on an international diet of Argentine corn, Kaffir corn, Canada peas and Red Cross pigeon grit, sacks of each of which would accompany them to the Arctic. They were also to be provided with twenty-five pounds of chewing tobacco as a disinfectant.[10] According to the *New York Times*, the pigeons had "been in training for several months in preparation for long flights in a cold country."[11] The aerologist was responsible for their care and feeding.

At the last minute, Byrd decided to take an additional pilot-mechanic. A fellow officer and aviator gave a glowing recommendation to an enlisted man serving on the USS *Richmond*, a light cruiser based on the west coast. Byrd saw to it that orders were issued instructing the man to report to Washington. Admiral Moffett thought this was a big mistake. If the sailor decided not to volunteer for the expedition once the mission was explained to him, the money the Department would have had to spend to cover his transportation expenses would have been wasted. President Coolidge, the commander in chief, was a stickler for economy. Byrd banked on his friend's assessment and figured that the man from the *Richmond* was bound to volunteer.

And so, late in May, lanky, unassuming Floyd Bennett strolled into Byrd's office. Byrd looked up across his desk. His first words to the man from the *Richmond* were: "Bennett, you want to go to the Arctic with me this summer to explore?"[12]

Bennett would not have passed muster with Donald MacMillan. He was five foot ten and had been married for eight years. "You bet I do," he said, and Byrd signed him up. It was the best personnel decision Richard Byrd would ever make.

Three planes, spare parts, spare engines, an eight-man navy unit, pigeons.... As the expedition grew beyond the carrying capacity of the Schooner *Bowdoin*, MacMillan intensified his efforts to find a second ship to accompany the *Bowdoin* north. Negotiations with the owners of the sealing vessel that Bartlett had recommended to Byrd were less than satisfactory. MacMillan finally settled on the SS *Rowena*, a 143-foot yacht that had been put on the market by Morrill Goddard, the sensation-mongering editor of the *American Weekly*, the graphic Sunday supplement of the Hearst newspaper chain. The *Rowena* had formerly been a French minesweeper. McDonald wanted to rename her the *Zenith*, but Gilbert Grosvenor and John Oliver La Gorce, president and vice president of the National Geographic Society, respectively, put their collective foot down. In those nobler and more dignified times, the crass commercial tie-in was considered inappropriate. Grosvenor and La Gorce decided that the "very graceful and proper thing" would be to rename the ship the *Peary*.[13] It was, of course, as MacMillan conceded, a fabulous gesture. Curiously, although MacMillan claimed to have bought the yacht (for "about $40,000 of my own money"), every indication points to McDonald subsidizing the purchase.[14] For all of McDonald's rampant egotism, he was content to conceal his largesse in this instance and maintain a fiction that elevated a friend.

The *Peary* was put into drydock in Brooklyn at the same shipyard where the *Roosevelt*, Robert Peary's steamer, had been refitted for her maiden Arctic voyage. The *Peary* was transformed into a combination aircraft carrier and icebreaker. A deckhouse at the stern of the vessel was removed to make room for three airplanes, and her bow was reinforced with one-inch steel plates, both above and below the waterline, and filled in with concrete to enable her to ram her way through the pack ice. The ship was christened on the twentieth of May in an afternoon ceremony at the Brooklyn waterfront. Admiral Peary's comely daughter, Marie Ahnighito Peary Stafford, did the honors, smashing a bottle of water retrieved from Eagle Island, her father's beloved home in Casco Bay. Mrs. Stafford was a celebrity in her own right. She was born in the High Arctic, during one of her father's early expeditions, and had been promptly acclaimed in the press for having achieved a "farthest north" for Caucasian infants. The newspapers called her the "Snow Baby."

The day following the ceremony, Amundsen and Ellsworth hopped off from Spitsbergen.

Roald Amundsen intended to name Keenan/Crocker/Bradley/Harris/Roosevelt Land "Arctica."[15] But he had been forced to practice a bit of deception—and for a typically Amundsenian reason: money.[16] The funds contributed by James Ellsworth and supplemented by donations from friends and acquaintances of Lincoln Ellsworth had not been sufficient to underwrite the expedition. Amundsen had to go to the Aero Club of Norway to make up the difference. The Aero Club refused to support a venture as risky and ambitious as a flight across the vast, unexplored regions of the Polar Sea but was willing to back a more modest project. Amundsen and Ellsworth signed an agreement with the Club to mount an aerial reconnaissance of the Pole and return to Spitsbergen. Privately, they had a secret agreement that if all went well, they would continue on to Alaska as originally planned.

The original and revised versions of Amundsen's plans confounded observers after his disappearance. No one could be entirely sure whether he had gone down in the eastern or western Arctic, or where to begin a search for survivors. By the twenty-fifth of May, the Norwegians had begun to organize a search-and-rescue operation to be launched from Spitsbergen. Amundsen and Ellsworth were then eighty-five hours overdue.

On the May 27, the National Geographic Society held a press reception for the MacMillan expedition. Richard Byrd was introduced to the media. He had been asked to prepare a brief talk on polar flying, and one of the topics he touched on was navigation. How do you steer a course from one place to another in a part of the world where the magnetic compass is unreliable? Byrd expressed his concern about the lack of instruments to compensate for the limitations of the standard compass. If he at least had a way to quickly ascertain the bearing of the sun, he said, he would immediately know where true north and south were and would be able to orient himself accordingly.

When he took his seat, the man sitting next to him turned to him and said, "Commander Byrd, I feel quite sure that your difficulty can be solved with a watch, and I'd like to explain it after the meeting is over."[17] The speaker happened to be Albert H. Bumstead, the chief cartographer of the National Geographic Society. An idea had dawned on him in a flash while Byrd was talking. Byrd and Bumstead had never met before. After the press conference, Bumstead took Byrd aside and excitedly sketched out his idea. Byrd was skeptical; the device Bumstead had in mind seemed too simple, too good to be true.

Bumstead said e would make one and test it out.

The following day, Byrd and MacMillan met at the Navy Department with Secretary Wilbur and Admiral Moffett to discuss the role of the American expedition in the Amundsen rescue effort. In Liverpool, at just about the same time, Grettir Algarsson was revising his plans in light of Amundsen's disappearance. Algarsson had been waiting impatiently for his blimp. The manufacturer with whom he had contracted had kept postponing the delivery date. Finally, Algarsson and Frank Worsley went to see the manager of the firm. The dirigible-maker admitted that the blimp-in-production would not be able to meet the contract guarantees: its range was little more than half the distance advertised. Algarsson decided to try to raise funds for an airplane. His goal now was not the Pole or the unexplored area but simply to join the search for Amundsen.

Everyone agreed that Amundsen was in some sort of predicament, major or minor. Gene McDonald was of course going to supply the MacMillan expedition with cutting-edge wireless radio equipment. The latest developments in the Amundsen story would be followed aboard the *Bowdoin* and *Peary* as the little flotilla made its way north. If Amundsen was still missing by the time the expedition reached Etah, the plan was for Byrd and his aviators to strike out to the north, rather than west. They would establish a fuel depot at Fort Conger and a base of operations at Cape Columbia, as Byrd had originally intended to do. The fliers would fan out from Cape Columbia to search for Amundsen. The exploration of the Polar Sea would be mounted from the northern shore of Ellesmere Island instead of from Cape Thomas Hubbard on the northern tip of Axel Heiberg.

On June 17, the Norwegian rescue mission arrived by steamship at King's Bay. The Government of Norway had deployed seven air force personnel and two seaplanes. Their assignment was to reconnoiter the ice north of Spitsbergen for traces of the missing explorers. One of the members of the party was a husky, twenty-six-year-old lieutenant named Bernt Balchen, fated to play a prominent role in the life and adventures of Richard Byrd. More than three weeks had passed since Amundsen and Ellsworth's disappearance.

That same day, the SS *Peary* embarked from the Boston Navy Yard. The steamer was due to proceed to Wiscasset, Maine, where the *Bowdoin* was taking on provisions. June 17 was Bunker Hill Day, a national commemoration of the 150th anniversary of the Revolutionary War battle. The departure of the ship was part of a program of festivities. Five thousand people assembled on the Charlestown docks, in the shadow of the Bunker Hill obelisk. A platform had been erected on the port gangway of the USS *Constitution*, the lusty frigate nicknamed "Old Ironsides" in the War of 1812. The historic ship had returned to Boston in 1897, one hundred years after she was launched from that city. The *Peary* was berthed beside her, the fuselages of three Loening Amphibians lashed side-by-side on the steamer's after deck. (The wings had been removed and stored in wooden crates.) Dignitaries gathered on the prow of the *Peary*. The distinguished assemblage included: Senators William M. Butler and Frederick H. Gillette, the latter a former Speaker of the House of Representatives; Alvan T. Fuller, the governor of Massachusetts; Boston's legendary mayor, James M. Curley, who had hosted a luncheon for MacMillan and Byrd at the Copley Plaza three days earlier; Assistant Secretary of the Navy Robinson; Charles Evans Hughes, a former justice (and future chief justice) of the Supreme Court, presidential candidate, and secretary of state (Hughes would give the keynote address of the Bunker Hill fest later that day at the annual meeting of the Bunker Hill Monument Association); Grover Loening; John O. La Gorce; and a buxom entertainer named Blanche Ring, famous for introducing the song, "Come Josephine in my Flying Machine." La Gorce raised an eyebrow (and doubtlessly others did, too) when Gene McDonald escorted Miss Ring aboard the *Peary*, accompanied by twenty male and female members of her troupe.[18]

She was not called upon to mount the platform and make a speech, but Ted Robinson and several principal office holders were. MacMillan spoke last, reiterating his intention to find both Amundsen and Harris Land. The Governor led the crowd in three rousing cheers. It was almost noon. At 12:15 p.m., a volley of cannonfire rattled the environs. Steamships blew their fog horns. A squadron of seaplanes from the Squantum Naval Air Station circled in precision formation at about a thousand feet overhead, their engines screaming. The *Peary* cast off escorted by six ships, three navy patrol craft, and three city fireboats, the latter punctuating the tumult with watery exclamation points spouted in geyser-like cascades.

6

TOWARD THE LOST ATLANTIS

*It would be amazing if the enormous space marked
"Unexplored Region" on maps of the Arctic turned out to
be only a frozen sea. Everywhere else in the
frozen north there is land.*

New York Times[1]

The next day, Thursday, June 19, four weeks after their departure, Amundsen, Ellsworth, and their party, ragged but alive and well, returned to Spitsbergen as passengers aboard a Norwegian sealing vessel. The story they brought with them was the first great survival epic of polar aviation. They had run into unrelenting fog within half an hour after taking off from King's Bay. There was also a strong headwind pushing against them, slowing them down. After eight hours in the air, each of the two planes had used up half the fuel in their respective tanks. They should have been at or near the Pole. Amundsen and Ellsworth's secret plan was to land at the Pole, leave one plane behind, fill the tanks of the other with the remaining fuel, and fly on to Alaska. But where were they? Amundsen glided down through the mist to find out, and Ellsworth followed suit. It was difficult to align a sextant with the sun and the horizon in a jouncing airplane. They both made safe landings in small pools of slushy water where the ice had split apart. Ellsworth's flying boat had sprung a leak, lost an engine and had to be abandoned. He had come down about three miles from the lead where Amundsen had landed; eventually the drifting icefields brought the two crews within half a mile of each other, and the expedition was reunited.

Celestial observations disclosed that they were 136 miles from the North Pole. They had struck north out of Spitsbergen on the 12th meridian and had been blown west of their course by an easterly wind. Finding a place to land on the boundless white expanse was one thing; getting *off* the Polar Sea proved to be infinitely more difficult. The slush in the pool where Amundsen had landed quickly turned to ice. The one Dornier Whale that remained airworthy was completely frozen in. The temperature was about 15° Fahrenheit. The only tools that were available were one long knife, one small ax, a couple of hunting knives that could be tied to the ends of ski poles to approximate axes, an ice anchor that could double as a pick-ax, a camera tripod, and three wooden shovels. With these implements they set to work hacking at the ice to dislodge the plane.

The Polar Sea, however, is a dynamic environment. The pressure of unseen geophysical processes continually reshapes the surface. Rows of jumbled ice would seemingly advance upon the plane while they slept. They had to haul the four-and-a-half-ton ship up onto a large ice floe to prevent it from being crushed. The ice continued to assail their position like a marauding army in a running battle. So time and again they had to decamp and lug the Whale out of harm's way, sometimes as much as half a mile. On four different occasions, they attempted to hack out a runway. Either a fog would descend and rot the ice they had worked so hard to smooth out, or hummocks of ice would close in and obstruct the track. There were five attempted take-offs on ice paths that didn't prove firm enough to support the plane.

Throughout the ordeal, Amundsen remained calm and collected. He established an orderly routine: regular periods for work, sleep, eating, and conversation. He had a peculiarly Norwegian outlook, a kind of fatalistic optimism, the feeling that, however grim the situation, it was always darkest before the dawn. His camp took on his personality and endured. As their rations dwindled, they spent three nights and two days shoveling out and tramping down one more runway. Their last-ditch effort was ultimately successful. They emerged from the Polar Sea the same way they had approached it—in a heavy fog—and came down in the waters off Northeast Land. A sealer happened to be trailing a walrus along the coast of this island, the northernmost in the Svalbard archipelago. The sailors turned into a bay to seek shelter from a breaking storm and encountered a Dornier Whale.

Ironically, James Ellsworth, Lincoln's father, had died of pneumonia at the age of seventy-five on the third of June. He would never know that his son had returned unharmed.

Grettir Algarsson had been unable to find the money to buy a plane. Shortly after news reached Liverpool of Amundsen and Ellsworth's reappearance, he gave up the idea of doing any aerial exploration in 1925. Instead, he and Worsley would explore under sail. They would mount a voyage to the waters between Svalbard and Franz Josef Land and conduct a search for Gillis Land, an island reported by a Captain Gillis in 1707 and never seen before or since. They embarked on June 22.

The way was now clear for the American expedition to find and claim Harris Land. Thousands of well-wishers poured into the slumbering river town of Wiscasset for the official send-off on the afternoon of Saturday, the twentieth. The Maine hideaway was MacMillan's home port and his traditional point of embarkation for Arctic voyages.

Thousands of red and yellow balloons were released when the *Bow-doin* shoved off at 2:38 p.m. from the old whaling wharf on the Sheepscot River and eased into the channel where the *Peary* lay anchored. Thousands of schoolchildren all dressed in white were assembled on a hillside overlooking the river; they were organized in such a way that seen from the distance they spelled out "MacMillan." All along the shore, thousands of voices cheered, hundreds of drivers honked their horns, and scores of weekend sailors tooted their whistles.

At the very last minute before the expedition departed, National Geographic chief cartographer Albert H. Bumstead arrived with the first two models of the new instrument he had patented, the gadget that had occurred to him while listening to Byrd speak at the press conference in May. Bumstead had won Byrd over during the initial trials of the device. Byrd would never again leave for an expedition without one.

The following day, the twenty-first, there was another send-off at Monhegan Island. The expedition had attracted so much attention that its departure was a national event, like the World Series. The quest for what one reporter called the "lost Atlantis of the north" represented America's aspirations for preeminence and security in a new era rapidly taking shape, an age of aerial commerce and aerial warfare, a future in which even the most powerful nations would be vulnerable to aerial attack. If the navy aviators found Harris Land, it was said, they would also find America's first line of defense against twentieth-century invaders. Never had an Arctic expedition embarked with such lofty expectations.

Nor had an Arctic expedition ever attained the status of an international provocation. The MacMillan-Byrd venture had inadvertently become a *cause célèbre* between the United States and three countries with whom America normally had the most harmonious relations:

Denmark, Norway, and Canada. The Danes were upset over what MacMillan had whispered to President Coolidge at the end of March—the inference that there was something rotten in Greenland. Norway and Canada had raised concerns over the issue of sovereignty and land claims in the Polar Sea. The Norwegians claimed Axel Heiberg Island and a couple of small islands immediately to the west of Axel Heiberg. The Canadians basically claimed everything north of Ottawa. Both countries were anxious about the American effort to annex Harris Land. The resulting diplomatic exchanges had the overtones of comic opera.

There was a celebration in Minnesota in the spring of 1925 to mark the centennial of Scandinavian immigration to the American Midwest. A Mr. C. H. Hambro, the chairman of the foreign relations committee of the Storthing, the Norwegian parliament, attended the festivities as the official representative of his government. Interviewed in New York a week before the departure of the MacMillan expedition, Hambro reminded the American press of the proximity of Norway and Norwegian territory (the Svalbard islands) to the Polar Sea. The lost Atlantis, he said, would be "Norway's nearest neighbor on the north. No land lies between us and the unexplored region. It is close to home, so to speak."[2]

The American press then reminded Mr. Hambro about the Monroe Doctrine. "The Monroe Doctrine," said the Norwegian, "can hardly be stretched from Pole to Pole."

Meanwhile, in Washington, an emissary of the Canadian government, the deputy minister of the interior, called on Secretary Wilbur, Admiral Moffett, and Richard Byrd. The deputy minister wanted Byrd to formally apply to the Canadians for permission to fly over Axel Heiberg Island. To do so, however, would imply that America acknowledged Canada's rights to an island claimed by Norway.

On the matter of land claims in remote wilderness areas, international law was perfectly ambiguous. Discovery in and of itself was not a sufficient basis to support a claim; discovery had to be followed by "occupation," although this itself was subject to interpretation. The Canadian government, pressing its contention that 1) the High Arctic belonged to Canada, and 2) the MacMillan expedition required permits for its proposed aerial survey of the region, officially informed the State Department that "posts of the Royal Canadian Mounted Police" had been duly established on Ellesmere Island and other sections of the "'Canadian northern territories.'"[3] To which the State Department replied that "it would like to be informed what constitutes a post of the Royal Mounted Police; where such posts have been established; how frequently they are visited; and to what extent, if any, and by whom, they are permanently occupied."

MacMillan not only wanted to annex Harris Land but also Axel Heiberg Island and the northern half of Ellesmere. He wrote to Secretary Wilbur on June 5, in order to find out what the Navy Department was willing to authorize him to do. "North of Cape Sabine," a site on the east coast of Ellesmere, just across Smith Sound from Etah, MacMillan said, "never a Canadian has set foot."[4] The secretary of the navy deferred to the secretary of state, Frank B. Kellogg. Secretary Kellogg and his minions were so befuddled by the matter that Kellogg finally turned to the National Geographic Society. The Secretary wrote to Gilbert Grosvenor on the nineteenth of June, the day before the MacMillan send-off, soliciting advice. But Grosvenor was in Wiscasset.

The upshot was that the expedition departed for the unexplored Arctic without any instructions whatsoever about what to do if Byrd and his aviators happened to find land there. The evening of the nineteenth, a Friday, Governor Ralph Owen Brewster (a Bowdoin man) hosted a farewell dinner at Wiscasset for MacMillan and Byrd. He told them to claim Harris Land for the State of Maine.[5]

Expeditions start out as abstractions, a fanciful idea of going to some strange, inaccessible place to accomplish a certain objective. People strive mightily to turn that idea into reality. The project takes shape over time and to its backers and supporters begins to look real. But it doesn't *feel* real to the participants until it gets underway. The moment it does, however, is tremendously exhilarating. There is an infectious giddiness, something like sitting down to a full-course meal and having the dessert first. The high spirits can be expected to last until the group gets out into the field and the various personalities that have been brought together begin to cope with their own expectations and each other.

For the 1925 MacMillan Arctic Expedition, the giddiness started to evaporate before the party reached Newfoundland. Serious tensions existed within the group which would never be resolved.

Although MacMillan used the navy to enlarge the scope of his project, he did not identify with the navy. Despite orders from Washington, he obstinately refused to take a standard, long-wave navy transmitter as a backup for the Zenith short-wave system. A number of flaws had been detected when the Zenith radios were flight-tested. Nevertheless, MacMillan left the navy equipment behind in Boston and in Wiscasset where it was subsequently ferried. A navy destroyer followed him to Sydney, Nova Scotia, with the old-fashioned whizbang "spark set" onboard and an ultimatum from the Secretary. MacMillan grudgingly allowed the navy apparatus to be transferred from the "government ship," as he disdainfully referred to it in an annotated diary, to the quarterdeck of the *Peary*, then looked the other way when his crew threw it overboard.[6]

He was a rugged individualist, a pathfinder of the Arctic frontier. In the midst of the modern world, he had managed to create a unique and satisfying niche for himself, and his highest purpose was to preserve it intact. He had installed Gene McDonald aboard the *Peary*, he told Grosvenor, "to look out for your interests and mine when dealing with the Navy personnel."[7] McDonald was as much of a freebooter as MacMillan, which was probably why they were such good friends. He was a star player, not a team man and was constitutionally incapable of acknowledging any authority higher than himself. The Navy Department and the National Geographic Society rightly understood that McDonald's primary purpose was to enjoy himself and to promote his product line. "Arctic Explorers," Zenith ads proclaimed that summer, "Stake Their Lives on Zenith Radio."[8]

The Geographic Society, too, had its own lookout, as MacMillan at least plainly understood. Gilbert Grosvenor and John La Gorce in addition to being president and vice president of the Society were also editor and associate editor of the *National Geographic Magazine.* Grosvenor had been hired as assistant editor of the magazine in 1899 and advanced to editor in chief in 1903. In those years, the Society was an organization of geographers. It had barely a thousand members, and its publication was as academic and insolvent as the *American Political Science Review*, or the journal of any other professional association. Grosvenor made the magazine enormously profitable by broadening its content. "Our interpretation of geography is very wide," he told the *New Yorker* in 1943. "When I see a subject that I think would be interesting to our million, two hundred thousand members, I don't scrutinize it to see if it's geographical." La Gorce added, "Behind the term geography is exploration. Behind that is adventure, and just over the hill is romance. Under Dr. Grosvenor, these three elements are stepped into closer focus. The chief has removed the technical padlocks from the science of geography."

Grosvenor became president of the Society in 1920. In 1925, there were about a million members. The business of the Society was to produce a continuing supply of exploration, adventure, and romance for the consumption of those million-odd readers. In a certain sense, the MacMillan expedition might be considered product development. The Society expected the navy to repeat the enterprise in 1926.

The quest for Harris Land would be a renewable resource. Grosvenor and La Gorce had assigned their star correspondent, Maynard Owen Williams, to the expedition to extract as much romance as possible from the first installment.

Williams sailed on the *Bowdoin*, a compact vessel with a commanding presence at the helm and a loyal crew. MacMillan had a democratic leadership style; he was always "one of the boys."[9] At the same time, he dominated every conversation he participated in, and his upbeat personality pervaded every nook, cranny and compartment of the schooner. A happy ship, she was largely exempt from the complexities of the developing subtext.

The *Peary*, however, seemed like a bottle filled with layers of different colored sand that would never be shook and blended. The captain was a portly, experienced seaman named George F. Steele. Stalwart, glum, taciturn, he had a round head like a snowman, a red nose, usually a pipe clenched between his teeth, a bull neck, and the circumference of a lighthouse. Steele came with the ship. He had been the master of the vessel for the past two years and had taken the prior owner on a cruise up the Newfoundland and Labrador coasts the previous summer. Byrd had wanted Bob Bartlett as skipper, but Bartlett had declined. Bartlett had been a seasoned Arctic hand when Donald MacMillan was a tenderfoot; his pride may have gotten in the way of accepting a subordinate role on a MacMillan expedition. (Bartlett had withdrawn from the Crocker Land expedition in the early stages of planning, perhaps for the same reason.)

Steele and his crew were, with one exception, all New Englanders—and most were Irish. (There were three deckhands named Mac-Namara.) They constituted one of three distinct factions aboard the steamer. The navy unit was the second. Quite a cosmopolitan aggregation, the detachment came from all over the United States and included Americans of English (Byrd), French, German, Scandinavian, and possibly Hawaiian descent. Byrd had selected two pilots who represented the navy in a series of international air races in the early '20s, Lieutenant Meinrad A. Schur of San Diego, California, and Chief Boatswain Earl E. Reber of Millville, New Jersey. Schur, thirty-one—his friends called him "Billie"—was a moonfaced, fair-haired flight instructor, stocky and sardonic. Reber, thirty-six, a swarthy, no-non-sense type, had seventeen years of service behind him and looked like Dick Tracy. The mechanics, in addition to Floyd Bennett, a country boy from northern New York State, were Nels P. Sorensen and Andrew C. Nold, both from the Midwest, and Charles F. Rocheville, a Californian. The aerographer (the weather and pigeon man) was dark-haired, dark-eyed Albert Francis, born in Hawaii and who may have been part Native Hawaiian.

The pilots were competent mechanics, and the mechanics were all expert fliers. Aerographer Francis, something of a utility infielder, was also a proficient mechanic, radio operator, and motion-picture cam-eraman. As individuals, Bennett and Reber impressed as the most mature and reliable, followed by tall, slim Sorensen; wiry Rocheville was the eternal optimist of the group; and Nold and Francis, the smallest and youngest—they were both about five feet, two inches tall and thirty years old—were the ladies' men.

Set against both the seafarers and the aviation unit was a third faction—the scientists and the professionals. There were five members of this group in all, three of whom sailed on the *Peary*: Dr. Walter N. Koelz, a slender, brainy twenty-nine-year-old naturalist; Jacob Gayer, a color photographer dispatched by the National Geographic Society; and Dr. Leo M. Davidoff, a resident at Peter Bent Brigham Hospital in Boston. A slight young man, about Koelz's age, with bad eyes and a dainty, girlish handwriting, Davidoff kept a detailed diary of the proceedings. He had a knack for caricature. About Gayer of the *National Geographic Magazine*, for example, he wrote: "[A] man of 40, of German descent and leanings—a queer, gray-haired, inelegant looking fellow, chews tobacco, yet pleasant withal, knows his job

thoroughly and is stuffed full of old German sagas and general information." Davidoff quickly bonded with Koelz and would assist him
in his wildlife collections. Another field researcher, Lieutenant Benjamin H. Rigg of the U.S. Coast and Geodetic Survey sailed with the
Geographic's Maynard Owen Williams on the *Bowdoin*. Rigg,
twenty-nine, a tide specialist in the tradition of Rollin Harris, had
done field work in Alaska and just returned from the Philippines
when he was recommended to Grosvenor for the MacMillan expedition. He and Williams augmented the science faction when the *Peary*
and *Bowdoin* were anchored together.

Each of these three groups had been molded in different ways by
their vocational experiences. The military men shaved every day, were
scrupulous about personal hygiene, and kept their uniforms clean and
their quarters neat and orderly. This set them apart from the seamen
who, Davidoff noted, "are surly, silent fellows with bad pyorrhoea ... [T]he incidence of pyorrhoea," he said, "is 100%." Like
the *Peary* crew, the aviators worked with their hands all day, operating, fine-tuning or repairing a piece of machinery. Had they not been
in the navy, most of these men would have been toiling on farms or
in factories. They were essentially blue-collar workers, coarse and
lowbrow, and this set them apart from the researchers and professionals.

Davidoff wrote:

> The naval men as a whole amuse me a good deal, they are
> apt to twit me about my Boston accent and my relatively
> mild expostulations. The other day, for example, they all
> nearly convulsed with laughter when in surprise at some
> previous remark I exclaimed "By Jove" ...

Byrd, a gentleman, a thinker, and a reader, would attempt to reach
out to the professionals but was not accepted by them. Davidoff,

for one, put him down as a conquistador. "A soldier, short of speech, handsome, chivalrous, brave to the point of foolhardiness," he wrote.

The spark-set incident had leaked to the press, causing sparks to fly between MacMillan and McDonald on one side and Byrd on the other. The issue soon fizzled and was forgotten, but the tensions and undercurrents beneath the surface of the expedition could not be contained for long. Another conflict surfaced halfway up the coast of Labrador; it was both inevitable and avoidable, and it threatened everything the principals hoped to accomplish under the midnight sun.

Summer appears briefly in the Arctic. It begins in the last week of June and continues through the first week in August. Flowers bloom across the tundra in this period, and mosquitoes thrive. The weather changes abruptly thereafter. August in the eastern Arctic is like November in the northeastern United States. The temperature drops and precipitation in the form of rain and snow increases. Richard Byrd's hallmark as an explorer, evident as early as 1925, was meticulous planning and thorough preparation. He had devised a prudent plan for the aerial survey of the Polar Sea. Two of the Loenings would streak out into the unknown from Cape Thomas Hubbard, the third would be held in reserve in case it became necessary to mount a search-and-rescue mission. In addition, he had carefully worked out a timetable for each aspect of the air operations.

Assembling the planes would be a major undertaking, and it would have to be accomplished on land. Basing his estimate on a twelve-hour working day, Byrd figured that it would take at least ten days to locate and clear a field at Etah, beach the amphibians, attach the wings, perform test flights, and enable his personnel to familiarize themselves with the use of compasses in the unusual magnetic conditions that obtain in the far north. It would take almost an additional week to put down a base or series of bases between Etah and Cape Thomas Hubbard. In other words, sixteen days of steady work would be required before the first pair of aviators set out from Axel Heiberg Island to explore the Polar Sea.

Byrd allocated six days for the search for Harris Land and three days for returning to Etah, disassembling the planes and hoisting them back aboard the *Peary*. That gave him a total of twenty-five twelve-hour working days for the entire program. To allow for weather delays he increased the total by 25 percent. The numbers told him that it could take as much as thirty-one days to accomplish his primary mission and that no time would be left over for the projected aerial survey of the Greenland ice cap, Ellesmere Island and Baffin Island. Byrd had consequently recommended that the expedition reach Etah by July 1 but was overruled; he now hoped that it would get there at least by the twenty-sixth. Even so, they would be out of the brief window of optimum flying conditions and well into the Arctic August before the Polar Sea operations began. Time, Byrd understood, was clearly of the essence.

MacMillan, however, assessed the situation with the savvy of an experienced Arctic mariner. He preferred to err on the side of caution and wait for the sea ice to break up a bit before exposing his ships to the danger of being crushed. He had therefore paused to celebrate the Fourth of July at Battle Harbor in southern Labrador, the site of a hospital founded by a world-famous physician and missionary, Dr. Wilfred Grenfell. Three days later, the expedition anchored at Hopedale, a village populated almost exclusively by Inuit, where the men purchased seal- and caribou-skin garments. Inland of the rocky coast rose a backdrop of hills lined with evergreens. MacMillan climbed a steep elevation, looked seaward between the trees and saw nothing but whiteness. "From the top of the hill it is apparently a solid pack up and down the coast," he wrote. "No opportunity for proceeding north as yet."[10]

That was on July 8. The expedition weighed anchor again on the tenth at 1:30 a.m. and four hours later put into a place called Windy Tickle, where MacMillan stopped to pick up a horsefaced young man named Abram Bromfield who had served as interpreter on his previous expeditions. Bromfield was out hunting and trapping, and did not return until 2:00 a.m. on the eleventh. MacMillan waited for him. MacMillan had intended to get underway later that morning but was dissuaded by a thick fog and a falling barometer. Instead, that evening McDonald produced a radio show starring Bromfield's colorful seventy-five-year-old, white-bearded father, Samuel, singing and accompanying himself on the fiddle, and spinning tales. It was broadcast to the United States.

Meanwhile, Byrd kept looking at the calendar and his watch. The irony of it all was that the expedition's best ice sailor (MacMillan) and its most knowledgeable flight engineer (Byrd) had never sought each other's point of view on the overall plan of operations. They might have decided that it probably made more sense to winter over at Etah and start flying the following spring. Conflicting outlooks, interests, and perspectives would continue to haunt the expedition and cripple its possibilities.

Certain members of the expedition, however, did see eye to eye. Floyd Bennett and Dick Byrd shared the same birthday: October 25. Bennett was two years younger than Byrd and between one and two inches taller. He was a quiet man, slender and handsome with a cleft chin, fair-hair parted on the left side, and the clean, good looks of the shy, straight-shooting hero of early Hollywood Westerns. He was born in a farmhouse near Warrensburg, New York, a small town about halfway between New York City and Montreal. The Bennetts were dirt poor—the family in fact was once admitted to the county poor house. There were five children, three boys and two girls. Some of the kids were placed in foster homes or other institutions. At the age of seven, Floyd, the middle child, went to Warrensburg to live with an uncle in a ramshackle cabin at the foot of a thickly wooded mountain. The stigma of poverty would leave an indelible mark on his soul.

His chief characteristics were taciturnity and adventurousness, both evident even in childhood. As a boy, he tended to keep to himself and once tried to run away with a circus. He wanted to be a lion tamer. At the age of fifteen, he saw his first automobile and became fascinated with the machine. He decided to go to vocational school to learn to be an auto mechanic and worked all winter in a lumber camp to pay the tuition. It was a fortuitous decision. He was a mechanical genius; he had the eye, ear, and touch to work magic with the internal combustion engine. Bennett completed a six-month automotive course four months ahead of schedule. He worked as a garage attendant, eventually opened his own repair shop, and joined the navy as a mechanic when the United States entered the First World War.

In 1919, the navy authorized flight training for enlisted mechanics. Bennett attended flight school at Pensacola and, like an artist, found his true medium of expression. Flying an airplane has certain elements in common with playing a musical instrument. The pilot has to manipulate several different strings or keys at the same time. The left hand operates the control wheel, the right hand the throttle, and the feet the rudder bar. Flying also has certain elements in common with ballet. Circling down and gliding to a landing, for example, is a graceful, dance-like maneuver. The proficient pilot executes it the way a dancer does, with fluidity and precision. But the pilot has to do it in the air, against a wind, and with lengthy extensions of human limbs. Floyd Bennett was a consummate aviator, a cockpit virtuoso. His mechanical ability and something indefinable—perhaps something in the very center of his being—enabled him to fly rhapsodies in the sky.

In 1924, the navy dispatched Bennett's ship, the *Richmond*, to southern Greenland to facilitate the arrival of a team of army fliers circling the world in stages. The army aircraft were about to depart eastbound from Iceland. Bennett flew over the coastal terrain scouting for possible landing sites. His enthusiasm for the aerial exploration of uncharted regions dated from that mission. Byrd and Bennett took long hikes together at Hopedale, roaming through the hills above the village. The temperature was in the mid-60s, and the mosquitoes alighted in heavy swarms. On the surface they may have seemed unlikely soul mates, one a humble farm boy with an eighth-grade education, the other a Southern aristocrat and Annapolis graduate. But both of these men were in many ways cut from the same cloth. The mechanically minded, analytical Bennett respected the commander's attention to detail as well as his elegant grasp of the logistical and technical aspects of the Polar Sea project. At the same time, the outgoing Byrd had his own quiet, solitary side, qualities the enlisted man exemplified and to which Bennett could easily relate.

Each would find the other tough and dependable in a pinch.

7

THE
WINDY PLACE

*The evil spirit of the Arctic is always watching
and can change success into misfortune and
failure within a few hours.*

DONALD B. MACMILLAN[1]

The standard marine sextant is a sighting device with built-in mirrors enabling the navigator to see two different things at the same time: the sun and the horizon. By adjusting the mirrors, the mariner brings the image of the sun down to the horizon and obtains the altitude of the sun from a scale on the instrument. The marine sextant wasn't suitable for air navigation because at high altitude the horizon line is not generally clear-cut. To compensate, Byrd developed an instrument that, in effect, took the vial of liquid from a carpenter's level and mounted it—horizontally, of course—on the front of a standard sextant. Looking through this instrument, one sees three things at the same time: the bubble, the center of the level and the sun. When the bubble is centered, the image of the sun can be brought down to an *artificial* horizon.

Because three things have to be aligned, the Byrd sextant is a more difficult instrument to master than the marine sextant and is slightly more prone to error. The mechanisms have to be finely adjusted to make sure that it sights correctly. Byrd was up on the bridge of the *Peary*, on July 12, taking sun sights and making these adjustments when he spotted smoke coming from the deck. He swiftly ran amidships and found a stack of life preservers on fire. They had been piled up against one of the three long, rectangular wooden crates containing the wings of the Loening Amphibians. The crates were stowed lengthwise on deck, just forward of the three airplanes and on either side of a smokestack. One crate was lashed to the railing on the starboard side of the smokestack, the other two on the port side. The fire had probably been ignited by fumes from the smokestack. Byrd tossed one of the life preservers overboard and opened a fire extinguisher on the rest. "Another minute," he wrote in his diary,

> and the flame would have ignited the oil and kerosene the [nearest] plane is soaked in and nothing in the world could have saved this ship with 7,600 gallons of gasoline around her decks.

The *Peary* crossed the Arctic Circle, latitude 66°30′, three days later at 10:30 a.m., en route to Greenland. Alone. The *Bowdoin* had damaged her propeller and returned to Hopedale to replace it with a spare. The steamer reached Godhavn on the sixteenth and another thing that could go wrong, did.

Coal had been discovered on the west coast of Greenland by American Arctic explorers in the nineteenth century, and was being mined in several locations by the Danes in the early twentieth. When MacMillan sailed down the Greenland coast in 1924, returning from his last expedition, he had the impression that there was a plentiful supply. He asked Gilbert Grosvenor to go through diplomatic channels and arrange for the Danes to provide about a hundred tons for the *Peary*. The steamer could only carry enough coal in her bunkers to reach Etah. Grosvenor made the necessary initiatives and was informed by the State Department that Copenhagen had authorized its representative in northern Greenland to deliver the coal, but only if the supply on hand was more than enough to meet the needs of the local settlements for the coming winter.

The *Peary*, of course, encountered the worst-case scenario.

The north Greenland mining industry was less productive than MacMillan had imagined. The governor had taken stock and found that he did not have *enough* coal on hand to last Godhavn and the surrounding villages through the long polar night. Under the circumstances, he could not release a hundred tons unless Copenhagen authorized the delivery and arranged to replace the fuel. This should not have come as a complete surprise. The Danish foreign office had specifically informed the American embassy "that it is very uncertain whether 100 tons may be available."[2] Grosvenor had received a telegram on May 26 from a State Department official summarizing the gist of the communication between Copenhagen and the American embassy. On June 13, the State Department sent him a copy of the note from the Danish foreign office; he forwarded the correspondence on to MacMillan two days later.

It seemed as if a hidden hand was poised to trip up the expedition at every turn, and at least one of the leading actors in the unfolding drama perfectly understood the situation. The *Peary* and *Bowdoin* maintained daily communication via short-wave with the expedition's respective sponsors, the Department of the Navy and the National Geographic Society. On the same day, July 16, that Governor Philip Rosendahl, the local representative of the government of Denmark, announced that he was unable to resupply the *Peary*, MacMillan sent the following dispatch to the NGS:

> We are making our third attempt to put on spare propeller.
> The Evil Spirit of the North, so familiar to the Eskimos,

has temporarily turned all of his attention to the white
visitors from the South. Unfortunately, we are having tides
with a rise and fall of only four feet.[3]

The *Bowdoin* had a ten-foot draft, and at least an eight-foot tide fall
was needed to beach the ship and replace the propeller.

Stark, rocky, treeless, and shaped overall like a deformed maple
leaf, Disko Island was not an idyllic vacation spot. Just off the west
coast of Greenland, up near the 70th parallel, it lies right below the
waistline of the continent. The stem of the leaf faces the mainland;
Godhavn is on the outer edge of the southernmost reticulation. About
150 people resided in the port in the 1920s; the majority were a mixture of Inuit and northern European ancestry. They lived in huts made
of sod and stone, and burned twigs, heather, and peat to cook their
meals. The prevailing odor was a "mixture of dog and human and
fish and particularly of skin and blubber and meat."[4] A visitor in 1926
called it the "aroma borealis." The *Peary* anchored here, awaiting the
outcome of a slow and agonizing diplomatic minuet as the navy and
the National Geographic Society induced the State Department to
cable the American embassy at Copenhagen.

While the diplomatic overtures dragged on, Byrd sat down and
calculated that 1,162 pounds of food and 600 pounds of spare parts
and mechanical equipment would have to be advanced to Cape
Thomas Hubbard to support the flights over the Polar Sea. He item-
ized the payload that each of the three airplanes would have to carry
to move this material in stages between Etah and two intermediate
bases en route to Hubbard, figured out that it would take something
like six round trips to establish each base, and specified the amount
of food, equipment, fuel, and oil each plane must carry to operate
with a margin of safety over the unexplored area. He typed up an

eight-page General Order on the nineteenth outlining the entire flight program.

While the steamer remained in limbo, the rest of its passengers occupied themselves according to their own lights. Floyd Bennett became interested in the sod houses of the native people, mound-shaped huts with a twelve to fifteen-foot entrance tunnel. He learned how to build one, knowledge, he thought, that might come in handy later. Gene McDonald learned to kayak.

A breakthrough came at last on July 22. Copenhagen informed the American embassy that it would authorize the release of eighty tons of coal if the State Department guaranteed payment.[5] John La Gorce was notified that same afternoon. La Gorce, in the name of the National Geographic Society, guaranteed the State Department that it would be reimbursed for the cost of the coal. However, Governor Rosendahl was not in direct radio communication with Copenhagen, nor did the local station on which he depended have the kind of sophisticated, experimental equipment that had been designed for the *Peary*. While his government had agreed to furnish the coal, Rosendahl had not received the necessary instructions.

Byrd and McDonald sent a volley of radiograms back to Washington. The secretary of the navy responded with a confirmation from the Danish Embassy of the arrangements with Copenhagen. The *Bowdoin* finally arrived at Godhavn at 5:00 a.m. on the morning of the twenty-fourth. At about nine o'clock, the entire expedition watched Rosendahl approach the harbor "in full regalia, epaulets, sword, etc."[6] The governor boarded the *Peary* and accompanied the steamer to the coal mines at Umanak, a settlement on the northern shore of Nugssuaq peninsula, some 180 miles north of Disko Island. Rosendahl understood the patterns of a traditional society. He knew the American sense of urgency would not translate and wisely resorted to pomp and circumstance to impress the native workers with the importance and official nature of the marathon loading duties they were going to be called upon to perform.

The *Peary* arrived at Umanak on the morning of Saturday, July 25, and tied up at a steep cliff. The mines were dark holes tunneled into the base of the cliff. Coaling began at 7:00 a.m. and ended twenty hours later, at 3:00 a.m. on Sunday, the twenty-sixth. At 4:30 a.m. on the day Byrd had hoped to reach Etah—July 26—the expedition first departed Umanak.

Ten days had been lost because MacMillan failed to acquire a coal tender or ensure a resupply. Ten long days, stretched to outsize proportions due to the twenty-four-hour daylight.

Ice conditions above the Arctic Circle can vary considerably. On the whole, it is not unlike cloud cover in the temperate latitudes. Ice floes, like clouds, could be small or large; they could be scattered across the horizon, or they could be thick and dense and block out the sea. But while frontal systems pass slowly, so that it may take a few days to run the gamut from a clear sky to overcast to breaks in the overcast, Arctic ice patterns change swiftly. The MacMillan expedition encountered the first wave at 4:30 on the afternoon of the twenty-seventh. A scattered layer of winter ice blown off the land, it was easily negotiated. At 5:00 p.m., the next wave arrived. They had entered an indentation of the Greenland coast called Melville Bay, usually referred to as the "dreaded Melville Bay," also known as the "Graveyard of Ships." Across the visual field and far into the distance spread boulders, crags and ledges of snow-covered, blue-tinted ice. MacMillan recognized it. "The pack itself," he noted in his log—the thick pack ice of the Polar Sea drifting south through the Canadian Arctic Archipelago.[7] It looked surreal, like miles of rocky terrain transplanted in patches from a frost-bound shore.

The most experienced ice pilot of the expedition, MacMillan came aboard the stronger ship, the *Peary*, and climbed the rigging to the crow's nest, where a jigsaw pattern of interlocking ice floes spread far and wide before his eyes. From this vantage point, he raised a pair of binoculars and remained aloft scanning the horizon for the thinnest ice and widest leads. He would shout directions down to Captain Steele on the bridge, who relayed the instructions to the mates on watch in the wheel house. "*Hard-a-port!*" "Hard-a-port!" "*Ease-t-starboard!*" "Ease-t-starboard!"

When all went well, the *Peary* broke the ice for the *Bowdoin*, the cakes grinding, cracking, and smashing against her bow. The steamer would lurch with the impact of each terrific crash. (Steady progress to her passengers felt and sounded like a series of highway collisions.) At other times, even with MacMillan hugging the mast, conning for leads, the steamer got stuck in the ice and much of the day was spent attempting to extricate her and the schooner.

In addition to heavy ice, the Scylla of Melville Bay, the expedition was also beset by its Charybdis—impenetrable fog. MacMillan cautiously waited out intermittent mists so thick the mountainous coastline was almost completely obscured in a rainy haze. Consequently, although the 500-mile passage just south of Etah was theoretically navigable in a day, the expedition didn't clear the ice until the thirty-first. "I seem to be the only one worried about this terrible delay. I wonder if the others realize how serious the situation is as regards having sufficient time to accomplish our mission," Byrd wrote, restless and impatient. "Should not have played game so damn safe."

The towering coastline of northern Greenland is cleaved with glaciers sweeping down to the sea. At 9:00 p.m. on Saturday, August 1, in the middle of a driving snowstorm, the expedition entered a break in the coastline and finally arrived at Etah, its designated base of operations. The heavy snow made it difficult to make out any of the features of the place. On the *Bowdoin*, at the sound of the ratchet wheel lowering the anchor chain, MacMillan's motion-picture cameraman emerged from the hatch with an envelope in his hand. Onnig D. Melkon was born in Cyprus and had immigrated to America at age eighteen, exactly eighteen years before the expedition. Squinting into the falling snow, he asked, "Where's the post office?"[8] MacMillan, who was standing on deck, swept an arm toward shore and simply said, "Look."

The ships were anchored in the choppy blue waters of a fjord about five miles long, sheltered from the pack ice drifting down the Greenland coast. The mouth of the fjord was to the west, and it opened onto Smith Sound, the channel between northern Greenland and Ellesmere Island. Far to the east, a dab of whiteness gleamed at the distant head of the fjord; the snow-covered glacier that had hewed out the canyon-like formation swept inland right above the water line. The rocky, snow-spattered cliffs that had been split asunder by the glacier framed the north and south sides of the narrow inlet. The cliff walls had a strange, iridescent quality and glowed with streaks of flaming orange and pale green; the orange was due to the dense and curious lichens that covered the boulders, the green to patches of grass growing on the slopes. Thin streams splashed down over the rocks here and there from the melting snow on the rim of the cliffs. The only signs of habitation were two large circles on one hillside, the last traces of igloos that had been erected in a bygone winter.

Etah, at 78°19′ N, was not a town. It was the Arctic frontier. Although the site had been used as a base by generations of American Arctic men, there is no evidence that English-speaking explorers had named it by spelling the word "hate" backwards. "Etah," in fact, is an Inuktitut word meaning "the windy place." Some 250 Inuit living in 1925 as their ancestors had for thousands of years roamed up and down about 400 miles of shoreline in northwest Greenland.

They were the pure strain, small, dark-haired, Asiatic-looking people, unlike the mixed breeds of Disko Island. Etah was the northern limit of their territory, the northernmost place where they could exist. Further north, Smith Sound, even in summer, was usually clogged with ice, preventing the hunters from going out in their kayaks and harvesting seal, walrus, and narwhal. Inland, the glaciers further north deterred the caribou herds.

The winds for which Etah was named and which slip down to the shore from the summit of the vast Greenland ice cap were howling when the MacMillan expedition dropped anchor. Small icebergs that had chipped off the glacier at the end of the fjord dotted the heaving waves. Fog descended to about one hundred feet above ground level. "What a God-forsaken place this is," Floyd Bennett was thinking.[9] To the aviators, the lay of the land appeared less than favorable. The Loenings were thirty-three feet long and had a forty-five foot wing-spread. They could neither be assembled on the *Peary*, because there was not enough room, nor on the water, because a wingless fuselage is unstable at sea and would topple over. They had to be erected on land, but the hills and rocks extended right down to the water's edge. There was only one small beach, a sandy, pebbly shelf that protruded about forty feet and was perhaps fifty feet wide—half the size of a major-league infield. It was too steep and abounded with large rocks. Byrd figured that flight preparations would take twice as much time as he had initially estimated.

"Nothing but rocks and ice, mountains and icebergs," Bennett noted in his diary. "Not one place to set up a plane. It looks like a hopeless job."[10] Work began the following day at 5:30 a.m. The temperature was around 32°F. Everyone from MacMillan on down rowed out to the beach and began prying up boulders and small rocks and smoothing out the sand. The beach was cleared by noon. The aviators then rowed back to the *Peary* and took apart the crates in which the wings were stored. The wings were left on deck; the lumber was brought ashore. Two lifeboats lashed together side by side and covered over with a layer of wooden planks served as a makeshift raft. The long sides and end-panels of each of the three dismantled crates were now laid down in the form of two parallel tracks leading from the water's edge up onto the cleared beach. The tracks were spaced far enough apart to match the width of the Loenings' landing gear. A couple of horizontal crosspieces were nailed under the tracks; they extended out on both sides like axles and were weighed down with heavy rocks to keep the ramp from being dislodged at high tide when the beach was flooded. The tracks had been completed in a drizzling rain and were in place by 3:00 p.m. Several trips were then made back to the *Peary* to raft the wings ashore and subsequently one of the amphibians. All hands hauled the fuselage off the raft and onto the tracks; the landing gear was lowered, and the ship was wheeled up the ramp to a work area. Had they not built a ramp, the wheels would have sunk into the soft sand. The fourteen-and-a-half-hour workday ended at eight o'clock that night.

Two planes were erected the next day in continued freezing temperatures and more rain and snow. The *Peary* and *Bowdoin* crews bent over and supported the wings on their backs while the aviators secured them to the fuselage. Bennett and the other mechanics had to take their mittens off and make some of the more delicate connections barehanded in the biting cold. That same day, MacMillan glided up the fjord in a motor launch and found two Inuit families; their homestead consisted of a winter residence, an igloo made of sod and rocks, and a summer home, a *tupik* or sealskin tent. MacMillan put the women to work making pants out of polar bear skins, the warmest trousers on earth. He wanted to be prepared for a forced landing on the pack ice of the Polar Sea. One of the Inuit seamstresses was a woman named Toocumah, who had made similar garments for the Peary North Pole expedition of 1908.

That evening two assembled biplanes, moored to their anchor buoys, floated placidly in the middle of the inlet. Byrd accorded Mac-Millan the honor of making the first test flight. The commander climbed down into the observer's seat in the belly of the amphibian designated NA- (or Naval Arctic plane) 2, below the two cockpits. Mechanic Charles Rocheville slipped into the rear cockpit. Pilot Billie Schur taxied into the wind, kicked in the throttle, pulled back on the control wheel (it was fully circular, like the steering wheel of an automobile), and ascended to 1,500 feet. The glacier below looked like a swirl of soft vanilla ice cream creeping inland. As Schur swung back over the fjord, his passengers waved to the Inuit, all of whom moved quickly into the little *tupik*. NA-2 landed successfully after a thirty-minute hop.

Bromfield, the interpreter, later asked the Inuit why they crowded inside the tent. They said they could not understand what held the flying machine up; they expected it to fall out of the sky, and when it passed overhead, they thought they were going to be killed. They all wanted to die together.[11]

By the evening of the third day at Etah, Tuesday the fourth, a dull, gray overcast day with intermittent rain, the last aircraft had been assembled and moored. Byrd and Bennett flew together for the first time at nine that evening when they took NA-1 up for a test flight.

They ascended to 5,000 feet in bitter cold air and turned west. The mouth of the fjord slipped behind them, Smith Sound stretched across their flight path. Out over the Sound, they noticed upon looking below the lower right wing that the channel north of Etah, as far as the eye could see, was completely lined with ice, "All as rough and corrugated as an old washboard," Byrd said.[12] They crossed the

Sound in fifteen minutes and approached Cape Sabine on Ellesmere Island. Byrd leaned out into the windstream for a look at the spot where eighteen members of the Greely party died of starvation. In the bitter cold, the exposed part of his face started to feel numb.

The eastern Arctic was once underwater and over the eons of geological time sea level has gradually decreased while the level of the land has risen. Arctic landforms generally have the appearance of raised beaches that were exposed as the sea receded. The Ellesmere coastline conformed to this pattern. Byrd found himself looking obliquely down on the eastern face of a wide, tan, snow-crested table-land sloping down to the water line at a forty-five-degree angle. The breaks in the coastline, canyon-like openings like Etah Fjord, were occluded with thick sheets of ice, motionless swishes of frozen whiteness.

As might be expected in the eastern Arctic in August, the next three days were heavily overcast with periods of steady rain erupting into violent squalls. During this period, when the rain let up a bit, Byrd put his aircraft through a series of routine tests to ensure that all systems were functioning properly. The radios had to be tested, the compasses had to be tested. Magnetic compasses are delicate instruments. The needle of a pocket compass can easily be deflected by metal on the person of the user or in the environs. Airplane compasses pick up a certain amount of error from the metal in the plane itself. The only way to determine the extent of deviation is to check the compass inside the plane against one outside of it. Deviation is noted and compensated for by placing small magnets in various parts of the plane.

There were fuel consumption tests and load tests. The Loenings needed a runway about a mile long to pick up enough speed to get airborne. Since open land wasn't available, all operations had to take place at sea. On a test run, however, NA-2 and -3 proved to be tail-heavy with a full load of fuel, emergency gear and survival rations—including material to be cached en route to the Polar Sea—and couldn't get off the water. Byrd decided to jettison a thirty-three-gallon emergency fuel tank that had been installed in the bow of each plane and move part of the load forward. With the weight distributed this way, the planes were able to lift off the fjord with sufficient fuel to fly about 300 miles from Etah, return, and still have enough gas left over in case the pilots drifted off course or had to circle around and wait for a fog to lift before landing at the home base.

Two decades after Kitty Hawk, the possibilities of aviation continued to be refined and enlarged. Unlike Amundsen, who pounced on aviation as a technology that could serve his purposes, Byrd saw himself as serving the development of that technology. Every test, every adjustment was part of the process of reaching the Polar Sea, part of the accumulated knowledge and experience that would enable polar aviation and aviation in general to advance to the next stage. The flight-testing and instrument checks, however, had a predictable effect on the other factions that constituted the expedition. MacMillan, McDonald, and the scientists and professionals became as restlessly impatient with the aviators as Byrd had been with the leadership on the outbound voyage.

Rigg, the Geodetic survey man, had established a tidal observation station; he had a machine with him—a tidal gauge—that automatically recorded the kind of data MacMillan had had to take down with pencil and paper in 1908 and 1909. Koelz, the naturalist, went out in the rain everyday collecting wildlife specimens, assisted by Dr. Davidoff. McDonald got out his kayak and went walrus hunting with the Inuit. During the first week at Etah, he made radio history, holding the first Arctic news conference. In the wee hours of the fourth and sixth, he and MacMillan were grilled via short-wave radio by reporters assembled at the Zenith radio station in Chicago. "Have you reserved seats for when Washington wins the World Series?" they were asked.[13] The Senators, the defending World Champions, were currently trailing the Philadelphia Athletics by three percentage points in the American League. "I'm afraid we won't be back in time to help Washington root for [Senators' president Clark] Griffith," McDonald answered.

On the fifth, the engine in the NA-1 developed a knock during a test run, and Bennett strongly recommended that it be replaced by a spare. This operation was conducted with the biplane bobbing up and down on the waves, and Bennett and Sorensen standing on the lower wings as one of three spare engines was lowered by the *Peary*'s boom. Three days had gone by and energetic, managerial types like MacMillan and McDonald wanted results. So far as they were concerned, the only results of the navy's efforts was that two planes failed to get off the water and the engine of the third had to be completely replaced.

On the evening of the seventh, Koelz and Davidoff were conversing in sign language with five amiable Inuit who had come aboard the *Peary*. Pilot Schur approached with drinks in his hands and gave one to each of the native people. He then indicated that in exchange for the drinks he wanted a bearskin. When the guests departed, he "doubled up with laughter," Davidoff wrote, "and explained that all he had given them was Listerine."[14]

This was precisely the wrong time for barracks humor. "The fact is that the naval contingent has been a disappointment from my point of view from the start," Davidoff was prompted to write.[15] Byrd, the commanding officer, tended to run on a bit about his ancestry, connections and access to "the great and near great." Davidoff and Koelz usually went out specimen-collecting at night, so Davidoff could be around in the daytime in case a medical emergency occurred. He may have been bagging specimens when Bennett and Sorensen worked around the clock in the cold and damp to finish installing the spare engine in the NA-1. But he apparently saw them or other members of the Naval Unit "gorge themselves on midnight lunches, wasting quantities of food unnecessarily and grow fat and even more dull, if that is possible, than before. Then," he said, "they rise late the next morning to make up for lost sleep. Meanwhile, the short spell of good weather may have come and gone and they sit and eat for another day."

After going without sleep to complete the engine installation, Bennett and Sorensen had reported for duty in the morning in case the weather cleared and it was possible to fly. However unfair, Davidoff's comments undoubtedly reflected the general opinion of the scientists and professionals. "And these are the heroes, these are the great Arctic explorers upon whom the eyes of the world are fixed!" he wrote, on the day of the Listerine prank.

They may know how to turn the wheels of an aeroplane but are otherwise lacking in all the accomplishments, all the refinements and all the graces of gentlemen.

⚡ 8 ⚡

THE SUN
COMPASS

From everywhere, it points toward the geographical pole.

ALBERT H. BUMSTEAD[1]

Ellesmere Island, the tenth largest island in the world, is a long, top-heavy, and stem-shaped splotch of ground that in outline looks like a human fetus just before it takes on recognizably human features and when its head is still curled against its body. The head is in the north, the tail is in the south. It is 500 miles long, about 255 miles wide at the head part, and two-thirds as wide at the tail. If turned upside down, it would resemble Great Britain. The two islands are roughly the same size; Britain is slightly larger. Both are in close proximity to smaller land masses immediately to the west. Axel Heiberg Island and Ireland are also proportionately the same size and shape.

Cape Thomas Hubbard at the northernmost tip of Axel Heiberg Island was just over three hundred miles due northwest of Etah, about the distance of Pittsburgh from New York. It was also the demonstrated limit of the cruising radius of a Loening Amphibian carrying the maximum load for a water takeoff. Byrd believed there was a time and place for the long, spectacular flight, but had never intended to try to reach the shore of the Polar Sea by hopping over Ellesmere Island in one fell swoop. Even if the amphibians had been able to get off the water with *all* the supplies necessary to operate out of Axel Heiberg, the engines would have had to work so hard to deliver the load that the strain would have lessened their reliability. For this reason, he had planned from the start to put down intermediate bases and proceed in stages. The 300-mile cruising radius confirmed his initial judgment. A spectacular dash to Cape Thomas Hubbard and back would have cut the fuel reserve and margin of safety much too close for comfort. Byrd wanted to establish at least one base in the interior of Ellesmere Island, about 150 miles from Etah—midway between Etah and the cape—so that if a pilot was flying between Etah and the intermediate base, or between that base and Hubbard, he would never be more than seventy-five miles from food, fuel, provisions, and a working radio.

MacMillan was confident that suitable landing places would be found on the surface of the numerous fjords that cut through Ellesmere. At shortly after nine o'clock on the evening of the eighth, a day of low-lying fog, squalls, and snow, the weather cleared sufficiently for an attempt to locate one. Bennett remained at Etah, repairing a faulty oil tank in the NA-1. Byrd climbed into the rear cockpit of the NA-3, behind Reber. MacMillan again occupied the observer's compartment of the NA-2, below Schur and Rocheville. On takeoff, a herd of about a dozen walrus blocked the mouth of the harbor. These massive animals wanted to fight it out with the planes, their shiny black bodies half out of the water. At the last minute they disappeared from view beneath the spray of the accelerating amphibians lifting off the waves.

The magnetic field that surrounds the earth is not uniform. The lines of force span the earth between the magnetic north and south poles. The forces of attraction cause the needle of our pocket compasses to spin from side to side in the direction of the poles. They also exert a downward pull on the needle. The vertical or downward-pulling component is negligible in the middle latitudes and can be disregarded. In the vicinity of the poles, however, where the lines of force converge, the vertical component is quite strong, and the horizontal component is correspondingly weak. The horizontal component is only about one-seventh as strong at Etah as it is in Washington, D.C. For this reason, although the magnetic compass is the principal steering instrument of an airplane, Byrd could not rely on it for direction-finding in the high latitudes. As a backup system, he had a more subtle and responsive instrument installed in each plane, an earth-inductor compass. This instrument, developed by the Bureau of Standards, made use of a fundamental principle of electromagnetism: a changing magnetic field generates an electrical field.

Two additional dials were mounted on the instrument panels of the Loening Amphibians for the operation of the earth-inductor compass. One was a compass card which the navigator adjusted to a desired course, the other was a steering indicator which showed deflections to the left or right. The instrument itself was connected to a coil, a pinwheel-like object mounted on the outside of the plane. A small motor made the coil revolve. The course-adjustment placed the revolving coil in a certain alignment with the earth's magnetic field. So long as the ship stayed on course, the coil remained in alignment, and the pointer on the deflection indicator read zero. If the plane started to veer off course, the coil generated a slight electrical current. The instrument was sensitive enough to detect the current, and the pointer consequently moved away from zero either to the left or right.

Over Smith Sound, the earth-inductor compass was sluggish but nonetheless functional. It had yet to be determined whether an airplane could be navigated with precision on a long flight in the polar regions. Roald Amundsen had navigated splendidly on a sledge journey from a base camp on the coast of Antarctica to the South Pole and back, but had been unable to steer with comparable skill in an airplane over the Polar Sea. In August of 1925, the future of polar aviation depended on Byrd's skill and the accuracy of the instruments he had assembled.

One of the complicating factors was that steering instruments such as the magnetic and earth-inductor compasses are oriented to the magnetic North Pole, while courses are plotted on maps oriented to the geographic pole. The former was then on Boothia Peninsula in the Canadian Arctic, about 1,200 miles south of the point attained by Admiral Peary in the Polar Sea. Byrd was flying *between* the two poles. He was also flying over largely uncharted territory. The variation between the two orientations was expected to be enormous, but the precise amount had never been determined. Fortunately, the device that Albert H. Bumstead had presented to Byrd just before the expedition left Wiscasset enabled him to ascertain this figure.

Bumstead had constructed a *sun* compass, a deceptively simple instrument that, as will be seen, allowed a navigator to determine true directions from the bearing of the sun. During one of the fleeting breaks in the perpetual overcast that hung over Etah since the day he arrived, Byrd had checked the magnetic instruments against the Bumstead compass and had calculated that the magnetic compasses were off by 103 degrees. Over Cape Sabine now, Byrd took some bearings with the earth-inductor compass of landforms that had been mapped by Peary almost a quarter-century earlier and discovered an additional "local" error of thirty degrees, probably due to previously undetected magnetism in the plane. This meant that to proceed on a straight line to the northwest, NA-2 and -3 had to steer a compass heading of due east!

The ships turned inland on this heading at an altitude of three thousand feet. Ellesmere is the northernmost island in the Canadian Arctic Archipelago and the most mountainous. The interior beyond Cape Sabine conformed to the pattern of high, sprawling tablelands with steep sides. Between them glistened fjords frozen over with ice and snow, or the smooth white icing of glaciers running down to the sea. The slopes of the plateaus were dusted with snow, the tabletop surfaces were rough, bumpy, and virtually smeared with a white wintry glaze. Over them descended layers of stratus clouds spread low across the sky in bands and streaks, the kind of heavy, dramatic weather that nineteenth-century landscape artists had portrayed in scenes of the American West.

In the belly of the NA-2, MacMillan enjoyed a new view of his old sledging grounds. A decade earlier he and Fitzhugh Green and their party had made their way across the same rugged terrain, heading for the same destination. He vividly recalled the scene for the *National Geographic*: "Stripped down to an undershirt and reeking with perspiration, we wallowed in snow thigh deep, yelling at our dead tired dogs until our throats were raw and our voices gone."[2] At the time, he had looked up at the sky and thought to himself, "Some day aviators will laugh at this." He knew from experience that the fjords he was looking down on usually thaw before the ice melts on the surface of the adjacent tablelands. But that had not happened in 1925.

Byrd noted that there was "very little open water in the fjords" to land on, nor were there long, flat stretches of open ground.[3] The ceiling remained low, the sun completely hidden. The overcast imposed another difficulty. Navigation begins with dead reckoning. You know where you started from, the direction you're traveling in, and how fast you're going. With this information, you can pretty well calculate your location. Navigators continuously make these running calculations, but dead reckoning is educated guesswork. The only way to eliminate the guesswork is to accurately fix your position from time to time and then restart the dead reckoning from the last positive fix.

There was no loran in the 1920s, no satellites, no Global Positioning System. Contemporary navigators relied on celestial observations to check and correct their dead reckoning position. The absence of the sun, however, meant that Byrd, in the lead plane, would have to find his way over the interior of Ellesmere Island and back *exclusively* by dead reckoning. This was an extremely tricky procedure in the air, because there was an additional element in the equation, and it was invisible: wind.

In 1919, when Byrd developed the bubble sextant, he had also evolved an instrument to measure wind drift, the extent to which an airplane is displaced off course due to the action of the wind. The apparatus was mounted at Byrd's right shoulder, on the starboard side of the rear cockpit of NA-3.

At first glance it partially resembled the upright telephones of the 1920s. What appeared to be the mouthpiece, however, was actually an eyepiece. As pilot Reber flew up the Ellesmere tablelands, Byrd looked through the eyepiece. He identified a blemish in the snow or a hummock of ice. A rotating arm projected at right angles from the base of the instrument. It was about a foot long and looked like the wooden rulers schoolchildren were using in those days, but was not a solid piece of wood. It was a narrow wooden frame with a wire down the middle. Byrd swung the frame over the object he was looking at and made careful adjustments until the blotch in the snow appeared to be running along the wire. A scale on the base of the instrument was so calibrated as to be able to tell him at a glance the velocity and direction of the wind. By timing the apparent motion of the blotch with a stopwatch, he could work out his *ground* speed, the speed the aircraft actually makes over the ground.

The problem of what course he had to steer to compensate for wind drift could now be solved by a series of computations. Using a mechanical flight computer, something like a circular slide rule, Byrd, in a matter of minutes could obtain the course he had to follow to correct for wind drift. On the outward flight, the drift indicator showed a crosswind from the north, and a course correction of some ten degrees was necessary. Interestingly, Byrd even had a backup system for the drift indicator. He had a bunch of smoke bombs in the cockpit, which produced black smoke to show up against snow and ice. He could have dropped a smoke bomb, then looked back over the tail of the amphibian. Radial lines had been painted on the horizontal stabilizer of the planes. The lines were arranged like the slats of a paper fan and were drawn five degrees apart. The approximate drift angle could be obtained by eyeballing the smoke as it floated aft past the graduated lines.

In effect, the amphibians were equipped with a large, external protractor.

Further on, the elevation of the formations increased. The plateaus seemingly rose to meet the descending layers of stratus. There were no passes ahead, and the landmarks behind were glazed with mist. Byrd instructed Reber to ascend to 3,800 feet to get over the clouds. Schur followed in the NA-2. They had flown a little over an hour out of Etah, covering a distance of about 120 miles, and the only way back now was by dead reckoning.

As they neared Smith Sound on the return leg, the drift indicator revealed a thirty-mile-an-hour gale pushing down from the north. Breaks in the cloud cover enabled them to find their way visually back across the channel. The waves were high when the amphibians landed in the harbor.

It soon started to snow and continued snowing for two more days.

A narrow, 300-mile long channel separates Axel Heiberg and Ellesmere Islands. Numerous inlets on the west coast of Ellesmere open on this channel. Cañon Fjord is one of the most breathtaking. It is an enormous rift in the coastline one-third the size of the Grand Canyon and almost as wide, and is shaped remarkably like a knee-high boot. The fjord courses fifty-five miles inland, from the northwest down to the southeast, then makes a ninety-degree turn at the "instep" and continues for another thirty miles. The "toe" of the boot points to the northeast.

A straight line drawn between Etah and Cape Thomas Hubbard runs diagonally across Ellesmere Island from the east to the west coasts. At about the halfway point, the straight line grazes the toe of Cañon Fjord. The straight line spans the length of the boot, from the tip of the toe to the top. Cape Thomas Hubbard, the northernmost point of Axel Heiberg Island, is about 135 miles from the mouth of Cañon Fjord, on a straight line running due northwest of Etah.

The straight line was Byrd's initial flight path. He wanted to put a base down in Cañon Fjord, but fog and clouds stopped him perhaps within twenty-five miles of the tip of the boot. Fog and clouds combined with the raised topography of Ellesmere Island produce extremely dangerous flying conditions. The aviator sees only a curtain of haze and may well fly into the side of a cliff. There were two alternate flight paths: one was to fly 135 miles due west of Etah to an inlet called Bay Fjord and establish a base there. Another great rift on the west coast of the island, Bay Fjord lay fifty to fifty-five miles south of Cañon Fjord. On subsequent flights, the aviators could hop from Bay Fjord northwest to Cape Thomas Hubbard, although this was a little like going from Phoenix to San Francisco by way of Los Angeles.

The second alternative was to proceed due north along the east coast of Ellesmere and put down a series of bases en route to Cape Columbia, the jumping-off point for Peary's sledge journeys. The northern route to the Polar Sea was about 25 percent longer than the Etah-Bay Fjord-Thomas Hubbard flight path, but Byrd believed there was a better chance of finding pools of open water for the amphibians to land on along the coast. He implored MacMillan to let him follow the shoreline, but MacMillan refused.

Again a clash of perspectives. Airmen are trained to look for possible emergency landing places as they fly. If the engine fails, the wings will retain enough lift to enable them to glide to a landing. Byrd scanned the terrain as he flew on the eighth but did not feel the plane could be put down safely on the crags and folds sprawling below his wing. In 1925, the aircraft engine was still an unreliable piece of machinery. He called the unit together at noon on the ninth and told his men he would not *order* them to fly over Ellesmere Island again. If they chose to follow him over Smith Sound, they would have to do so as volunteers. The navy men understood the situation but remained as game to carry out their mission as Byrd himself.

MacMillan, however, had the foot traveler's conception of safety; he knew the country and was concerned about what would happen in the aftermath of a forced landing. Each amphibian carried an inflatable life raft. Accordingly, MacMillan worked out a water route by which the downed airmen could make a journey to the east across the interior of Ellesmere Island.[4] When their rations were consumed they could live off the creatures that inhabited the land: musk ox, Arctic hare, eider duck, glaucous gulls. The Inuit reported that the Royal Canadian Mounted Police had erected a shack on the coast, near Cape Sabine, a likely ploy in their campaign to establish Canadian sovereignty in the High Arctic. It was unoccupied but said to be well stocked with food. MacMillan suggested that the survivors wait there for rescue. He apparently felt that a line of retreat along the northern route would have been too long to prove viable and that another Greely starvation drama might play out. "I was most vigorously turned down," Byrd wrote, of his proposal to reach the Polar Sea via Cape Columbia.[5]

On Tuesday, August 11, the stubborn mist hanging over Etah finally lifted. This was the first sunny day since the expedition arrived. "At about 4 AM the clouds cleared off," Davidoff reported, "and all the mountains around us with their snow-covered peaks and red, green and purple sides glowed in the sunlight." The three amphibians departed at 10:40 that morning for Bay Fjord. Byrd and Bennett took the lead in the NA-1 and flew at 7,000 feet. Schur and MacMillan in the NA-2 and Reber and Nold in the NA-3 followed at 4,000 feet. Banking northwest of Cape Sabine, they cut across now familiar points and promontories jutting out into Smith Sound. The peninsulas looked like the long necks and bodies of petrified dinosaurs with their heads submerged for a drink. The steep, snow-glazed plateaus that framed the fjords and rolled inland were dozens of miles long. Pilots Bennett, Reber, and Schur preferred to keep these surfaces under them as they flew. If the engine quit, they were prepared to lower their wheels and put the plane down right on top of the mesas. They probably would have died in the attempt. Later that fall, the navy subjected a slightly modified version of the Loening Amphibian to a series of performance tests. The landing gear, the test pilots said in their report were "not of a very rugged construction. Adequate for smooth fields and carrier work. Not well suited for cross-country operations."[6] Byrd's misgivings about forced landings on Ellesmere Island were right on the mark.

For twenty minutes they followed Flagler Bay, which curves sharply inland to the west for about thirty or forty miles. The head of the Bay narrowed into a riverbed threading through the vast central highlands like a long and twisted piece of string. The topography of central Ellesmere is starker than the coast. Across the horizon swept the distant, jagged ridgelines of hundreds of sharply peaked mountains. The sides of these ranges were as creased and folded as crumpled pieces of paper. Some of these formations rose to elevations as high as the altitudes of the planes; some rose even higher. "The sun beating down on the endless slopes," Byrd wrote, "threw a constant glare in our eyes."

Heavy stratus was moving in from the west, the bands and streaks resting on the jagged ranges like a lowered curtain. There was a pass running through the rolling tablelands immediately to the south. Bennett steered for the gap, ascending to 7,300 feet. Byrd plotted a course to Bay Fjord some fifty miles away. The bright sunlight enabled him to try out on this flight the navigation instrument that would prove indispensable to his career as a polar explorer.

When timepieces were made of gears and springs and had circular dials, boy scouts were taught a simple procedure to orient themselves if they got lost in the woods. They pointed the hour hand of their watch directly at the sun, then they looked at the dial and imagined a straight line halfway between the hour numeral and twelve o'clock. That straight line ran north-south. If you know the time of day, the corresponding position of the sun is an indicator of direction. Similarly, before clocks were invented, direction, in a certain sense, served as an indicator of time. In the northern hemisphere, the gnomon, the shadow-casting marker of a sundial, always faces true north. During daylight hours, so long as the dial is inclined for the latitude of the site and the sun is shining, the shadow will show you the position of the sun relative to true north, or, in other words, the correct time. The sun compass is a steering device that makes use of these relationships. The modern sun compass was conceived by Roald Amundsen as a navigation aid for his aborted 1924 transpolar flight. But the connection between time, the sun, and direction probably occurred to the ancient mariners of many of the world's cultures. Evidence has recently been unearthed in southern Greenland that the Vikings used a primitive device of this nature.[7]

Amundsen's instrument was manufactured by a German optics firm. It was basically a periscope some eight inches high mounted at eye level above the pilot's flight controls. The device was adjusted for the course to be followed, and a timing mechanism was activated. Looking into the sight, the pilot saw crosshairs. The plane would then be put into a turn. The periscope was so designed that a mirror image of the sun would appear in the middle of the crosshairs when the airplane turned to the desired heading. You maintained course by steering the plane in such a way as to hold the image steady.

The timing mechanism rotated to stay in alignment with the sun and was embedded in the top of the periscope. The sun never sets during the brief Arctic summer nor, of course, from an earthbound point of view does it stand still as the day proceeds. It appears to swing around the sky like clockwork starting in the north at midnight local time and making a full circle over the next twenty-four hours through the east, south, and west. The Amundsen instrument effectively extracted useful information from the apparent motion of the sun, but on the whole the precision engineering embodied every virtue except simplicity.

What if you kept the clockwork mechanism but eliminated everything else? What if you made a clock with a circular dial and the clock had one hand and it took that single hand twenty-four hours to go around the dial? You would, in effect, be able to track the position of the Arctic sun at a glance. This is substantially what Albert H.

Bumstead pondered while he listened to Byrd's remarks on polar navigation during the press conference at the National Geographic Society. "I pictured myself standing at the north pole," he explained years later,

> and seeing the sun go around me once every twenty-four hours with a regularity of motion exceeding that of the most perfect time piece. I thought of a watch lying flat on the ground, and how, if it only had a twenty-four hour dial instead of the usual twelve hour dial, the hour hand, once pointed at the sun, would keep itself pointed at the sun as long as the watch ran.[8]

The Bumstead sun compass is a slow clock; there are twenty-four numerals on the dial, and it takes twenty-four hours for its single hand to revolve around it. The twelve and six o'clock positions on an ordinary clock are 12 noon and 12 midnight on the Bumstead dial. The three o'clock position is 6:00 p.m. The nine o'clock position is 6:00 a.m. The hand of the clock is a gnomon, a shadow-casting device. It is thick, pear-shaped, and has an upraised pin on the end that points to the numeral. If the hand is set to the correct time, the sun is out, and you turn the instrument toward the sun, at a certain point the pin will throw the shadow of the sun down the middle of the hand. The clock is now in alignment with the sun, and you are facing true north. If you also had a magnetic compass, the difference between the direction indicated on the compass and true north would be the exact amount of variation in the locality where you are standing.

The beauty of the Bumstead instrument is that it can also be used to steer by. The dial on Bumstead's device is exactly two-and-one-quarter inches in diameter; the entire clock and its casing is about the size and shape of a small jar of Noxzema. The mechanism can be tilted up and down, and resembles a miniature version of the huge searchlights that were lit up in front of Hollywood movie palaces in the 1920s for the premiere of a motion picture. The up-and-down adjustability allows the navigator to tilt the clock to the precise angle (latitude) between the equator and the place where the instrument is being used.

You can tilt a searchlight up and down, and you can swing it left and right. The Bumstead clock also happens to be mounted on a circular plate that swivels. That plate is a compass card. The navigator can select any course by turning the plate. As the plate moves, the clock moves with it. This throws the sun and the hour hand out of alignment. If the airplane is turned so that the shadow of the sun is brought back into alignment with the hour hand, the pilot has found the desired heading. By keeping the hour hand aligned with the shadow, the aviator keeps the ship on course.

Byrd turned the compass card to a true west-southwesterly course of 250 degrees and adjusted the angle of tilt to the latitude. The time was 12:07 p.m. The hour hand was pointing slightly to the right of 12 noon. Byrd banked the airplane until the shadow fell down the length of the hour hand and knew he was on a heading straight for Bay Fjord.

Bennett did most of the flying with Byrd taking over now and again as relief pilot or to correct the heading. En route to Bay Fjord, Bennett signaled for Byrd to pass the logbook. The roar of the Liberty motor made it impossible for them to communicate verbally; in the open-cockpit days, aviators stuffed their ears with cotton to prevent nerve damage and hearing loss. Bennett returned the log with a note written across a blank page: "Will you fly for a few minutes?"[9]

The aft cockpit had a stick control instead of the control wheel installed in the forward compartment. Byrd took the stick and busied himself maintaining altitude and heading. Flicking his eyes from the white-spattered horizon to the instrument panel and back, he was astonished to see Bennett haul himself out of his cockpit and climb onto the lower wing. The oil pressure gauge was reading dangerously high. Byrd scanned the surface for a place to land, but saw nothing, he said, "but jagged and snow-covered mountains and cliffs, and water full of rough ice."[10] Air temperature was, he estimated, perhaps fifteen degrees below zero. Either from clogging or another effect of extreme cold, excessive pressure had built up in the system that supplied oil to lubricate the moving parts of the engine. An engine failure—or worse—was imminent, and if Byrd tried to put the plane down, they would die.

Both he and Bennett were wearing a full set of furs—caribou parka, polar bear pants, sealskin mittens, and sealskin boots (with a sheepskin lining procured from the U.S. Navy). These garments were much too warm to walk around in at Etah but proved insufficient in the air. Byrd was freezing sitting in the cockpit. Bennett, out in the windstream of the plane, had to be numb with cold. He crouched over the engine, holding on with one hand to the struts between the upper and lower wings. In his free hand, he held a wrench; he had clamped the end of the wrench on the cap of the oil tank and attempted to unscrew it.

All that stood between them and either a blown engine at 7,300 feet or a crash landing in the crumpled hills was a two-dollar wrench and one wrist. Somehow Bennett knew that the trouble was in the oil tank and that if he got the cap off, the pressure that had built up in the tank would be relieved. He managed in his precarious position to apply enough leverage, removed the cap, and consequently saved his and Byrd's life.

Reber found himself in a predicament at about the same time. The NA-3 was having difficulty gaining enough altitude to fly over the increasing cloud cover. The white glare, meanwhile, was giving Reber a touch of snow blindness. He decided to turn back. When Reber disappeared from view, Schur turned the NA-2 around. Schur wanted to catch sight of the NA-3; if Reber was forced down, Schur would at least be able to report his position. He picked Reber up momentarily, then lost him again and resumed the west-southwesterly course.

MacMillan was in the aft cockpit behind Schur; the observer's cabin of NA-2 was unoccupied. Presently, Schur turned to MacMillan and shook his head. "Below us now," MacMillan wrote, "was a tumultuous sea of clouds with not a peep hole to the earth."[11] The stratus cloud is not white and puffy but rather a wall of gray mist that forms relatively close to the ground. That wall was rolling in under the airplanes, making it impossible to even search out a place to land if it became necessary to descend. Schur thought it futile to continue. Up to this point, he could find his way back to Etah by visually retracing the flight path through the pass. He, too, decided to get back while the getting was good.

Bay Fjord, like Cañon Fjord, was a boot-shaped inlet, just a few sizes smaller. The outlines were remarkably similar. The heel and toe of both fjords were at the eastern end, and the toes of both boots pointed north. Byrd and Bennett flew up the length of Bay Fjord, which runs fifty-five miles due west from the heel. A patchy blanket of vapor was suspended over the fjord and extended across the badlands on either side like smoke hanging over a burning town. Byrd could see the surface of the fjord here and there, and what he saw beneath the patches of mist was a rough white floor with some dark slits and cracks. The mouth of the inlet opened onto a channel called Eureka Sound, which was about half as wide as Bay Fjord was long. They approached the juncture within thirty minutes and found the entire water system practically one solid sheet of snow-covered ice.

9

IN THE MIDST
OF CHAOS

Happiness in the north is a very important factor,
in fact, one of the most important contributions
toward success in any undertaking.

DONALD B. MACMILLAN[1]

The lofty expectations with which the expedition departed and the failure of the aviators to perform up to those expectations threatened to divide the expedition along its fault lines. Among the civilian contingent, there now resonated "a loud undercurrent of opinionated discontent." This was Dr. Davidoff's phrase. Davidoff himself filled his entire diary entry of the eleventh with a devastating critique of the Naval Unit. "The aviators," he wrote, "after spending—wasting—about 8 hours of this first good flying day, started off at noon and returned in about three hours without having landed … "

> Great God! there may be hardships in landing, in the inhospitable country, in the inclement weather, in the unforeseen

failure of the planes to perform—but what I can't see is how a group of men sent up to accomplish what appears to be an important mission, insist on eight hours at least of sleep—nay, often stay abed until 10 or later in the morning, never mind the weather, the one good day in 14, leave their preparations until that good day arrives and spend the best part of it in loading their ships and tightening their motors.

(He obviously had never heard of a preflight inspection.)

"The whole business is entirely demoralized," he went on, "even MacMillan is beginning to throw up his hands in despair, and but for him everybody would be cutting everybody else's throat or run away south with the steamer ... "

"This, to me, at least," he fumed, "is the greatest display of inefficiency, corruption, soiled politics that has ever taken place."

If I have learned nothing more, I have at least learned how the U.S. Navy spends its money and in what hands it is entrusted.

He was so angry he put his fountain pen down for a week, except to say: "Until I can write something more cheerful I shall desist from this diary, for to me it is a sad state of affairs."

Under the circumstances, MacMillan appears to have conducted himself judiciously. He understood the impact the elements had been having on Byrd's flight plans, figuring all along that one "good north wind"[2] would clear out the fog and clouds, and "one week with the hot sun [would] soon melt the ice [and] enable us to do our work."[3] He was, however, increasingly critical of the Loening Amphibian. MacMillan thought it was the wrong airplane for the job; the maximum load it could carry on water maneuvers was about 1,000 pounds less than expected. He doubted whether the aviators could make enough trips back and forth to equip the bases Byrd envisioned and still reach the unexplored area of the Polar Sea before the Arctic winter arrived at the beginning of September.

MacMillan met with Byrd on the twelfth and asked him if he realistically felt he had a chance to accomplish the mission.[4] Byrd answered in the affirmative. He was thinking of the straight line that connected Etah and Cape Thomas Hubbard. If he could put one base down on the eastern coast of Ellesmere Island, find a way to Cañon Fjord and establish a second base there, he could cross the Polar Sea before the expedition had to leave Etah.

Gene McDonald brought a huckster's sensibility to the MacMillan Arctic Expedition. That evening, he gathered a dozen Inuit men, women, and children in the salon of the *Peary* for a radio broadcast.[5] The native people performed their traditional chants to the beating of a kiloute, a drum-like instrument resembling a tennis racket. It was made entirely of walrus parts: the tusk (the ivory handle), the spleen (the drum membrane), and the rib (the drumstick). The instrument was only to be played by an angekok, a shaman, or, literally, "miracle worker." The Etah musicians referred to themselves as "Angekok of the Stars and Skies." The selections included the "Song of the Snow Bunting," the "Song of the Raven," and the "Song of the Fox." The performance reportedly sounded like the rah-rah-rah of the Notre Dame cheerleaders when the Four Horsemen crashed through the Army defensive line. It was transmitted live to Chicago and created a stir in broadcast circles but failed to propitiate the Evil Spirit of the North.

Gale-force winds blew up from the south on the twelfth, howling day and night. No flights were possible. The thirteenth was an unmitigated disaster. Another gale struck, this time from the north and northwest. The wind kicked up the waves, and the continuous thrashing so battered the NA-2 that the seams parted where the metal plates joined on the lower hull, the part of the fuselage that rode on the waves; the forward compartments filled with water and she began to sink, nose first. The aircraft was in water up to her propeller shaft before the crew got a line around the shaft and hauled her out of the fjord. She would be out of commission for the duration of the expedition.

On the fourteenth at midday, the two surviving planes landed on a spot of open water in one of the long, icy inlets that scalloped the coastline of Ellesmere Island opposite Etah. The flight crews—Byrd and Bennett in NA-1, Schur and Sorensen in NA-3—pulled on rubber boots and spent the next hour and forty-five minutes hauling ashore 100 gallons of gasoline, ten gallons of oil, camping gear, a Primus stove, a rifle, 120 rounds of ammunition, and 200 pounds of food, including fifty cans of pemmican, seven pounds of erbswurst—a pemmican-like preparation of condensed pea soup—five pounds each of sugar and tea, ten pounds each of butter and powdered milk, twelve pounds of bacon, twelve cans of crackers, and six cans of cod liver oil in case of stomach trouble.

Within four hours of returning to Etah, Byrd, and Bennett took off with another load for the cache. Andrew Nold accompanied them in NA-3 and to carry as much additional supplies as possible flew without a relief pilot. When they circled down over the fjord, however, they were devastated to find that masses of drift ice had been blown into the inlet, and the thawed channel the planes had landed on earlier was no longer clear.

While hunting for another base, the two planes became separated. Plane to plane radio communication was not possible. Nold got lost and turned back for Etah. He knew enough to steer west to return east, but his instruments may have been malfunctioning. He inadvertently flew due north and would have run out of fuel and smashed into the jagged highlands below if Byrd and Bennett had not caught up with him.

The best flying weather seemed to coincide with the hours just before and after midnight. The winds were calm, the sky relatively clear. Late on the evening of the fifteenth, stuffed to their metallic gills with another load of food, fuel, and gasoline, the amphibians once again hopped off Etah harbor. The sun was just to the right of their course and just above the horizon. The layers of stratus that streaked across the horizon were illuminated by its fiery glow. A landing was made and a second cache established on the shores of a bay just to the north of the previous site. A curtain of fog descended and finally dissipated by about 4:15 a.m. NA-3 then developed engine trouble. Byrd and Bennett ascended to 5,000 feet in NA-1 and assumed a heading for Cañon Fjord.

The nose of the airplane pointed across a seemingly endless range of mountains chiseled by previous ice ages into raw, pyramid shapes. The formations were a few thousand feet high, broad-based with sharp, snow-capped peaks. Three sleek white highways curved one way then another through the mountains and out toward the horizon; they converged at a distant juncture, revealing themselves to be branches of one amorphous glacier. The sides of the mountains were so steep they seemed to be nearly vertical. A featureless wall of gray, smoky stratus rested right on top of the range, the snow-streaked summits disappearing in the clouds. The success of the expedition clearly depended on reaching Cañon Fjord, the strategic halfway point on a straight line to Cape Thomas Hubbard and the Polar Sea. "Get a look into it if you possibly can," MacMillan had told them, "but do not attempt anything in clouds or fog as you did the other day. We can stand failure of our plans but not a serious accident."

They slipped over one of the lower elevations, "just under a cloud bank," Byrd said.

The charts the aviators carried with them were based on the piece-meal cartography of nineteenth- and early twentieth-century explorers. The High Arctic would not be systematically mapped until aviation matured and airplanes were bigger, faster and more reliable. Ahead on the horizon, disappearing beneath another barrier of low stratus, was a second range that did not appear on Byrd's charts. These mountains were higher; modern topographic maps show elevations in excess of 5,000 feet, the altitude at which Byrd and Bennett were flying. Between the two ranges was a ragged gash of a valley described by Byrd in four words: "magnificent, stupendous, awful, terrible."

> I can [he said] compare it only with our own Grand Canyon, except that this was more terrifying than beautiful. Nature had wrought this in a ruthless moment, though it had required eons of time as we would measure it. There were crevices dividing the rock masses in which a fair-sized city might be placed.

Francis, the aerographer, could utilize the radio to tell NA-1 what the weather was like at Etah, but there was no advance warning of storm systems brewing on the far side of the mountains. Now a gale swept up out of the south. A single-engine, thirty-three-foot airplane is as much at the mercy of a roaring, forty-mile-an-hour wind as a three-inch leaf. There is perhaps nothing in existence as petrifying as being confined inside a small plane encountering extreme turbulence. A frightful sensation, intense and visceral, overcomes the occupants, the bottom-falling-out feeling you get in the pit of the stomach when the roller coaster plummets straight down over the precipice. But unlike the roller coaster, there is no scaffolding, no track, and no reassuring connection to earth. The rim of the bowl of horizon rises high overhead and out of view as you go plunging down, hurtling, dropping hundreds of feet. Then back up again, up to the blue horizon, followed by another sickening plunge.

The air was the roughest in Byrd's experience. "The currents battered our plane unceasingly," he said, "tipping it up and sweeping it sidewise until we seemed to be swinging like a pendulum through space." Byrd was afraid they would be thrown into a tailspin and come spiraling down on the boundless composition of snow, rock, and glacier etched below. Bennett had the wheel, battling on in an almost futile effort to hold the plane straight and level. From time to time, he would glance over his shoulder at Byrd, his goggles masking his eyes. He showed no distress. He was looking to see how Byrd was doing, to find out if the commander wanted to turn back.

The Byrd-Bennett partnership was sealed during these moments of sheer terror. Byrd had recognized Bennett's superior piloting skills; now he saw what Bennett was made of, and Bennett simultaneously took Byrd's measure. They almost crashed—several times—but did not reverse course until they were satisfied that NA-1 could not ascend with its heavy load of emergency gear to a high enough altitude to clear the wall of mist that rested on the second range.

The storm that battered Byrd and Bennett over the mountains blew all day and was followed by snow flurries at night. While falling snow dusted the decks and portholes of the expedition vessels, McDonald staged one of the most convincing demonstrations in the early history of radio. During the run-up to the MacMillan expedition, he had persuaded the navy to install short-wave equipment on the USS *Seattle*, the flagship of the United States Fleet. The fleet was about to embark on a goodwill tour of the Pacific. On August 16, the *Peary* and the *Seattle* established two-way voice communications.[6] The flagship was now anchored off Wellington, New Zealand, halfway around the world from Etah. McDonald had brought the Inuit singers and musicians back for a repeat performance and had invited the fleet commander, Admiral Robert E. Coontz, to stand by to receive them. According to legend, the conversation between Coontz and McDonald went something like this:

"Your signal's not coming through, Commander. I hear something, but it doesn't sound like singing. Sounds like … college yells."

"Yes sir, you're receiving us loud and clear!"

The storm cleared away the clouds and fog. Weather-wise, Monday, August 17, heralding the third week of August, was "a good day," according to Donald MacMillan, "slightly overcast" in the morning "with a north wind," but "a beautiful afternoon, easily the best we have had since leaving the Labrador." It was therefore painfully ironic that on this fine day one of the two remaining planes was out of commission. The engine of NA-3 was removed and had to be replaced with the last remaining spare. Byrd wanted to take off that night in NA-1. "Begged MacMillan to let Bennett and me go today to Cañon Fjord but he would not agree," Byrd wrote in his diary. "Wonderful day. Probably last chance." MacMillan, he said, "seems to have given up." He "seems to be in a great hurry to pack up and go back. Wonder what is in his mind."

Ice was forming on the lakes around Etah. The tiny flowers were past their bloom. The days were comfortable, the temperature ranging from the mid- to upper-30s, but in the evening the thermometer plunged below freezing. A thin layer of ice had formed on the surface of Etah Fjord the previous night. MacMillan had learned to read the story the land was telling him. Winter was coming. A realist, he therefore found it increasingly difficult to picture himself in an airplane this season looking down on the continent he believed existed within three hundred miles west of Cape Thomas Hubbard.

His primary concern was time. Two years earlier to the day, the *Bowdoin* had dropped anchor at a spot eleven miles north of Etah called Refuge Harbor. MacMillan had wintered over there, allowing the schooner to be frozen in. The ice in Smith Sound had broken up on schedule in July of 1924, but Refuge Harbor never thawed. The crew had to burn their way out—they filled buckets of smoldering ashes from the galley stove and cast the ashes out on the ice in two long, parallel lines to open up a lead. MacMillan rammed the ship through the lead and nearly capsized her on a sunken ledge. He didn't want the ice to get a toehold on his ship again. Moreover, this year neither the *Bowdoin* nor the *Peary* were provisioned for the winter.

One plane flying solo violated the protocol of the expedition. If forced down in a pool of water on Ellesmere Island, it would, like Amundsen's plane, be locked in when the slush froze. The NA-1's radio was out of order. No one would know where to look for her, and the temptation would be too great to prolong a search beyond the time when the ships could easily get underway for the voyage south. For these reasons, MacMillan had vetoed the flight of August 17.

The most difficult command decision had yet to be made: How much longer could they sit tight at 78°19′ N? How much more time could MacMillan give the Naval Unit to attempt to reach the Polar Sea? "If fiords are clear of ice possibly work can be done," he radioed to the National Geographic Society that day. "If no landing places can be found on water or land success doubtful." Being a blunt and pragmatic man, he dealt with these issues in the only way that made horse sense: he focused on results. He wrote Byrd a cordial letter on the seventeenth saying, "I have decided to await [sic] here at Etah one week more to give you and your men as much time as possible to put down a cache of provisions."

> If, at the end of that time, you and the men under
> your command believe that, given three days more, the

Expedition can reach a point on the Polar Sea at least two hundred miles west from any part of Axel Heiberg Land, I will gladly remain. If, at the end of that time, I receive no favorable report from you as to progress made, I shall assume that the work cannot be done.[7]

Two hundred miles into the Polar Sea would surpass the distance MacMillan had pushed his dog teams in 1914. That was the yardstick to which he held the Loening Amphibians.

After the storms, the rain, the snow and the fog, a period of fair weather now descended on northern Greenland. Davidoff, who had resumed his diary on the seventeenth, likened it "to our Indian summer, quite cold, but really splendid clear days." NA-3 would be ready for ready for takeoff on the twentieth with a new engine and a new wing. All boded well. It was therefore with supreme astonishment that Byrd deciphered a coded message from the Navy Department that he received on the nineteenth. It read:

MacMillan recommends that no further attempt be made to establish bases for flight over Polar Sea. Recommends leaving Etah to further explore Baffin Land, Greenland and Labrador. Please confer with MacMillan and make comment immediately.[8]

Expeditions are among the most exhilarating and the most monotonous activities human beings can undertake. Faraway, unfamiliar places are exciting, but the unfamiliar becomes routine only too quickly. Members of expeditions have a lot of time on their hands and few diversions. Most of that time is spent talking. Unless people are actively engaged in an ongoing project in a specific camp, the conversation is usually about going somewhere else. When word got out that MacMillan had given the aviators another week, the navy men were pleased, but Maynard Owen Williams, Jacob Gayer, Benjamin Rigg, and Leo Davidoff were upset. The scientists and professionals could not wait to see the last of Etah.

Williams had been a missionary, foreign correspondent, and world traveler when he joined the staff of National Geographic in 1919. One month older than Byrd, he had more name recognition among the public at large than any member of the expedition other than MacMillan. He wore wire-rimmed glasses and a floppy hat with the brim turned down and, wandering around Etah, must have looked like a vacationing executive pining for a trout stream. Williams and his ungainly, tobacco-chewing colleague, Gayer, had taken pictures of the scenery around Etah when the sun came out on Saturday the fifteenth, and stayed out for a change. Gayer had shot the first color photographs of the Arctic. The visual possibilities of the fjord and glacier had rapidly been exhausted. Rigg had compiled as much data for the Coast and Geodetic survey as could be extracted from the rise and fall of the tides, and Walter Koelz, the naturalist, had collected countless specimens of the small mammals, birds, and plants that managed to thrive at 78° north.

Measured against their own work and McDonald's short-wave experiments, the efforts of the Naval Unit seemed to the scientists and professionals to be without result. The midnight sun was due to set for the first time the following week. As the season for exploration wound down in the Arctic, the different factions that had been amalgamated into the expedition inevitably began looking to their own interests and agendas. What about the Viking ruins? What about Baffin Island, the fifth largest island in the world? Williams, Gayer, and Rigg complained to MacMillan that the longer the expedition persisted at Etah, the less time remained to chance to take pictures or collect data at the other ports on the expedition itinerary. Koelz would have joined them had he not departed on a field trip to an Inuit village twenty miles distant.

As Davidoff had prophesied six days earlier, MacMillan now indeed did throw his hands up in despair. He had made a sound management decision, but the expedition was coming apart as a result, and he saw no way to hold it together. In a fit of pique he sent a radiogram on the evening of August 17 to Washington, passing the buck to the National Geographic Society. "I am convinced that the Navy planes cannot do the work," he began. "This is the opinion of Williams, Gayer, Koelz, Riggs and nearly every man on board both ships. The Liberty engines are not standing up. The last spare engine is being installed."

> Three propellers have been installed. We have been here eighteen days. Two depots have been established but only ninety miles from ship. We have one thousand miles to go in addition to another one thousand to establish advance station. This must be done in ten days.[9]

It was 300 miles from Etah to Cape Thomas Hubbard, another two hundred miles to MacMillan's benchmark in the Polar Sea, and an equivalent distance to return. MacMillan reckoned that the amount of back-and-forth flying necessary to ferry supplies from Etah among one or two intermediate bases to reach Cape Hubbard would amount to an additional thousand miles. "We are simply wasting time and defeating all other objects of the expedition," he continued.

> By leaving Etah now your men can all do a big and valuable work. These are the facts. I leave it entirely to your judgement as to what I shall do.

Gilbert Grosvenor was in Europe, and Secretary of the Navy Curtis Wilbur was apparently on vacation as well. John La Gorce and Assistant Secretary Ted Robinson were minding their respective stores. Robinson at the moment was acting secretary of the navy. Upon receiving the MacMillan missive, La Gorce immediately conferred with Robinson, and both were apparently stunned at this development.

Robinson, according to La Gorce, "deemed it advisable to send Commander Byrd a cipher radio asking for his opinion."[10] Byrd composed the following reply:

> MacMillan did not inform me that he wanted to give up undertaking. Have conferred with MacMillan and he agrees that we should keep on flying to accomplish our mission. We will have two planes ready to fly tomorrow night.

MacMillan seems to have been trying to appease two irreconcilable factions. Coded messages were to be responded to in code. Byrd put the three sentences in cipher and submitted it to McDonald for transmission. Looking at the message, McDonald saw a series of four-digit numbers. Just three days earlier, Byrd had written in his diary about McDonald, "He seems to be suspicious of everything and everyone." To put McDonald's mind at ease, Byrd explained the gist of the message. McDonald said he would send it through, but went back on his word. By the morning of the twentieth, Byrd learned that the cipher had not been sent, and he and McDonald were once again at loggerheads.

McDonald thought he was helping MacMillan by denying Byrd input in the decision-making process transpiring in Washington. He formally took the position that there was "no reason why [the message] should not go in plain English as there is nothing in it of a confidential nature."[11] It's not difficult to guess what was really on his mind. If Harris Land was not in the cards this season, there was only one other way the expedition could make headlines and promote Zenith Radio, and that was to find the Viking ruins and prove that the Norsemen had discovered America. (Ten days later, on the return journey, McDonald wanted to send out a story that the *Peary* was running out of coal and would have to burn her own woodwork for fuel; he thought it would be good publicity.)

Meanwhile, Williams, Gayer, and Rigg dispatched a radiogram of their own, informing La Gorce that "The success of Navy plans seems impossible."

> If we leave now we can make stops in Greenland, Labrador and possibly Baffin Land ports with every possibility of more human interest stuff and scientific specimens and data than has been so far secured.[12]

By the time Byrd was allowed to get a response through to the Navy Department, the National Geographic Society, in the person of John Oliver La Gorce, had already endorsed MacMillan's finding. The NGS "will stand by your judgement," La Gorce had replied.

> We concur with proceeding upon further plans of Expedition.[13]

This was what MacMillan wanted to have happen. The decision had been made for him. All that remained was for him to rationalize it. He sent a letter over from the *Bowdoin* on August 20, formally notifying Byrd of the cancellation of the aerial mission. "Since talking with you yesterday, I have talked with the majority of your men who declare that it will be impossible for us to carry out our plans," he said.

Last night, the head of Etah Fjord froze over as it did the night before. A forced landing in Cañon Fjord or Eureka Sound would certainly result in a freezing in of the plane and a detention of the Bowdoin for fifteen months. In view of the fact that all other work as planned by the National Geographic is being prevented by our delay I have decided to prepare for home at once.

From Byrd's point of view, MacMillan had turned 540 degrees in three days, and the rapidity of these about-faces must have made Byrd's head spin. He sat down and carefully drafted a reply. "I am distressed beyond measure that we won't try again for the Polar Sea," he said, "and I beg you to reconsider your decision."

Of course I realize that you are using your best judgement and grant that it may be far better than mine only I do feel that we still have a chance to succeed. I would like to take that chance.

"Today is the 20th," he went on, "and I think that with four or five good days we could get out over the Polar Sea by using relief pilots."

I don't want to enter into any controversy with you about what my men think, but I have had the impression that they still want to try for the Polar Sea. In fact, they expressed themselves to that effect today. Do you not before we leave desire to explore the unexplored parts of Ellesmere Island beyond Sawyer Bay towards Cañon Fjord?

Byrd suggested that Gayer or Williams accompany the aviators "for some good photographs." And "do you not think it a good move to photograph the fjords beyond Cape Sabine?"

Having served nine years in the Virginia state legislature, Harry Flood Byrd, Richard's older brother, won his party's gubernatorial nomination while Dick was in Etah. Since the Byrds were Democrats in a largely Democratic state, the primary victory gave Harry a virtual lock on the general election. Sometime over the course of the MacMillan expedition, Dick must have received word of the primary returns and in some fashion celebrated his brother's victory. He must have casually let it be known among his shipmates that his brother was going to be governor of Virginia. The story then made its way through the grapevine and must have been distorted in transit so that by the time it reached the *Bowdoin*, Richard had become the Byrd with political ambitions.

This is the only way that what Donald MacMillan personally believed about Richard Byrd makes any sense. MacMillan pegged the Washington-based aviator as a "slick politician" trying to accomplish spectacular feats in the Arctic in order to win a future election.[14] Months later, he told Fitzhugh Green in confidence that Dick Byrd's dream was to be governor of Virginia and that he "definitely made that statement to Schur." (Green thought MacMillan's views were so off-the-wall he dictated a memorandum on the conversation immediately after the explorer left his office.)

Byrd was a smart man, and on August 20 he made a strong appeal, but it was too late. There would be no further flights across Smith Sound. MacMillan dismissed Byrd's appeal as political grandstanding.

With exemplary timing, at the precise instant when the relations between the leading actors at Etah became most strained, an almost incongruous episode of opéra bouffe occurred. The SS *Arctic*, a venerable Canadian icebeaker, arrived at Etah carrying an expedition launched by Ottawa to uphold the sovereignty of the Dominion in the far north. The Canadians were on their way across Smith Sound to finish building the RCMP station just up the coast from Cape Sabine. Exchanging pleasantries with the master of the ship, the equally venerable Canadian Arctic explorer, Captain Joseph E. Bernier, seventy-three, and the expedition leader, George P. Mackenzie, Byrd described the flights he and his unit had made over Ellesmere Island.

Shortly thereafter, Mackenzie's secretary, one Harwood E. R. Steele, boarded the *Peary*, located the commander of the American naval detachment and inquired as to whether the MacMillan expedition "was in possession of a permit from the Government of Canada authorizing them to fly over Ellesmere and other islands in the Canadian Arctic Archipelago."[15] Byrd said he didn't think the expedition had such a credential. Whereupon he was apprised that Commander Mackenzie was prepared to issue one. Byrd said he would take the matter up with MacMillan.

The *Arctic* had not sailed in secret. Washington was well aware of the Canadian expedition. That very day, La Gorce had sent MacMillan a radiogram outlining the protocol to be followed, and the Navy Department had dispatched a copy to Byrd. "To avoid embarrassing diplomatic situation," La Gorce said,

> it is essential you obtain license or permit from Mackenzie or Bernier of Canadian SS Arctic to land and explore Baffin Island or other territory south of Ellesmere Island.[16]

The message concluded: "Situation most delicate."

Barely hours after wrestling with MacMillan over the fate of the Polar Sea mission, with the tension still thick between them and a few sparks still flying, a deeply frustrated and quietly fuming Richard Byrd found himself conferring with the *Peary* man over an inane, diplomatic formality. In matters of life and death, Donald B. MacMillan could be relied upon to make the prudent and correct decision. But when it came to diplomacy, he was just too plain ornery to bend. He had a vague notion of having read in a newspaper prior to embarking from Wiscasset that the Canadians had granted the expedition all necessary permissions. Such a news item would have had no official standing. But from this position, MacMillan would not budge.

Later that afternoon, in full dress uniform and without an overcoat, Byrd boarded the *Arctic*, formally presented himself to Mackenzie, thanked him for having offered to grant permission to fly over Canadian territory, and respectfully informed him that he had referred the offer to Commander MacMillan.[17] MacMillan, Byrd said, stated that the required permits had already been granted and that notification of the granting had been received in the press.

Mackenzie, incredulous, then summoned as a witness the first officer of the *Arctic*, a Quebecois named Lazare Desire Morin. Affidavits were subsequently taken from both First Officer Morin and Harwood E. R. Steele.

Byrd made two brief entries in his diary over the next couple of days. The first line eloquently summarized his feelings. It read: "A remorseless cruel universe grinding out its destiny." The second revealed his principal source of comfort. "To have Marie in the midst of chaos," he wrote, "that is enough."

PART 2

THE MAN IN
THE CRISP
NAVY WHITES

☰ 10 ☰

F.F.V.

*My boyhood days and associations
were the happiest in my life.*

RICHARD E. BYRD[1]

Almost ten years after the Peary-Amundsen-Bartlett conferences, the Polar Sea had still not been traversed by air.
Byrd estimated that the Naval Unit had logged a combined airtime of over seventy-five hours in the High Arctic and that
the loops traced by the three planes over Smith Sound and Ellesmere
Island added up to some 5,292 miles flown west of Etah. This was a
remarkable achievement for the open-cockpit era; in modern terms,
Byrd pushed the outside of the envelope, perhaps to the limit of its
elasticity in that time and place.

By aerographer Albert Francis's calculations, half the time the
expedition had spent at Etah the weather had either been adverse or
severe. The Arctic winter of 1925 arrived early, and the ice conditions
that season had been exceptionally bad. The failure of the MacMillan
expedition, however, wasn't entirely or even fundamentally due to ice
or adverse weather—the problem was that the expedition could not
weather adversity. The clashing factions and personalities could have
harmonized had the stars aligned favorably and smashing results been

achieved. But the expedition was such a conglomeration of ill-fitting parts that any setback was bound to exacerbate the tensions that existed between them.

MacMillan started late and sailed slowly and conservatively up the Labrador coast. Those decisions were defensible. But he made one single management error: he failed to adequately provide for a resupply of coal. That error pushed the flight schedule back one week, into the predictably stormy month of August. The wheels of the "remorseless cruel universe" grinding out the destiny of the expedition were set in motion.

Nothing seemed to go as planned. Francis brought the ten navy carrier pigeons ashore the second day at Etah and erected a coop on the bluffs overlooking the small beach where the biplanes were assembled. He set them loose a few days later to acclimate themselves to the environs. Six failed to return. A seventh was lost on a subsequent "exercise flight" from which the three survivors returned "in an excited state." Unfortunately, the skies over the fjord were controlled by the local predators. Arctic falcons prey on small indigenous birds called auks. Hundreds of thousands of these auks abound in the rookeries around Etah. They endure by virtue of superior speed and maneuverability, and could fly rings around the pigeons. The navy birds fraternized in the air with flocks of auks. The elite and highly trained carrier pigeons were reportedly worth $200 apiece, but the navy apparently neglected their basic combat training.[2] When the falcons swooped down, the pigeons were sitting ducks.

Byrd and Bennett made one more exploratory flight before the expedition departed for the south, and Albert Francis accompanied them as cameraman. MacMillan authorized a hop over the Greenland ice cap. On August 22, the day the sun would dip below the horizon at midnight for the first time that season, NA-1 ascended to eleven

thousand feet and turned inland over Verhoeff Glacier, the white icing
that lined the roofs of the coastal mesas above Igloodahouny, an Inuit
campsite fifty miles down the coast from Etah. The edge of the glacier
had the same washboard-like texture of Smith Sound, but the innu-
merable corrugations were separated by deep crevasses in the ice.
Further inland, the vast sheet of ice became smooth and firm.

The sky was clear, visibility unlimited. Byrd estimated he could
see a hundred and fifty miles in all directions—behind him, to the
west, as far across Smith Sound as the interior of Ellesmere Island.
Ahead, to the east, the ice sheet spread to the limits of the horizon
and gradually rose in the distance to an elevation equal to the altitude
of NA-1. Its whiteness dazzled so brightly the aviators could hardly
judge how high they were flying above it.

With a falling barometer and the rising probability of a gale
advancing on Etah, "the Windy Place," MacMillan thought the plane
could be more safely disassembled at Igloodahouny, "the Place of
Many Camps." The temperature was so cold above the ice cap that
when Bennett landed on the ample beach to await the *Peary* and the
Bowdoin, neither he nor Byrd nor Francis could open their hands and
relax the tight grip in which they held their instruments.

No exploration of Baffin Island or of the interior of Labrador
occurred. The expedition slipped down the coast of Greenland and
across Davis Strait with the winter squalls nipping closely at its heels
only to be occasionally overtaken by violent snowstorms. MacMillan
found some Norse ruins to venerate and ponder during a stopover in
southern Greenland. But he, Captain Steele, and their respective crews
had all they could do to bring the *Bowdoin* and the *Peary* back to
New England intact.

The National Geographic Society estimated that 16,162,300 lines
of reportage had been written about the MacMillan expedition in the

2,409 daily newspapers published in the United States at that time.[3] The expedition introduced Richard Byrd to America. Over the course of the summer, he had become the third most celebrated pioneer in the new field of polar aviation, only trailing Roald Amundsen and Lincoln Ellsworth in name recognition. Richard Byrd entered the national consciousness as a dashing figure in a crisp, white uniform adorned with a gleaming pair of golden wings. He looked like a movie star and occupied the center of attention with manly grace. He knew who he was, he was doing what he wanted to do, and he was doing it at exactly the right time.

The explorer Richard Evelyn Byrd was the third member of his illustrious family to bear that name. The second was his father, and the first, the explorer's great-grandfather, a fifth generation Byrd. The first Richard Evelyn was born in 1800, exactly 130 years after the first Byrd arrived in America; from there the family traces its lineage back an additional six hundred years. When William the Conqueror crossed the English Channel and landed at Hastings in 1066, one of the men-at-arms who fought at his side was a warrior named Hugo LeBrid. The polar aviator was a direct descendant of the Norman invader. William and his Norman followers were themselves descendants of Norsemen who had previously conquered the northwest coast of France and had settled there by the early 900s. The explorer Richard Byrd had Viking genes embedded in the very strands of his DNA.

Hugo's immediate descendants became tradesmen. His grandson, Thomas, a vintner by profession, anglicized the family name, changing it from LeBrid to Bird. Thomas's son, John, gentrified it, substituting "y" for the more pedestrian "i". John Byrd lived and worked in London as a respectable, middle-class goldsmith. His father-in-law, Captain Thomas Stegge, had accumulated vast holdings in the colony of Virginia, which had passed to his son, Thomas, John's brother-in-law. John Byrd had two sons, the eldest standing to inherit the family business. Stegge Jr. did not have any children. The uncle offered to make the younger Byrd his heir if the nephew came to Virginia. In 1670, eighteen-year-old William Byrd set foot in the New World and became the forerunner of an American dynasty.

Three years after his arrival, William married and married well. His bride, the former Mary Horsmanden, was a descendant of several royal houses of Europe. Her regal ancestors included a king of England (Edward III), a king of Hungary, a Byzantine emperor, two Crusader kings of Jerusalem, and five French monarchs including the legendary Charlemagne. Their son, William Byrd II (1674–1744), was the first star of the American branch of the family. An attractive and charming gentleman, he was a wit, a lover, and an eloquent defender of the Virginians' rights. He held numerous offices in the colonial government, led expeditions to survey the borderlands between Virginia and North Carolina, and founded the city of Richmond. Perhaps his most singular contribution to the Old Dominion was his own brilliance. The second William usually started the day by reading works in Hebrew, Greek, and Latin. He built Westover, one of the most fabulous estates in American history, and within its stately confines accumulated a library of 3,600 volumes, the largest privately owned library in America during his lifetime.

William cultivated an interest in science, botany, and medicine, writing learned treatises on these subjects. But his most celebrated writings remain his diaries. A frequently quoted passage describes a typical day at Westover with his first wife, Lucy:

> In the afternoon my wife and I had a little quarrel which I reconciled with a flourish. Then she read a sermon in Dr. Tillotson to me. It is to be observed that the flourish was performed on the billiard table.[4]

William had three children with Lucy, one of whom died in infancy, and four with his second wife, Maria. His firstborn and eldest daughter, the legendary Evelyn (pronounced to this date by the Byrds as *Eee*velyn), was an ethereal beauty, the most ravishing of all the plantation ladies of the colonial aristocracy. Evelyn never married. As a young girl, she had had a relationship with a suitor of whom her father disapproved. After William broke it up, she withdrew from the social whirl. She died mysteriously at the age of thirty, perhaps of a broken heart, and remains celebrated in Virginia folklore as the tragic heroine of a storied era.

William Byrd II had inherited 26,231 acres of plantation land as well as a couple hundred slaves, and increased the family assets by leaps and bounds. He had expanded his real estate holdings to 179,423 acres upon his death. His son and heir, William Byrd III, however, squandered his patrimony. Westover was sold out of the family in 1814. The third William commanded a regiment in the French and Indian War and joined forces with another regimental leader, Colonel George Washington. Unlike his friend from Mount Vernon, William III remained loyal to the crown during the Revolution. One of his sons joined the Continental Army, while the other became a Redcoat. After the war, the latter, Thomas Taylor Byrd, became the first of his line to settle in the Shenandoah Valley.

The first Richard E(*ee*)velyn Byrd (1800–1872) was the sixth son of Thomas Taylor. In many ways, Richard I set the standard for the generations to follow. He was a lawyer-politician, a calling the Byrds gravitated to as naturally as the Barrymores to stage and screen. He also exemplified the chivalric code so much a part of Southern culture following the publication of the novels of Sir Walter Scott. Scott's romantic vision of medieval kingdoms reinforced what upper class Virginians wanted to believe about the era of the great plantations. By adopting the conduct celebrated in the tales and instilling the code in their young, prominent Virginians managed, in a sense, to create the reality in which they believed.

In 1861, the mistress of an estate called Belle Grove was murdered with a meat cleaver. The alleged perpetrator—one of the housemaids, a free black woman—awaited trial in Winchester, the cultural and commercial crossroads at the northern end of the Shenandoah Valley. This occurred a year and a half after the incendiary abolitionist John Brown attempted to single-handedly topple the plantation system, and less than thirty miles from Harpers Ferry, the site of the paramilitary operation masterminded by Brown. The terrorists failed to ignite a slave revolt but succeeded in inflaming emotions on both sides of the Mason-Dixon Line. Under the circumstances, the plight of a black charged with the brutal murder of a white was not a popular cause in northern Virginia. Everyone agreed that the defendant was entitled to counsel, but of all the lawyers who practiced in the vicinity, only one was willing to take her case. The first Richard E. Byrd, a distinguished attorney who had represented the Valley in the state legislature and at the "Reform Convention," a constitutional convention that had convened in Richmond during the mid-1850s, volunteered his services free of charge.

Richard did not win an acquittal, but as his client happened to be pregnant, he was able to wrangle a stay of execution. Shortly thereafter, war was declared. Historians disagree as to whether Winchester, some eighteen miles farther north than Washington, D.C., changed hands seventy-one or seventy-two times during the Civil War; but when the Union forces first occupied the town, the prisoner was released. Richard joined the Army of Northern Virginia and served as a staff officer throughout the war. His son, the sixth William Byrd (1828–1896), also bore a saber in the Confederate cause. William had studied law at the University of Virginia and settled in Texas after receiving his degree. He opened a law office in Austin and edited the local paper, the *Austin Gazette*. Just three years after he first crossed the Red River, he became treasurer of his adopted city.

As Adjutant General of Texas, the sixth William organized the
regiments that marched east and fought like wildcats under the Stars
and Bars from the Seven Days' Battles of 1861 right through to Appomattox. William quickly traded his administrative position for a field
command in the west. In March of 1864, Lieutenant Colonel William
Byrd, commanding officer of Fort De Russy, Louisiana, was forced to
surrender his post when Union forces massed against the small outpost
at the beginning of the Red River Campaign. William spent the
remainder of the war in prison.

Virginia lost more than a war at Appomattox. It lost its splendor,
and it lost its identity; it literally ceased to exist as a state. The home-
land of four of the first five presidents of the United States had become
Military District Number One and would continue in this nebulous
status for the next five years. The countryside had been so ravaged by
the fighting that an estimated 600,000 of its citizens—more than one-
quarter of the state—emigrated in the 1880s. Although William had
married and started raising a family in Texas before the war, he moved
his family back to his native valley at the end of the bloody struggle.
Perhaps helping to rebuild in an era of hopelessness, lawlessness, and
humiliation satisfied the code of honor he had inherited.

William had been seriously wounded in battle and returned to
Winchester, in the words of one obituary writer, "broke in health and
wealth."[5] His eldest son was the second Richard Evelyn Byrd (1860–
1925), and his grandson was the polar explorer.

The senior Richard E. Byrd, along with his brother-in-law, Con-
gressman Henry Delaware Flood, and United States Senators Thomas
B. Martin and Claude A. Swanson, were known as the "Big Four" of
Virginia politics in the first quarter of the twentieth century. Byrd won
a seat in the Virginia House of Delegates in 1906 and was elected
Speaker of the House in his second term, something no other delegate

had ever accomplished—before or since. A brilliant, erudite man with a photographic memory, his character and attainments apparently made a lasting impression on everyone acquainted with him.

Twenty-five years after Richard's death, his eldest son, Harry, received a letter from a fellow Virginian, Douglas Southall Freeman, the Pulitizer Prize–winning biographer of Robert E. Lee and George Washington. "This morning, about sunup, for no discoverable reason, I fell to thinking again of your Father," Freeman began. The sixty-five-year-old author said he had known "almost all the conspicuous Virginians of the last half-century" and wanted to pass on his recollections "to those who will cherish them."

"Your father," he continued,

> had the most acute intellect possessed by any Virginian of my lifetime, and with it he had absolute, unhesitating courage and—what is perhaps less familiar—the most complete candor in dealing with press and public that ever I had the privilege of observing. I never knew him to balk at any question put to him concerning any public issue.[6]

At the national Democratic Party convention of 1912, Richard opposed the other three members of the Big Four and supported Woodrow Wilson for president of the United States. Wilson, born in Staunton, Virginia, five counties south of Winchester, had gone to college with Byrd. Personal loyalty trumped politics; Byrd later managed Wilson's campaign in the Old Dominion. He had physical as well as political valor, beginning his career practicing law in Winchester and serving as county prosecutor for twenty years before running for the state legislature. Whenever a crime had been committed in the hills, he would drive his buggy up into the Blue Ridge and calmly administer justice in the middle of a family circle of hairtrigger Hatfields or McCoys.

It was customary for Speakers of the Virginia House to preside for no more than three two-year terms and then relinquish the gavel. As Richard had no enthusiasm for resuming a seat on the floor of the chamber, he stepped down in 1914 and returned to the courtroom. He was appointed U.S. district attorney for the western section of Virginia and opened a law office in Richmond. Small, stocky, studious, he wore wire-rimmed glasses, kept his hair clipped short, and was known for his oratory and fighting spirit. Like his grandfather, he had a penchant for sticking up for the underdog, often taking the cases of defendants who could not afford to retain him. He was also something of a character.

He was not above hurling inkwells and other objects across the courtroom at his opponents. When his son Harry ran for governor, he attended one of the candidate's rallies armed with two pistols. He told his ten-year-old grandson, Harry Jr., as he dressed for the occasion, "A man has threatened to kill your father. I plan to sit in the back of the hall and if there's any shooting to be done, I'll shoot first."[7] He was a crack shot as well as a proficient drinker. Although he worked in the legislature to restrict the sale of alcohol, he consumed it liberally. He had a cabin in the mountains where he would retreat on occasion to binge. He should (and probably could) have become governor. Perhaps, as journalist Charles J. V. Murphy, a friend and early biographer of his son, Richard Jr., had supposed, he may have been too learned and too scholarly to really enjoy politics.

In 1886, Richard married a woman with as formidable a personality as his own. Eleanor Bolling Flood was a descendant of several First Families of Virginia, including the Delawares. Thomas West, the twelfth Lord Delaware, was appointed governor of Virginia in 1609. Miss Bolling, as Eleanor was called, was fond of saying that when the Byrds arrived in the Old Dominion, her ancestors sold them the land on which they built Westover. Like her husband, Miss Bolling came from a family of lawyer-politicians. Her grandfather, Charles James

Faulkner, had served in both houses of the Virginia state legislature and in the U.S. House of Representatives, and had been appointed ambassador to France by President Buchanan. Within a year of her marriage, her uncle, who also bore the name of Charles James Faulkner, would be elected to the U.S. Senate, and her brother, Hal, a future member of Virginia's Big Four, would proceed to Richmond upon winning a seat in the House of Delegates.

The law, the ministry, and the military were the most acceptable callings for the men of the First Families. There was, however, only one role available to the women. They became ladies. As in the courtroom, at the pulpit, and on the battlefield, successful practitioners required superior intelligence, presence, and a certain amount of theatrical flair. Eleanor Bolling Flood played her part magnificently. She was a lovely, brown-eyed Virginia belle, petite, erect, and strong-willed. She liked having people around her and was accustomed to being the center of attention. The liveliest part of any social gathering at which she was present, even as a silver-haired grandmother, was usually the corner in which she held forth. She was cool and commanding in a crisis, and abrupt and direct when annoyed. But as her outbursts were inevitably followed with an irresistible display of soothing charm, even her stings were delightful.

She had a great zest for life. She liked the company of men and paid more attention to the little boys of her extended family than to the little girls. She was also intensely patriotic. In later years, she went to the movies twice a week, attended by her grandson, Harry Jr. It was customary in those days for the American flag to be projected on the screen at the beginning of the show and for the National Anthem to be played. More often than not she would cry upon the presentation of the colors. She believed in doing one's duty, telling the truth, and, most of all, in right and wrong.

Miss Bolling was born at Selmo, her father's plantation outside of Appomattox. Her parents, Major Joel West and Eliza Faulkner Flood, may have liked the quiet and isolation of the countryside, but Selmo could not quite contain their daughter's high spirits. Eleanor escaped to Winchester to attend the Episcopal Female Institute. The boarding school occupied a two-story building in the heart of town and had been founded in 1874 by a group of concerned citizens, among them William Byrd, Richard's father. William was also a member of the Board of Directors.

Fitzhugh Green interviewed Mrs. Byrd in the twenties and reported that, "Her early married life was like a chapter out of a historical novel. Just two months after she met Richard Evelyn Byrd, she married him. Her age was nineteen."[8] Although the Floods, like the Byrds, had been wiped out financially by the Civil War, Richard was a young man of excellent prospects. In his first year of married life, he was doing well enough to afford a sumptuous, three-story Victorian manor house near the railroad tracks at the western end of town. The homestead had the general shape of a wedding cake with square layers and was set back behind a long hedgerow; except for the sloping roof, which was green, the building was cream-colored and partially covered with ivy. From the wraparound veranda, Mrs. Byrd would wave to the engineers of the Cumberland Valley line as the trains emerged from the woods that bordered the property and made a slow turn to the station on the next block. Here at 326 Amherst Street, four blocks from the courthouse and city hall, the couple enjoyed a comfortable middle-class existence and raised three rambunctious sons.

Richard Evelyn Byrd Jr. was born on Amherst Street on October 25, 1888, the middle child. The eldest, Harry Flood Byrd, named for Miss Bolling's brother, arrived one year earlier and the youngest, Thomas Bolling Byrd, followed Richard one year later. All of the boys had distinct personalities: Harry, the most serious and industrious of the trio; Tom, the most introspective. Dick was the most spirited.

"That boy is a case," their grandmother, Jane "Jennie" Rivers Byrd, said of her middle grandchild. "Some day I hope he writes a book, because he certainly has had a lot of fun, and it would be a shame to keep it all to himself."[9]

Dick proved unpredictable. He once decided that the family cats were dirty and proceeded to bathe them. His next problem was to dry them out. He solved it by hanging them up by the tail on the clothesline. The consequent howling was heard all over the neighborhood. Dick loved to make and fly huge kites and send up hot air balloons. He also made small parachutes and jumped out of windows with them. "He was always on top of a house or some tree," his mother told an interviewer. "Danger was all that thrilled him."[10] He was said to have climbed all the trees in Winchester; according to the same source, there were very few roofs in town that he had not scrambled over.[11]

At the turn of the twentieth century, Winchester was a small and unhurried community of slightly over five thousand people. It was easily walkable from one end of town to the other and remains so today. There were brick sidewalks, and the streets, commercial and residential, were lined, by and large, with two- and three-story wooden or brick buildings. The older, plainer structures dated back to the Colonial era. The newer ones, including municipal buildings such as City Hall and a central firehouse, exemplified the ornate Victorian and Beaux-Arts influence. Most of these buildings are still standing. They were not then, nor are they now packed together in a row as in crowded, northern cities, but were separated from one another by a dignified amount of space, and even the more modest dwellings were fronted by a stately white portico. The spacing makes the town seem exceptionally still and genteel.

In this setting, the three Byrd boys enjoyed an idyllic childhood. They rode horses, swam in mudholes, and played football, baseball, and field hockey. Along with other west-enders, they fought running battles with the kids from other parts of town. In these encounters, Dick, the smallest and thinnest of the Byrds, was usually the most aggressive. The brothers, as might be expected, also fought among themselves. Their father, known around Winchester as either Mr. Dick, or—to distinguish him from his namesake—Big Dick, taught his boys to shoot and box, and reportedly promoted sparring sessions and other rough-and-tumble competitions between Little Dick and Tom. Tom was lengthening by the day and would eventually tower over his siblings, and Dick had all he could do to maintain an edge over his kid brother. According to one story, amiable Tom, at age eight, finally blew up after Dick, nine, wrestled him to the ground and rubbed his face in the dirt. The eight-year-old picked up a knife and chased Dick down the hall and up the stairs. With the enraged Tom on his heels, Dick locked himself in one of the bathrooms, climbed out the window and either up or down the lightning rod, depending on two different versions of the tale, while Tom hacked away at the door. Another story has it that the adolescent Harry and Tom repeatedly picked on Dick.[12]

Early on young Dick dedicated himself to a physical fitness program to compensate for his stature. He would continue to exercise regularly all of his life. Despite the roughhousing and sibling competitions, the brothers had an "all for one, and one for all" credo and would remain close and supportive as adults.

Richard Jr. inherited his moral code from both his mother and father, particularly the former. He acquired the outgoing side of his personality from his mother, and from her he learned to be strong, persistent, and determined. He also learned self-control. Miss Bolling was described as "convivial, but not effusive," and not given to emotional displays.[13] When her youngest son went swimming, failed to return, and a heavy rain began to fall that evening, she calmly gathered the neighbors and set in motion plans for a systematic search. During these preparations, a soaked Tom sheepishly entered the house. "She didn't rush to him, gather him into her arms, and burst into hysterical sobbing as many a woman might have done," one of the neighbors told Fitzhugh Green.

> She told him to go into the bathroom, take off his drenched clothing and wait for her. She thanked those who had come to help, and had coffee and sandwiches for us before we had time to leave. From tragedy, the moment was turned adroitly into celebration. Not once through it all had Mrs. Byrd lost her head.[14]

Years later, when Fitzhugh Green became Richard Byrd's first ghostwriter, Byrd wrote his friend one of the most revealing letters of his life. Referring to a magazine article Green had in mind, Dick said, "Please do not let me express in the story too much emotion. There is something in me that is extremely adverse to expressing of emotion publicly, or in any public document."[15] That something was implanted by his mother.

From his father, he acquired the solitary, philosophical side of his character. His favorite pastime was taking long hikes through the countryside with a fox terrier named Judy and, sometimes in addition to the terrier, a St. Bernard named Jack. As an adult, he looked back on these hikes as being extremely formative experiences. "I guess," he once said, "while spending so much time walking through the woods, I learned to have a great interest in the laws of nature and became convinced that, although civilization got away from a state of what we called 'nature,' which is the real effort of civilization, we still did not get away from the cosmical processes any more than the earth can get away from them in following its path around the sun."[16]

When Byrd embarked on the MacMillan Expedition, he brought a small library with him: two textbooks on navigation, three of Robert Peary's books on polar travel, a treatise by William Ernest Hocking, a professor of philosophy at Harvard, and a number of academic tomes that Hocking, a personal friend, had given him. Hocking was a worldly philosopher with mystical leanings. In 1918, he had written *Human Nature and Its Remaking*, a meditation on the further growth and development of human beings as a species. It examines this subject from the point of view of psychology, sociology, political science, and eastern and western religions, ultimately concluding that human nature responds "to something hailing from beyond nature." Byrd read the book on the trip north and ate it up.

Richard's adventurousness, however, was unprecedented. It seems innately his own, a part of himself that came into the world with him. His boyhood hero was a war hero, Lieutenant Richmond Pearson Hobson, U.S.N. (Hobson won acclaim during the Spanish-American War for sinking an expendable American naval vessel in Santiago harbor in an effort to bottle up the Spanish fleet.)[17] His idol was Captain Adam C. "Kit" Carson, an attorney who worked in Mr. Dick's law office in Winchester until he enlisted in the army to fight in Cuba. Carson hailed from Enniskillen, a borough of Northern Ireland. Scotch-Irish, a descendant of the Scotch settlers of the region, he and Dick met when the future explorer was five or six. Kit was as high-spirited as the boy who idolized him. When he returned from the war, he brought Dick over to the camp in Washington where his regiment was billeted, dressed him up in an ill-fitting lieutenant's uniform, and allowed him to march in the ranks when the troops passed in review before President McKinley. Carson's regiment was mobilized to put down the Philippine Insurrection, and after the nationalist army was defeated Captain Carson became Judge Carson. Having won back-to-back military engagements in the Caribbean and South China Seas, American policymakers supposed that the solution to the unrest in the former Spanish possession was grafting American-style institutions on the archipelago. Accordingly, Kit was appointed to preside over the Eighth Judicial District of the Philippine Islands, an appointment that precipitated the defining episode of Richard Byrd's youth.

Carson wrote the boy a letter from his new post suggesting that Dick come out to the islands and pay him a visit. The suggestion may have been playful, but Dick took it very seriously. He had been dreaming of traveling around the world and jumped at the chance. But first he had to sell the idea to the prospective sponsors of the expedition— his parents, who were understandably opposed. "I could hardly believe my ears when Dick asked if he might go," said Mrs. Byrd, "but I soon learned that he meant it in all seriousness."[18]

The Byrd boys were expected to act like gentlemen in the presence of their elders. Dick quietly and most respectfully avowed that he would never forgive his parents if they did not allow him to go. He also hinted that he would run away from home in the general direction of the Philippines if he had to.

His mother said:

> I was aghast at the thought of his traveling such a great distance alone and living in a military camp, especially since Dick was not what you might call a husky boy. As his father and I realized how much it meant to him to carry out his plan, and perhaps feared that he might enforce his threat to go without permission, he was told that he could go.

Eleanor fervently hoped the whole notion was just a passing fancy and that Dick would eventually change his adolescent mind. But she always recognized that her adventurous middle child was different from ordinary youngsters, and she knew instinctively that she could best serve her boys by getting out of the way of their possibilities. On August 9, 1902, she accompanied Dick to Washington, where he boarded a westbound train on the first leg of his journey. Saying good-bye to him, she said, was "one of the most trying ordeals I have ever experienced."

"That day," Byrd told Charles Murphy, "my face was full of poi-son oak and I could hardly see because my eyes were so swollen. My mother was not given to weeping, but she wept that day. I felt more than a little blue myself."

He was two and a half months shy of his fourteenth birthday.

At San Francisco, young Dick boarded a military transport whose first port of call was Nagasaki, Japan. The western North Pacific, however, is the breeding ground of typhoons, particularly in the sum-mer and fall. The steamer ran into one which its skipper called the worst he had seen in fifty-two years of seafaring. The torrential rains driven by hundred-mile-an-hour winds shattered the railings, smashed the lifeboats, toppled the smokestack, and washed the debris—smoke-stack and all—right out to sea. So high did the waves mount that when the ship plunged down over the crests, it dropped with such terrific force that the passengers and crew feared the steamer would break in two. There were wives and dependents aboard, and the male passen-gers were each assigned one of them to look after. Byrd was sent to comfort a schoolteacher who had been strapped in her bunk for safety's sake as the towering waves continued to surge. Steadying himself with one hand, he applied cold compresses to her forehead with the other.

"I thought it was a wonderful storm," he remembered. "I didn't know enough to be afraid."[19] He brought the same sense of wonder and discovery with him to the Philippines, where only a surface calm prevailed. While the United States pursued a high-minded program of pacification and Americanization, guerrillas continued to lurk in the bush, waging a resistance movement against what they perceived to be an army of occupation. Americans in this period possessed a Kipling-esque faith in their country's cause, and Dick, like any romantic lad, wanted to play a heroic role in the national crusade.

He became a favorite of Governor Bernardino Monreal of Sorsogon Province in southern Luzon, where Kit Carson held court. On Dick's fourteenth birthday, Monreal made him a deputy sheriff and formally issued a proclamation to that effect. He was also officially granted permission to carry a revolver. With a Smith & Wesson in his belt, Dick eagerly saddled a pony and rode with the constabulary on their pursuit of insurrectos and ladrones. On one occasion, the posse sprinted twenty-seven miles inland to the scene of an ambush. The party spent several days in the jungle, trying to track down the perpetrators who had seemingly vanished without a trace. Nothing of consequence was observed except for a lovely volcano. The experience so far proved too tame for an imaginative boy. Just before the constables broke camp, the fourteen-year-old started down the trail by himself and was surprised by a mob of ladrones who jumped out the bush, whirling their bolos in the air. Byrd wheeled his pony around, galloped back to camp and was almost shot out of the saddle by one of his fellow peace officers who stood sentry. The man's hand was trembling when the boy dismounted.[20]

In December of 1902, Dick toured Samar Island with Kit's brothers, Sam and Charlie Carson. Sam was an army doctor. The principal sight on the itinerary was Balangiga, the place where Company C, Ninth U.S. Infantry was massacred on September 28, 1901. A year later, another deadly foe plagued the island: cholera. The disease is highly contagious. Sam Carson was one of three American officers assigned to a detachment of about one hundred Filipino scouts. When one of the soldiers succumbed to the epidemic, others were quickly stricken. Dick thought he was going to die. He had been assisting Sam in his duties and had taken the pulse of the first victim when the

soldier reported to sick bay. He and the American officers were evacuated to a nearby hilltop as the disease continued to ravage the biv-
ouac area below. There they dined on parrots and monkeys, and for
Christmas added a bit of canned plum pudding to the regular bill of
fare. Sam Carson finally smuggled the boy aboard an outrigger that
ferried him up the coast to a place where he could catch a ship for
Manila.

In 1896, Richard Byrd Sr. had bought his hometown newspaper,
the *Winchester Star*. Little Dick regularly wrote colorful letters home
from the Philippines, and his father had these dispatches printed in
the paper. In February of 1903, he was back in Sorsogon, sharing
Judge Carson's quarters. "In the next room the Judge is holding
court," he wrote his mother, "as it is the custom for a judge to have
his room next to his courtroom and of course it is all held in Spanish
as the Filipinos do not understand English."

> There are two men in there whom the Judge is sentencing
> to be hung, and they take it just as if nothing was going on.
> They do not even change their expression. There is a scaf-
> fold which you can see from my window on which six men
> were hung last year.[21]

Carson's brother Charlie, Dick added, "saw them hung."

After Dick had romped around the islands for nearly a year, the
Judge put him on a British tramp steamer bound for Europe and the
States via the Indian Ocean, the Red Sea, and the Suez Canal. In the
Red Sea, the second mate forgot to wind the chronometer. Since you
must know the exact time in order to fix your position by celestial
navigation, the ship was effectively lost. The captain had to steer due
west into the setting sun and could not be certain where he was until
he hit Madagascar.

When Dick landed in Boston on July 10, 1903, he was met not only by his mother but also by a pack of reporters who wanted to know all about his adventures. He had developed a love for the sea and an awareness of the mysteries of navigation. The whole pattern of his adult life had been established.

⟛ 11 ⟛

MARIE

*She is my anchor to windward
and my compass.*

RICHARD E. BYRD[1]

One of the industries that enabled the South, Virginia in particular, to recover in the aftermath of the Civil War was tourism. As railroads expanded across the region, Southern entrepreneurs began to capitalize on their greatest natural resource: their climate and scenery. Modern hotels were erected in Virginia's drowsiest hamlets, and luxurious resorts sprang up throughout such spectacular locations as the green rolling countryside between the Blue Ridge and the Allegheny Mountains. Soon Northern legions once again descended on the Shenandoah Valley, but this time as vacationers. Winchester promoted itself as a spa, the "Queen City of the Valley." A brochure published by the city at the turn of the twentieth century boasted of a low death rate, pure mountain air, pure mountain springs ("Purest water gushes from two springs of unusual capacity and is piped to every home"), and a dry climate.[2] "The summer nights," it was said, "are usually cool however hot the days that follow.

"During the summer," the brochure went on, "the summer cottages are all occupied, private boarding houses filled to overflowing and hundreds of resort seekers are passing through the city."

One of the more exclusive facilities in town was the Winchester Inn, located on the west side of the city on a hill just below Amherst Street. There, on a hot June, July, or August day sometime in the 1890s, Richard E. Byrd Jr. met a sweet, slender, brown-haired, and brown-eyed little girl from Boston, Massachusetts. Her name was Marie Donaldson Ames. They were both about seven years old. Marie was two and a half months younger than Dick and already demonstrated a considerable talent for music and dance. She was playing the violin at a recital when they first encountered one another.

Marie was a proper Bostonian. Her family resided on Beacon Hill, and they could trace their lineage back to the passengers on the *Mayflower*. Her father, Joseph Blanchard Ames, was an investment banker. As a child, Marie was "a shy, timid little girl with lovely brown eyes."[3] Dick Byrd was drawn to her from the start. Just before his twenty-fifth birthday, he composed a long letter to Marie in which he reviewed the history of their relationship in the form of a fable. "Once upon a time," he wrote, "there lived in a beautiful sunny land, a small boy—never mind his name—and one day this boy met a little girl."

> He had seen her before, but not until then did he notice how active and straight and graceful she was. Right away he liked her and they became friends. The little girl was a stranger and when it came time for her to go to her home in the Northland the boy was sorry and always, when she had gone, he carried in his mind an image of his new friend.
>
> Once a year thereafter, when nature had completed her adornments of green foliage and the birds sang their joy at

living, the girl came back to the beautiful land. Together
she and the the boy wandered over green fields and shaded
paths and they were happy with each other, and everything
took on brighter colors; even the birds sang more sweetly.

Marie had a younger sister, Katharine, but no brothers. Byrd had no
sisters. They made a deal: Dick would be the brother Marie never had,
and Marie would be his sister. As time went on, the very idealistic
Dick began to perceive that his summer playmate's inner qualities were
as agreeable as her outward appearance.

The fable continued:

The girl was beautiful and good and pure. She was sweet
and innocent too and for every living creature she had a
natural love and sympathy. Her heart was tender and true
and nothing was more beautiful than her mind. To the
youth was given a keen perception and all of this he saw,
and more too: he had a glimpse of her radiant soul; and
for the first time the boy experienced a deeper feeling than
friendship....

One summer (and it just might have been the one following the Philippines trip, for there is nothing like high adventure to give a sensitive
boy the manly courage to reveal his innermost feelings), Dick and
Marie were out horseback riding. Their ponies at a walk descended
single file down a gentle slope, Marie in the lead. Out of the blue Dick
blurted out, "Marie, I love you."

Marie was taken aback. She was a bold young lady (she didn't
ride sidesaddle), but for many long moments she remained silent,
speechless. When she was finally able to talk, all she said was, "I don't
know what to say." She thought of Dick as her best friend, as the
brother she never had. That was the extent of her feelings; but after

that ride, she was considerate enough not to ever refer to herself as his "sister" again.

Richard Byrd and his brothers first attended a small private school one block from home. Miss Jennie Sherrard, a Victorian schoolmarm who awarded silver stars to pupils distinguishing themselves in subjects such as elocution and penmanship, conducted classes in a two-room schoolhouse behind 226 Amherst Street. The main house was owned and occupied by the Massies, who were cousins of the Byrds. Miss Jennie's sister, Miss Lizzie, ran a boardinghouse nearby. Tom, Dick, and Harry then transferred to John Kerr Public School, a gray, two-story building only four years older than the eldest brother. The public school, six blocks from home, had eight classrooms. The brothers attended preparatory school at the Shenandoah Valley Academy, which their father had attended. Founded in 1865, the Academy occupied several sites in and around Winchester. In the 1890s and early 1900s, it sprawled over twenty acres on the south side of Amherst Street near the Winchester Inn.

On September 1, 1904, Dick entered the Virginia Military Institute, following in the footsteps of his grandfather, William, who graduated from VMI in 1849. Dick was not quite sixteen when he matriculated; the college gave him credit for his year of world travel— one of the reasons he was admitted at such a young age. From this time forward, Winchester would remain Dick Byrd's hometown, rather than his home. He kept up a correspondence with Marie over each succeeding winter. The fable he composed in 1913 picks up the thread of the story. "Once a year," he wrote, the nameless youth of the tale

would return to his boyhood's land: a visitor to his home.
There he would meet the girl and each time he returned he

told of his love, for it was deep and true and would as soon die as the sun would grow cold. But she loved him as a friend; yet he hoped and their love and beautiful friendship continued.

Dick, the smallest as well as the youngest member of his freshman class, waxed sensitive about his size. Freshmen at VMI are called "rats" and have just about as much status as rodents. Byrd took the attendant hazing in stride, until a large upperclassman made an unkind remark about his stature. He was prepared to duke it out with the big cadet, but the latter's peers intervened.[4] No one in the ranks of the cadet corps ever said anything about Byrd's size again. Byrd's classmates at Lexington remember him as modest, gentlemanly, and inquisitive. "He was very considerate of others as evidenced by his being especially helpful to three Chinese cadets who were in their rat year," said an alumnus who roomed with Byrd as a sophomore.[5] What most impressed his brother rats was his valor; he may have been frail and thin, but "he had the courage of a lion."[6] During some rough-and-tumble in the barracks, Dick smashed his hand through a glass pane in the door of his room. His arm was cut from the palm to the elbow. "A tourniquet was applied to his upper arm," said the roommate. "The doctor arrived and promptly closed the wound with fifteen stitches—all accomplished without benefit of anesthetic. Dick was silent throughout."

At 140 pounds, he played quarterback on the junior varsity squad. He particularly distinguished himself on the gym team. His specialty was the flying rings, and there wasn't any aerial stunt he was unwilling to try. The gym team put on an exhibition at the 1905 commencement. Two members were seriously injured in practice sessions, attempting to perfect a routine on the rings; Byrd was asked to take their place. One of the witnesses to the performance said, "He swung himself from one ceiling-end to the other like a carefree elf, and while high in the air he would turn two flips and land on his feet as gracefully as a cat.[7]

> "There was about him," the observer said, "a Peter Pan mixture of simplicity and manliness. Each feat he performed was the result of long and persistent practice; but in practicing he would essay risks that no other cadets would dream of taking."

At the end of the freshman year, rats are allowed to wear their white uniforms for the first time. But before the first-year men in those days officially made the transition from rat to sophomore, they had to run the gauntlet. The upperclassmen would arm themselves with belts, broom handles, old shoes, sticks, and bayonets, and proceed by lining up along the stoops and stairways. On that day, instead of running down the steps like the rest of his classmates, Dick Byrd "walked as leisurely as if he were on a moonlit promenade."[8] While some of the upperclassmen took their whacks, others were so affected by his manly bravado that they went easy on him. He got off with less punishment than the rest.

Byrd and three classmates spent each Sunday for several weeks of their sophomore year exploring a network of caverns about two miles west of the college. It was a typical Byrd expedition. According to his roommate, he "soon learned where they were and carefully made his plans to explore them, gathering the equipment he thought he would need such as a number of battery lights and a large quantity of very heavy string." Strange, sculpture-like formations appeared in the beam of his flashlight as Byrd and his friends followed the underground passageways. On one of these excursions, at what had appeared in the darkness to be a dead end, the boys discovered a hole slanting downwards at a forty-five-degree angle. It was just about man-size and head first into it dove Dick Byrd. He emerged inside of another huge limestone gallery and returned to the barracks covered with mud.

Byrd finished twelfth among the 104 members of the freshman class, and sixteenth among the seventy-six sophomores. His best subjects were mathematics and Latin. An English teacher told him he had "a promising career as a writer."[9] After two years, he left VMI because he had his heart set on attending the Naval Academy. His mother had encouraged him to apply to Annapolis. Ever perceptive, Mrs. Byrd understood that the military would provide a legitimate outlet for her adventurous son.

In 1906, Harry Byrd, the go-getter of the family, expanded the Byrd newspaper empire. Richard Sr. was not a businessman. He bought the *Winchester Star* as a platform for his opinions; his principal journalistic interest was writing editorials. By 1903, the paper was going broke. Harry persuaded his parents to let him drop out of school to manage the *Star*. He put the business back on its feet by practicing the same pay-as-you-go regimen he would later apply to the government of the Commonwealth of Virginia. Three years later, he decided to branch out and began publishing the *Martinsburg Evening Journal*. Dick went with Harry to Martinsburg, about twenty miles northeast of Winchester, and became circulation manager.

Byrd passed the written examination for the Naval Academy in the spring of 1907. A vacancy, however, was not expected to open up for twelve months. The future explorer spent the academic year of 1907–08 at the University of Virginia, where his brother Tom studied. Dick went out for football and played a few big games as a substitute quarterback. He basically marked time at Charlottesville until his appointment to Annapolis came through. "I am afraid that football, etc. keeps me from studying as I should," he wrote Marie. The "etc." included an incident Byrd was not particularly proud of, but which he nevertheless confided to her in detail. As a rite of initiation of a certain social club on campus, Byrd and a friend were told to take hashish and report to the club later in the evening. The drug obtained was in pill form. After taking the amount of pills the club members had specified, Byrd said he and his friend "found that we had taken nearly four times too much for the pills were of one grain and we had thought that they were 1/2 grain."[10]

Byrd's friend gasped. He figured they were both done for and insisted that they go to the hospital. "Personally, I didn't think that we would die," Byrd wrote. "I didn't care to go and consented only on the consideration that he shouldn't tell them that I had taken any of the stuff." But by the time they got to the infirmary, "my friend fell against the wall and got blue in the face. My hands were cold but his forehead was much colder and he couldn't answer me. Naturally you know what I thought." The doctor immediately administered a stimulant. About that time Byrd started to keel over. The doctor realized he, too, had been popping pills and prepared another hypodermic.

"Soon after that," Byrd said, "I became unconscious and the next thing I remember they had us out in the cool night air throwing cold water on us and carrying us along trying to make us walk so as not to go to sleep." His pal remained in the hospital for a week. Having a stronger constitution, Byrd was released in two or three hours after admission.

On May 28, 1908, Richard Byrd entered the U.S. Naval Academy. In the interval before the academic year began in the fall, the 226 members of the incoming class were put through a daily regimen of rowing, target practice, seamanship, physical training, and drills, and ceremonies. They were also subjected to the will of such swaggering, imperious upperclassmen as Midshipman Fitzhugh Green, a fourth-year man of whom it was observed, "he reads orders in a voice which

causes the knees of the plebes to knock violently together."[11] Their
first conversation was initiated by Green and went as follows:

> **Green:** Hey, who are you?

> **Byrd:** Midshipman Byrd, suh.

> **Green:** Where from?

> **Byrd:** Vuhginia, suh.

> **Green:** Think you're good looking, don't you?

> **Byrd:** No, suh.

> **Green:** All right. Forward march!

> **Byrd:** Aye, aye, suh.[12]

Byrd blended in effortlessly. "Personally, I like the life here and think
that a boy could put in four years at no better place," he wrote Marie,
after his first two months. He appreciated the team spirit that quickly
developed as a result of the training and indoctrination. He was always
someone who could look around him and discern what was going on.
"In the course of time," he said in the same letter, "the members of
the class begin to think alike in regard to certain unwritten laws that
exist only at the Naval Academy, and then the spirit has found its level
and becomes crystallized."

The Academy emphasized athletics, which Byrd adored. He won
a doubles championship in tennis during his plebe year, giving the
credit entirely to his partner and roommate, Garland "Froggy" Fulton
of Charlottesville, Virginia, one of the best players and best students

in the freshman class. Byrd represented his class on the Midshipmen's Athletic Association, went out for the football, wrestling, and gym teams, and participated in some extracurricular boxing as well. In the fall of 1908, one of his fellow plebes was beaten up by two large upperclassmen. "The whole academy became indignant," Byrd said, "and a class meeting was held and according to the Annapolis code of honor, the honor of the class was at stake." Two members of the class were selected to participate in a rematch with the offenders. Byrd was one of them. Although his opponent outweighed him by fifteen pounds, Byrd had the superior technique. In his own words, he and his classmate gave the bullies "a square deal." According to his medical records, he was treated afterwards for a bruised hand.

Byrd sustained a series of injuries in athletic competition at the Academy, one of which would have a dramatic impact on his career. In his sophomore year, he was Welterweight Wrestling Champion and a second-string quarterback on the varsity football team. The starting quarterback and best all-around athlete at the Academy broke his neck in a Navy-Villanova game on October 16, 1909. Byrd played against Princeton two weekends later and wound up under a pile of heavyweights. When the defensive line was peeled off of him, he could not get up; he had sprained his right ankle. He was back on the field on November 18, hobbling through a practice session.

Each summer, the midshipmen were assigned as the crew of a battleship that embarked on a practice cruise. At the end of his second year, Byrd reported aboard the USS *Massachusetts*, which set sail on June 4, 1910, for the Mediterranean. Once on the high seas, he came down with typhoid fever and spent the summer at the Royal Naval Hospital at Plymouth, England. Although the football coach at the Academy wrote Byrd, telling him to get well and that he saw him as captain of the team in the fall, there would be no scrimmages for him in 1910.[13] He had lost too much weight and was too debilitated to allow back on the field. He was sidelined by a thigh injury in 1911.

When he could not play football, Byrd turned to gymnastics. He was captain of the gym team his senior year. The Navy tumblers were in close contention for the intercollegiate championships in 1911–1912. Byrd spent Christmas week of 1911 trying to get the hang of a fantastic stunt on the flying rings that he was sure would propel the team past Yale, its closet rival, in an upcoming meet.

There were two parts to the maneuver, and they involved turning two full circles as he dangled from the rings. First, swinging high over the floor, he would smoothly raise his legs up. Then with his heels pointing to the ceiling, he would continue to spin over and complete a back flip. At the end of this maneuver, he would look like he was flying. His stomach and legs would be parallel to the ground, his outstretched arms clinging to the rings. The muscles of his upper arms would appear corkscrewed from the turn, as if he had dislocated his shoulders. For this reason, the maneuver was termed a "dislocate."

Next he would bring his legs up again, point his heels at the ceiling once more, and execute another back flip. This time, however, he would let go of the rings. He would fall as he spun over, but as he fell he would catch hold of the rings once more. The entire maneuver was called a dislocate-cutoff-catch. An extremely difficult combination, a stunt Byrd said, "that I have heard since I have been over here, sooner or later always broke the necks of the professionals who did it."[14] Marie had written him two letters asking him not to attempt the dislocate combination. He would have listened to her; he always did. But he had not yet received those letters. He had performed the stunt successfully the week before Christmas. On December 28, 1911, he tried it again.

That day, he swooped higher over the gym floor than he had ever swung before. He was aware of a hush down below as the members of the team watched the captain perform his breathtaking routine. He spun into the dislocate and came out of it perfectly, his body parallel to the ground. Now he brought his legs up again and went into the cutoff. He released his grip, then, going for the catch, caught hold of only one ring. Reaching out in desperation, he fell to the varnished floor. Fortunately, his feet hit the ground before the rest of him did, but he had fallen about seventeen feet. He couldn't pick himself up. His right foot—the one he had injured in the Princeton game—was numb and literally bent out of shape.

Byrd's right ankle was found to be both fractured and dislocated. He spent the next two months in the Naval Hospital at Annapolis, and during this time requested and received permission to take his midterm exams there. Dick's ankle bones had still not knit by the end of February, prompting his Uncle Hal to pull a few strings and have him transferred to the Naval Hospital in Washington, D.C. The doctors in the capital decided that Byrd's ankle needed to be strengthened before any further surgery. For the next several weeks, his foot was repeatedly exercised, massaged, and soaked in hot water.

"You say you don't see how I can walk around with a broken bone. I can feel it crunch when I walk," he told Marie, "but it doesn't worry me." He was, however, worried sick about graduating with his class. It was not uncommon for a midshipman to be "turned back" and repeat a year of instruction, but Byrd would have none of it. He kept his nose buried in his textbooks while his was leg was being treated, and although his doctors would have preferred to operate in the spring, he requested that he be sent back to Annapolis so that he could take his six annual exams. The tests were so fiercely difficult that other factors, such as class standing, could compensate for a poor grade. Byrd could not fall back on his class work because he had been out for too long. He returned to the Academy at the end of March, buckled down to his studies, and through sheer determination managed to pass every test. Marie knew he would. "If anyone could accomplish the impossible," she said, "it would be you." On May 31, 1912, firm union of the ankle bones was finally found to have taken place.

Of the 226 midshipmen that were admitted to the Academy in 1908, seventy had been winnowed out over the next four years. Byrd graduated sixty-third of the 156 who received diplomas on June 7, 1912. In *The Lucky Bag*, the Annapolis yearbook, his classmates wrote the following about him:

> Richard Evelyn Byrd, Jr., athlete, leader in all things, friend, gentleman. From the time we entered as plebes until the present, Dick has been putting his whole heart into everything he does, whether it be a little meeting that took place behind the old hospital, or in the gym, or on the football field. No man deserved more from Fate, and got less, than he.[15]

The "little meeting" referred to the boxing match of his plebe year. The yearbook writers went on to list his record of illnesses and injuries. Through it all, they said, he did not complain. "He was the same old cheerful Dick."

Marie, accompanied by her mother, had visited the Academy on numerous occasions at Byrd's invitation and had attended dances there. The writers knew he was in love. They went on:

> Most of the time Dick wanders about with a far-away, dreamy look in his eyes, and one often wonders whether he knows whether he is going or coming. He's suffering from a malady that gets us all sooner or later. He has already lived a life rich in experience, and he will live a life richer still, but he will always give to life more than he asks.

Marie Ames, in her early twenties, was still slender and still had the same lovely brown eyes she had as a child, but now, a relative observed, "a different spirit shines through them."[16] She was not a raving beauty but was certainly an attractive, intelligent, and accomplished young woman. Throughout her life, people who came in contact with her admired her for the kind of person she was: sweet, gracious, and genuine. She was about five foot five with a perfectly oval face, a straight nose, and a soft and gentle glow that radiated from within.

She had been educated at a private school in Brookline, Massachusetts, and at a convent in Paris, and was studying for a career as a concert violinist. She also studied dance and had appeared as a solo dancer in Boston in 1911 at the Vincent Club, an exclusive organization of society women that staged variety shows for charity. Marie had performed a Spanish gypsy dance. She and her best friend, Dick, swapped photographs at this time, and she sent him a publicity picture taken for the show. She was photographed in costume, decked out in a peasant blouse and fiesta skirt; large round earrings dangled from each ear. In the picture, she struck a tempestuous pose, tossing her right hand high in the air, clutching a pair of castanets. Her stage name was "Sylvia Rose." "Signor Ricardo Byrdette presents his compliments," wrote Byrd.

She was one of the few people in the world—maybe the only person—from whom he would not hide his feelings. "What I love in you," he told her in 1910, "is your beautiful soul, so tender and sympathetic, indeed in such accord with mine that my heart strings have been touched, never to vibrate again except in unison with yours."

Like all precious things you are hard to get, but when once got you will not go from hand to hand like some cheap article. Your heart will never be won but once, for such is the way of a great soul and therein lies your priceless worth.

When Byrd received his commission and his orders, and as Marie pursued her own career path, the times and occasions that had brought them together in the past inevitably began to dwindle. Upon graduation, he was detailed to the *Wyoming*, the newest and mightiest battleship in the Atlantic Fleet. After a temporary stint training recruits for the *Wyoming*, he joined the ship at the Brooklyn Navy Yard, where the superdreadnought was fitting out at the end of 1912. "Now that my ship will be so much away and you will seldom be in Winchester," he wrote, "I will, in all probability, gradually and quietly drop out of your life."

> Good by Marie. May gladness be yours throughout the new year and may peace and happiness be with you always. May he, who knows all, so conduct your destiny that only those things will come into your life that will revert to your ultimate good. This is my constant prayer for you.

"Good by again dearest Marie," he concluded.

"Mr. Byrd," said the captain of the *Wyoming* in a periodic fitness report, "will make an excellent officer. Is a young man of exceptionally fine and agreeable character, and excellent moral character. Is very zealous and painstaking."[17] But while Dick threw himself (wholeheartedly as usual) into the busy routine of a junior officer on a man-of-war, he silently suffered an awful longing. "Can it be? Has she gone out of my life?"[18] he asked himself. As he put it in the fable he later composed about the boy from the sunny land,

> For him, there was no happiness and his wound constantly ached and seemed passed healing.

Standing long watches on a steel deck put more pressure on Byrd's weak ankle than the joint could bear. He kept neglecting the pain and swelling, until he fell down a gangway on the *Wyoming*. He wound up back in the Naval Hospital in Washington, where this time the surgeons cut a u-shaped incision over the round part of the ankle, cleaned out some loose fragments, and nailed what remained of the ankle bone to the bottom of his leg bone.[19] Byrd was first led to believe that a silver nail had been used and got a bit of an ego boost; he later found out that the nail was a common variety, no different from the ones embedded in the beams of the hospital.

On May 1, 1913, just about a week after the operation, a letter with a familiar handwriting arrived in the mail. Marie was distressed to hear that he was back in the hospital. A few weeks later, he received a couple of ties she had knitted for him. "I thought that, what with the Vincent Club, and music and society you had probably forgotten all about me," he said.[20] He was discharged from the hospital on August 1 and given six weeks' sick leave. They met back in Winchester and enjoyed the rest of the summer together, as in years gone by. Something new had slowly been crystallizing within Marie Ames. She, too, had been trained to hold her emotions in check, but she saw things clearly now. Her feelings for Dick Byrd had always been deeper than she had allowed herself to realize. As they wandered together over hills they first climbed as children, she told him that she loved him with all of her heart and that her love was ever growing.

He sat down and wrote the long, lyrical tale of their relationship shortly after she left for Boston. It concluded with a different sort of flourish than that referenced by his ancestor, William Byrd II:

> Such was the power of love that his wound was healed, and all unhappiness died, buried in the grave of the past. No poet ever dreamed a thing more beautiful than the unfinished story of this boy and girl.

A six-year commitment was required of the young men who accepted an appointment to the U.S. Naval Academy: four years of instruction at Annapolis followed by a two-year apprenticeship at sea. During those six years, they were not allowed to marry. Richard Evelyn Byrd Jr. and Marie Donaldson Ames waited no longer than was necessary. They took their vows in Winchester on January 20, 1915.

⫶12⫶

GREAT LOVE
COMES FIRST

*Go where he may, he cannot hope to find
The truth, the beauty pictured in his mind*

SAMUEL ROGERS
1763–1855

In *The Lucky Bag*, the Annapolis yearbook, the blurb devoted to each graduate was traditionally introduced with an appropriate quotation. The above lines, from an 1819 poem entitled "Human Life," introduced the two paragraphs about Richard Byrd that appeared in the 1912 edition. The quote aptly described one aspect of Byrd's character: Byrd the dreamer and visionary who meditated on nature and civilization, and was often seen absorbed in thought. But there was a part of him that neither his classmates nor future shipmates ever saw because he kept it hidden, and ironically it was perfectly captured in the next four lines of the same poem:

But if by chance an object strike the sense,
The faintest shadow of that Excellence,
Passions, that slept, are stirring in his frame,

Thoughts undefined, feelings without a name!

The secret Richard Byrd was a man consumed with passion. He did not love lightly. Marie was and had always been an ideal partner in his mind, someone who possessed every quality he desired in a woman. He adored her, worshipped her, and felt a soaring joy in his marriage, an inexpressible happiness that grew and intensified and became almost impossible to contain. It dominated his thoughts as well as his emotional life. Byrd habitually thought in terms of processes and dimensions larger than himself. As a boy walking through the woods, he contemplated the laws of nature. As a world-famous aviator, he would speculate on the role of aviation in the evolution of humankind. In the same way, as a young married man, he thought of his union with Marie as being part of something larger. Since they had grown up together, knew each other so intimately and admired each other so thoroughly, he believed that there was something finer, purer, deeper about their relationship than the ordinary variety.

"I thank God that we have found real love," he had written during their engagement,

> as different from the average so-called love as bad is from good; as dark is from light; as Earth is from heaven.

In his mind, like in the songs of the mystical poets, real love was connected with the harmony of the universe and ideas of spiritual development. It was rare, elevating, and transformative, a love that "surpasses everything earthly," a part of the everlasting, "a glimpse into Heaven." The couple transformed by true love would, in turn, help elevate their fellow men and women. Early in 1914, he wrote:

> Through our life we must walk hand in hand among the people with a Christ-spirit. We may not leave any

monuments or posthumous glory behind us; but as we walk along the path we will strive to carry an atmosphere with us that will refresh with its quality those within its compass.

Five months after they had gotten married, he echoed this sentiment. "Dearest," he said, "there is eternity behind us and eternity before us and out of the unknown God brought us together and joined us in love, so let us cling closely and give some account of this wonderful thing God has given us one for the other." Again and again, he emphasized that "To give to the world the best that is in us we must live our lives together always."

The problem was that an officer in the U.S. Navy was trained for leadership and command on a ship at sea, and the navy made no special provision for the passions that stirred within the wiry frame of its most happily married ensign. Byrd had done well in the service. Following the operation on his ankle, the treating physicians recommended a period of less strenuous duty. Byrd was reassigned to a smaller ship, the battleship *Missouri*, half the size of the *Wyoming*. He reported for duty on September 27, 1913, and was immediately made executive officer, due to a shortage of personnel available for the position. In the spring of 1914, the *Missouri* was detailed to Annapolis to participate in the Naval Academy's annual practice cruise. The middies were due to cross the Atlantic that summer. Meanwhile, the Wilson administration contemplated a police action against Victoriano Huerta, a military dictator coughed up by the Mexican Revolution. Richard Byrd had no intention of sitting out a shooting war. "If we fight," he told his fiancée, "I *shall not* go over with the midshipmen." He wound up on the armored cruiser *Washington*, which departed for Vera Cruz at the end of April. A week later the ship was diverted to Santo Domingo to broker a truce among serial revolutionaries in Haiti and in the Dominican Republic.

In the West Indies, Byrd was cited on two occasions for saving crewmembers from drowning. There were 861 men aboard the *Washington*, the equivalent of a battalion in the army. Battalions are broken down into a number of companies. Similarly, the crew of a man-of-war is separated into divisions. Each division has its own guns to man or its own part of the engine room to operate. Just as junior officers in the army are in charge on the company level, junior officers in the navy run the divisions. Byrd seemed to have no difficulty getting results. He had observed early on that a "discontented crew is never an efficient one."[1] This understanding, the relationship between morale and efficiency, would remain central to the leadership principles he adhered to throughout his career. "I have my division running now without a ripple," he wrote home. His captain, Edward W. Eberle, the future admiral and chief of Naval Operations, called him, "A very energetic and promising young officer."[2]

That summer, a slot became vacant on the *Dolphin*, a dispatch boat that had been put at the disposal of the secretary of the navy, Josephus Daniels. The Secretary had the prerogative of selecting the officers who served on his yacht. When informed of the vacancy, Daniels remembered a junior officer he had met at the dedication of a Y.M.C.A. building at the Brooklyn Navy Yard. While touring the facility before the start of the official ceremonies, he noticed that a Bible class was in progress. Daniels, a newspaperman by trade and a political reformer by temperament, was himself a regular churchgoer and Sunday school teacher. He led his entourage into the classroom and sat down. The class was being conducted by a young ensign who "was visibly embarrassed but stuck to his text."[3] Daniels later invited the ensign to attend the dedication ceremonies and occupy a seat on the platform next to the fleet admiral and other senior officers. As a result of that meeting, Ensign Richard E. Byrd Jr. was encouraged to put in writing an idea he had for a corps of Y.M.C.A. officials to be assigned to American naval vessels as a means of alleviating the coarseness of shipboard life. It didn't hurt that Daniels, a Wilson supporter, had attended the 1912 Democratic Convention and during the proceedings had befriended the only member of Virginia's Big Four who stood out for his candidate—Richard E. Byrd Sr.

The cruiser *Washington* was anchored off Santo Domingo City when orders were received reassigning Dick Jr. to the secretary's yacht. He joined his new ship on October 12, 1914. The *Dolphin* was larger than a gunboat and about equally well-armed. It carried a crew of 117 men and fifteen guns, and, like any navy vessel, was required to spend a certain amount of time sailing on a prearranged course for drills and target practice. War had broken out in Europe while Byrd was in the Caribbean. In the spring of 1915, a couple of months after he and Marie had married and moved into an apartment in Washington, the *Dolphin*'s home port, the yacht was pressed into service for neutrality enforcement duty. Fourteen German ships were interned at various ports along the eastern seaboard from Newport News to Boston; they were said to be plotting to make a dash for the Atlantic, some carrying American coal to resupply warships on the high seas. This would be a clear violation of the neutrality laws. The navy was mobilized to turn back those vessels. The *Dolphin* patrolled the waters off New York, but saw no action. Later in the year, she sailed up and down the East Coast ferrying Secretary Daniels on a prolonged inspection tour.

Byrd continued to make a sterling impression on everyone he met. He was occasionally detached for temporary duty aboard the *Mayflower*, the presidential yacht, and became great friends with the assistant secretary of the navy, a New York patrician with a zesty smile and an irresistible personality. His name was Franklin Delano Roosevelt. "I like Roosevelt," he told his wife. "He is far from brilliant but he is very ambitious and a good diplomat." Dick Byrd, of course, was not lacking in ambition either, but at the moment he wasn't thinking about his career or worldly success. He was thinking about his bride.

"You are so perfectly dear and precious and when you put your arms around my neck and your face against mine I am beside myself with happiness and love and tenderness and I generally say something that is idiotic," he wrote from New York. He thought about Marie constantly and wrote everyday, often twice a day. "Darling," he said, "there are no two ways about it: I'm miserable away from you. And the contrast to my great happiness with you is almost more than I can bear." He daydreamed of residing with her at Westover, imagining her standing on the great front porch of a colonial estate. Above all, he desperately wanted to have a home and a home life. "I can not," he declared, "and will not look forward to a life of separation from my darling who I love so absolutely that there's nothing much outside of her." Referring to a conversation with a shipmate who had adjusted to the navy lifestyle, he wrote, "If I minded separations as little as does he I would be ashamed of being married." He was absolutely clear in his own mind about his priorities. "I put you and our love first before everything," he told Marie. "Great Love doesn't come to many dearest and when it does it must come first in spite of the fact that people cannot understand the attitude."[4]

The commanding officer of the *Dolphin*, Captain Ralph Earle, had first met Richard Byrd at the Naval Academy when Earle did a tour as a disciplinary officer at Annapolis. They got along famously and remained friends for decades; Earle retired as an admiral to become president of Worcester Polytechnic Institute in Worcester, Massachusetts, and saw to it that the college awarded Byrd an honorary degree in 1928. As commander of the *Dolphin*, he described Byrd in these words: "calm, even-tempered, active and painstaking."[5] Neither Earle nor anyone else attached to that ship suspected the depth of emotion concealed behind the cool façade of their efficient young ensign. Nor were they even remotely aware that he had made the most momentous decision of his life. He had decided to get out of the navy if he could do so honorably.

He believed he could.

His right ankle had become a chronic sore spot. He was still unable to stand a routine, four-hour watch without pain and occasional swelling. The pain had become acute in the summer of 1914, while Byrd served aboard the *Washington*. A cast had been put on his foot at that time to take the pressure off the ankle, and he had had to hop around the deck on crutches for a couple of weeks. The pain worsened for a while after that procedure, but gradually improved. The condition basically remained unchanged. Byrd often traded watches with his fellow officers so that he might do his duty at night when he could sit down. Examined again in November of 1914, it was observed that his feet no longer matched: the bony part of the ankle on the inside of the right foot was enlarged and was also lower than the equivalent projection on his left ankle. A month later he was given special exercises to strengthen his right foot. The exercises became increasingly difficult to perform.

In the middle of April 1915, he wrote to his Uncle Hal, confiding his desire to be retired.

Henry D. Flood was now chairman of the House Foreign Affairs Committee. He was also a friend of Dr. Francis S. Nash, a member of the navy's Board of Medical Examiners and the senior member of the Naval Retiring Board. Byrd asked his uncle to discuss the ankle injury with Dr. Nash and prevail on Nash to recommend his nephew for retirement. In June of 1915, Byrd would become eligible for promotion, having served three years as an ensign; in order to be considered for promotion, however, he first had to pass a physical. "The time for the Retiring Board to act," he told Hal Flood, "is when I go up for promotion the last part of next month or the first part of June."[6]

Byrd came up before the Medical Examiners on July 16, 1915. He was found "not physically qualified to perform all his duties at sea, owing to lameness in his right leg, on prolonged exercise." The board moved slowly, recommending that he "be further examined physically after six months under service conditions to ascertain the extent of his incapacity." On January 26, 1916, the Board of Medical Examiners reconvened and certified that "Ensign Richard E. Byrd, U.S. Navy, is incapacitated for service by reason of lameness in right ankle joint contracted in the line of duty, and he is therefore not qualified to perform all his duties at sea, and we do not recommend him for promotion."

Byrd could have endured the sore ankle and gone on standing his watches. The injury merely limited him to a four-mile hike when he got off-duty instead of the ten or fifteen miles he felt he had the stamina to cover.[7] It was a damn nuisance, but he could have toughed it out. He crossed the Rubicon when he brought it to the attention of the medical board. No glory awaited an officer who failed to advance with his class. He had encouraged Marie to continue her studies in music and dance, but of her own volition she had put down the violin and bow, and had retired "Sylvia Rose" to become Mrs. Richard Byrd. Now, he returned the gesture. He threw his navy career right out of the window.

He was summoned before the Retiring Board on March 2, 1916, and "did not desire to question the medical members, to rebut their evidence, nor to make a statement."[8] He was retired as of March fifteenth that year. In accordance with customary military procedure, he was elevated, as he retired, to the next higher grade, lieutenant, j.g.

But the navy would not let Richard Byrd go.

It had been estimated at this time that after two years of battle, the first major war of the twentieth century had consumed between three-and-a-half and four million lives, nearly as many as had been lost in all of the conflicts of the previous century.[9] For almost a year and a half now, the opposing armies in Europe had been deadlocked across a front that extended for 450 miles across Belgium and northeastern France. Casualties on the western front ranged from 5,000 to 50,000 per day. The fighting had meanwhile spread to Italy and the Balkans, and, due to the advent of submarines, even the international shipping lanes were threatened. Industrialization and mass production had made possible a warfare of unprecedented fury and scale. The Atlantic Ocean no longer seemed large enough to prevent the United States from being drawn into the conflagration.

In May of 1916, the Navy Department offered Byrd the assignment of going up to Rhode Island and bringing the Naval Militia of that state to a condition of readiness. He figured he was needed; moreover, the logistics were right. Byrd's father-in-law, Joseph Ames, had died shortly after Dick and Marie's wedding. His sister-in-law, Katharine, had married an indirect descendant of George Washington and resided in Philadelphia. Marie's mother, Helen, consequently lived all alone. While Byrd worked in Providence, he and Marie could move in with Mrs. Ames and have a life together in a Boston townhouse.

Byrd took the job. His official title was instructor-inspector, but his duties ranged from organization to recruitment. He threw himself into every task in his usual wholehearted manner and even proved himself adept at marketing military service. "I knew war was coming," he said. "I had been speaking all over Rhode Island trying to get recruits, which at first was very difficult to do. But when I began to say, 'Do you want Rhode Island to be a second Belgium?' and when we put on several parades the recruits began to come in."[10]

The Naval Militia had lacked a commander for a year when Byrd arrived in Providence on June 9. After six months on the job, he was appointed commander by Rhode Island Governor R. Livingston Beeckman. When the U.S. declared war on April 7, 1917, Byrd said, "we mobilized the whole state militia within twelve hours."[11] Governor Beeckman received a letter of commendation for that feat from the secretary of the navy. Beeckman, in turn, wrote Secretary Daniels, giving Byrd most of the credit.

For the first time, Byrd's administrative abilities became a matter of record. While serving at the Rhode Island post, he registered for a couple of economics courses at Harvard Graduate School. Apparently, he was looking toward life after the navy but didn't have time to pick up an advanced degree. Shortly after the declaration of war, Daniels brought him back to Washington where he found himself eventually installed as secretary of an Army-Navy Commission on Training Camp Activities. The chairman was a thirty-four-year-old New York attorney named Raymond B. Fosdick, who would return to private practice in the twenties and represent John D. Rockefeller Jr. One of the members of the commission was a sports legend—athlete, coach, author, and businessman Walter Camp, the "Father of Modern Football."

The Commission was an interesting social experiment that sought to ensure that recruits retained their ties to civil society while they made the transition from civilian to military life. A precursor of the USO movement, the Commission worked with local churches and lodges and such national organizations as the American Library Association, the Knights of Columbus, and the YMCA, to establish a program of recreational activities which, it was hoped, would reduce alcohol abuse among servicemen and check the spread of venereal disease. Fosdick concentrated on the army half of the Commission's work and left the navy responsibilities to Byrd. "He turned out to be a ball of fire," Fosdick said, "full of ideas and energy, eager, tireless, and up to his ears in work."[12]

Fitzhugh Green had married a Philadelphia socialite less than five months before the call to arms. "The war made separation natural," he said. "The war made everything exciting."[13] It understandably prompted Dick Byrd to revise his priorities. American troops had arrived on the western front while Byrd waged a relentless campaign against, as the literature of the Training Camp commission put it, the "MENACE FROM IMMORALITY."[14] A young man who at the age of fourteen had been a pistol-packing deputy in the Philippines could not at twenty-eight abide being sidelined in Washington while his generation prosecuted a "war to end all wars." Byrd did his utmost to get out from behind a desk. He actually proposed that the navy send him to the trenches. The rationale was that by learning what modern trench warfare entailed, he could help the navy and Marine Corps develop amphibious landing techniques. "I am intensely and profoundly interested in the matter," he wrote in a memo, "and am prepared and anxious to go into the trenches for the necessary knowledge."[15]

Byrd even recruited one of the most influential members of the Senate Committee on Naval Affairs, Claude Swanson, to lobby for the idea. It was shot down, but he had a back-up plan in mind. Byrd's interest in aviation was first kindled during his plebe year at the Naval Academy. The disciplinary officer assigned to his floor at Bancroft Hall, the Annapolis dormitory, was an air power aficionado who held late-night bull sessions on the subject; Byrd attended regularly. That officer was Lieutenant Ernest J. King, a future admiral, chief of the Bureau of Aeronautics, commander in chief of the U.S. Fleet, and chief of Naval Operations. Other attendees included Jerome C. Hunsaker, who would go on to study aeronautical engineering at MIT and design the NC flying boats and the airship *Shenandoah*; Byrd's roommate, Garland Fulton, future head of the lighter-than-air division of the Bureau of Aeronautics; and Donald W. Douglas, the eventual founder of the Douglas Aircraft Company, manufacturers of the D.C. airliners. King was so influential as a proselytizer that Fulton maintained that the entire structure of U.S. Naval Aviation was built by King's disciples in Bancroft Hall.[16]

Byrd had made his first flight in an airplane in the early part of 1913 while attached to the battleship *Wyoming*. Since then, in one guise or another, aviation was never more than a half step away from him. In the summer of 1915, as the retirement process dragged on, the *Dolphin* put into Portsmouth, New Hampshire, and Byrd ran into an old navy buddy named Frenchy Lamont. "He is an aviator and wants me to come into the Aviation Corps—says I'm made for it," he wrote Marie. A year later in Rhode Island, Byrd organized three new divisions of the Naval Militia: Engineer, Marine, and, due to his personal interest in aviation, Aeronautic. The Militia acquired an airplane and sent it off to war during the mobilization.

Nothing in Byrd's personal correspondence suggests that he had done any serious thinking about his future upon finding true love. The national emergency, in a sense, enabled him to find his true calling. Standard procedures no longer apply when a nation mobilizes for war. Corners are cut, exceptions are made. New possibilities arise. Byrd's zeal, energy, and adventurous spirit impelled him to reach literally for the sky. He went up before the same Board of Medical Examiners that had found him physically incapacitated for duty at sea and pleaded for a chance to serve in the air. Despite all the influence he was able to bring to bear—Swanson and Martin in the Senate, Flood in the House, Nash on the board itself—it was a tough sell.

But he put it across.

✈ 13 ✈

OUT OF SIGHT
OF LAND

*I don't believe in waiting for opportunity
to knock at the door.*

RICHARD E. BYRD[1]

The beach at Pensacola in February of 1918 was a composition of blazing sunshine, blue waters, and wooden wings. A deck had been hammered down on the sand, and a cluster of hangars had been erected on it. Ramps slanted down from the deck right into the sea. Floatplanes were launched by rolling them down the ramps on little wheeled trucks. Here and there a crescent of white sand obtruded from beneath the deck. The drone of aircraft engines drowned out the sound of the lapping waves. Dick and Marie Byrd had driven down to the air station together and taken a room at a local boardinghouse. Having a new and exciting window of possibility open in his life and his wife alongside him to share the experience was as much happiness as Dick Byrd had known since the day he got married. He was in a jaunty mood when he reported for duty. As soon as he had a chance, he walked out between the hangars and along the deck that swept to the edge of the sea. At that moment, an airplane, a single-engine trainer, plummeted out of the sky and into the bay killing the two occupants, a student pilot and a flight instructor.

Richard E. Byrd Sr. had no use for this passing fancy called aviation. When his son left for Pensacola, he solemnly told Dick goodbye, figuring he would never see him again. As Richard Jr. watched a boat full of orderlies, medics, and divers motor out to the crash site, the "romance of aviation" suddenly seemed to wear a bit thin. While the wreckage and victims were fished out of the sea, he ran into an old classmate, Nathan B. Chase. Chase was the quietest and most assuming member of the Naval Academy's class of 1912. He was physically frail and had not participated in any sports at Annapolis. Today, he would be called a "nerd." Naturally, he had taken a good-natured ribbing from the "jocks," including Dick Byrd. Although he and Byrd had actually been close friends, Chase now saw a way to even the score.

He gestured to a seaplane that had been flight prepped and asked Byrd if he wanted to take a spin. "I'm frank to say that was not the moment I would have selected to go up," Byrd said.[2] Nevertheless, he donned a leather helmet and goggles, stuffed his ears full of cotton, and climbed into the open cockpit. Down the ramp went the plane and into the water. Chase took Byrd up to 4,000 feet, an altitude so high the hangars could barely be distinguished. For the next forty minutes, he dived and rolled and looped over the sea, and put the airplane through every stunt and maneuver he knew.

Human beings, unlike birds or fish, were not made to exist in a three-dimensional medium. We were made to move hither and yon over a flat surface. So long as we do—other things being equal—our nervous system remains in equilibrium. But the minute we add a vertical axis and find ourselves pulled abruptly up or down (think of a fast-moving elevator), a fire alarm goes off in a visceral nerve center and our muscles tense in anticipation of doom. Chase was used to it. Byrd was as dizzy as a drunkard, and the mass of sensitive nerve fibers in his stomach squealed in unison at every plunge.

Then Chase let him take the controls.

Despite the abrupt introduction to aerobatics, Byrd took to the air as avidly as if the vowel in his last name had been an "i." "He used to go up with any one who even said he could fly," one of his instructors recalled. "He risked his life more times than any other beginner I ever saw in flying after hours with some of the rawest pilots on the field. He seemed to feel that if he could only be in the air he could learn, regardless of how crude the man manipulating the plane might be."[3] He soloed after nine hours and fifty minutes of dual instruction. Having made the first solo, student pilots are allowed a certain latitude to buzz around on their own and raise their comfort level in the air before receiving advanced instruction. Byrd used this period to become what he called a "landing specialist."

He made fifty-six landings in the next eight days of solo practice and over seventy solo landings spanning the next month. The point of this exercise was to thoroughly prepare himself to cope with various in-flight emergencies. Airplanes fly because the wings create lift, a force equally as strong as gravity. Lift is developed when the wind meets the leading edge of the wing at the proper angle and flows smoothly over the wing surface. If the smooth airflow is interrupted, the wings lose lift. In this situation—called a "stall"—suddenly nothing whatsoever holds the ship up, and it drops like a stone even if the engine is running perfectly.

The biplanes employed as training aircraft by the navy in 1918 were one step up from the flying platforms of 1913 in which Byrd had his first flight. The wings still looked like a wide box kite, but there was a fabric-covered fuselage now that fit between the struts and spars of the upper and lower wing. The plane was cumbersome in the air and the engine prone to failure, and either a stall or an engine failure in some configurations could lead to a spin and certain death. Nathan Chase had told Byrd to always maintain his airspeed and he would be all right. This is due to the intricate relationship between airspeed and the aerodynamics of lift. On takeoff, for example, if you try to climb at too steep an angle, you will both lose airspeed *and* interrupt the smooth flow of air over the surface of the wing. On landing, the situation is reversed. If you are not gliding down at a steep *enough* angle, you're liable to come in too slow and lose lift. A stall can be fatal in such circumstances because the pilot is flying too low to have room to recover. So Byrd taught himself to keep an eye on the airspeed indicator and methodically practiced recovering from simulated engine failures and incipient stalls, and making a safe landing. He did this in climbs, in turns, and at high and low altitude, and the practice would save his life in several instances.

Nathan Brown Chase of Washington, D.C., died in an airplane crash at Pearl Harbor in 1925.

"Flying training during the war," Byrd said, "was like being on the firing line and I believe there were a bigger percentage of casualties then there were in the front line trenches."

> Every day or so we lost some friend, but no one stopped to mourn about it and not many seemed to bother much about it. The casualties, of course, were caused by the great rapidity with which we were trying to turn out the flyers.[4]

On one takeoff, just as Byrd had gotten off the water and was barreling forward at sixty miles an hour, he collided with another student pilot who had come in for a landing at about the same speed. The planes were wrecked, but the pilots suffered only bruises and embarrassment. His closest call occurred on the return leg of a cross-country flight that had taken him some one hundred miles east of Pensacola. He ran into the edge of a thunderstorm, where the turbulence was so severe it almost bucked him out of the sky. He managed to keep control of the plane and put her safely down on the waves, where he waited for the storm to subside. He had his share of luck but survived flight training basically for the same reason he survived his polar expeditions: careful and meticulous preparation. He received his wings on April 7, 1918, and became Naval Aviator Number 608.

Since Byrd was an officer and one of the few Annapolis graduates to come through Pensacola, he was retained at the station as an instructor and accident investigator. In the first capacity, he taught navigation at the training center's ground school. In the second, he had to pick through the wreckage every time a plane fell out of the sky and try to figure out what had gone wrong. He often found himself looking over the mangled remains of his friends. In his own words, unedited for publication, Byrd described the scene of one accident as follows. A seaplane had crashed at low altitude over land:

> Mechanic thrown a few feet clear—broken into many pieces but face calm, even serene. Face not scarred—left leg at a crazy angle—toe pointing backward—right leg looking like a Z. Clothes torn—covered with oil. Pilot caught in wreck. Terrible gash in head—left side of face mashed in—leg broken at right angles, making a right angle. He was apparently trying to talk and was moving. Took about ten minutes to cut him loose. When doctor arrived, pronounced the pilot dead, said that he had a smash over the heart that caused death instantly, and yet I know that he moved for four or five minutes.[5]

Accident investigation proved such traumatic duty that Byrd had to reconcile the horror of it with his own sense of values. He came to terms with the mounting death rate at Pensacola by characteristically viewing it from the perspective of something larger than himself. This was the pioneering of a new technology, he reasoned; in the long run the benefits would surely outweigh the cost. In the short run, aviation would help win the war.

The Germans had concentrated three and a half million men on the western front over the winter of 1917–18. By the spring, the kaiser's legions had opened a furious offensive against the British and French, coming within striking distance of Paris. "We were all begging for foreign duty orders," Byrd said.[6] But the senior aviators didn't believe the fledgling pilots were ready to fly in a combat zone. Byrd nevertheless had the knack of making things happen. The navy had commissioned aviation visionary Glenn Curtiss to begin production of a new series of flying boats, mammoth multi-engine bombers capable of flying across the Atlantic Ocean, a feat that had not yet been accomplished. Designated the NCs or navy Curtiss planes, their mission would be to bomb German warships at their home ports.

Crossing the Atlantic, like the Polar Sea, was the sort of spectacular flight that would appeal to Dick Byrd. It would be more than a benchmark in aviation, it would be a milestone at the crossroads of history and science, commerce and international relations. It would change the way Americans and Europeans looked at the world, and the way they lived and did business. No one gets to be Speaker of the Virginia House of Delegates by wishing on a star. No one becomes chairman of the Foreign Relations Committee of the U.S. House of Representatives by waiting for the telephone to ring. Byrd came from a long line of movers and shakers. He grew up surrounded by people who knew how to achieve because they in turn had learned from the example of their successful parents. He inherited this skill right along with his name. Although barely out of flight school, he decided to promote himself for the choice assignment of piloting the NC-1 to Europe when the first of the big new flying boats came off the assembly line. In May of 1918, he confidentially wrote to Walter Camp of the Fosdick commission to get the sports legend behind the idea. He suggested that Camp contact the Aero Club of America to build support for the venture.[7] At the same time, he began applying his imagination and creativity to developing new procedures and techniques to overcome the limitations of conventional aircraft.

Byrd lined the beach with drums of burning gasoline, took off into the darkness, and with the dots of flame onshore to guide him made what might have been the first night landing on water anyone had ever deliberately attempted.[8] He also undertook the first series of flights out of Pensacola in which an aviator intentionally flew out of sight of land. Byrd collaborated on this venture with twenty-nine-year-old Lieutenant Walter Hinton, chief flight instructor for multi-engine seaplanes at the training center. With Hinton, Naval Aviator Number 135, at the control stick, Byrd conducted the first experiments in air navigation over the open sea. As a result of these exercises, he came to the conclusion that some sort of bubble attachment would have to be affixed to a mariner's sextant to provide the ocean flier with an artificial horizon. Otherwise, with the actual horizon so often indistinct to an aviator or obscured by clouds, it would be impossible to measure the altitude of a celestial object.

On July 9, 1918, Byrd dispatched a memo to the chief of Naval Operations formally requesting permission to make the transatlantic crossing in the NC-1. He may have had a fraction of the flight time of a senior naval aviator, but nevertheless considered himself "well qualified" on the basis of specialized knowledge and preparation.[9] The NC-1 wouldn't be flight-tested for another three months. Byrd's initiative, however, did not go unrecognized. He was sent up to Nova Scotia in August, where German subs had become increasingly active.

Byrd was given command of U.S. Naval Air Forces in Canada. His mission was to establish two air bases, one at Halifax, the other at Sydney, and to patrol the coast for U-boats. He took Walter Hinton with him. Aviation was something of an afterthought at the Navy Department in this era. The Halifax base, where Byrd made his headquarters, consisted of thirty large tents. They were occupied in due time by some 150 men, but none of the enlisted personnel knew anything about aircraft. They were Marine technicians; they could break down steam, gasoline and Diesel engines into their constituent parts, but they didn't know how to put a biplane together. Two disassembled seaplanes arrived in crates on Canadian Railway flatcars. It appeared at first as if the engines were missing, but the motors eventually turned up in a freight car. The bombs the aviators were supposed to drop on the submarines were nowhere to be found.

When the first plane was erected on the beach, Byrd and Hinton climbed into the cockpit "with some trepidation," Byrd admitted. "We did not know whether or not it would fall to pieces."[10] They flew over the city on a test flight and caused panic in the streets. In a *War of the Worlds* type of hysteria such as Orson Welles would later wreak on the radio, the citizens imagined they were being invaded by the Germans. "There were a number of screams, we heard afterward," Byrd said, "and a number of women fainted. We were requested not to fly over again." The second plane was assembled the next day. Byrd borrowed some depth charges from the warships in the harbor and started to patrol the coastal waters.

The weather was awful. Along the rugged banks of maritime Canada, warm, moist, late summer breezes circulating up from the Gulf Stream met water previously cooled in the Polar Sea. The result: persistent fog. Due to the winds cascading up and down the cliffs, the air was perpetually rough. Worst of all, from Byrd's point of view, the enemy was nowhere in sight. He once thought he saw a periscope protruding from the deep. This was about thirty miles southeast of the entrance of Halifax harbor, towards the end of September 1918. He and Hinton had been following up a report of a sub at that location. Byrd was just about to drop a depth charge when he realized he was looking down on a spar floating around on the waves. Marie had joined him at Halifax earlier that month. He had been living in a tent like the rest of his men until she arrived, then moved with her into a small house that had been built on the base. There were two more planes at his disposal by then, and one ray of hope concerning the transatlantic flight.

The navy had ordered Byrd to locate a suitable beach on the coast of Newfoundland where a large seaplane could refuel, presumably, for the long hop across the Atlantic Ocean. He and Hinton interpreted this to mean that Washington had given the NC flight the go-ahead. Buoyed by this notion, they devoted themselves in their spare time to picking up the transoceanic flight planning where they had left off at Pensacola. They tried out smoke bombs and flares as objects a navigator could eyeball to determine wind drift when flying out of sight of land. Byrd plotted courses for an Atlantic hop in a series of stages from Halifax to Newfoundland to the Azores. He met a British naval officer at Halifax, a Commander W. T. Walker, who had devised a crude bubble sextant; he bought the instrument and took it up on a flight with Hinton to put the artificial horizon to the test.

Walker had made the bubble glass an integral part of the small telescope on the sighting end of a standard sextant. He added an appendage to the bottom of the telescope tube, near the eyepiece, to house the bubble glass. In order to see the bubble when taking a sight, Walker put a mirror inside the telescope. There was a hole in the tube over the place where the bubble appendage was attached. This enabled the user to look through the telescope and see the celestial body and the reflection of the bubble at the same time. The bubble was too sensitive to be easily centered; the image of the celestial body was inverted, making life a little more complicated for the navigator; and the mirror took up about half the diameter of the tube and limited the field of vision. There were a number of other problems as well. Byrd thought the bubble idea was fundamentally sound but needed further development.

In Western Europe, the Big Push was underway. The Allies had repelled the Germans at the Second Battle of the Marne, which took place over the summer of 1918. In September, just about the time that Byrd almost bombed a piece of flotsam, nine hundred thousand American doughboys started to force their way through the Argonne Forest. Dick's younger brother Tom was one of them. Tom Byrd had gone overseas as an infantry lieutenant, served heroically, and made captain by the time the Armistice was signed on November 11. State Senator Harry Byrd had been appointed fuel administrator for Virginia by the Wilson administration and in that capacity made sure that military installations and defense industries in the Old Dominion had an adequate supply of gasoline and coal. Harry was the father of two children, but "for the remainder of his life," said his biographer, Ronald L. Heinemann, he "was nagged by conscience for failing to enlist."[11] Dick Byrd, the most sensitive of the brothers, told Fitzhugh Green in 1927, "I have never gotten over the fact that I did not get into the fighting and am most reluctant to talk about the war."[12]

He consoled himself after the Armistice with dreams of the Atlantic crossing. As the Canadian stations demobilized, he sent a memo from Halifax to Washington on December 4, 1918. "Hostilities being at an end," he wrote, "it is again requested that I be detailed to make a trans-Atlantic flight in an NC-1 type flying boat."[13] Unbeknownst to him, another and more experienced airman submitted a similar proposal two months earlier. Commander John Henry Towers, Naval Aviator Number 3, had been a passenger in a seaplane on a flight over Chesapeake Bay in June of 1913. This was in the pre-cockpit days when pilot and passenger sat in front of the engine. They were cruising at about 1,600 feet when a sudden downdraft yanked the aircraft right out from under them. The pilot fell to his death. Towers caught hold of a strut and held on to the plummeting plane. As the aircraft neared the water, another gust of wind leveled the wings and broke the freefall. For a moment, the plane flew straight and level—but upside down. Then the ship rolled into another dive and hit the water near Annapolis Harbor. Towers suffered severe bruises over his entire body but reached the dock, directed a search for the remains of his companion, and was able to walk unassisted to the Naval Hospital.[14] He was the only person, so far as anyone knew, to fall 1,600 feet without a parachute and survive.

Jack Towers had received his wings in 1911; his instructor was Glenn Curtiss. He became a flight instructor himself. He was posted at Annapolis during Byrd's senior year, 1911–1912, where he taught Washington-based officers to fly. He and Byrd may have met at this time. Their paths might have crossed again early in 1913, when Towers commanded a naval aviation unit during fleet maneuvers at Guantanamo, Cuba. Towers developed the catapult method of launching airplanes from the deck of a surface ship and led the pioneer naval aviation detachment that participated in the police action at Vera Cruz. He was assigned to the office of the chief of Naval Operations during the World War and was the only staff officer at this post with an aviation background. Byrd reported to him from Halifax.

Byrd traveled to Washington in November or December of 1918, met with Towers, and discussed his work on navigating out of sight of land.[15] The secretary of the navy approved the transatlantic flight on February 4, 1919. Jack Towers was given command of the operation two days later and in less than a week had established a Trans-Atlantic Flight Section within the Navy Department. He brought Byrd onboard to develop the necessary instruments and handle all other aspects of the flight planning dealing with navigation. Towers was three years older than Byrd and, like Byrd, a Southerner. He hailed from Georgia. They would become great friends; within two years, Jack would have a son, and Dick would be the godfather.

Great enterprises are rarely if ever the exclusive province of one government or one people. As in the quest for the transpolar flight, there was renewed competition for the transatlantic hop. At the moment a Swedish aviator was in northern New Jersey, awaiting the completion of a powerful twin-engine seaplane being assembled for him by a Newark manufacturer, and several British expeditions were in the running for a £10,000 prize put up by the *Daily Mail* for the first ocean flight. As the navy entered the race, Dick Byrd set out to perfect the bubble sextant.

He went to see one of his best friends, his Academy roommate, Garland "Froggy" Fulton, a rising star in the lighter-than-air branch of naval aviation, then in charge of the aviation division of the navy's Bureau of Construction and Repair. Byrd asked Froggy to assign "an expert instrument man" to work with him.[16] Fulton reached into his Aviation Accessory Department and produced a civilian employee, one Luis de Florez. De Florez had graduated from MIT the same year Byrd had graduated from the Naval Academy. He was a mechanical engineer, an inventor, and a Naval Reservist, and had already devised an early turn-and-bank indicator and other flight instruments for the navy. He was also the man who conceived the safety belt and shoulder harness. Like Byrd, he had a stellar career ahead of him, and—like Byrd—he knew it.

Byrd showed de Florez the Walker sextant and pointed out its various limitations, starting with the slim telescope and narrow field of vision. He suggested that de Florez make a new Walker-type sextant but with a fat telescope. Another possibility was to separate the bubble attachment from the telescope and put the bubble on the outer limb of the sextant. De Florez seemed keen on the outer-limb design. The NCs were due to hop off from Newfoundland by the middle of May, when there would be a full moon. They were being assembled in New York and would therefore have to depart on the first leg of the flight—New York to Newfoundland—by the second week of May.

Byrd was concerned with getting results in the shortest possible amount of time. He instructed de Florez to make two prototypes, one with the fat telescope and one with the bubble on the outer limb; he would try them both out and see which worked best. This was the beginning of a sub-plot that would develop alongside the transatlantic flight and end in a quasi-judicial proceeding verging on screwball comedy.

Byrd was responsible for instructing the transatlantic fliers in rapid methods of celestial navigation. He also had to supply them with every item of equipment they might conceivably need to find their way over the ocean: compasses, charts, watches, radio sets, radio direction-finding aides. Under his direction and prodding, the Aviation Division of Naval Operations produced a lightweight, compact version of a drift indicator developed by an Italian aeronaut, Colonel Arturo Crocco, for use in dirigibles. Byrd procured a stockpile of flares which could be fired from the bow of the NCs; by sighting down through the drift indicator on the burning flares, the transatlantic navigators would be able to tell by how much and in what direction the wind was pushing them off course.

He checked back with de Florez at the beginning of March and found that the engineer had made an "outer limb"-type bubble sextant but had failed to carry out the second part of his instructions and produce a Walker-type sextant with a fat telescope. Byrd was, in his own words, "rather sharp" with de Florez for not providing an alternative but soon found that the bubble on the outer limb gave good results. The prototype was rather cumbersome, however, so he put de Florez to work on building a simplified version. The new model was completed in April. It was much more satisfactory but not yet a functional sextant. The most serious flaw was that on taking a sight, the bubble and the celestial object could not be seen clearly at the same time. If the user focused on the sun, the bubble would appear blurred, and vice versa. The whole purpose of using the bubble as an artificial horizon would be defeated.

Byrd eliminated this problem by a stroke of genius: he inserted a half lens in the eyepiece. He worked out some other adjustments and subsequently delivered the advanced prototype to the Naval Observatory at Anacostia in the District of Columbia. The Naval Observatory made the bubble sextants that were used on the transatlantic flight.

The NC flying boat was the most startling and majestic aircraft of its day and time. It appeared only fourteen years after the death of Jules Verne and almost seemed as if it had sprung from the author's imagination. It was an enormous biplane. The upper wing was 126 feet long, only four feet shorter than that of a Boeing 707. The lower wing measured ninety-four feet. The two wings were connected by a network of wires and struts. Four engines were mounted between the upper and lower wings, and the entire wing assembly was balanced on top of a gray, forty-five-foot-long hull. The hull, the part of the aircraft designed to float on water, was initially modeled on a whaleboat.[17] The design was tested and considerably streamlined. The end result had so much aerodynamic swoop it looked more like a whale than a boat. The tail assembly was connected to the hull and the wings by an additional twenty-five foot network of wires and struts. If Captain Nemo had been an aviator and the *Nautilus* had been an aircraft instead of a submarine, it would have resembled this mammoth coupling of box kite and longboat.

There were four NC's at the inception of the mission, but a fire broke out in the hangar on two occasions, and the wings of one ship had to be cannibalized for the repair of another. At 10:00 a.m. on the morning of May 8, 1919, the three remaining NC's embarked on the first leg of the Atlantic crossing. Jack Towers commanded NC-3.

Lieutenant Commander Patrick N. L. Bellinger, a rugged South Carolinian who had served on submarines prior to getting his wings, was commanding officer of NC-1, and Lieutenant Commander Albert C. Read, a small, quiet New Englander with sharp eyes and sharp features, took charge of the NC-4. Bellinger was Naval Aviator Number 8; Read was Number 24.

Air navigation was such a new wrinkle that the role assumed by the commanding officer of each flying boat was not pilot, but navigator. Byrd had tutored Towers, Bellinger, and Read in the use of the bubble sextant and the theory and practice of navigating while out of sight of land. By specializing in this art, he had made himself indispensable to the success of the mission. Towers had gone to bat for him and secured permission for Byrd to accompany the NC-3 as far as Newfoundland to work out any potential kinks in the instruments developed under his supervision.

The pilot and co-pilot sat side by side in an open cockpit built into the hull just forward of the wings. The mechanics occupied a cockpit just aft of the wings, and the radio operator was positioned a little further aft. As the aerodynamic hull was ten feet across at its widest point and seven feet high, a crewmember could step down from his station and move forward and aft through the roomy interior. But he couldn't do this standing up. He would have to crawl. He would worm his way through a crawlspace that went under the fuel tanks, which were lined up single file in the middle of the hull, and under the dangling feet of the other crewmembers, who were perched on raised benches.

The commander-navigator, however, sat forward of the pilots at a table in the belly of the hull. Here he could spread his charts and communicate with his crew by telephone, but he could not see where the ship was heading or much of anything outside of his compartment. To take a sun sight or check his drift, the commander had to move to the forward end of the hull and raise himself up through a circular hatch originally installed for a machine-gunner. He would stand erect in the wind to shoot the sun or lean over the rim of the hatch to sight down into the drift indicator.

Towers described the scene in the flagship as follows:

> Byrd spent the afternoon vibrating between the forward and after cockpits, trying smoke bombs, sextants, etc. My cockpit was not very large, and with all the charts, chart desk, sextants, drift indicator, binoculars, chronometers, etc., stacked in there, very little room was left. As I wore a telephone all the time, wires were trailing all about me, and Byrd and I were continually getting all mixed up like a couple of puppies on leashes.[18]

The transatlantic hop was every bit as much of a national undertaking as the flight of *Apollo 11* sixty years later. The full resources of the U.S. Navy had been committed to ensure the success of the mission. Sixty destroyers were deployed along the projected flight path of the flying boats from New York, New York, to Plymouth, England, to provide logistic and emergency support. Most of the ships of this flotilla were stationed across the ocean at fifty-mile intervals. Four hours after getting underway, NC-3 received a radio message from NC-4 indicating that an engine had been lost and a forced landing might have to be made. No one aboard the flagship was worried. It was assumed that Read would descend within sight of the first of four destroyers stationed between Cape Cod and Nova Scotia.

NC-4 wound up losing two engines, coming down on the waves with no help in sight and taxiing one hundred miles to a naval station on the coast of Massachusetts. Towers and Bellinger reached Halifax without incident, landing near the base that Byrd had built from scratch less than a year earlier. The two flying boats departed Halifax for Newfoundland on May 10. When NC-3 flew out of sight of Nova

Scotia, Byrd climbed up to the hatch in the bow of the hull, leaned over the rim and looked down through the sight of the drift indicator. Under any circumstances, riding in the forward hatch would have been an exciting experience. The immense.wingspread and the four roaring engines were above and behind him. There was nothing in front of him or below but the thin air and the boundless sea. He was cold, despite being bundled up in four layers of clothing. He wore two pairs of long flannel underwear, a uniform and, as an outer garment, a heavy, fleece-lined, leather flying suit. Clad in this cocoon, his head and upper body completely out in the open, he had the wind in his face and the feeling of being propelled forward over the waves on the nose of a thundering, unseen force. As dramatic as the physical sensations was the reading of the drift indicator. If the instrument was to be believed, they were being pushed off their course by a number of degrees. Byrd climbed back down and asked Towers to take a sight. Towers went up into the daylight and got the same result.

They huddled together among the wires and paraphernalia of the little chart table and made an historic decision. They decided to trust the instrument and direct the pilot to alter his heading accordingly. "When we hit land exactly where we hoped to, we knew that the first drift indicator had proved its worth," Byrd said. "And I knew then that at last an airplane could be navigated without land marks. I was delighted."[19]

At 5,000 feet above the coast of Newfoundland, Byrd and Towers took turns looking down from the round hatch and saw hundreds of tiny white objects on the dark surface of the sea. To Byrd, they resembled sails; to Towers, grazing sheep. They were icebergs, the first seen by Byrd in his career. Two hours later, NC-3 landed just behind NC-1 at Trepassey, a fishing village about sixty miles southeast of St. John's. This was Byrd's last stop. He had fervently hoped that somewhere along the route from New York he would be officially transformed from an advisor to a full-fledged crewman. But although he had the support of Towers and Bellinger, orders were received at Trepassey relieving him of any further connection with the flight of the NC's and attaching him to another project.

Albert Read, whose Yankee countenance seemed to his classmates at the Naval Academy to have been cast in plaster (they called him "Putty"), made two more forced landings en route to Newfoundland but arrived in time to depart with Towers and Bellinger on May 16.[20] The three planes were separated first by darkness and then by fog. Towers and Bellinger both reached the vicinity of the Azores; in an unrelenting mist, each landed on rough seas to avoid flying blindly into a mountain. Both the NC-1 and -3 suffered heavy damages. Ironically, it was Putty Read who found a rift in the fog. NC-4 landed in Horta Harbor on one of the smaller of the Azore Islands and continued on to Lisbon and Plymouth to complete the world's first transatlantic flight.

The lighter-than-air branch of naval aviation had also wanted to compete in the transatlantic crossing. The C-5, a dirigible less than one-tenth the size of *Shenandoah*, embarked from a naval station at Montauk Point, Long Island, for Newfoundland on the fourteenth of May. She arrived safely at St. John's twenty-five hours and forty-five minutes later and, on the basis of that performance, received the green light to attempt a transatlantic flight to Ireland. Byrd was ordered to join the C-5 at St. John's and assist with the navigation.

As soon as the dirigible descended, her weary flight crew disembarked and went to bed.[21]

A ground crew of some one hundred men took over to moor the airship. Just then a gale blew up. The ground crew, holding on to the ropes of the airship, fought a tug-of-war with the raging winds and ultimately lost. The C-5 blew out to sea, never to be seen again. And along with her went Byrd's hopes of flying across the Atlantic in 1919.

≡14≡

USEFUL

When a man makes himself useful
he will be kept around.

Richard E. Byrd[1]

When Byrd returned from Newfoundland, he became involved in three business ventures. One was the tire business. The future explorer was the principal shareholder and president of the Tire Shop, a retail outlet at New York Avenue and 12th Street in northwest Washington. He was drawn into the company through a sailor who had served under him at Halifax and had since returned to civilian life. Byrd went after national distributorships and dreamed of opening branches in Winchester and throughout the Shenandoah Valley. At the same time, he bought two airplanes and had associates fly them from city to city and take people up for rides. They charged twenty-five dollars a ride at first, but the market forced them to cut the price to fifteen. Like any good entrepreneur, Byrd learned the value of advertising. He did considerable advance work in Pennsylvania before dispatching the planes to that state in the summer of 1919, making $4,000 in one week.

Byrd remained in the tire business for about two years and eventually turned a profit, but he lost money on the aviation end. One plane crashed within a year, and the other needed major repairs. His third potential money-making activity was the marketing of the bubble sextant. He sounded out two manufacturers in New York, one of whom offered him 20 percent royalties on each sale. But when he attempted to file a patent on the instrument, he found that Luis de Florez had beaten him to it.

This, in Byrd's opinion, was a "direct steal," a "dirty trick."[2] It was "underhanded."[3] It was decidedly not the conduct of a gentleman. Byrd had strictly observed the code of honor in his relationship with Commander Walker. He kept Walker informed about his own work with the artificial horizon and pledged that

> if I ever make any money on this sextant I intend to let you know about it and to let you have your proper share.[4]

But he could not abide people who failed to uphold his own standards. He initiated an "interference" with de Florez's patent application, claiming priority of invention. The motion was heard by a board of examiners of the U.S. Patent Office, and the proceedings dragged out over a period of three years.

The actual sextant that was used on the transatlantic flight and became standard issue in naval aviation at this time consisted of a fat telescope with a half lens in the eyepiece *and* a bubble level on the outer limb. By all rights, it should have been called the Byrd-de Florez sextant. It represented the combined efforts of an accomplished navigator and a talented engineer, and the only reason they were never able to reach an equitable arrangement with one another was because they were just too much alike. They were both blazingly energetic, aggressive young men with no time to waste. De Florez's family was as aristocratic as the Byrds. He was born in New York but spent part of his childhood on the continent, in the palaces of his relatives in

France and Spain. He was a small man with fair hair, a waxed mustache and a quick mind who spoke five languages and habitually dashed, rather than walked, up and down the corridors of his workplace. In the first five years after the Armistice, he reportedly made three-quarters of a million dollars on his patents, which, in addition to aviation aides, included certain mechanical processes for the production of gasoline. He was a consulting engineer to the oil industry while simultaneously working for the navy. During World War II, de Florez had himself activated as a captain in the regular navy. He presided over his own bailiwick in the naval bureaucracy, the Special Devices Division, and won national acclaim for inventing a series of realistic flight simulators employing motion pictures of attacking enemy fighters. "He is undoubtedly the most dynamic officer in the United States Navy," said the *New Yorker* in a 1944 profile, "and it is unlikely that any other navy could match him."

Be that as it may, during the testimony-taking phase of the patent case, Richard Byrd repeatedly upstaged Luis de Florez. De Florez hired a large New York law firm to represent him in the interference. Byrd consulted with a Washington-based patent attorney, but elected to represent himself. On one occasion, he actually took his own testimony, asking himself questions and then answering them.

"What is your name, age, residence and occupation?" he asked himself.

He answered: "Richard E. Byrd, Jr; thirty-one; Twenty-four hundred Sixteenth Street, Washington, D.C.; Naval officer."

"Have you read the counts of the present interference?"

"Yes."

He proceeded to elicit a 2,000-word statement from himself giving his version of the genesis and development of the bubble sextant. He subsequently deposed three witnesses he had summoned in his own defense: Commander Patrick Bellinger, Lieutenant Commander Garland Fulton, and Lieutenant Walter Hinton.

Having honed his trial skills, Byrd went up to New York two months later to cross-examine de Florez. The opposition had attempted to present de Florez as having prior knowledge of celestial navigation. "In taking a sight of the sun," Byrd asked him, "what are the corrections that would have to be made to the observed altitude of the sun to get the true altitude?" "What corrections would it be necessary to make to an observed altitude of the sun from an airplane with an artificial horizon sextant?" "Please explain in detail the difference between taking a sight using the sea horizon and using the sextant which is the subject matter of this interference?" De Florez's attorney objected seven times to this line of questioning, on the basis of immateriality and irrelevance.

On November 4, 1922, the Patent Office finally reached a verdict. It was decided that neither Byrd nor de Florez could be awarded the patent because it had already been taken out by an Englishman (whose surname, oddly enough, was Evelyn) two years before Byrd and three years before de Florez were born.

Byrd pursued his business interests while continuing to serve on active duty in the Aviation Division, and he pursued them because, as a retired officer, his position was rather precarious. While juggling tires and airplane rides, he told one friend, "If the Navy ever kicks me out, I won't have to look for a job."[5] To another he wrote: "My own status is still indefinite. I do not know how long I will be in the service and why they have not kicked me out long ago I do not understand."[6] But as with the transatlantic project, he continued to specialize in areas that would receive the navy's highest priority and remained the indispensable man.

In the months after the Armistice, a familiar pattern began to play out in the armed forces of the United States. Aviation had emerged as a powerful new weapon, one that could alter the very nature of war.

Now the army and navy had to undergo the difficult task of adapting to innovation. Some of the highest-ranking members of the military, including General Billy Mitchell, could see what aviation would become and believed that its potentialities rendered conventional weaponry obsolete. Mitchell argued for the creation of a Department of Aeronautics, a cabinet-level agency co-equal with the army and navy. Aircraft and airmen would be removed from the existing services and concentrated in a new organization with new leadership. Byrd and other naval aviators wanted to remain in the navy. To shore up naval aviation, Byrd took the lead in pushing for the creation of a Bureau of Aeronautics within the Navy Department. Since the authority to revise the organizational chart of the navy would have to come from Congress, Byrd, by necessity, began to specialize in legislative relations.

Mitchell, like Byrd, came from a political family. His grandfather was a bigwig in Wisconsin state politics, and his father was a U.S. senator. The general had attained his wings in 1916 and commanded the aviation arm of the American Expeditionary Force during the Allied drive to victory on the western front. He was a crafty infighter skilled in the art of the legislative ambush. Working through one of his congressional supporters, he succeeded in appending to an army appropriation bill a provision that would place aviation shore stations under army jurisdiction. In one fell swoop, five naval air bases would have been wiped off the chessboard.[7] Byrd set out to counter the maneuver by adopting Mitchell's methods. He established personal relationships with the members of the appropriate congressional committees and took the time to discuss the naval point of view with each of them individually.

In this way, he slowly rallied support in both houses and built the kind of coalitions necessary to advance the cause of the Bureau of Aeronautics. Meanwhile, he and Mitchell continued to wage a shadow war of moves and countermoves. When the Bureau bill was first introduced in the Senate, the general had a time bomb slipped in between its clauses. He contrived to have the legislation amended in committee to require the head of the Bureau to be a pilot. A navy bureau would naturally be helmed by an admiral. Since no aviator had yet been elevated to flag rank and no admiral knew how to fly, the bill was guaranteed to self-destruct even if it became law. Byrd defused the amendment by having the language changed. As a result of his efforts, the Bureau chief was merely required to have flown as an "observer."[8] He made deft use of another Mitchell weapon: the hearing. Byrd disarmed the Mitchell forces by pointing out in testimony before the House and Senate Committees on Naval Affairs that the proposed Bureau was merely a matter of "internal departmental organization."[9] It was intended to bring about "greater efficiency in the administration of Aviation." It had "no bearing whatever on a United Air Service." It was no big deal.

Ironically, the greatest opposition to the Bureau occurred within the Navy Department itself. Certain admirals felt that appropriations for aircraft would come at the expense of battleships. There was also at this time a cultural divide between navy aviators and non-aviators. The fliers regarded their duty as being so hazardous that they deserved special consideration. The situation was exacerbated by the fact that the majority of navy aviators were not Annapolis graduates and had not been indoctrinated to put the service as a whole above any of its separate divisions. Looking back on this period nearly a decade later, Byrd said,

> The younger fellows even began to have what bordered on contempt for the non-fliers. They were fairly wild, did a good deal of drinking and felt that they should not be held to account for what they did, and got somewhat spoiled. On the other hand, it is true that they were more or less on the firing line most of the time.[10]

Meanwhile, the regular, seafaring navy officers, for their part, also "carried things too far, especially the older ones who would not admit that aviation had any value."

> Some of the older admirals got very much down on avia-
> tion and helped to make progress difficult. There still is
> much feeling against flight pay.

The latter point of view was summed up by an admiral who once said in Byrd's presence, "Aviation and your young flying aristocrats is use-less and a drag on the Navy. If I had my way I would wipe the whole business off the map." Byrd became a reconciler within the service. As an airman, he was naturally accepted by the younger group, and, as a regular officer with an impeccable family background, he was equally accepted by the older faction. He represented naval aviation to the rest of the navy, while at the same time representing the navy position *on* aviation to the House and Senate.

The civilian leadership of the navy was more flexible and forward-looking than the fleet admirals. Byrd had quickly enlisted Franklin Roosevelt as an ally in the Bureau drive; he and the assistant secretary had gone moose hunting together in the fall of 1919 and were on the best of terms.[11] Secretary Daniels proved equally sympathetic. But the first director of naval aviation that Byrd served under, Captain Noble E. Irwin, an officer of the old school, opposed the Bureau of Aero-nautics. Irwin returned to sea in July of 1919 and was succeeded by Captain Thomas T. Craven, who initially resisted the idea before becoming a supporter. Craven completed his tour in January of 1921 and was replaced by a man who would become the best friend Rich-ard Byrd or Naval Aviation would ever have in the service.

Captain William Adger Moffett, the "Father of Naval Aviation," was fifty-two when he reported for duty in Washington. A white-haired man, neither larger nor more distinguished-looking than the average member of a small town chamber of commerce, he was a born leader and one of the most brilliant and respected naval officers at sea or onshore. Moffett ran the Great Lakes Naval Training Station during the war, the largest facility of its kind in the world, and turned out more and better-trained sailors in 1917–18 than any other installation in the United States. He had a genuine interest in aviation that began at Great Lakes, where he established an aviation school financed at first by the contributions of civilian enthusiasts. In December of 1918, he was given command of the super-battleship *Mississippi*, the crown jewel of the Pacific Fleet. The *Mississippi* rewrote the book on naval gunnery under Moffett's stewardship, posting the highest scores in the service. Moffett broke all existing records by an adroit innovation: he used airplanes for artillery spotting. He combined expert seamanship and efficiency with tremendous people skills. He took a personal interest in each officer and enlisted man under his command and was said to have once read a homesick sailor to sleep. His crew worshipped him and chipped in to present him with a dress sword when he was reassigned to the Navy Department after a two-year tour.

With Moffett onboard and Byrd working at full throttle, the Bureau of Aeronautics came into existence on July 12, 1921. Moffett became the first chief of the Bureau and a rear admiral at the same time. He and Byrd would work closely together in the new Bureau and establish a mentor-prodigy relationship. On July 21, in a stunning demonstration of air power, a bomber squadron dispatched by Billy Mitchell sunk the *Ostfriesland*, a dreadnought-class battleship surrendered by the demilitarized Germany. The war between Mitchell and the navy would continue until the general's court-martial in 1925.

In the summer of 1920, the JL, the American version of the sleek, all-metal monoplane that had been developed in Germany, flew in stages from New York to Los Angeles and back to the East Coast again, pioneering a transcontinental air mail route. A year later, the navy had its own all-metal monoplanes. In May of 1921, while struggling to get the Bureau bill passed, Byrd drafted a proposal for a solo, non-stop transatlantic flight in one of these aircraft.[12] He was asked to wait until the bill became law before submitting the proposal. Twelve days after the legislative fight was won, he redrafted the memo, and it was forwarded with Moffett's endorsement.

The flight plan had all the Byrd trademarks: it was simultaneously daring and careful, and, above all, used ingenuity and imagination to extend the range of a limited technology. The immediate precedent was a record flight that had been made within a month of the departure of the NC's on the dramatic hop from Newfoundland to the Azores. Two British aviators, Captain John Alcock, pilot, and Lieutenant Arthur W. Brown, navigator, had taken off in a twin-engine biplane from St. John's on June 14, 1919. Heading east across the Atlantic, they ran into a dense fog affording only occasional glimpses of the ocean. One of those glimpses was particularly startling because the ocean was in the wrong place: it was above them instead of below. Having only rudimentary instruments, they were unable to tell in the mist if they were flying level with an unseen horizon. They finally landed in a bog on the west coast of Ireland, some thirty-five miles north of Galway Bay, their initial target. The plane nosed over on the impact.

Alcock and Brown survived and were heralded for accomplishing the first non-stop transatlantic crossing. Two weeks later, a long, cigar-shaped British dirigible, the R-34, departed from Edinburgh, Scotland, completing a successful round trip to New York. R-34, in effect, completed two non-stop crossings, one westbound and one east. The only casualty occurred when the airship arrived in Long Island. A carrier pigeon (one of two aboard the R-34) made an unscheduled flight through an open window and was unable (or unwilling) to rejoin the dirigible for the return voyage. Alcock and

Brown retained the transatlantic honors for a flight in a heavier-than-air craft when Byrd set out to recapture the glory for the navy and for the United States.

He intended to surpass Alcock and Brown by flying from St. John's to England. Byrd planned to fly solo in order to carry extra fuel to increase the range of the best available airplane. He was confident that he could fly and navigate at the same time, and that, unlike the NCs, he would not require the logistical support of any surface vessels at all. However, he faced a rather interesting problem: the maximum range of a JL-type monoplane fell significantly short of Ireland's east coast. His plan for coping with the discrepancy was inspired. The prevailing winds in the Atlantic at the middle latitudes were westerly, with a velocity at five or six thousand feet of about twenty or thirty miles an hour. Allowing for the fact that the wind might not be squarely on the tail of an eastbound aviator, Byrd figured he could reckon on a tailwind component of at least fifteen miles an hour.[13] That fifteen-mile-an-hour tailwind would boost his ground speed and effectively increase the range of his aircraft by 330 miles, enabling him to outfly his predecessors while maintaining a more than ample margin of safety. His backup plan was to equip the plane with airbags to keep it afloat if he had to ditch at sea, and carry flares and smoke bombs to signal passing steamships.

With the election of Warren G. Harding, a new Republican administration had assumed office in 1921, and it fell to the new assistant secretary of the navy to pass on Byrd's proposal. Colonel Theodore Roosevelt, the eldest son of the twenty-sixth president (and the second Roosevelt to inherit the sub-cabinet office once held by his father) urged Byrd to shelve the flight plan for the time being. Roosevelt felt it made more sense to wait for the development of an airplane with a longer range and a more reliable engine. The colonel stuck to this position, and Byrd ultimately conceded. The outcome may have prolonged his life. Like the Polar Sea, the Atlantic Ocean would not be easily conquered.

As in 1918, when Byrd first requested permission to fly across the ocean, he received a consolation prize. The navy had purchased the R-38, a new British airship undergoing a preliminary series of test flights. An American crew stood by in England to take possession of the dirigible and to fly the ship across the ocean to the United States once the trials were completed. Byrd was dispatched to join the crew and assist in the navigation. He embarked from New York on August 13, 1921.

The R-38 was the largest rigid airship that had yet been built. She was 695 feet long with a gas capacity of 2,700,000 cubic feet. If stood on end among the skyscrapers of lower Manhattan in 1921, she would have been the second tallest structure in the City of New York. (The sixty-five-story, 792-foot Woolworth Building was only ninety-seven feet or some seven stories higher.) Like the R-34, the first airship to cross the Atlantic, R-38 was a silver, cigar-shaped dirigible, but longer, faster, and more powerful. Her U.S. Navy designation was ZR-2. Only three pioneer transoceanic flights had been successfully accomplished by 1921: NC-4, Alcock and Brown, and R-34. The impending voyage of R-38/ZR-2 would mark the fifth time in history that the ocean was crossed by air (giving R-34 credit for two flights because she made a round trip), the fourth non-stop transatlantic flight, and the third such flight by lighter-than-air technology.

The dirigible was based at an airfield near Howden in northern England. Byrd arrived in London on the evening of August 20, a Saturday. At the office of Admiral H. C. Twining, the American naval attaché, he subsequently learned that the British planned to subject ZR-2 to a prolonged trial flight on Tuesday and Wednesday, the twenty-third and twenty-fourth. For the better part of two days, the dirigible would cruise round and about, and ultimately land at

Pulham in southern England (the air base from which she would depart for the United States when she was certified to be airworthy and the British relinquished control). Of the forty-four American naval personnel billeted at Howden during the trials, only seventeen would be permitted to accompany ZR-2 on the flight to Pulham. Byrd was told that he had better report to Howden on the double to make sure his name was on the list.

He set out on Monday the twenty-second, missing the early train and only reaching the airfield that evening. The number of Americans who had wanted to participate in the flight far exceeded the available room. Byrd's name had been deleted from the list while he was in transit. The personnel selections had already been posted, and the British were averse to making last minute changes. Byrd and the skipper of the American crew, Commander Louis H. Maxfield, decided to be diplomatic and allow their hosts to run the show according to their own proclivities.[14] Maxfield was Byrd's cousin by marriage. His executive officer, Lieutenant Commander Emory W. Coil, was a friend of Byrd's and a classmate at the Academy. The senior engineering officer, Lieutenant Commander Valentine N. Bieg, was another friend and a fellow Virginian. Byrd received a warm welcome from them and other crewmembers of his acquaintance but could not help but notice a certain apprehensiveness they all seemed to share.

The initial trials had not been completely successful. Part of the inner skeletal structure had buckled and bent on a nine-hour test flight in mid-July, and at the time the ship had been cruising on less than full power. Those sections had subsequently been reinforced. The American sailors assigned to the airship were calling her a "lemon."[15] No one was more concerned than Coil, the X.O. Emory Wilbur Coil, a fair-haired, exuberant fellow, played the mandolin and habitually wrapped his buddies in bear hugs. He had been turned back one year at the Naval Academy and consequently graduated with Byrd's class instead of with the class of 1911. Bad luck had continued to plague him. He had lost both his wife and mother early in 1919 and had since remarried. Later that year, he had been given command of the dirigible C-5, the airship to which Byrd was supposed to transfer after the NC's had reached Trepassey. Coil had lost the C-5 to a raging wind and with it his chance to mount the world's first non-stop transatlantic flight. He had a premonition that the ZR-2 would never reach the States. Another crewman had dreamed that the ship blew up over the River Humber.

On the morning of the flight, Byrd boarded the dirigible with Coil. They climbed up from the control car to the envelope and proceeded down a central ramp that spanned a distance equivalent to the length of three city blocks. On either side of the walkway loomed the monstrous bladders swollen with the hydrogen gas that lifted the ship. American and British personnel responsible for monitoring the valves of the gas cells manned various duty stations under the vaulted ceiling. If it were possible for Byrd to relieve one of the enlisted members of the American contingent, he might still be able to make the flight. It was suggested that a sailor named William J. Steele, a mechanic, might be expendable. But when Byrd caught up with him, Steele demurred at having to remain at Howden. He had his family with him, had sent his dependents on to Pulham, and looked forward to joining them there.

It would not have been gentlemanly to pull rank. Shortly after 7:00 a.m. that Tuesday morning, Byrd stood in the shadow of the airship with the ground crew, as the sleek silver leviathan ascended in the sunrise and circled slowly towards the south. He returned to London, intending to join ZR-2 at Pulham on Thursday the twenty-fifth. Byrd was beginning to feel as if it were 1919 all over again, that he was destined once more to be the odd man out. The lifting capacity of ZR-2 was as yet unknown, but it was clear that the ship could not comfortably lift the maximum load it was designed to carry aloft. If someone were to be left behind to lighten the load, "I will have to be that someone," he thought.[16] He sat down and wrote two letters in London, one to his wife and one to Admiral Moffett. He told Marie that it would probably be another two and a half weeks before the airship was ready to embark on the transatlantic flight, and he confided that after travelling all the way to England, he might well be put in the embarrassing position of having to watch the ship depart without him. He wrote to Moffett in an attempt to forestall that eventuality.

"Now, Admiral," he said, "you are familiar with my way of anticipating matters that are of vital importance and it is of the most vital importance for me to make this trip."[17] He said he would explain upon his return.

> Therefore provided that my making the flight would in no way interfere with the air ship's mileage but would be of considerable assistance in a navigational way, I do not want to be left behind because of some imaginary reason.
>
> What difference could the weight of one man make with a lift of some 40 to 50 tons?
>
> Nor do I want to cut out of the trip even a [mechanic] or a rigger. That would make me feel very badly indeed …
>
> I am merely giving you my thoughts in the matter as you are the best friend I have got in Washington.

It was more than likely that cables would shoot back and forth between London and Washington before any final personnel decisions were made. Byrd had done all he could. While still in London on Wednesday evening, August 24, he stepped out of a barbershop, grabbed a newspaper, and learned that ZR-2 had exploded over the River Humber.

The airship had not descended at Pulham due to thick fog. She flew back up the coast to northern England and circled lazily over Hull, a city on the Humber, at about 1,200 feet in calm air. During these maneuvers, a series of flight tests were performed. ZR-2 was due to return to her home base, Howden, twenty miles west of Hull, once the tests were concluded. At about 5:38 p.m., a sharp right turn was made to test the rudder controls. As the stern swung into the turn, the ship broke in two. The fracture occurred about three-quarters of the way from the nose to the tail. The forward section burst into flames and exploded in mid-air; it exploded again just as it hit the water. There were thirty Englishmen aboard the dirigible in addition to the seventeen Americans, and of the forty-seven crewmen only five survived.

Byrd was immediately detailed to Hull to take charge of the American end of the salvage operations. He was the most senior of the American naval officers assigned to the ZR-2 who remained alive. He arrived at high tide. The Humber was several miles wide, and at high water the current was swift and the surface was choppy. The remnants of the airship could be seen about a mile from the dock: some twisted girders protruding in triangular shapes like tent poles. For the next ten days, Byrd went out at low tide with the tugboats and wrecking barges as the rough water was repeatedly dragged. Maxfield's body was found ten miles downriver from Hull. Bieg was in a tangle of wires and girders at the rear of the control car. Coil was located among the fractured girders; he had stationed himself at the part of the ship where he suspected the structure was weakest. His remains were recovered on August 28. Three days later, the river surrendered William Steele. Most of the bodies were burned; some could only be identified by their teeth. The widows were not allowed to view the remains.

On Wednesday, September 7, two weeks after the disaster, a funeral service was held at Westminster Abbey. An RAF contingent in jodhpurs and high boots marched at the head of the procession followed by American sailors in their white caps and white leggings. The honored dead were carried on gun carriages. A military cortege is organized in reverse order of rank. Byrd followed in the rear, marching beside the coffins of Maxfield, Coil, and Beig, marching with death. For two long weeks of mortuary duty, he had been living in a state of emotional duress. Working side by side with the British through the worst of it instilled in him a vision of international harmony. The loftier dimensions of the tragedy were the only aspects he preferred to dwell on.

Dick Byrd liked the winters in Washington because he liked the cold.[18] His opinion of the winter of 1921–22 is not recorded, but it may have been favorable. Late in January of 1922, a storm swept through the mid-Atlantic states producing twenty-eight hours of continuous snowfall in the nation's capital. When it was over, the city had to plow itself out from under twenty-nine inches of snow, the largest accumulation that had ever been recorded in the District of Columbia up to that time. At about 9:00 p.m. on Saturday night, January 28, 1922, the ceiling of the Knickerbocker Theatre collapsed under the massive pressure of the snow on the roof. Inside, an audience of perhaps 500 men, women, and children were enjoying "Get Rich Quick Wallingford," a silent comedy, while the orchestra in the pit provided spirited accompaniment. When the roof fell in, it brought the balcony down with it. As the balcony gave way, part of the rear wall collapsed. Some three hundred people were buried under the debris.

The theatre stood at the intersection of 18th Street and Columbia Road in northwest Washington, in an exclusive residential district near Embassy Row and the National Zoo, about a mile and a half from the White House. One of the first passersby on the scene was

Richard Byrd. Byrd made his way through the rubble and snow and spent the balance of the evening helping to liberate the survivors from the slabs of concrete, masonry, and steel beams in which they were imprisoned. An army captain named Hills and his wife were trapped beneath several layers of balcony and roof. Byrd crawled through the debris to reach them and had other rescue workers run out and get jacks, hacksaws, and other tools which were then passed to him. Directly overhead stood a portion of the balcony that had not yet fallen but was ominously teetering. Byrd worked for at least three hours under the pile-up to extricate the Hillses, "all the while," according to one eyewitness, "lying on his back or stomach with plaster falling on top of him."[19] Had the hanging fragment of balcony collapsed in the meantime, Byrd himself would have been killed. "I wasn't born with much instinct of self-preservation," he once said.[20]

Byrd had still been in the tire business at the time of the ZR-2 tragedy and had still been pushing the sextant case. While he was away in England, Marie had looked after both matters. Dick's passion for his wife had not dimmed after seven years of marriage. "I'm crazy to see you. I've missed you terribly," he wrote from Hull.

> Dearest if you even dream a cl-x while I'm away it'll make me unhappy for they are mine and I love them. What do you think of me for writing this way.

Their first child, Richard Jr., was born on February 19, 1920. A year and a half at the time of the airship crash, he was described by his mother as "a very noisy determined youngster with a quick temper." Marie was in the early stages of her second pregnancy when the Knickerbocker incident occurred. As late as that year—Byrd would turn thirty-four in October of 1922—he still saw his future as being outside of the navy. "I feel that I have made good in the Navy and I hate to leave it," he told a friend, "but if a man is ambitious I don't think that there is much future in this country in the Army or the Navy."[21] Byrd's Uncle Hal had died in December of 1921; sometime after the funeral, Dick had had an audience with an old friend of Hal's, the New York financier Thomas Fortune Ryan. Ryan hinted that he would give Byrd a job if and when Byrd went on the inactive list. But as far as the navy was concerned, Richard Byrd was still the indispensable man.

In February of 1922, a joint congressional committee drafted a bill to reconfigure the military pay rate. For the first time, a soldier, sailor, or marine would be paid on the basis of both rank and length of service. The measure was supposed to save more than twenty-eight million dollars a year over the next six years. The chairman of the committee, Senator James Wolcott Wadsworth Jr. of New York, said, "I feel that this measure embodies the most scientifically drawn pay rate that this Government has ever had."[22] The terminology disguised the fact that military pay was essentially going to be cut by more than a hundred million dollars over the next six years. Byrd was assigned as point man for a joint service committee mobilized to refute the scientific theories of the joint congressional committee.

Slightly different versions of the measure passed the House and the Senate. The two bills then went to a conference committee to iron out the differences. The legislation that emerged from conference, however, contained a number of provisions that seemed to have taken some of its proponents by surprise. The length of service component had been mysteriously increased from 40 to 50 percent of a serviceman's overall pay, which had the effect of raising military salaries. The rations and subsistence allowance for officers and enlisted men who lived off post had been increased, and a clause voted by the House to cap the pensions of retired officers had vanished from the printed page. Although the new measure, as one exasperated representative from Texas put it, would "not save a cent," the conference report was accepted by the Senate without opposition and passed the House by a vote of 202–50.[23]

Byrd was commended for his efforts by both the army and navy and was asked by the navy to go immediately to work on the Appropriations bill for 1923. He disliked being a lobbyist and once offered to fight a superior officer, a commander, who called him a "politician." The commander backed down. Nevertheless, he was good at legislative relations—for two reasons. In the first place, he lobbied like a gentleman. As he would advise his nephew years later, when future Senator Harry Byrd Jr. started writing editorials in the *Winchester Star*, he took exception only to an opponent's position on the issues, never involved himself in personalities, and always showed respect for the other fellow and his point of view. He was also a superb strategist. As in his quarterback days, Byrd selected the plays and called the signals for the whole Navy team. When legislation needed to be advanced, he would first "attempt to locate the vulnerable spots of the enemy." Once he figured out who on Capitol Hill needed to be called or placated, he would then hand the ball off to either Admiral Thomas Washington, the head of the Bureau of Navigation, or to one of his aides; Admiral Robert E. Coontz, the chief of Naval Operations (later commander in chief of the U.S. Fleet); or Ted Roosevelt, the assistant secretary. "So it is," he boasted privately, "I slide through and actually get more credit than if I worked like a dog."[24]

Evelyn Bolling Byrd was born on September 5, 1922, and Katherine Ames Byrd would arrive on March 24, 1924. Marie had gone home to Boston to have her babies, and she and Dick eventually established their household permanently in the Ames townhouse on 9 Brimmer Street. Dick liked the Boston winters better than those in

Washington.[25] He and Marie didn't celebrate their anniversary every year on January 20, they celebrated on the twentieth of each month. Marie was (and would remain) a silent partner in all of his activities, his closest confidant and advisor.

He remained in the service, instead of leaving to make money with Thomas F. Ryan in 1922, because he was loyal to the navy, and the navy asked him to stay on. In 1923–24, he devoted himself to another naval operation that made him an even more valuable player. He traveled around the country organizing reserve Naval Aviation units. In an era of a downsized military, Byrd sought to establish a cadre of trained aviators and aviation mechanics that could be readily mobilized in a national emergency. He set up these units in New York, New England, and Chicago, accomplishing the mission on a shoestring budget. He was doing this work when he learned that the navy was soliciting applications for a pilot to join Roald Amundsen's transpolar flight team in 1924. Amundsen had not yet declared bankruptcy. "In five minutes," Byrd said, "I wired in to the Department offering my services."[26] He was turned down because he was married. The pilot who was eventually selected was merely engaged.

In July of 1924, Byrd's partner on the out-of-sight-of-land experiments, Walter Hinton, hopped over the Amazon rain forest in a seaplane, and in a nine-month period logged some 12,000 miles flying out of sight of civilization as an aerial scout for a geographical expedition. It was, certainly, an exciting time to be alive, and Byrd itched to participate in the spectacular adventures that continued to enrich the era.

He may not have realized it at the time, but everything he had done in his adult life had put him in a perfect position to organize an expedition of his own. He had a solid core of support in the Navy Department, starting with Admiral Moffett, who considered Dick Byrd "the most able young officer with whom I have come in contact"[27] and "an officer of the highest type in every respect."[28] He had a legion of admirers in Congress, including almost every member of the Senate and House Committees on Naval Affairs, as well as Nicholas Longworth, who would become Speaker of the House in 1925.[29] And he could count among his friends such prime enablers as Raymond B. Fosdick, and Franklin and Ted Roosevelt.

Wherever Byrd might have gone and whatever he might have done, he had the energy and imagination to accomplish something new, bold, and noteworthy. But if he had not put great love first in 1915 and conspired to be retired, if he had had a conventional naval career, even if he had gone into aviation, he would have been uprooted every two years and transferred from ship to ship or from post to post. He would have been unable to serve continuously in Washington, D.C., at the heart of the naval command, from the triumph of the NCs to the tragedy of *Shenandoah*, and to solidify so formidable an array of personal relationships.

Late in 1924, a movement was started to gain Byrd a promotion via an act of Congress, the only way possible for a retired officer to be promoted. The rest of his class had advanced to lieutenant commander while he languished as a lieutenant. Old family friend Claude Swanson, one of the ranking members of the Senate Naval Affairs Committee, took the lead, and both Roosevelts pitched in and wrote letters to several legislators on Byrd's behalf. The measure became law on February 10, 1925.

"I could accomplish more as Lieutenant Commander than as a Lieutenant," Byrd said. "I acted at once. My eyes were on the North Pole."[30]

PART 3

THE GREATEST
STORY OF THE YEAR

15

LIGHTER VS. HEAVIER

I am more convinced than ever that far northern Arctic work will never be done by heavier than air machines.

DONALD B. MACMILLAN[1]

There is no part of the world aviation cannot conquer.

RICHARD E. BYRD[2]

R ichard Byrd started planning his second assault on the Polar Sea before he left Etah at the conclusion of his first. He had a two-stage plan. He intended to reactivate his original idea of a flight to the North Pole and the unexplored area northwest of Ellesmere and Axel Heiberg Islands. But the flight would be mounted in the spring when firm snow covered the ice and an airplane equipped with skis could find places to land. Since Melville Sound was impossible to navigate so early in the year, Byrd was inclining to Spitsbergen or Point Barrow as the initial base of operations. He expected to find land in the Polar Sea. After the spring expedition, he would sail to Etah and winter over at the RCMP station near Cape

Sabine. In March, he would set out by dog sledge to the shore of the new land to locate landing fields and cache supplies for a resumption of the aerial survey. The bases would be in place before the next series of flights began. Byrd's talent for making friends extended across cultural and linquistic barriers. He had particularly hit it off with an Inuit hunter named Noo-Ka-Ping-Wa and had arranged for this man and several of his comrades to sledge him across Smith Sound after the ice formed in the fall of 1926 and come back for him in the spring of 1927. MacMillan's man, Abie Bromfield, interpreted.

The Arctic frontier casts a formidable spell on the seeker after horizons. Floyd Bennett shared Byrd's fascination for the endless sweep of glacier, cliffs, and sky. He had a notion of wintering over with the Inuit some day.[3] He just wanted to have his own food with him; he didn't think he could subsist on raw seal and polar bear. Byrd was too wary now to reveal his plans to all and sundry, and certainly not within earshot of Donald MacMillan. He confided only in Bennett, and the two of them began formulating a new venture during the stormy passage home.

Roald Amundsen and Lincoln Ellsworth had also started planning a new expedition before they left the Arctic in 1925. They had come to the conclusion that the transpolar flight could not be accomplished in an airplane, at least not at the present stage of development of heavier-than-air technology, and had decided to acquire a dirigible. Coincidentally, while Amundsen and Ellsworth were en route from Svalbard to Oslo, the Zeppelin Company held a press conference in Berlin to announce plans for a German polar expedition. The company proposed to build the largest airship in the world, a Polar Zeppelin costing two and a half to three million dollars. Funds would be raised in a myriad of small contributions by appealing to the patriotism of the German people.

Lighter-than-air technology had international adherents. In Italy, Colonel Umberto Nobile of the Italian Military Aeronautic Corps had designed a new kind of dirigible that combined the strength and range of a huge rigid airship with the economy of a blimp. Nobile designed *semi*rigid dirigibles. He reduced the internal skeletal structure of the rigids to a metal keel that extended from bow to stern along the bottom of the ship. From both sides of this horizontal spine, a series of curved bracing supports radiated outwards like an open rib cage. The gas bags that elevated the ship rested on this cradle. On March 1, 1924, Nobile had launched the N-1, a semirigid half the size of the U.S. Navy's *Shenandoah*, but more than 50 percent larger than the blimp Byrd had initially wanted to buy from Goodyear. The N-1 had attracted a considerable amount of attention, and Amundsen and Ellsworth thought it might be within their budget. They opened negotiations with Nobile and the Italian government on their return to Europe, striking a deal in the first week of September 1925. For $75,000, the explorers acquired a 348-foot long, hydrogen-filled balloon. A repurchase agreement enabled the Italians to buy back the ship for $46,000, if she were returned to them in good order at the end of the transpolar flight. The net cost ($29,000) was less than the price of one of the Dornier Whales with which the Norwegian and the New Yorker had set out from Kings Bay four months earlier.

The new Amundsen-Ellsworth venture was announced in Oslo at a meeting of the Aero Club of Norway on September 9, about the time the storm-battered MacMillan expedition had reached the southern tip of Greenland. Byrd had demonstrated that an airplane could be navigated in the polar regions, but had not shown that it could outdistance a dog team. Amundsen's conversion to lighter-than-air was a seminal event in the quest for the transpolar flight and predictably touched off a controversy over the utility of the airplane. By the time the *Peary* and *Bowdoin* had arrived in American waters, Byrd and MacMillan had declared themselves on opposite sides of the dispute.

MacMillan joined Amundsen and Ellsworth in dismissing heavier-than-air technology as an instrument of polar exploration. He allowed for the superiority of the dirigible, "if air transportation is to be used."[4] But, he told a reporter, "I am still of the opinion that the dog is King of the Arctic and that more can be learned when he is employed." Byrd also gave an interview when the expedition returned home. "With a little more time and a better season than we had," he said, "airplanes can penetrate the unexplored parts of the Polar Sea."[5]

The problem with heavier-than-air machines, amply illustrated by the Loening Amphibian, which Byrd insisted had been "the best available plane" in the summer of 1925, was that, relative to the dirigible, the airplane had limited range.[6] It could only carry so much fuel and, in consequence, could only fly so long and so far. "Airplanes would be all right," Amundsen told the press, if they could cross the Polar Sea without having to land.[7] But if you had to put them down on a shifting icefield, he said, to refuel or make celestial observations, "there would always be grave doubt whether they could get up again." He had also found it impossible to shoot the sun with precision in a plane cruising at close to a hundred miles an hour.

Dirigibles could hover over one spot, to make the sun less of a moving target, and they could descend to an altitude low enough for a navigator to aim a standard mariner's sextant at a clear horizon line. The problem with lighter-than-air machines, however, was fragility, a limitation underscored on September 3, 1925, when the *Shenandoah* was wrecked in a thunderstorm over Ohio. En route to St. Louis, on a tour of the Midwest, the airship formerly promoted for a transpolar flight encountered a roaring, seventy-mile-an-hour squall. *Shenandoah* twisted in the violent wind and was torn apart, broken into three drifting, detached pieces. The aft, midsection, and nose each contained a number of gas bags that checked their respective descents, but the control car ripped loose of its attachments and plunged 7,000 feet to the ground. Fourteen men were killed, including the captain of the ship, Byrd's friend Zachary Lansdowne.

Asked for his reaction to the *Shenandoah* disaster, Amundsen said, "I'd rather fly over the Arctic Circle in a dirigible than over Ohio."[8] He planned to embark from Kings Bay in the spring when the air over the Polar Sea was smooth and clear, and storm systems usually didn't develop.

The lighter-heavier controversy nevertheless carried over from the close of the 1925 Arctic exploration season to the preparations for 1926.

Less than a month after the *Shenandoah* tragedy, another aerial tour ensued over the Midwest. This was a successful, upbeat event that ultimately proved to be of tremendous significance for polar aviation. On September 28, seventeen heavy-duty airplanes took off from the Ford Airport at Dearborn, Michigan and began a seven-day, 1,900-mile circuit that would take them in a wide loop as far west as Omaha, Nebraska, and then as far back east as Cleveland, Ohio. Edsel Ford conceived the tour as a way of promoting commercial aviation. As a prospective aircraft manufacturer, he was interested in demonstrating that transport planes could carry passengers and freight from town to town on a regular basis without mishap. So he devised a schedule of takeoffs and landings in eleven cities across half a dozen states and invited his competitors to help him simulate an airline. Entrants that finished the course on schedule would qualify for a trophy.

One of the manufacturers attracted by the Ford competition was a boyish, energetic thirty-five-year-old Dutchman who had gotten into the airplane business in Germany before the First World War.

Anthony Herman Gerard Fokker, test pilot, designer, and entrepreneur, had made a fortune equipping von Richthofen and the rest of the German aces during the war and slipped out of the country in disguise after the surrender. He donned the uniform of his landlady's son, a soldier, walked past a pair of policemen posted outside his house, drove to the railroad station, and boarded the next westbound train. According to one account, he owed over fourteen million marks in back taxes. Fokker relocated to Amsterdam and established a new company. The inventory consisted of about 200 airplanes and 400 engines his loyal German employees eventually succeeded in smuggling across the border in six exceptionally long freight trains.

Fokker was in the United States during the spring and summer of 1925 to reconnoiter the American market when he heard about the Ford Reliability Tour. Anthony Fokker as a self-promoter was not far behind Gene McDonald. He sent a cable to his Amsterdam plant instructing his people to take their top-of-the-line, single-engine monoplane, the F-VIIA, and add two additional engines. The operation was completed within eight weeks. Fokker returned to Holland, flight-tested the new trimotor himself, then had the plane disassembled and shipped to America for the Ford tour.

Eleven planes completed the cross-country loop with a perfect score, making each of the stops along the way within the stipulated time frame. Although it was not a "race" per se, and there was no special award for arriving in the lead, the first airplane to land back at Dearborn at the end of the circuit was the Fokker trimotor. Anthony H. G. Fokker was one of eight passengers aboard.

◥ 16 ◤

IN DEFENSE
OF THE
LITTLE JITNEYS

*I gave my [Greenland] movies for the first time in my
home city the other day, and a quarter of the city
turned out. It is astonishing the interest people
take in polar things.*

RICHARD E. BYRD[1]

Individually, any one of the three dramatic events of the 1925
Arctic exploration season would have been sufficient to focus the
attention and energy of the western world on the Polar Sea:
Amundsen's return from the dead; his gallant commitment to resume
the quest for land, this time in a dirigible; and Byrd's serial flights over
uncharted airspace without the loss of a single pilot or plane. Collectively, the result was mesmerizing. Each development was like the
chapter of an epic novel that Americans and Europeans were simultaneously absorbed in reading. Increasing numbers of people waited
breathlessly for the next plot twist. Minor characters attempted to
project themselves into major roles, and almost anyone wealthy

enough to finance a polar venture was happily disposed to buying themselves a passing mention in the unfolding narrative.

Two more Polar Sea expeditions were announced before the end of the year. In Paris, on November 17, 1925, a French lieutenant announced plans to travel across the surface of the Polar Sea in a caravan of motor vehicles. The veteran Norwegian explorer, Captain Otto N. Sverdrup, was said to have invented a foolproof motorized sledge, a vehicle supposedly able to float across leads of open water like a boat, haul itself onto the ice floes and rumble over pressure ridges at up to about fifteen miles per hour. Sverdrup, seventy, had accompanied Nansen on the polar drift voyage of 1893–96 and later traversed the High Arctic on his own. A half dozen of his "mystery sledges" were being built for the French expedition. Two of the six sledges would carry seaplanes with folding wings; the planes would be assembled on the ice and perform reconnaissance operations. The expedition planned to embark in the summer and travel from Spitsbergen to Point Barrow. Applicants were expected to prove their mettle by passing an endurance test in a Parisian refrigeration chamber.

Two days before Christmas, the City of Detroit announced its own expedition. Detroit had already established itself as the automobile capital of America. Edsel Ford and other leading citizens had visions of their town becoming the aviation capital as well. The Detroit Aviation Society was formed to promote these visions; Edsel was a member of the Board of Directors. The organization raised $53,000 or some 40 percent of the projected cost of an ambitious effort to fly north of Point Barrow and through what Vilhjalmur Stefansson called the "Pole of Relative Inaccessibility," or the center of the Arctic ice pack. The Ice Pole was about 400 miles west of the North Pole. Stefansson was one of the organizers of the Detroit Arctic Expedition. The leader was his protégé, Captain George Hubert Wilkins, thirty-seven, an Australian cameraman, pilot, and naturalist.

Wilkins had been with Stefansson on the ill-fated voyage of the *Karluk* in 1913. When the ice closed in and Stefansson abandoned ship, he took young Wilkins and his cameras with him in the small party that eventually made its way to shore. Wilkins spent the next four years learning survival skills under Stefansson's tutelage. He would later say of his mentor, "he taught me to work like a dog and then eat the dog."[2] Wilkins cranked a motion-picture camera and took still photographs all across the western Arctic. Returning home in 1917, he joined the Australian Flying Corps, received his wings and a commission, and flew photoreconnaissance missions over the western front.

After the war, he participated in two British Antarctic expeditions, including the last Shackleton venture. The Detroit Arctic Expedition was his first leadership role in polar exploration. He intended to search the Beaufort Sea for Harris Land (if he found it, he was actually going to name it for Rollin Harris) and ultimately continue on to Spitsbergen, pioneering the air route Amundsen had forsaken in 1923.

Meanwhile, in England, Grettir Algarsson had found a backer and was looking for an airplane. Algarsson and Worsley had attained a farthest north of 81°15′ on their 1925 Arctic cruise and returned to London on November 8 of that year. Their most newsworthy sighting was a "dark appearance" in the waters east of the Svalbard archipelago.[3] They believed it was Gillis Land, the fabled island supposedly glimpsed by an early eighteenth-century mariner and never seen again, but theirs was a minority opinion. The lead line of an item in the contemporary press summed up the majority position: "Grettier [sic] Algarsson, Canadian explorer, and Commander Frank Worsley find mirage."[4]

Three weeks before Algarsson's return, a construction crew was dispatched from Oslo to erect a hangar at Kings Bay to house Amundsen's dirigible. Algarsson felt that it was already too late to put in an order for an airship. He elected to try to get a jump on Amundsen in a heavier-than-air vehicle. This may have been the idea in the back of the minds of two other would-be transpolar fliers, a pair of Norwegian naval aviators who proposed to fly across the unexplored area from Arctic Russia to Alaska via a pair of seaplanes.

Unlike the rest of his competitors, Richard Byrd could not drop everything and devote himself full time to organizing an expedition. When the *Peary* returned to Wiscasset, he found himself smack in the middle of a raging controversy over military aviation. In the immediate aftermath of the *Shenandoah* disaster, Colonel William Mitchell, the army's rambunctious advocate of air power and a unified air service, had released a statement to the press that ultimately provoked the court-martial he had been seeking to focus attention on his crusade. Mitchell blamed the loss of the airship on "incompetence in the Navy Department" and "criminal negligence." He believed the ship had been "about fifty percent overweight" and charged the Navy with cutting corners and failing to observe proper safety precautions.

Mitchell had been a Brigadier General up until April of 1925, when he lost his job as assistant chief of the U.S. Army Air Service. He held the higher rank by virtue of that office, but was no less controversial as a colonel than he had been as a general. He went on firing off one allegation after another about the mismanagement of the army and navy air services, and while he was at it, he criticized the Navy for bungling its role in the MacMillan expedition. The Navy, he said, borrowed "some airplanes from the Army that were entirely inadequate to the work at hand." And, "as far as can be learned from a distance, they had a cat-and-dog fight all the way up and back, between MacMillan, the pilots and the Navy Department, and, of course, got nowhere and did nothing." The Colonel apparently had so much on his mind, or had gotten so carried away with his verbal strafing of the War and Navy Departments, that he accused the Byrd

Naval Unit of having failed to achieve the wrong goal. "Is there an airman who does not know," Mitchell asked, "that with the little jitneys they took up there the pole could not be reached?"

President Coolidge quickly resorted to ritual and ceremony to allay the public's concerns about the Mitchell charges: He appointed a committee to investigate the situation. Mitchell appeared before the Coolidge "Aircraft Board" on October 1, and referred to the airship catastrophe as a "treasonable" offense.[5] "So far as the trip to the Arctic is concerned," he said, "that was done in a haphazard manner."[6] Mitchell said the Loening Amphibians "were designed for work in the tropics and the Caribbean Sea. You can't do things like that and get away with it always."

On the sixteenth of October, four days after he arrived back in Washington, Byrd was summoned before the president's Aircraft Board. He defended the Amphibians and denied that the aviators and MacMillan fought like cats and dogs. "MacMillan," he said, "deserves most of the credit for the fact that the officers and men and planes are back safely."[7] A week later, Byrd's father died, unexpectedly, at the age of sixty-five. Such was his homecoming.

Mitchell was charged on October 24 with making statements "of a nature to bring discredit upon the military service." The court-martial convened on the twenty-eighth. The trial recessed for Thanksgiving, and when it resumed on Monday, December 1, Byrd was called to testify for the prosecution. The proceedings were typically contentious. "Are you a graduate of Annapolis?" asked assistant prosecutor Major Allen W. Gullion. "Are you a descendant of the Byrd who settled or founded Richmond, Virginia?" This was an attempt to establish the purity of Byrd's bloodlines, in an America where society news commanded almost as much press coverage as sports. The attorney for the defense, Congressman Frank R. Reid of Illinois, immediately leaped to his feet. "I object to these anthropological questions," he said.

Reid was a working class Irishman who had worked his way through college and law school. He had supported Billy Mitchell in Congress and volunteered his legal services pro bono. Major Gullion quickly established that the witness had been an aviator for seven years, had flown twelve or fourteen different types of airplanes, had recommended the Loening Amphibian for the MacMillan expedition, and felt that the Arctic planes had performed "very well." During the cross-examination, Reid made Byrd revisit the spark set flap and tried to extract the admission that the purpose of the expedition had been to sell Zenith radios. The explorer rejected the implication.

"Was it absolutely necessary for your safety to have the Navy radio set?" Reid asked, zeroing in on the controversy.

Byrd: It was advisable.

Reid: Was it necessary?

Byrd: I would not say it was absolutely necessary.

Reid: The kind of radio equipment made no difference to you when you left this country?

Byrd: Yes, it did.

Reid: Then I ask you again, was the radio equipment that the Navy wanted you to use necessary for the safety of your ships in the Arctic region?

Byrd: And I answer again that it was not absolutely necessary but it was very advisable to have it.

Reid continued to press Byrd relentlessly on every aspect of the expedition from its inception to conclusion, but the explorer stayed with him:

> **Reid:** Did the Navy Department hurry you in your preparations for this trip?

> **Byrd:** No, I hurried the Navy Department.

> **Reid:** You hurried the Navy Department?

> **Byrd:** Yes.

> **Reid:** Are you not part of the Navy?

> **Byrd:** I did hurry myself, if that is the question you ask.

> **Reid:** Did you find the Pole?

> **Byrd:** We weren't looking for the Pole.

Grover Loening testified the same day, expressing resentment at Colonel Mitchell's having called his airplane a "jitney."

The Colonel was found guilty later in the month. By then the federal funding cycle had entered the legislative phase again. Admiral Moffett launched the navy PR campaign for a major budget increase by releasing a report pleading for more money for naval aviation. The Department wanted to maintain the Naval Air Station at Lakehurst, New Jersey, where *Shenandoah* had been based; it wanted to buy an experimental all-metal dirigible from the Ford subsidiary, the Aircraft Development Corporation; and it wanted more airplanes and more aviation personnel. The appropriations bill was due to come before the House in January. Dick Byrd's considerable political skills were pressed into service on behalf of the navy's spending program.

As for his own project, he remained focused but secretive. He realized that the navy and the National Geographic Society had been chastened by the controversial outcome of the MacMillan expedition and that neither agency would be inclined to sponsor another polar epic in the near future. His next project would have to be a private expedition with which he hoped and expected the service and the scientific community might be willing to cooperate. The first order of business was to amass some private capital behind the undertaking. Byrd was given leave by the navy, following MacMillan's lecture before the National Geographic Society, to present a series of illustrated talks on the 1925 expedition. He had an engagement in Detroit at the beginning of November and tried to schedule a meeting with Edsel Ford, but was unable to obtain an audience with Ford until December 7. "It was a big moment," Byrd wrote. "Should he deny a subscription, there would be no 1926 expedition for me."[8] Edsel gave Byrd a tour of the Dearborn factory, and, to Byrd's relief, was more than willing to make good on the financial support he had pledged prior to the advent of the MacMillan venture.

Over the next couple of weeks, Byrd worked out an agreement with John D. Rockefeller Jr.'s people, principally Raymond B. Fosdick, that Rockefeller would continue to follow Ford's lead and match whatever contribution Ford was prepared to make to the prospective expedition.[9] Byrd at last felt he had enough backing to take the next step. While in New York three days before Christmas, he called Lakehurst to confer with Lieutenant Charles Bauch, the dirigible expert with whom he had corresponded in March. The superior range of an airship could not be easily ignored.

Bauch had survived the last flight of the *Shenandoah*. He was unavailable when Byrd phoned, and the call was answered by another lieutenant, Clinton Havill; Havill had led one of the salvage teams that had been dispatched to Ohio to recover the bodies and sift through the wreckage. Byrd wanted to talk about the availability of navy blimps for a transpolar flight. Havill advised him that a dirigible at least 50 percent larger than the blimp he had considered using earlier in the year would be necessary for the flight. "Do you think," Byrd asked, "that lighter-than-air has a better chance than heavier-than-air?" Havill said, "If the equipment is right, I think lighter-than-air has the best chance."[10]

Four days after Christmas, Bauch wrote to Byrd, endorsing the lighter-than-air option. Bauch had taken charge in the aft section of *Shenandoah* when she started rolling and vibrating like an airplane in a spin, and her struts started to snap. The gas bags in the overarching structure had checked the freefall, and fortunately only one of his men was killed when the breakaway stern hit the ground. Professional risk-takers, however, do not dwell on tragedies. Bauch, like Havill, confined himself to the logistics of lighter-than-air, which were exceedingly complicated and expensive. He projected a ground crew of a hundred men. In addition, a hangar would have to be built to protect the ship from high winds, and a large and costly steamship would have to be chartered to transport the men, the building material, and the hydrogen gas. The gas cylinders alone would weigh over two hundred tons.

"I expect to use a dirigible this time of 350,000 cubic feet capacity—150,000 cubic feet larger than the one we contemplated using last year," Byrd confided to Gilbert Grosvenor, writing from Boston just before the New Year.[11] He had not yet submitted a proposal to

Admirals Moffett and Eberle or to Secretary Wilbur. He wanted to put it to them personally when he returned to Washington after the holidays.

Grosvenor seems to have shuddered when he read the letter. "I appreciate your writing me so confidentially of your plans," he replied. But, "naturally, I dislike to see such a good friend as you again embark on so perilous an undertaking as conducting a dirigible across the Polar area."[12]

There weren't many people in America—or on earth—at this time who knew more about polar aviation than Richard Byrd. Even with only one Arctic season under his belt, his experience was a valuable commodity. The organizers of other prospective expeditions saw the handsome commander as a person who could instantly lend credibility to their own projects and consequently tried to recruit him. Robert Anderson Pope, a Harvard engineer who had lived and worked in the Arctic, wanted Byrd to take charge of the aviation end of an Ivy League expedition. Pope subscribed to the geopolitical theories of Vilhjalmur Stefansson and Fitzhugh Green. He believed that the nation that controlled Harris Land would be the dominant air power in the Western Hemisphere. Accordingly, he had scheduled a fundraising dinner at the Harvard Club in New York at the end of January. He intended to appeal to the patriotic sentiments of the eastern elite to finance an aerial survey of the unexplored area north of Point Barrow. The All-American Expedition would get underway in the summer and cover the same icefields the Detroit expedition expected to reconnoiter in the spring.

Professor William H. Hobbs, chairman of the Department of Geology at the University of Michigan, was planning an expedition to Greenland and tried to enlist Byrd to make more flights over the icecap. Hobbs was a pioneer meteorologist. He had studied the circulation of polar and equatorial air masses and had drawn some conclusions about the effects of Greenland weather systems on the North Atlantic shipping lanes. He wanted to test those propositions in the field. He asked the navy for a ship and had been turned down; consequently, he decided to try a MacMillan approach. If he could manage to get naval personnel attached to his expedition, with Richard Byrd in command of the unit, he thought he could prevail on the service to provide a couple of seaplanes for reconnaissance work.

Finally, just after New Year's, Byrd was summoned to Detroit where he was offered the position of second in command of the Wilkins expedition. Byrd politely declined to sign on with Pope or Hobbs but seriously considered joining forces with Wilkins. They were the same age (Wilkins was born one week after Byrd) and were at the same stage in their careers—both on the verge of a major breakthrough as expedition leaders. They got along famously.

George H. Wilkins had been molded by a desolate setting. The youngest of thirteen children, he had been raised on a farm on the edge of the Australian outback. The nearest schoolhouse was a five-mile hike across the desert. He kept to himself as a child, remained a loner as an adult, and was at his best working alone or in small groups in bleak and remote locations. A big, rugged-looking man with a receding hairline and a black goatee, Wilkins fit the popular stereotype of the brawny explorer. But despite the ferocious appearance, he was an agreeable and modest fellow. He had spent the last couple of years leading a natural history expedition in his native land for the British Museum and had earned about $15,000. He had planned to invest the proceeds in an airplane and fly over the western Arctic in search of the land he and Stefansson had failed to find a decade earlier.

The businessmen that comprised the Detroit Aviation Society enlarged upon Wilkins's plans. By the time Byrd and Wilkins met at the Cadillac Hotel on January 2, the scale of the expedition had more than tripled. The Fokker trimotor had been the talk of the Ford Reliability Tour, and a new model, one with an increased wingspan, had been brought over from Holland for the Wilkins flight. A single-engine Fokker had also been acquired, as well as an experimental three-engine airplane the Fords had rushed into production. An overland division of the Detroit expedition was going to haul supplies from Fairbanks to Point Barrow in a fleet of Ford tractors, and a transpolar flight to Spitsbergen had been tacked on to the agenda in addition to the search for land.

Dick Byrd was an ideal candidate to manage this enterprise, whose business affairs, according to Wilkins, "were a hopeless muddle."[13] Wilkins had magnanimously agreed not to claim Harris Land for Australia, since the undertaking was backed by American money. With Byrd aboard, the expedition would have an American naval officer in the field to make the claim for the United States.

Charles Bauch had told Byrd that Goodyear was the only company in Europe or America presently equipped to manufacture a non-rigid airship with a gas capacity in excess of 300,000 cubic feet. Byrd queried his contacts at Akron and learned on January 5 that the company already had one on hand. The dirigible, designated the CM-5, had been acquired from the French government five years earlier. It had a volume of 320,000 cubic feet and was offered to Byrd for $18,000. Byrd now envisioned an ambitious program of virtually non-stop Arctic exploration that would span the better part of the next eighteen months. He would leave for Alaska with Wilkins in February and help organize the flights that were scheduled to be mounted from Point Barrow in March. In the meantime, a staff led by Floyd Bennett would prepare the groundwork for Byrd's own expedition, which would depart in April.

Byrd was leaning toward Spitsbergen as his base of operations. The Svalbard islands were halfway between Norway and the Pole, and the passage north from Norway was navigable in the spring. The archipelago extended as far north as the 80th parallel and was centrally located there between Greenland, to the west, and the Franz Josef Islands, to the east. Amundsen and Ellsworth had acquired a 672,000 cubic foot dirigible with a range of 3,500 miles, and were planning a direct flight from Spitsbergen to the Pole and beyond. While Amundsen had the track record and Ellsworth the resources to finance a top-flight aircraft, Byrd would have to work within the constraints of a more limited budget. His flight plan necessarily had to be more conservative, but he studied the maps and arrived at a brilliant alternative to an ambitious transpolar flight.

He would fly from Spitsbergen, either in the CM-5 airship or a trimotor airplane such as Wilkins was using, 550 miles to the northwest to Cape Morris Jesup, the northernmost point of land in Greenland—and the world. The Pole was only 430 miles due north of Jesup; the heart of the unexplored area of the Polar Sea was an equivalent distance due northwest of the Cape. By setting up an advance base at Jesup and stocking that base with a resupply of fuel, he and Bennett would subsequently be able to fly to one of those destinations, return, refuel, and hop off for the other. The range of the trimotor or the CM-5 were, at best, half that of the Italian dirigible. Byrd would—if he got there first—nevertheless survey about 60,000 square miles of the Polar Sea that no human being had ever seen. If he found Harris Land on these flights, or even an island north of Morris Jesup, he would name it Ford Land, for Edsel Ford. The initial survey would be completed by late spring, when the stratus clouds begin to mount in the Arctic.

The party would depart by the beginning of summer. In mid-August, Byrd would find a ship to transport him to Etah, perhaps accompanied by Bennett. As he had worked out with the Etah Inuit before the MacMillan expedition departed for the States, he would winter over at the RCMP shelter on Ellesmere Island. In March, he would advance bases by dog sledge to the shore of the Polar Sea and mark out the landing fields he would need to pick up the aerial survey right where he had left off.

Gilbert Grosvenor had agreed with Byrd's assessment of his chances of getting money from the NGS. He had been brutally honest. "I do not think it wise to ask our Board of Trustees to make another grant to Polar exploration," he said, "as I am confident that the Trustees would not approve the expenditure of further funds from the National Geographic Society for Arctic exploration in 1926."

The key to launching the Spitsbergen operation was to obtain as much material assistance from the Navy Department as possible. To do this, Byrd had to build support for the project among his mentors in the command structure. But getting the undivided attention of every link in the chain of command took time, particularly in January, with the appropriations bill on the floor of the House of Representatives. "My plans are nothing like definite enough yet to publish," Byrd wrote in answer to a newspaperman's query. "The wheels turn slowly—much too slowly to suit me."[14]

The conservative scale of the proposal appealed to the navy brass. They were not dreamers but pragmatic men who had built impressive careers by getting things done. Looking at things strictly from the practical standpoint, Byrd's chief boosters—Moffet, Eberle, and Wilbur—all urged him to drop the idea of going with Wilkins as second-in-command and to concentrate on his own plans. Byrd himself began to question the wisdom of soliciting donations from the wealthy for an expedition in April and May, while preparing to put his life at risk in March. He resigned from the Detroit expedition, expressing sincere regret in a letter to Wilkins. "I have enjoyed knowing you," he said, "and I hope that we may see more of each other in the future. I am extremely anxious to do anything that I can for your expedition, and therefore I beg of you to call on me if there is anything I can do."[15] Byrd sent the Australian one of his sun compasses.

Earlier that day, Friday, the twenty-second, the end of the third week of January 1926, Secretary Wilbur had spent an hour with Byrd going over the expedition plans. They had spent an hour together the previous day. They met again the following week, on Wednesday, the twenty-seventh, one day after the House trimmed and passed the navy budget measure. Wilbur told Byrd on that occasion that while he approved of the "general project," he wanted to "think over the specific plan."[16] The secretary thought Byrd should fly out of Point Barrow, although Spitsbergen was 400 miles closer to the Pole.[17]

By now, Amundsen's dirigible, the N-1, had been renamed the *Norge*, a Scandinavian word for Norway, and Colonel Nobile, the designer of the airship, had been hired to pilot the craft on the transpolar flight. Wilkins was preparing to leave Detroit for Seattle on the first leg of his journey to Alaska, and would be accompanied by his new right-hand man, Major Thomas G. Lanphier, an army pilot and squadron leader. The Ford trimotor Wilkins was due to take with him had been destroyed along with three other planes when the Ford hangar went up in flames on January 17. But the two Fokker airplanes acquired by the expedition had arrived disassembled in New Jersey, at the Dutch company's American facility, and were about to be shipped west by rail.

On January 30, Byrd finally got the go-ahead from Curtis Wilbur and announced his intentions to the Washington press. He not yet resolved the lighter vs. heavier question in his own mind. He had neither an aircraft for the polar flight nor a steamship for the North

Atlantic voyage. And, other than Floyd Bennett, who would serve as second in command, he had not recruited a single member of the expedition.

≡17≡

LATE ENTRY

The big thing first is to get results. Economy is second
to that, but it is a damned important second.

RICHARD E. BYRD[1]

On January 23, Richard Byrd received a check for $20,000 from Edsel Ford, $5,000 more than Ford had pledged in 1925. John D. Rockefeller Jr. followed suit and wrote a check for the same amount on February 5. An additional $5,000 was contributed by a pilot, aviation booster and Naval reservist who also happened to be the head of one of the oldest and wealthiest families in America. Vincent Astor, thirty-five, came into some seventy million dollars when his father, Colonel John Jacob Astor IV, went down with the *Titanic* in 1912, the largest inheritance in American history at that time. Most of the money was in real estate in New York City. Astor had learned to fly in 1915. As a youth, he aspired to go to Annapolis and become a career naval officer, but his father objected. He received a commission and served at sea during the Great War, and remained active in the reserves after the Armistice.

Two other prominent New Yorkers wrote checks during the initial phase of Byrd's fundraising, one a transplanted Virginian, the other the son of a transplanted Virginian. Thomas Fortune Ryan, seventy-four, was the most successful Wall Street financier ever to migrate north from the Old Dominion. A poor country boy, he became one of the leading monopolists of the robber barons era, organizing syndicates that controlled mass transit, public utilities, banking, and insurance in New York and other cities, as well as railroads, tobacco, rubber, coal, and oil. Ryan bankrolled Tammany Hall, the infamous political machine in New York, and was also a major player in Virginia politics. He maintained a residence in the county where he was born and raised, and had been particularly close with one of Virginia's most powerful politicians, the late Congressman Henry Delaware Flood, Dick Byrd's uncle.

Ryan died in 1928, leaving an estate more than commensurate with his middle name; his worth was estimated at between two and three hundred million dollars. The "Great Opportunist," as he was popularly known, contributed $2,500 to the Byrd Arctic Expedition. So, too, did Peter Winchester Rouss, fifty-one, son of the New York dry goods king, Charles "Broadway" Rouss. The elder Rouss started out in business in Winchester, Virginia, Byrd's hometown, married a local woman, and retained close ties with the southern community long after he moved north. Peter had presided over the family business since his father's death in 1902.

With $50,000 deposited in the National City Bank of New York, Byrd was sufficiently confident of going north in 1926 to begin organizing an expedition. He also realized that $50,000 was hardly sufficient to finance the purchase of the Goodyear blimp, 220 tons worth of gas cylinders, the construction of a hanger plus the upkeep of a hundred-man ground crew, in addition to the basic costs of sailing to Spitsbergen and back. "Therefore, regardless of the respective merits of airships and airplanes," he wrote in a long memo to Wilbur, summarizing his plans, "the latter must be utilized."[2]

If Thomas Fortune Ryan had been more generous to the nephew of an old ally, Richard Byrd might have entered history as a pioneer aeronaut.

Anthony Fokker had created a sensation in aviation circles with his trimotor transport plane, the F-VIIA-3m. After the Ford Reliability Tour, he shrewdly allowed the army to flight-test the aircraft, then arranged for the ship to tour the eastern seaboard. The airplane promoted itself. On January 27, the trimotor made a twelve-hour hop from Jacksonville, Florida, to the Fokker plant in Hasbrouck Heights, New Jersey, just outside of New York. There were three stops en route, including Washington, D.C. Byrd drove out to the airfield that afternoon to have a look at the plane. Despite the attendant schmoozing, at the end of the day the total flight time from Jacksonville to New Jersey was close to a speed record set in 1922 on a flight from Palm Beach to New York.

At the control wheel was a naval reservist, Lieutenant George R. Pond. Pond was interested in Byrd's plans but wrote a week later to say that he was unable to join the expedition. Pond, in his own words, had "already piloted 'old faithful' through some 17,000 miles of intensive cross-country flying in rain, sleet, snow and fair weather, from Canada to Cuba (over seventeen states and two 'foreign' countries), and through every conceivable landing condition."[3] His honest appraisal of the plane: "The ship is a *good* ship; none better. With good piloting and ordinary practical care in operation," he said, the airplane "will take you anywhere in the world within its cruising range."[4]

The Fokker trimotor placed second on the Wright Aeronautical Corporation's list of the twelve best airplanes of 1925. Many observers, Dick Byrd included, believed that it heralded, in Byrd's words, "a new era in aviation progress."[5] Contemporary twin-engine aircraft could not cruise on one motor; the Fokker could continue flying on two engines if one failed. With a light load, it could fly a short distance on one engine. Based on U.S. Post Office statistics of airmail operations, Byrd calculated that for every 200 miles in the air, the chances of a forced landing in a trimotor were one flight in 1,649 takeoffs.[6]

The Detroit expedition had ordered a brand new Fokker. Factory-fresh aircraft require a substantial amount of flight time to ensure their airworthiness. Byrd inquired about the availability of the prototype. The 17,000 hours Pond had accumulated meant that the original trimotor had been flown "long enough," Byrd thought, "to get the usual kinks out of it."[7] Fokker offered to sell the airplane for $25,000, $12,500 down. Byrd would have preferred to acquire a Ford trimotor, out of loyalty to Edsel. But since the hangar fire, Edsel did not have a competing product. With Edsel's blessing, Byrd accepted Fokker's terms on February 10 and concluded the deal three days later.

Byrd's contract with Fokker's American operation, the Atlantic Aircraft Corporation, did not include the three engines. He was counting on the navy to furnish the motors and provide a surface ship. The service declined to do either, both in compliance with the Coolidge administration's emphasis on economy and to avoid the impression that the project was a "Navy" rather than a "private" expedition. Byrd's target embarkation date was April 1. This gave him less than two months to produce a full-scale expedition almost entirely on his own. Richard Byrd, however, had the energy, discipline, and determination to turn a pipe dream into a blueprint and a blueprint into reality.

He started by going before the U.S. Shipping Board, a federal agency that was legislated into existence in 1917, to help manage the logistics of waging war in Europe. Its role was to put together a large enough fleet of merchant vessels to transport men and materiel across the Atlantic Ocean. After the war, the Board was responsible for the disposition of all the ships it had seized, bought, requisitioned or had built. By 1926, the remnants of the "emergency fleet" were in the process of being liquidated. Byrd asked the Board to lease him a steamer at the nominal rate of $1 per year. The Shipping Board located a suitable derelict, the SS *Chantier*, a 350-foot-long cargo ship with a 3,500-ton displacement. As she was in mothballs off Staten Island and due for the scrapheap, there was no objection to a charter at the proposed rate.

The *Chantier* had been out of commission for five years. She had been stripped of everything worthy of salvage and, had it not been for the Byrd expedition, would never have seen the high seas again. A survey conducted in 1923 found her to be structurally sound but "not well cared for."[8] She was in dire need of a makeover. The decks had to be wire-brushed and painted, the machinery was rusty, the booms were "split, soft and weather-beaten," the wiring was in poor condition, and parts of the engine were "rusted or slightly rusted." The Shipping Board put thirty-five men to work overhauling the freighter. She was required to carry insurance, however, and a snag developed over the cost of the policy. It would be another month before the situation was resolved.

While dickering with the insurance underwriters, Byrd made a brilliant acquisition, recruiting George O. Noville, a thirty-six-year-old Manhattan business executive as flight engineer and third in command. Noville worked for the Vacuum Oil Company, a firm that in five years would merge with Standard Oil of New York to form the Mobil Corporation. He had enlisted in the navy after graduating high school and showed such promise that he was sent to Columbia University to study aeronautical engineering. He was commissioned in the Naval Air Service in 1916 and flew combat missions over the Italian front during the World War. After the Armistice, he pioneered the airmail service both as pilot and superintendent. He was back in a navy uniform in the summer of 1924, in charge of a fuel depot established in southern Labrador for the benefit of the army round-the-world fliers.

Noville was bright, effective, and perpetually on the make. He brought a bit of whoopee to the Byrd-Bennett team. Byrd was upright and personable; Bennett, upright and taciturn. Both were monogamous and temperate. Noville was a devil with women and an incorrigible drinker. He was divorced and had a daughter from his failed marriage, a circumstance far less common in the twenties than today. Everyone called him "Rex." He may have had the squarest jaw in polar exploration. He wore a pince-nez, a prim accoutrement that for many years had lost its prissiness due to having been popularized by Theodore Roosevelt. Noville had the physical proportions of the twenty-sixth president as well. He was a brisk-looking man, slightly smaller than Byrd and heavier set, with brown hair smoothly parted and pomaded. A physical fitness fanatic, he had been the Navy broad jump champion for seven years. He currently held the rank of lieutenant in the Naval Reserves and was an expert on the lubrication of aircraft engines.

Byrd and Noville had known each other since about 1922. Noville's company had offered to donate engine oil to the MacMillan expedition, and he and Byrd had communicated during the preparations for that trip. Byrd was concerned about the effects of extreme cold on lubricating oil; he did not want to encounter over the Polar Sea a repeat of the in-flight emergency that had forced Bennett out on the wing of the Loening Amphibian. It made perfect sense, therefore, to bring an oil specialist to Spitsbergen to attend to the problem. Byrd sealed the deal with three words: "Go to it."

Noville gave the expedition a vigorous presence in New York. He kept an eye on the overhaul of the *Chantier* and was also responsible for hiring a captain and chief engineer and stocking the ship with stores. Dozens of men were required to operate the steamer: seamen, firemen, oilers, coal passers, cooks. The crew was recruited from Washington, where Byrd was assisted by Bennett and another reserve officer, Lieutenant Robert C. Oertel, a tall, twenty-nine-year-old aviator from Augusta, Georgia. Byrd wanted people he could trust, who would work hard and follow directions. He knew where to find

Richard E. Byrd. © OHIO STATE UNIVERSITY

Roald Amundsen. © OHIO STATE UNIVERSITY

Alton Parker, George "Rex" Noville, Dick Byrd, and Floyd Bennett in conference on the *Chantier*. © OHIO STATE UNIVERSITY

Crossing the Delaware. © OHIO STATE UNIVERSITY

The *Norge* arrives at Spitsbergen. © OHIO STATE UNIVERSITY

Amundsen's mast as it looks today. © S. BART

The *Josephine Ford* prepared for flight. © OHIO STATE UNIVERSITY

Byrd and Bennett minutes before takeoff. © OHIO STATE UNIVERSITY

The interior of the *Josephine Ford*, looking aft from the cockpit.
PHOTOGRAPH TAKEN BY AUTHOR AT THE HENRY FORD

The view looking forward. PHOTOGRAPH TAKEN BY AUTHOR AT THE HENRY FORD

The *America* at Roosevelt Field. © OHIO STATE UNIVERSITY

Byrd and Noville at Roosevelt Field, with Bert Acosta pinch-hitting for
Floyd Bennett. © OHIO STATE UNIVERSITY

George Hubert Wilkins, an
explorer who looked like one.

Richard E. Byrd.

Young Marie Donaldson Ames
of Boston, Massachusetts.

them. He and his aides obtained lists of naval and Marine Corps reservists and put out a call for volunteers. They were soon inundated with responses.

Oertel, the son of a physician, an eye, ear, nose, and throat man, argued in favor of the existence of land in the Polar Sea from an entirely new angle: the theory of probability. The high latitudes, he reasoned, were dotted with islands.[9] In fact, there wasn't 200,000 square miles of the known Arctic that was entirely devoid of solid ground. The odds, he cheerfully concluded, were heavily in favor of finding land in an unknown region five times as large. Byrd liked optimistic, upbeat people. He made Oertel fourth in command of the expedition.

The list of entries in the polar derby changed throughout the winter. The German Zeppelin project was scratched due to the acute economic problems of the Weimar Republic. The two Norwegian lieutenants who had a notion to fly across the Polar Sea from Arctic Russia quickly faded back into the obscurity of their granite cliffs and fiord cities. On February 16, Robert A. Pope's All-American Expedition officially joined the field. As chief pilot, the slot Byrd had declined to fill, Pope had enlisted Lieutenant Leigh Wade, the leader of the team of army fliers that had circumnavigated the globe in 1924. The expedition was augmented by the journalist and world traveler Lowell Thomas. A correspondent in the late war, Thomas had made a flying visit to the Middle East, stumbled upon T. E. Lawrence, and filed the dispatches that transformed the desert campaigner into a matinee idol. Thomas himself had become a media star in the process and would continue exploiting the same formula—equal parts drama, history, romance, and adventure—for the rest of his life.

The Ivy League party planned to fly out of Point Barrow in July. The French "mystery sledge" expedition was also gearing up for a summer departure; the French were leaning toward wintering over at Spitsbergen or the Franz Josef Islands before starting out across the ice floes the following year. Algarsson was busy organizing in England for a getaway in May, but no one was paying attention to him. Wilkins and Amundsen were the men of the moment.

Wilkins had left Seattle on a steamship bound for Alaska on February 13. Major Lanphier, the officer assigned to claim new polar land for the United States, sailed up the Pacific coast with him. Awaiting them at Fairbanks was a twenty-nine-year-old lieutenant in the Army Air Service, a former barnstormer and bush pilot named Carl Benjamin Eielson. Eielson, a transplanted Alaskan, had flown the mail out of Fairbanks without mishap until the government canceled his contract because the route was considered too dangerous. He would eventually be recognized as the "Father of Alaskan Aviation." Wilkins saw in him what Byrd saw in Floyd Bennett.

The airship *Norge* had meanwhile been stripped down, reinforced, and reconditioned for the polar crossing. On the twenty-seventh of February, Colonel Nobile piloted the dirigible on a six-hour test flight from Rome to Naples and back. The only hitches were the traffic jams that occurred when Neapolitan drivers stopped to gawk at the monstrous gray, torpedo-shaped balloon circling over their city. Amundsen had been on a lecture tour of the United States and Canada since the fall. He was passing through Edmonton the day of the test flight and was asked, "What new thrill is there for you after you have conquered both poles?" He said, "Nothing, probably, but marriage. Although I have yet to find the girl."[10]

He sailed for Oslo on March 6; Ellsworth had preceded him by several weeks. While Amundsen journeyed home, a supply ship departed Norway for Kings Bay. It carried part of the steel framework of a mooring mast and the first of 250 cylinders of hydrogen gas.

Byrd's fundraising brought him in contact with additional mem-
bers of the American aristocracy who, like Edsel Ford and Vincent
Astor, had a direct connection with aviation. Godfrey L. Cabot of
Boston, Massachusetts, for example, sat at the very apex of Beacon
Hill society. In fact, a popular old rhyme had it that in "good old
Boston, the home of the bean and the cod, the Lowells talk to the
Cabots and the Cabots talk only to God." Godfrey Lowell Cabot
ascended a little closer to the Almighty when he learned to fly in 1915
at the age of fifty-four. A leading industrialist in the gas and oil business, he patented the first system for refueling planes in the air and
was the first President of the National Aeronautic Association, an
organization founded in 1922. Another Boston contributor, Porter
Hartwell Adams, a descendant of the second and sixth presidents of
the United States (John Adams and John Quincy Adams), was a first
generation aeronautical engineer, one of the first private citizens to
own and operate an aircraft, a founder of the National Aeronautic
Association, and chairman of its Executive Committee. Richard
Farnsworth Hoyt (Harvard, 1910) commuted to work in the summer
in a flying boat which he piloted between his Wall Street office and
an estate on the Massachusetts shore. Hoyt was in banking and
finance, sat on the boards of numerous companies and was chairman
of the board of the Wright Aeronautical Corporation. In three years,
he would engineer the merger of the firm with the Curtiss Aeroplane
and Motor Company, and become chairman of the board of the new
entity, the Curtiss-Wright Corporation.

Hoyt understood that exciting projects like a flight to the North
Pole and the search for land in the Polar Sea would stimulate public
interest in aviation and hasten the eventual acceptance of the airplane
as a means of everyday travel. Through his influence, Wright
Aeronautical contracted to sell Byrd four engines and spare parts at
cost. The engines were a major innovation. They were air-cooled
radial engines, the latest model in the company's innovative, 200 hp,

nine-cylinder "Whirlwind" series—a high-end product. The proto-type—the J-1—was introduced in 1921. Byrd acquired the J-4, the fourth generation Whirlwind. Fokker had installed the same type of engines on the trimotor for the Ford Reliability Tour, and they had performed splendidly for George Pond on his accumulated 17,000 miles of flying.

The cylinders of an air-cooled radial engine are arranged around the crankshaft like the spokes of a wheel and are simply exposed to the airstream to prevent the motor from overheating. The air-cooled engine has fewer moving parts than a water-cooled engine and weighs less. A lighter engine meant that the same airplane could carry an overall heavier load, i.e., more gasoline. More fuel meant the aircraft could fly a longer distance without having to land. The Wright Com-pany agreed to buy back the fourth or spare engine if returned in good condition and to make a donation of $4,000 when paid in full for the equipment. The total bill was $21,420.

The supply of well-heeled industrialists with pilot licenses, how-ever, unfortunately lagged behind the project's escalating expenses.

One of the most significant meetings Byrd had in New York wasn't with a contributor but with an old pal from the Naval Academy, Fitzhugh Green. In 1924, Green had been assigned to the Office of Naval Intelligence in New York. He may have been the first staff officer in either the army or navy to specialize in media relations. He was essentially a navy propagandist. He came from Missouri, from an old Colonial family, a sturdy, blocky middleweight with smooth, sandy hair, small eyes, and a solemn and gloomy demeanor. Green had been lost on the ice for several days in a howling blizzard during MacMillan's Crocker Land Expedition; the experience may have left a permanent imprint on his face. Twelve years later now, he still wore the habitual expression of someone squinting hopelessly into stiff winds and blowing snow. Despite the sullen appearance, he was a lively writer. He had published the first half of a projected two-volume history of the U.S. Navy, a pair of action-packed thrillers about a fictional alter ego, the two-fisted navy lieutenant Bliss Epley, and numerous articles in popular magazines about exploration and adventure. The print media in those days was an elite preserve managed by a clique of talented professionals who came from the right families and had attended the right schools. Green's social standing, writing ability, and Annapolis background enabled him to make the right connections. "My work," he told a superior officer in Washington, "is divided into two parts: writing and conniving."[11] To Byrd he explained: "My game is to act as a confidential adviser to various editors and publishers so that the public mind is gradually moulded into a pro-Navy state."[12]

He was particularly close with publisher George Palmer Putnam, grandson and namesake of the founder of G. P. Putnam's Sons and one of several generations of Putnams who helped run the family business. A sharp, angular-looking man in the crisp, clean-shaven, pinstriped patrician mold, Putnam, thirty-nine, was one of the first media wheels to grasp the increasing fascination of the Jazz Age public with explorers and adventurers. He published books by adventure personalities and—such was the spirit of the times—was at this moment planning his own Arctic expedition. Putnam was preparing to embark for Etah in June with one of his authors, Captain Bob Bartlett.

To ply his trade as an Arctic mariner, Captain Bob needed a ship, and his more sympathetic patrons finally bought him one, a sleek, ninety-three-foot long Gloucester fishing schooner, the Cadillac of the North Atlantic seaways. On the maiden voyage, Putnam and Bartlett were going to retrace the route of the MacMillan Expedition to Smith Sound, ostensibly to collect wildlife specimens for the American Museum of Natural History. The Putnam Arctic Expedition had lined up a couple of naturalists to handle the research end. The scientific staff would eventually be supplemented by a lasso-twirling cowboy, an expert archer, a book writer, a juvenile book writer, and a cameraman from Pathé News, the newsreel outfit.

G. P. Putnam knew how to spin off derivative products. He was a dynamo in wire-rimmed glasses, a man who always seemed alert, aware, and in a hurry. In addition to publishing books and organizing an expedition, he simultaneously did business as George Palmer Putnam, Inc., a literary and public relations agency. Fitzhugh Green played a number of key roles in the Putnam media enterprises—writer, ghostwriter, and right-hand man. Green put Byrd in touch with Putnam, and Dick Byrd suddenly had himself an agent.

Previously, Byrd, on his own, had sold the newspaper rights to his expedition to Current News Features, a Washington-based syndication service. His competitors made similar deals. The explorers were obligated by virtue of these transactions to write dispatches and feature stories covering all phases of their adventures. Wilkins earned $25,000 for signing with the North American Newspaper Alliance, and Ellsworth, negotiating for Amundsen and himself, extracted $50,000 from the *New York Times*. Byrd received an advance payment of exactly $5,000.

He stood to make more money depending on how close he came to accomplishing the twin aims of his project, the flights to the North Pole and the unexplored area of the Polar Sea. He would, in effect, be paid by the milestone. On the Pole flight, for example, he would get $1,666.66 for each degree of latitude he conquered north of 84°, an additional $6,666.66 for reaching 89°, and another $6,666.66 bonus for attaining the Pole itself. A slightly different incentive structure would reward him for passing the 70th, 90th, and 100th meridian of longitude on the search for polar land. If every incentive were met, he could realize in excess of $70,000, in addition to the sum advanced.

But the deal contributed precious little to the revenue side of his ledger when he signed the document on February 13.

A week after Byrd shook hands with Putnam, Putnam and Green had lunch with Emanuel Cohen, the head of Pathé News, and got Byrd the same terms for the motion picture rights that Pathé had offered Amundsen ($5 per foot of newsreel footage, 50 percent of the net receipts for feature films). Putnam also wrangled a $2,500 cash advance out of Cohen; Amundsen wasn't offered anything up front, which is perhaps the reason he didn't sign with Pathé.

The media contracts kept Byrd afloat—literally. Arctic expeditions were not considered good insurance risks. He was unable to obtain satisfactory terms from commercial underwriters, the latter refusing to issue a policy on the *Chantier* for anything less than total loss. Further, the insurers insisted on a provision that exempted them from making good on the policy unless the salvage and recovery costs equaled $150,000—almost four times what the ship was worth in the first place. Since the vessel had to be insured, there was only one solution. The Shipping Board itself assumed the risks, and Byrd's charter rate was increased by a premium of $968.75 per month. When the *Chantier* was finally delivered on March 25, Byrd paid $3,876 down, one dollar for the ship and three thousand eight hundred and seventy-five dollars for insurance coverage for the first four months.

On that day, the Fokker trimotor made its first flight since being reconditioned for the Byrd expedition. The plane took off from the Fokker plant in northern New Jersey and flew east over Manhattan Island out to Curtiss Field in the undeveloped marshlands of Mineola, Long Island. George Pond was in the pilot's seat; Dick Byrd and Floyd Bennett flew as observers. The ship had originally been designed to carry up to ten passengers, but the passenger seats had been removed and two extra fuel tanks now occupied the forward end of the flight cabin. The extra tanks supplemented the two fuel tanks in the center of the high wing. The wing tanks were standard equipment for the Fokker trimotor, each having a capacity of one hundred gallons. The extra tanks were slightly larger and could hold 110 gallons each. In addition, a compact, lightweight wireless set had been installed in the flight cabin, and a small table had been provided for the navigator and his instruments and charts. The plane had also acquired a name.

Byrd had asked Edsel Ford to name the aircraft. Ford made a logical suggestion and then a patriotic one. He suggested naming the plane in honor of a polar hero, say, Peary or Scott, or for President Coolidge's wife, Grace, a popular first lady. *Peary* recalled the 1925 expedition, an outing Byrd hoped to surpass, and *Scott* an outcome he hoped to avoid. The *Grace Coolidge* perhaps lacked a certain ring to it. In the end, Byrd decided to express his gratitude to his chief benefactor by naming the ship for the third of Edsel's four children— his only daughter, three-year-old Josephine.

The *Josephine Ford* performed gorgeously on her maiden flight over the metropolitan area. She was a fabric aircraft. Her sleek, streamlined fuselage consisted of a metal skeleton sheathed by a handsome, navy blue canvas cover. A highly varnished wooden wing with a thick leading edge extended over the top of the fuselage. Her name and the name of the expedition were displayed on both sides of the fuselage, "JOSEPHINE FORD" centered over the words "BYRD ARCTIC EXPEDITION." The nomenclature appeared near the tail assembly, in crisp, white letters on the blue background. An additional word—"FOKKER"—was emblazoned in white on the middle of the fuselage, also on both sides of the aircraft and in bigger letters. And a billboard-size "FOK" and "KER" (blue letters on a white background) were spread across almost the entire underside of the wing on each respective end. The publicity-conscious Anthony Fokker contractually prohibited Byrd from removing the company markings for a month after the expedition.

A big ship for her era, the *Josephine Ford* was forty-nine feet two inches long, fifteen feet longer than a Loening Amphibian. Her single wing measured sixty-three feet three inches from end to end, an eighteen-foot longer wingspan than the Loening. Her size, the color scheme—the blue and white of the navy uniform—and the sturdy, maplewood wing, gave the ship a bold, dynamic profile. She looked ready to brave uncharted airspace. A few days later, Bennett put the *Josephine* through some load tests at Mineola.[13] Sitting next to him in the co-pilot's seat was Lieutenant Alton Parker, U.S. Marine Corps, a thirty-year-old Mississippian who had joined the expedition as a reserve pilot. Parker had been a mechanic at Pensacola when Byrd was learning to fly; Byrd later recommended him for flight training. He and Bennett found that the ship could lift 5,524 pounds, at least 500 pounds more than Fokker thought she could. Her fuel consumption was 30 percent lower than expected, her range conceivably 30 percent longer.

In a christening ceremony in Rome on March 29, a silk Norwegian flag was hoisted at the stern of the *Norge*, and the Italian airship formally became a Scandinavian vessel. This was at Amundsen's insistence; he would not fly under any flag other than that of Norway. At the same time, the name of the undertaking the ship made possible was officially changed to the Amundsen-Ellsworth-Nobile Expedition. The international cast of characters could now proceed to the Arctic in perfect unity. Amundsen and Ellsworth left Rome shortly after the ceremony to return to Oslo. They would depart for Spitsbergen by boat in a couple of weeks and supervise the preparations underway to receive the airship. Nobile continued to direct the work of outfitting the dirigible for its flight from Rome to Nome.

Two days after the event in Rome, George Wilkins and his version of Floyd Bennett, Carl Ben Eielson, took off from Fairbanks, Alaska, on their first flight to Point Barrow, ferrying some 3,000 pounds of supplies. The omens had not been favorable for Wilkins. He had christened his airplanes at Fairbanks on March 11, the whole town turning out on an airfield covered with a foot of snow. Later that day, after the single-engine Fokker had been dubbed the *Alaskan*, and the trimotor the *Detroiter*, Wilkins proposed to take the latter aloft for a test flight. A newspaperman who had helped clear the snow inadvertently walked into the barely visible blur of a spinning propeller and was killed instantly.

A week later, both planes were smashed on succeeding days. Eielson and Major Lanphier, the second-in-command, were trying to get the feel of the airplanes, when first Eielson in the *Alaskan* and then the major in the *Detroiter* lost lift and stalled at the head of the runway while coming in for a landing. The landing gear was severely damaged on both planes. In addition, the tractors that were supposed to haul supplies overland to Point Barrow failed to make headway and were finally replaced by dog teams.

By the thirty-first, however, the *Alaskan* was airworthy again. Wilkins and Eielson hopped off north-northwest for the jagged white creases of the Brooks Range, the mountains standing between Fairbanks and the tundra sloping down to the Arctic coast. They picked up a tailwind, ran into clouds, and, when the haze finally cleared, found themselves looking out on the rough icefields of the Polar Sea. As there was sufficient fuel in reserve, Wilkins decided to plunge forward for a spell. By the time they turned back south and pointed the ship towards Barrow, Wilkins estimated that they had flown 140 miles out from shore, or seventy miles farther into the Polar Sea than the *Karluk* had sailed in 1913. Since they had had at least thirty miles of visibility, they had actually surveyed one hundred miles of territory in the western Arctic that no human being had ever seen.

⟩18⟨

THE SPORTING ELEMENT

All three of us—Amundsen, Wilkins and myself—
are seeking to discover new land and also to conquer
the Arctic from the air. It is not exactly a race,
but the element of competition is there.

RICHARD E. BYRD[1]

Charles John McGuinness, a roguish Irishman who joined a Byrd Antarctic expedition some years later, was asked why he wanted to sail to the bottom of the world. "Ef there'd'a been a dacent war goin' on," he said, "Oi wouldn't!"[2] This may at least partially explain why the impending penetration of the unexplored area of the Polar Sea by aircraft excited the media to such an extravagant degree in the spring of 1926. The *New York Times* called it "the greatest news story of the year."[3] The nation's leading newspaper carried eleven front-page articles on the quest in March of 1926, and more than double that number in April, when Wilkins was finally airborne and Byrd and Amundsen departed for the Arctic. The *Times* assigned two correspondents to Spitsbergen, one to accompany Byrd, the other Amundsen and Ellsworth, and contracted to print dispatches from Norwegian and Italian journalists who flew as passengers aboard the *Norge*.

In mid-March, another *Times* correspondent set out to haul a wireless radio hook-up 1,500 miles overland from Nenana, Alaska, to Point Barrow, in order to pick up transmissions from the explorers in the home stretch and relay news of their discoveries back to New York. Nenana, about fifty miles west of Fairbanks, was the last stop on the railroad at that time and the only transportation north was by dog team. The *Times* man was accompanied by a wireless operator on loan from the U.S. Army Signal Corps. They didn't bring a generator, expecting to use one already at Point Barrow. Whenever a settlement was reached, the reporter would file a dispatch for the paper via telephone or telegraph. These stories, datelined Ruby, Nulato, Candle, and Kotzebue, Alaska, were hair-raising accounts of blizzards, thin ice, and unruly dogs. They were printed on the front page.

No one was more adept at playing to the media and building up the excitement than Roald Amundsen. In one of the feature stories published in fulfillment of his newspaper contract, he began to speculate on what he might find in the Polar Sea. Suppose, he said, there was a large landmass at the top of the world. Well, what if one of the hundreds of whaling ships that had gotten stuck in the ice floes of the Bering Strait had been carried by the ice to the shores of that land? The crew of a whaler consisted of about fifty men, "and they always took native hunters and women with them," Amundsen said. If they struck land, he continued,

> they would have been able to build houses with the timbers of the ship, they would have had a large store of provisions to keep them until they got in stores of food from the seals and other sea animals and from the birds. They would have found a comparatively mild climate in the summer months. The sun would have been warm for a good part of the year.

They could have lived, multiplied and thrived, but they would have been cut off forever from civilization by the drifting ice.[4]

"It would be the most dramatic and amazing discovery in all human history," Amundsen wrote. "To see people, live human beings, on any land in the midst of the Arctic ice would make the traveler in a dirigible pinch himself hard and blink many times to make sure he was awake. It just couldn't be, and yet it is not impossible. Nothing is."

This lovely piece of ballyhoo appeared in newsprint on Easter Sunday, April 4. On that weekend, a convoy of four large trucks and a tractor-trailer proceeded from Mineola to Brooklyn, escorted by a squad of motorcycle police. The tractor-trailer was first in line, the flatbed bearing the fuselage of the *Josephine Ford*. The truck immediately behind it carried the wing of the Fokker. The trimotor had been flight-tested for ten hours before being disassembled; there were no kinks, no hitches. She was completely airworthy. The third van held a small biplane, a Curtiss *Oriole*, which Byrd had acquired primarily for the benefit of the cameramen that would accompany his expedition; Pathé News helped defray the cost of this airplane. The last truck was loaded with the motors of the two planes and other parts and fittings.

The departure of the *Chantier* had been held up for a few days because at the last minute the tail shaft was found to be cracked and had to be replaced. She had been moved from dry dock to the Brooklyn Navy Yard, and when the convoy from Mineola arrived at Berth 10, at the foot of Clinton Avenue, it had to fall in behind a long line of trucks. All day Saturday and Sunday, vans arrived with equipment and provisions for the voyage, including forty tons of food, a six months' supply. The crates, barrels, and boxes were unloaded and hauled up the gangplank by the volunteer crew augmented by a platoon of prisoners summoned from the Navy Yard brig.

The Standard Oil Company had donated eighty-five barrels of gasoline. Remington had provided firearms; Underwood, typewriters. Manufacturers and wholesalers in virtually every industry had furnished a creaking shipload of products either gratis or at cost. Late in March, Edsel Ford had made a further contribution of ten thousand dollars, increasing his subscription to thirty thousand and, again, Rockefeller followed suit. Thanks principally to their largesse, Byrd had raised a total of $74,000 from individual subscribers. But despite the generosity of his numerous suppliers, he had spent close to one hundred thousand dollars and was personally in the hole for the balance.

Putnam had arranged a lecture deal just before the Easter weekend, but there was no money advanced. The only way Byrd could conceivably meet his obligations was to make a newsworthy flight over the Polar Sea and cash in on his media contracts after the fact. His chief fear, accordingly, was not a forced landing on the pack ice. It was that something would happen at the get-go to prevent the expedition from ever getting underway. He would not therefore tempt fate and allow the airplanes to be lowered into the hold of the *Chantier* over the weekend because both Saturday the second and Sunday the third were windy, blustery days.

Every time an expedition turns around it seems to incur one more expense. There is always another item that has to be bought, another fee to be paid. The deficit would climb to $32,000 by the time Byrd returned to New York. He was nevertheless determined to economize. Instead of buying a new diary, he used the same one he kept on the MacMillan expedition, a symbolic victory in the battle of the ledger. He had written a long entry in that hardbound volume under January 1, 1925, so long it had spilled over to January 3. He had not picked the diary up again until June 20, the day the *Peary* and *Bowdoin* departed from Wiscasset. The pages for the period between January and June were all blank. April 2, 1925, was a Thursday. Byrd opened the diary to this page, crossed out "Thursday," wrote "Monday," crossed out "2," wrote "5," and began keeping a journal of the 1926 expedition.

Monday, April 5, 1926, was the day the *Chantier* shoved off from the Brooklyn Navy Yard. "I cannot get over my astonishment that there is so much public interest in our expedition," he wrote at the end of that day. Some two thousand well-wishers had gathered at the dock of the Navy Yard and hundreds of visitors toured the ship. The earliest arrivals watched a team of derricks hoist the *Josephine Ford*'s sixty-three-foot wing off the pier, hold it more or less level and parallel with the ground, and ease it carefully over the deck. It was twelve feet wide and two-and-a-half feet thick at the center and tapered at the ends; when raised from the horizontal, dangling from a sling, it stood as tall as a Brooklyn tenement. Seamen steadied it over the forward hold. Like a Brobdingnagian sword-swallowing act performed in slow motion, it was slowly lowered to rest beside the fuselages of the *Fokker* and the *Oriole*. A wooden bulkhead had to be demolished to make way for the wing as the lowering proceeded. The entire operation took six hours and was supervised by Floyd Bennett; when it was over, the airfoil had been interred without a scratch. An hour later, a piece of lumber that had been used to rig the sling plummeted into the hold. It landed between the Fokker wing and the *Oriole*, narrowly missing three men.

Byrd's instruments—bubble sextant, sun compass, earth-inductor compass, drift meter—and his and Bennett's Arctic furs and survival gear were displayed on the main deck of the *Chantier* for the edification of the visitors. Such was the state of American civilization in 1926 that none of these irreplaceable items were stolen. Many of the guests were young women who had arrived in Easter finery to bid farewell to husbands or sweethearts among the crew. Rex Noville had invited a blonde bombshell named Sigrid Matson of Jackson Heights to see him off. At least half a dozen of his other female acquaintances apparently arrived on their own initiative and were scattered on every deck. Noville was in charge of the loading of supplies, an activity that continued practically up to the moment of departure. Lines of blue-jackets with sacks on their backs were still filing up the gangways and companionways. A blur with a firm jaw, Rex went racing from deck to deck directing traffic and kissing another girl-friend goodbye. To one of them, a writer from the *Herald Tribune* heard him say, "I thought I told you not to come on out here from Oklahoma."

Along about midday, Vincent Astor's yacht, the *Nourmahal*, approached the pier. Aboard were Richard Byrd, his brothers, Governor Harry and apple-grower Tom Byrd, numerous friends and acquaintances, Navy Yard officials, Shipping Board officials, and, apart from Edsel Ford who was otherwise engaged, almost everyone who had made the expedition possible, from money men like John D. Rockefeller Jr. to media wheels George Palmer Putnam and Emanuel Cohen. Marie Byrd, who preferred to remain out of the limelight, had toured the *Chantier* and bid her husband goodbye earlier in the day. She was three months pregnant with their fourth child.

There was a reception and lunch aboard Astor's yacht. Rockefeller, pressed into service as MC, had given an impromptu talk on how the international competition for the transpolar flight might aid the cause of peace by bringing the industrialized nations of the world closer together. Sometime that afternoon, Arthur Hays Sulzberger, publisher of the *New York Times*, reached into his pocket and gave Byrd a 1922 Liberty silver dollar for luck. At close to 4:00 p.m., Byrd shook hands with Sulzberger, Rockefeller, and the others, and ascended the gang-plank of the *Chantier*. Rockefeller, dressed for the spring chill in topcoat and bowler hat, turned and said, "I wish I were going." The Navy Yard band played "Auld Lang Syne." Byrd stood on the prow, waving his cap, a slender, erect figure in navy blues on a rusty, tar-streaked deck. His thoughts as the steamer backed stern-first into the East River were recorded in his diary.

"I have never seen such kindly feeling," Byrd wrote. The decency and sincerity of a wealthy and enormously powerful man like Rockefeller moved and inspired him. "I must keep the expedition on a high plane in every particular," he thought. He reflected on the many exhausting days and weeks of reaching out to total strangers. How precious and indispensable was each individual expression of support. "There are not words enough in the dictionary with which to adequately thank these people," Byrd thought. "I feel very inarticulate and unworthy of all this. I think of the expedition not as mine but as 'ours,' the boys with me and America's."

Sailors on a nearby cruiser stood at attention. As the *Chantier* glided into Upper New York Bay, she passed an old ship currently berthed on Staten Island and employed as a tugboat, the SS *Roosevelt*. A generation earlier, that same ship had brought Robert Peary and his aides Bob Bartlett and Donald MacMillan to the northern shore of Ellesmere Island, the base from which Peary had mounted his successful dash to the North Pole.

"This day has proved that there is a lot of romance and spirit of adventure in this great country," Byrd thought. "I have received hundreds of telegrams and letters from all over the country. I have simply been overwhelmed."

In Rome that day, Pope Pius XI received and blessed the flight crew of the dirigible *Norge*. The airship was scheduled to depart three days later on the first leg of its Arctic journey. Colonel Nobile plotted a course to Spitsbergen that bypassed the North Atlantic as much as possible because of the risk of encountering a seasonal storm. He also wanted to make rest and fuel stops along the way. This restricted the flight path to cities that had the infrastructure to receive and house an airship. Oslo had to be included in the itinerary because Amundsen wanted his countrymen to have a chance to see the ship;

a mooring mast had been erected outside the city especially for the occasion. As a result, the planned route over Western Europe resembled the trajectory of a Hoyt Wilhelm knuckleball. The first stop was 1,200 miles to the northwest, at the airfield near Pulham, England, a London suburb. The *Norge* would subsequently fly northeast to Oslo, east to Leningrad, and then north to Kings Bay.

A heavy wind blew down from the mountains outside of Rome and across Ciampino Flying Field on the morning of Thursday, April 8, the day of the scheduled departure. The *Norge* stayed inside her hangar that day and remained grounded on Friday, the ninth, when the winds picked up and the sky was overcast. Finally, at 9:30 on the morning of Saturday, the tenth, a fair weather day, the airship flew over waving crowds of well-wishers that had assembled in the streets of the Eternal City, and then headed for the coast of France. The only thing Mussolini, the Italian premier, had asked of Amundsen before agreeing to sell him the airship was that he retain some of the original crewmen for the transpolar flight. Accordingly, a half dozen Italians watched from the celluloid windows of the control car or the engine gondolas as the blue Mediterranean appeared on the horizon. The rest of the crew consisted of six Norwegians, a Swede, and a Russian, almost all of whom had been with Amundsen on previous expeditions. Two of the Norwegians had been forced down on the ice with Amundsen and Ellsworth in 1925. The Italians were small men and were all mechanics; at any given time, three of them rode in the gondolas and monitored the engines. The Norwegians were huge and served as co-pilots, helmsmen, and navigators. The Russian, a naturalized Norwegian, was a radio operator; the Swede, a meteorologist. The Italians wore brown jumpsuits and round, military-style parade caps with shiny visors. On chains around their necks they wore religious medallions that had been blessed by the Pope. The Scandinavian contingent wore heavy sweaters or tweed hunting jackets. Nobile, the pilot, gave orders to the flight crew in English, the lingua franca.

Five additional guests and correspondents were also aboard for the first leg. That made a total of twenty-one men, eighteen of them crowded into a space thirty feet long and only six feet wide, about the size of a trolley. The raw footage is deceptive because the control car was partitioned. The flight controls were in the prow, and a radio room and toilet had been installed in the aft section. Most of the passengers and crew were confined to the middle cabin. There were four chairs in the control car: three were in the prow, the fourth was in the midsection and occupied by the navigator. Everyone who was not manning the controls or fixing the position of the ship had to stand around the navigator's table or sit on the floor.

The walls of the control car were made of canvas. There was no heating or cooking system because of the danger of striking a match in the general vicinity of over 600,000 cubic feet of hydrogen. Each man was allotted two sandwiches, and water bottles and a thermos of hot coffee were passed around. If sunlight streamed through the ample windows, it was warm and pleasant in the car; when the sun slipped behind a cloud, it became awfully chilly. A trap door in the ceiling enabled the crew to pass between the tiny control car and the massive envelope of the airship. One could stand at the foot of a metal ladder in the control car and look up through the opening at the keel that ran along the length of the dirigible. The survival gear to be loaded at Spitsbergen would be lashed to the ribs of the keel. Bending one's head all the way back, one saw the dark underbellies of the bulging gas bags that elevated the ship. The control car was just below the prow of the airship. The mechanics could ascend the ladder, walk aft along a narrow gangway a couple hundred feet and climb down into the three gondolas housing the engines that drove the airship forward. They had to wear rubber-soled shoes because the nails in ordinary shoes could produce sparks when their feet met the metal walkway, and they had to look where they were going. Aft of the control car, there was nothing below the catwalk but empty space and the bottom of the airship. Anyone who fell off the walkway would probably plunge clear through the fabric shell to the surface of the earth. There was no guide rail, no handholds. During a storm that blew up over France, Nobile sent a half-dozen men up the ladder and spaced them out along the wobbly gangway to trim the ship. They weren't allowed to move a muscle until the *Norge* crossed the English Channel.

The dirigible threw out her ropes and was hauled down to the ground and into a hangar at Pulham late on the afternoon of Sunday, April 11, after spending twenty-nine hours en route and several additional hours maneuvering to land. During the time the *Norge* was aloft, Wilkins had made a second flight ferrying supplies from Fairbanks to Point Barrow and back. He had hurt his right arm in a freak accident at Barrow and would be out of action until the end of the week.

Byrd had taken a number of small American flags to be carried over the ice in the *Josephine Ford* as souvenirs for the supporters of his expedition. He and his aides had seriously considered attaching those flags to harpoons so that if land was spotted in the Polar Sea, he could hurl "the Stars and Stripes" from the door of the plane and the flag would be planted in the snow. American sovereignty over the hypothetical territory might not have stuck so easily, but patriotism and the feeling of the country's honor being at stake permeated the atmosphere of the Byrd expedition. That was one of the elements that bound together the fifty-one men who sailed with him to Spitsbergen.

There was something robustly American in the very makeup of this aggregation. Hundreds of young men who read about the expedition wrote letters or applied in person pleading to be accepted as volunteers. Some of these adventure-seekers were sized up and signed on, so that while most of the crew were reservists who had served long hitches in the navy or in the Marines, the ship's company as a whole represented a broader spectrum of American life. They were working stiffs and college boys, immigrants and professionals, well-to-do men and hand-to-mouth men, the kind of conglomeration that might have been found in the grandstands of Yankee Stadium, the Polo Grounds, or any ballpark in the country in those egalitarian days before sky boxes, and they had rolled up their sleeves and were ready to pitch in and go to bat in support of a magnificent pennant drive.

The stalwart ship's captain, Michael J. Brennan, a native of County Clare, Ireland, first shipped out—under sail—at the age of fifteen. He immigrated to the United States in 1910 and became an American citizen. An erect and dignified seamen, Brennan smoked a pipe, favored bow ties and cardigan sweaters, and wrote Kiplingesque verse about the Irish when no one was looking. Chief Engineer Thomas B. Mulroy was, inevitably, a large, pink-faced man, dark, jowly, beetle-browed, and indefatigable. Brennan, Mulroy, and three other ship's officers had served in the navy during the World War, switched to the merchant marine after the Armistice, and had been referred to the expedition by the Shipping Board.

The deckhands included two Wall Street brokers who had been infantry officers in France and war heroes. One of them, Jonathan Duff Reed, had been awarded five battle stars and a Purple Heart with an oak-leaf cluster. He was in the burlap business and hoped to avoid, he later wrote, "another sweltering New York summer," which often arrives at the end of May. The day he left to board the *Chantier*, he hung a sign on his office door: "Out to lunch."[5] Joseph de Ganahl (Harvard, 1925), the son of a Texas oil millionaire, came aboard with luggage in hand and said he just had to go. Byrd thought he had the right spirit and took him on as a coal passer. Two West Point cadets also showed up at the last minute. They were looking for a place to hide as stowaways when Robb Oertel caught up with them. Oertel decided to sign them up rather than ship them out.

The professions were represented by William C. Haines, a meteorologist assigned to the expedition by the U.S. Weather Bureau; Dr. Daniel P. O'Brien, a physician on loan from The Johns Hopkins University Hospital; and R. Harold "Doc" Kinkade, a field engineer detailed by the Wright Aeronautical Corporation to nurse the Whirlwind engines. All were in their thirties. Some of these men—Mulroy, de Ganahl, and Haines, for example—would embark on future Byrd voyages. Mess boy Epaminondas J. Demas, twenty, a bellhop at the Hotel Washington in Washington, D.C., would come of age with the Byrd expeditions. Demas was born in Corinth and had emigrated from Greece at the age of twelve to join a pair of older brothers who had already established themselves in America. A small, serious fellow known as "Pete," with a thick crop of dark hair, Demas aspired to a career in aviation. His brother, Nick, was a short-order cook at a restaurant frequented by Dick Byrd and had gotten to know the explorer because Byrd loved Nick's salads. When Nick told Byrd about his brother's career aspirations, Byrd said to send Pete up to the State, War, and Navy Building; he'd be happy to talk to the young man. The day Demas arrived at the Bureau of Aeronautics, he found Byrd and Admiral Moffet discussing the finer points of Einstein's Theory of Relativity. He was devoted to Byrd ever since.

An all-American outfit of this nature of course had to include someone from Brooklyn. Richard W. Konter, a chief radioman in the navy, had retired after twenty-nine years in the service to ship out on the *Chantier* as an ordinary seaman. Konter had sailed up and down the South Seas and the China Sea and had survived typhoons and the Boxer Rebellion. Around his arms coiled a pair of dragons that had been tattooed in Shanghai. He played all of the string instruments (and other instruments) and brought a half-dozen ukuleles, a banjo, and several harmonicas aboard the *Chantier*. The ukulele had emigrated from Hawaii to the U.S. in the 1920s and was all the rage. Konter wanted to introduce the instrument to the "Eskimos."

He didn't know that there weren't any in all of Svalbard. He was forty-four and slender with a long nose and crooked smile and was the life of the party.

After leaving the Brooklyn Navy Yard, the *Chantier* anchored the next day off Staten Island to adjust the compasses and square away the sacks, trunks, barrels and boxes that had been piled up on the decks and in the companionways, a potential calamity in case of heavy seas. Everyone chipped in to lug the stores—the doctor, the meteorologist, even the two cameraman assigned by Pathé News. The competition supplied by Amundsen and Wilkins happily fostered an infectious spirit of cooperation. Getting the *Chantier* to Spitsbergen and the *Josephine Ford* aloft was the single aim to which the entire ship's company subscribed, the common identification. Deckhand Alexander Geisler, a bodybuilder who worked out at a Washington gym Byrd attended and had become friends with him, vowed not to shave again until Byrd and Bennett flew over the North Pole.

A motorboat meanwhile drew alongside the freighter, carrying another individual who had packed a suitcase and aspired to join the expedition. She was a very attractive young woman who claimed to be a journalist, but was not permitted to climb aboard. She had asked for Noville.

On the seventh of April, the first day on the high seas, Byrd discovered a shipmate he didn't know he had. After dinner, heading for his stateroom on the upper deck, he thought he saw a familiar face in the shadows. He raised a flashlight he was carrying, switched it on, and found himself looking into the furtive eyes and pockmarked faced of Malcolm P. Hanson, a thirty-two-year-old radio engineer who worked at the Naval Research Laboratory in the District of

Columbia. "I confess to being a stowaway," Hanson said. The previous year Byrd had consulted with Hanson on the radio equipment for the MacMillan expedition. Hanson had designed a transmitter for the *Chantier* and had been given leave to come up to New York to install the equipment. The system was not working properly when the ship weighed anchor. The radio room was directly across a corridor from the generators and engines, and the induction noises interfered with the signal. Hanson had been working day and night on the set and decided on the spur of the moment to stick around until the problem was licked, even though he had not been authorized by the Navy Department to sail with the ship.

Hanson was courting trouble with his employer, but his act exemplified the group spirit that took hold of the expedition. He was also destined to go south with Byrd, as was another crewmember who from the outset contributed mightily to morale: a lively fox terrier contributed by Dr. Anita Maris Boggs of Washington, D.C., educator, philanthropist, and co-founder of an international goodwill agency, the Bureau of Commercial Economics. The dog arrived in New York with the name of "Dynamite," which matched his personality. Some of his shipmates called him "Frosty" for his pale coat. But the name that stuck was "Igloo."

Twenty minutes before midnight on the evening of April 13, the *Norge* glided out of the English hangar, assisted by a 200-man ground crew, ascended rapidly in the darkness and headed straightaway for the North Sea. Twenty crewmen and guests made the journey to Norway. The Italian motormen bought camp stools in England so they wouldn't have to stand for the duration of the flight or sit on the floor. But the stools were cheaply made and collapsed under the weight of the Norwegians. The *Norge* also had a canine mascot, a demure little brown and white female named Titina. Coincidentally, she was also a fox terrier. She belonged to Colonel Nobile and was in the arms of one of his friends during the farewell ceremonies at Ciampino. At the last moment, Titina leaped aboard the control car; she would remain a member of the crew and accompany her master to the Arctic. There is no indication that Igloo and Titina ever met.

Throughout the night the sea surged and raged, and a heavy fog closed in. When it lifted by morning, the southern coast of Norway appeared on the horizon. Three Norwegian Navy seaplanes buzzed out of the granite cliffs to escort the *Norge* up the coast to Oslo. Thick crowds had assembled in each coastal town en route; handkerchiefs, hats, and flags were waved aloft like so many dabs of color in an expressionistic painting. Amundsen's dirigible was the first airship ever to visit Norway, and the entire country seemed to have turned out to celebrate its arrival. The narrow streets of Oslo, the capital, were densely packed and erupted with a tumultuous bellow, clearly audible to Nobile and his crew over and above the sound of their own engines. The aeronauts were probably unaware that the shopkeepers of the city had locked their doors, offices were closed, and children were excused from school, or that among the tiny figures waving from the roof of the parliament building were the heads of the government.

A mooring mast had been erected on an airfield outside of the city. King Haakon VII and fifty thousand cheering spectators gathered on the field, as Nobile circled and started his descent. Brass bands played, glee clubs sang, banners were unfurled. That night the barometer fell. Rather than remain exposed on the mast, Nobile departed for Leningrad, his next stop. He flew into a thick fog and heavy winds. The icy gusts struck hard, whistling through the rigging of the airship and pitching it about like a surface ship on a stormy sea. It became impossible for the crew to stand up without falling into one another. Stiff with cold, they lay side by side on the cramped floor of the navigation compartment.

The gale lasted through the next morning. By noon, the mist cleared. There was land below, but it was impossible to tell where they were or how far off course the ship had been blown. Nobile descended close to the ground, where people could be seen looking up at the airship. Notes were written in English and in German and dropped from the control car. They read: "Where are we, north or south of the Gulf of Finland? If south, please hold arms up; if north, cross arms."

Whether the citizens responded or not is a matter of dispute. Eventually railroad tracks were spotted. The helmsman followed the tracks to a station, someone raised a pair of binoculars, read the name of the town on the station sign, and someone else looked at a map. In any event, Nobile figured out that he was in Estonia and went on his way.

He and one of Amundsen's men had traveled to the Soviet Union at the beginning of the year to make arrangements to land in the worker's paradise on their flight to the Arctic. At about eight o'clock on the evening of April 15, the *Norge* descended on an airfield outside of Gatchina, a snowbound town some thirty miles south of Leningrad. A Red Army ground crew eased the dirigible into a hangar the Soviets had agreed to make available. That same day, the Bolsheviks formally annexed any new land that might be discovered on the Eurasian side of the North Pole.[6]

19

THE SOUL OF HONOR

B stands for Bennett, we see him each night
the rest of the day he keeps out of sight

THE *CHANTIER* SHOVELFUL[1]

Up in Warrensburgh, New York, Floyd Bennett's hometown, it was said of the aviator, "He never talked much and seemed interested in nothing but motors and automobile engines. People who tried to strike up a conversation with him could get him to comment on nothing but the weather. Sometimes he refused to talk about that."[2]

When the *Chantier* embarked for the north, Bennett's whereabouts was a mystery to the volunteer crew. They had all met Byrd, but the second in command was something of an invisible man. Joe de Ganahl, the Harvard grad, set out in search of the missing aviator one day and finally found him in the lower hold, at work on the *Josephine Ford*.[3] Bennett was determined to have the engines completely overhauled, the instruments installed and all systems inspected and fully operational by the time the ship reached Spitsbergen.

He was the hardest working man on the expedition. An accountant and ex-Marine officer who sailed as supercargo on the *Chantier* said in an interview after the return journey that "Bennett was looked up to" as much as Byrd was. The two of them were "so much alike as to be almost the same man. They are both quiet, modest men, always pleasant, ready to kill themselves with overwork, never irritable, never angry."[4]

Their personalities meshed perfectly, and the expedition took on their most conspicuous characteristics: concentrated energy and good humor. There was no shortage of the latter. Many of the reservists had had technical training and were mechanics or electricians in the service, but seamanship is a specialized art. Of the fifty-two members of the ship's company, only nine (the captain, the first, second, and third mates and five of the crew) were experienced and competent mariners. With an amateur crew aboard, the first two weeks at sea were a veritable comedy of errors.

At the outset of the voyage, one of the Wall Street brokers was ordered to run and get the fire hose. He scoured the forecastle and could not find one. Thinking the ship was on fire, he grabbed a fire extinguisher instead. He had no idea that the task immediately at hand was to spray the mud off the anchor and the anchor chain as it was raised off the bottom, customary procedure at sea. None of the experienced sailors onboard could ever remember this being done with a fire extinguisher. Another landlubber standing watch one night kept reporting "Light dead ahead! Light dead ahead!" Roused from sleep, Byrd and Captain Brennan found that the light source the ship was in danger of colliding with was the evening star.

Brennan did a commendable job of holding his Irish temper ... for a while.

A West Point cadet was assigned to the galley to wash dishes. He hated the work and after breaking twenty dishes in two or three days was relieved from the mess detail and asked to audition for the job of steering the ship. However, neither the cadet nor any of the first few applicants were up to the job. "Several times I thought we were going to the *South* Pole," said Tom Mulroy, the chief engineer.

> It was quite discouraging at times, when we were trying to make speed with the old girl to watch her maneuvers due to the green helmsmen. I don't think there is a letter in the alphabet she didn't make.[5]

Byrd's cabin was right next to the captain's. "Just about the time some helmsman would get at right angles to the true course," Byrd said, Mike Brennan would poke his head out of the porthole, "and believe me I could hear some choice language through the partition. 'You blankety, blankety landlubber, there isn't a man on the ship who can steer!'"[6]

Jonathan Reed recalled the night when Brennan raised his sextant to an overcast sky to get a shot at the moon but nothing was visible in the overcast. At West Point, "moon" was a derogatory term for a failing cadet. When the captain, with his customary profanities, wondered aloud where the moon was, the West Pointer flunking sea duty innocently piped up, "Here I am, sir." Reed concluded his account of the incident here, saying, "I won't go into any detail as to what happened after that."

These stories made the rounds of the ship, were repeated at the mess table and contributed to the lore of the enterprise. At night, the crew would gather in the dining saloon and play checkers, chess, and cards. Konter, who developed into an expert helmsman with no prior experience at the wheel, would play the ukulele, distribute the instruments he brought with him, give music lessons, and strike up a band. Byrd would entertain with card tricks and then take on the winners of the evening's chess and checkers matches. He had been winning shipboard tournaments since his ensign days and was the best player of either game on the SS *Chantier*. "There are mashed fingers, sea sickness, men tired out, etc.," he wrote in his diary, "but all are happy and I believe I can say we have a happy ship."

After five days at sea, Rex Noville somehow found out that the crack New York reporters had observed him kissing a different woman goodbye on each deck of the *Chantier* and had included this detail in their coverage of the departure. He sent Sigrid Matson a radiogram pleading with her to disregard the "ridiculous stories" in the press.[7] "Our last talk," he said, "settled everything." With this off his mind, he settled down to business. He and Oertel were such efficient managers that Byrd was able to leave the details of running the ship to them and Captain Brennan. While Bennett worked on the plane, Byrd worked out a flight plan for the long hop to Peary Land and the Pole.

Peary had reached the northern tip of Greenland in 1900 and thought he had found an island. A quarter-century later, no one knew if he was right or if, as other explorers contended, the sprawl of ground named for the admiral was in reality a peninsula. The latter supposition would turn out to be correct. Peary Land is an area the size of Maine, Peary's home state, and its chief feature is an unusually dry climate. There is so little precipitation that despite the extreme cold the snow remaining on the surface after the summer melt-off is too sparse to turn into an ice sheet. Peary reported a smooth, light layer of snow accumulating over the winter and the absence of an ice cap. On the basis of these observations, Byrd felt that he and Bennett would find a suitable place to land and establish a base for further operations.

It was essential to receive accurate information about weather conditions at Spitsbergen before they flew a return leg from Peary Land. Byrd prepared written instructions for the *Chantier* to broadcast a local weather report every fifteen minutes, on the hour, quarter hour, and half hour.[8] If it was clear to land at Kings Bay, the report was to be preceded by the letter "E," a single dot in Morse code. The dot would be repeated five times. The sequence of five dots would itself be repeated five times. If the landing field were obscured by fog, Byrd wanted the weather report to be preceded by the letter "T," a single dash. That signal was to be repeated four times in a sequence of five consecutive repetitions.

Typically, Byrd had a backup plan in case of radio failure. He had bought signal kites from a manufacturer who had written him back in March. These kites were five and seven feet long and rolled up like an umbrella when not in use. If for any reason the *Chantier* believed the *Josephine Ford* had *not* picked up the transmissions and fog had descended, Byrd directed that signal kites be flown at either end of the field and at a sufficient altitude to get above the mist. Attached to the kites would be a device Noville had invented to automatically set off smoke bombs. The rising smoke would be seen for miles. If the fog was high enough above ground level for the plane to penetrate and safely land, this information would be conveyed to the aviators by trailing a pennant or small flag from the kites.

If the plane was forced down, the aviators would transmit a series of long dashes and attempt to report their position. If they went down within a hundred miles of Spitsbergen, the *Chantier* was instructed to patrol the edge of the pack ice and enlist as many ships in the search as possible. If a forced landing were made within "easy walking distance" of Greenland, Byrd and Bennett would head for Peary Land and follow the coastline of Greenland or Ellesmere Island down to Etah. This was potentially a 600-mile hike. The Putnam expedition was scheduled to depart from New York in June. Putnam had arranged to rendezvous in southern Greenland with another of his authors, the great Danish explorer Knud Rasmussen, an expert sledger. Rasmussen was going to sail further north with Putnam and Bartlett. If the downed aviators were lucky, Rasmussen would arrive at Etah in time to organize a search party.

Byrd did not spell out in his contingency plans the worst-case scenario. If he and Bennett were forced down in the vicinity of the Pole, they would have to replicate one half of Peary's 800-mile sledging journey to 90° north and back to the nearest point of land. Peary had dogs, support parties, and the benefit of twenty years' practice. Byrd and Bennett had no experience negotiating pressure ice. They would be unassisted—there was not the slightest possibility of Rasmussen reaching them that far north—and they would have to manhaul. "We should starve and freeze, and fall from exhaustion before we were through. And we'd probably be 'through' long before we got back to land," Byrd wrote two years later.[9]

En route to Spitsbergen, he merely wrote out a list of instructions for Noville to follow in case he had "a forced landing away from base and the *Chantier* returns to the States without me." He wanted Noville to "put the ship out of commission as soon and as economically as possible. My reason for this," he said, "is that every cent spent comes out of my estate." Noville was to salvage and sell as much of the expedition's equipment as possible to help the estate pay off the debts Byrd had incurred organizing the expedition, and work with Fosdick and Putnam to "see that I am done justice in so far as my contracts are concerned." The Shipping Board, he added, "should refund the Expedition the amount of the broken tailshaft."

It was characteristic of Byrd to keep the short odds of completing a long manhaul to himself; it was also characteristic that he quietly took every possible precaution to increase his and Bennett's slim chances of surviving the worst case. Checking the emergency gear, he found that his outfitter, Abercrombie & Fitch, had forgot to include one of the most indispensable items, a Primus stove. Byrd arranged for one to be picked up by a *New York Times* reporter due to join the expedition in Norway. On the seventh night at sea, he stayed up late typing a three-page inventory of the emergency rations and survival equipment he and Bennett would have to haul across the ice on their sledges. The following day he compiled an exhaustive list of some one hundred different pieces of flight equipment, starting with the survival gear and including navigation aids, fire extinguisher, tools, and spare parts. On the ninth night at sea, he stayed up weighing each item on the master list.

The amount of "storage space" on an aircraft is measured by the pound. Considering the amount of fuel and oil the plane had to carry, there was only room left over for 1,400 additional pounds, and that included Byrd and Bennett. "The weight has to be kept down to a minimum and yet there are so many things we should have to add to our safety," Byrd wrote in his diary. "We think this may leave us with 1,800 miles cruising radius but as to that we can't tell until we reach Spitsbergen and actually try out the plane."

Byrd had decreed that no one was to be served breakfast after 8:30 a.m. The *Chantier*'s dining table was too small to seat everyone; only half the ship's company could be served at a time. Under these circumstances breakfast could drag on all morning, and the cooks would be late preparing the next meal. So the crew was asked to be in for the morning meal by 8:30. After staying up one night until 2:00 or 3:00 a.m. working on his flight plans, Byrd walked into the galley at 8:36 a.m. Noticing the clock on the wall, he walked right out again. Mess boy Pete Demas brought a couple of soft-boiled eggs, which Byrd loved, and some toast and oranges to the commander's state-room, but Byrd sent it back without a bite.[10] He would not exempt himself from any rule.

By mid-April, when the *Norge* descended on the airfield outside of Leningrad, Amundsen and Ellsworth had departed for Kings Bay, and the sore-handed Wilkins was about to embark on his third flight ferrying fuel from Fairbanks to Point Barrow. Since all three expeditions had been provided with cutting-edge radio equipment, they could keep tabs on the progress of their rivals. Byrd had a slight advantage in this department. Frederick T. Birchall, managing editor of the *New York Times*, had met Byrd and apparently fell under the spell of his personality. Birchall sent radiograms to the *Chantier*, passing along tidbits gleaned by his correspondents. According to one of his missives, "Best information dirigible arrives Spitzbergen [sic] May 1st."[11]

The *Chantier*, meanwhile, was about halfway to Norway and had encountered headwinds and high seas. She was making no more than eight and a half knots. Byrd asked Mulroy if anything could be done to make better time. The chief engineer had already been considering the problem and had an idea. Byrd had filled his bunkers with over 1,500 tons of coal, enough for the voyage to Spitsbergen and back. He was not going to make the same mistake MacMillan had made the previous year. The airplanes were in the forward hold; three-fifths of the fuel supply, close to 900 tons, was stored in the after hold. The ship was consequently drawing twenty-one feet aft and just sixteen feet forward. The imbalance was slowing the ship down. Mulroy suggested redistributing the 900 tons to the side bunkers.

"Is that all?" Byrd said. "Well, that's easy."[12]

The entire expedition started taking shifts shoveling coal. Byrd and Bennett pitched in and took their turn as well. The emptying of the after hold continued almost right up to the time the *Chantier* reached Spitsbergen. The men sang as they shoveled:

> Sweet little coal bunker
> don't you cry
> You'll be empty
> bye and bye
> When our commander is
> crossing the Pole
> We'll be in the bunker
> shoveling coal

Byrd suspected the little ditty was contributed by meteorologist William Haines, a round, slow-moving man who, the explorer said, had "a secret sense of humor."[13] Haines emerged from the expedition with the nickname "Cyclone."

Amundsen and Ellsworth arrived at Spitsbergen on April 21. On the twenty-fourth, the *Chantier* dropped anchor off the coast of Trondheim, Norway, where Malcolm Hanson transferred to a tugboat that brought out three new expedition members: an ice pilot named Isak Isaksen and two London-based media people, a *New York Times* correspondent and a third Pathé News cameraman. The reporter, William Bird, brought a Primus stove with him and a thousand dollars worth of additional supplies, including new dishes.

Hanson had solved the interference problem by erecting a radio room at the stern of the ship, up on the poop deck. The "room" consisted of a shelter made of tarpaulin which protected the equipment but not the operator. On stormy nights, the radiomen had to wear a couple of wool sweaters, slickers, and a leather aviator's helmet to withstand the wind and rain. Since the seas were generally rough and the waves often rose so high they washed over the deck, operating the receiver was, in Hanson's words, "like tuning a set tied to the back of a bucking bronco." Byrd had interceded with the Navy Department on Hanson's behalf; so long as the engineer returned to Washington expeditiously he would not be penalized for absenting himself without leave. The crew gave him three cheers when he went over the side.

The rendezvous off Norway was the last time letters could be posted back to the States. Byrd seized the opportunity to write to his oldest child, his only son, Dickie. "Daddy is way out on the ocean on his big ship," he said.

We have 53 men on board the ship. There are 10 men to
steer the ship and 15 men to fire the boilers and keep the
engines going. (I see where your mommie is going to be
asked a lot of questions.)

Tomorrow, I give this letter to a man who is going to
meet us in a boat and he will take it to another big ship and
it will come all the way across the water to you.

In a few days daddy will be in a country where there is
no darkness, no night and where there is a lot of ice and
snow and polar bears. Then daddy is going to fly a long
way over that ice.[14]

He enclosed one of Konter's harmonicas and added, "Daddy loves you
and misses you very much." In his leisure hours, Byrd had been reading Robert Scott's journal of his march to the South Pole, the last great
manhauling epic of the heroic age of polar exploration. The ordeal
ended in a tent within eleven miles of a supply depot. Scott and his
sledging party had no food or fuel, were ravaged with scurvy, and
suffering from exhaustion. Outside, a blizzard was raging. The diary
was found among their dead bodies.

En route from Norway to Spitsbergen, Byrd wrote another, longer
letter to his son, one that would remain among his effects and be delivered in the event he met a similar fate. The second letter, handwritten
on three sheets of Byrd Arctic Expedition stationery, with writing on
both sides of each page, was not composed in language comprehen-
sible to a six-year-old. It was intended to guide the child through manhood. "My precious boy," Byrd began. "This letter is to be read twice
by you on your eighth birthday then again on your fourteenth birthday,
your sixteenth and once every four years after that."

I am writing at sea in my cabin. The sea is very rough and
icy winds are blowing from the icefields of the Polar Sea.

We arrive at Kings Bay tomorrow and from there I am to take a hazardous airplane flight over the Polar Sea which is a cold and frozen ocean.

If by hard luck I do not get back this is my farewell to you my dear boy, which I know you will take very seriously and all your life I hope you will try to follow what I ask you to do.

When you reach manhood I will be only a vague memory to you, like a dream it will be. But now I am a very real factor in your life. Your sweet mother can tell you how I adore you. But even she does not realize the depth of my affection for you. You are everything a son should be— devoted, unselfish, thoughtful, generous and honorable with an unusual sense of justice. You have I am thankful to say many of your mother's traits.

Byrd's message was both simple and profound. He enjoined the boy to take his place as the man of the family and look after his mother. At the same time, by devoting himself to his mother, the boy would cultivate the qualities Byrd saw and admired in her. He wrote,

I have loved your mother since we were little children and I have never known her to do an unkind or an unjust thing. She is the sweetest, purest human being I have ever known or have ever heard of. She is an angel, too good I am afraid for this world. My boy I worship her. She is the kind who never hesitates to sacrifice herself for those she loves and then think nothing of it nor look for credit.

Youth is cruel and thoughtless and has little consideration for age; but I believe you will be an exception to this rule. I believe that you will always try to help your mother over the rough place just as you would like to do even now as a child. She is very, very proud of you and so don't let shade or stain darken your name. Anything dishonorable that you would do would break her heart.

Whatever comes up you will find her the best sport you have ever known. I have never met a man whose sense of fair play and sportsmanship equalled hers. She is a thoroughbred—every inch of her.

My last words to you my boy are to beg you to consecrate your life to two things—first to understand, cherish and protect your mother and secondly to emulate her in all matters. Model yourself as much as you can after her for she is the finest person in the world.

Byrd went on in this vein for another page and a half. Summing up in conclusion, he wrote,

And so my boy I will end where I began, follow your mother's advice and try to make yourself as much as possible like her with her great sense of honor. She is the very soul of honor.

"Always," he said, "put honor and your mother first."[15]

The same day Byrd wrote his farewell letter to his son—the twenty-eighth—he sent a brief and friendly radiogram to his foremost rival, Roald Amundsen. Byrd and Amundsen had met in Washington on October 21, 1925. The Norwegian had arrived in the capital a week after opening his lecture tour at Carnegie Hall in New York. After shaking hands that morning with President Coolidge at the White House, he stopped by the Navy Department to thank the Secretary and his staff for having been prepared to divert the MacMillan expedition to his and Ellsworth's rescue. Before he stepped out on the stage of Poli's Theatre that afternoon, he was introduced by Richard Byrd.

Lincoln Ellsworth came down to Washington for that lecture. Afterwards, when he, Amundsen, and Byrd had a chance to speak privately, Byrd confided his plans for a 1926 expedition. He sounded out Amundsen about any objections the Norwegian might have had to Byrd's using Kings Bay as a base. Amundsen said, "We will welcome you with open arms."[16]

Amundsen and Byrd exchanged messages during subsequent months, pledging mutual support. Isaksen, the ice pilot who had met the *Chantier* at Trondheim had been recruited by Amundsen for the Byrd expedition. "Please arrange for our ship *Chantier* to go alongside dock at Kings Bay immediately upon arrival tomorrow night Thursday about six PM," Byrd radioed:

> I wish to offer you any help we are capable of. We have fifty men aboard. Kindest wishes and best regards to you and all members of your expedition from all members of our expedition and my personal greetings to you.[17]

The *Chantier* steamed into Kings Bay at about four in the afternoon of the twenty-ninth. From the prow of the steamer, it was impossible to even see the small pier. A Norwegian naval vessel, the *Heimdal*, a gunboat, was blocking it.

20

VIKING
VALOR

Amundsen was not above a white fib now and then,
if it made someone happier or if it extricated him
from some trivial embarrassment.

LINCOLN ELLSWORTH[1]

In the decade since Roald Amundsen attended the Hunter's Fraternity dinner in New York with Robert Peary, the Arctic had completed the process of weathering his Nordic face. His hair was as white as snow and his complexion as ruddy as the glare of the midnight sun. The reflection of the sun turns the endless icefields into gleaming vistas, the glare punishes the eyes and forces the explorer to constantly squint. Amundsen's eyelids were consequently heavy and the corners of his eyes deeply wrinkled from his additional exposure to Arctic glare. His cheeks were seamed and seared from so many more seasons of bitter winds and blowing snow. He was three months shy of his fifty-fourth birthday now, but looked ten years older than his chronological age. Judging from the wear and tear on his face, the casual observer might suppose that he was close to what was then the end of the average human lifespan.

But he was also a giant of a man erect and agile with rock-hard upper body development. One's first impressions upon meeting him therefore were partially inaccurate and practically incongruous: advanced age, health, and strength. The combination amplified the sense of power he projected. His most prominent feature was his nose, a large protuberance as bold and curved as an eagle's beak. The size of Amundsen's nose has actually been recorded. A Seattle sculptor measured the explorer's physiognomy for a bust that was completed after the subject went north in 1926. The nose was three inches long. Amundsen's face, the artist declared, was "one of the strongest that I have ever modeled."[2] He was a striking figure. A newspaperman accompanying the Norwegian on a stroll through midtown Manhattan in the fall of 1925, when Amundsen was in town to lecture at Carnegie Hall, noticed the way New Yorkers reacted to him. "On the avenue, as he walks toward Forty-second Street," the reporter said, "there are whispered words of recognition. But the passer-by would not have to know that this is Amundsen. He would look twice or three times, because he is also obviously a personality."

> He has the Viking look that a few sea captains, a few aviators and a few explorers still possess. It stands out in a city crowd almost as markedly as though he were striding along in the garb of skins and furs which he wore last June at latitude 87 degrees 44 minutes north.
>
> One imagines he might pause at Fifth Avenue and Forty-second Street, call for volunteers to man his next expedition and make up the crew between traffic whistles— so powerful is his personal magnetism.[3]

Amundsen reportedly flinched just once in the aftermath of the forced landing of the Dornier Whales. According to Lincoln Ellsworth, he "trembled like a leaf as he stood facing that vast, silent mass of expectant humanity that waited to greet us on our return from the '25 flight."[4] In Oslo, following his triumphant homecoming, Amundsen received the welcome news that his ship, the *Maud*, had finally been released from the ice floes with which she had been drifting since the end of 1922. The floes had carried her along the Siberian rim of the Arctic rather than across the Polar Sea to the North Pole. She arrived in Seattle in October of 1925 after having departed from that city more than three years earlier. As soon as the ship made port, three members of the expedition hurried to Rome to join the flight crew of the *Norge*. "The observer sees at a glance why men follow and trust Amundsen," wrote the New York reporter. "Looking at him, it is hard to imagine him in death or defeat."

Amundsen came from a land of long winters and a culture of long silences. His ancestors arose mysteriously out of the east, overran Scandinavia, and ranged far to the west long before there was such a thing as "history" to keep a reliable and accurate record of their voyages. He was as much a product of his culture as Byrd was of industrial America. About Byrd, there seemed and felt something new, vibrant, and contemporary. Amundsen personified the millennia, the inexorable march through time of an ancient seafaring people. On his personal stationery, his name was written in the upper right-hand corner in small gothic letters. No font could have been more appropriate.

If Byrd transformed himself into an expedition leader the modern way, by self-study, pluck, and salesmanship, Amundsen did it through the Old World process of apprenticeship and exposure. He was born into a shipping family, the youngest of four sons. At the age of fifteen, he read Sir John Franklin's account of his early expeditions to the western Arctic and resolved to follow in Franklin's footsteps. Amundsen was sixteen when Fridtjof Nansen electrified Norway and the world by leading the first ski party across Greenland. Nansen's celebrated crossing reinforced young Amundsen's polar fantasies.

He undertook a rigorous program of exercise to harden himself and embarked upon ski tours of nearby mountains and woods to develop his proficiency in wilderness travel over ice and snow. He entered medical school at the behest of his mother, but dropped out when she died and went to sea. His first voyage was aboard a sealer plying Arctic waters. At twenty-five, he was engaged as second mate on a voyage to Antarctica organized by a Belgian naval officer, Adrien de Gerlache de Gomery, an inexperienced go-getter who, in Byrd fashion, sprang full-blown into a leadership position. The ship, the *Belgica*, set sail in 1897; its chief medical officer was Dr. Frederick A. Cook.

Cook had three Arctic expeditions under his belt, including one with Peary. He was an agreeable shipmate with keen insights, and Amundsen was eager to learn all he could from him. The *Belgica* made polar history, becoming the first ship to winter over in Antarctica. Cook saved the expedition during the dreary months of darkness by persuading the party to eat fresh seal and penguin meat. Vitamin C had not yet been discovered, but Cook suspected that there was something in fresh meat that served as an antidote to scurvy, and he was right. When the sun reappeared, he saved the expedition a second time by finding a way to release the ship from the ice in which it was locked.

A quarter of a century later, the sixty-one-year-old explorer was accused of having perpetrated an oil swindle and convicted of mail fraud. Peary had died a national hero; Cook had survived in disgrace. During his 1925–26 lecture tour, Amundsen stopped off at the Federal Penitentiary at Leavenworth, Kansas, to visit his old shipmate. He spoke kindly about Cook to the press and refused to take sides in the Cook-Peary controversy. For this heresy, the National Geographic Society canceled a lecture date. Amundsen made no apologies. Back in New York in early March of 1926, at the conclusion of his tour, he received in the mail an embroidered linen tablecloth that Cook had made in prison. "I am more touched by this gift," he told a reporter, "than by almost anything that has happened to me in a long time."[5]

He was equally adept at accommodating public opinion as he was at defying it. His youthful dream had been to negotiate the Northwest and Northeast Passages and to plant the Norwegian flag at the North and South Poles. After the *Belgica* expedition, he set out to accomplish the first task but packaged the project as an effort to locate the North Magnetic Pole. He knew that he needed to present a valid scientific research agenda to secure financial backing. Amundsen spent two winters in the heart of the Northwest Passage, learning from a new group of mentors, the native people of King William Island. The sledging and survival skills he absorbed completed his polar apprenticeship.

In 1909, he was preparing to check off his next two Arctic goals when word spread through Europe that first Cook and then Peary claimed to have reached 90° north. Amundsen understood that there was a marketing element in exploration and that either Cook, Peary, or both had satisfied the world's demand for the conquest of the North Pole. So he changed Poles and competed with Scott for the distinction of being the first to attain 90° south. Amundsen won by masterfully combining Inuit sledge methods with Norwegian ski techniques. He subsequently received enough recognition to solicit backing for a northern venture. By then, the prospect of undiscovered land in the Polar Sea had supplanted the poles in the public imagination.

Amundsen's determination to accomplish the transpolar flight was widely admired. His ever evolving plans—from biplane to monoplane to twin-engine flying boat to transoceanic dirigible—paralleled the evolution of aviation itself and endowed his quest with an heroic rather than quixotic quality. Cheering crowds turned out at each landing as the freighter he and Ellsworth boarded at Trondheim, the *Knut Skaaluren*, slowly made its way up the Norwegian coast.

Passengers included members of the *Norge* ground crew and corre-spondent Russell Owen of the *New York Times*. The Arctic Circle crosses northern Norway. The hours of darkness progressively dimin-ished each day of the open-sea passage from Tromsø to Spitsbergen.

Amundsen brought a phonograph with him; he set it up in the dining saloon every night, where the passengers gathered after dinner, and played records until it was time to go to sleep. He loved Amer-ican popular music. The evening's journey towards the strange, faraway world of twenty-four-hour daylight was accompanied by tunes like "Swanee River" and "Old Black Joe." The last song before lights out was always "Home Sweet Home." The men inevitably lapsed into an emotional silence when they listened to it. "Captain Amundsen sat, pipe in hand, smiling reflectively at the machine," Owen reported. "Mr. Ellsworth lounged on the cushions, staring at the ceiling."[6]

Amundsen was renowned for his ability to consume virtually any slop whatsoever. In thirty years of polar wanderings, he had spent a fortune and acquired fame and a cast-iron stomach. He had neither a wife nor a family nor much in the way of worldly possessions—nothing but charts and dreams and a certain restless energy. What drove him on, what made him pursue the transpolar flight from year to year? He gave vague answers to the question, whenever he bothered to answer it. "It's all I know," he once said.[7] In one of the newspaper articles that appeared under his byline, he spoke about "the quiet, the absolute peace which surrounds one" in the polar regions. "Men sometimes go mad when isolated in the Arctic or the Antarctic," he wrote, "but I like it. There is no sense of loneliness, only peace and quiet and freedom."[8]

Peace and quiet is all very well, but Amundsen resided in Oslo, not New York or Chicago. He could hardly be portrayed (or portray himself) as a fugitive from the machine age, nor had he sacrificed his life and bloom to a search for noise abatement. The Arctic quest appealed to him at a deeper and more visceral level. A rare hint of the inner Amundsen appears in an obscure memoir by one Eva Alvey Richards, an American who lived and worked in northern Alaska as a teacher and nurse. Richards recalled a conversation she had with Amundsen in the kitchen of Maynard-Columbus Hospital in Nome. Amundsen had arrived in Nome in August of 1923, to plan a new transpolar flight in the aftermath of the crash of the JL monoplane. He was still thinking in terms of airplanes at this point.

"Amundsen liked kitchens," Richards wrote. "He was always at home in them. One morning, when he sat in a rocker beside the stove while I kneaded bread into loaves, we spoke of the lure of the Arctic and the grip it takes upon our heart strings—something the explorer [Anthony] Fiala had written had set us on the subject."

> "So," he mused, "does it draw one—like a chilled man seeking warmth of an open fire, as alcoholic spirits attract a man who would forget his enemies, but more as a man, long separated from the homeland, approaches the bountiful board spread in his honor, laden with the many dainties he has not tasted since his youth—so I think it draws one."

"And even as he spoke," Richards remembered, "his voice held the brave and high resolve—the lure—to cross the Pole by plane, and his steady eyes of blue had that light within their depths such as is only vouchsafed to those who have looked long and far over vast and frozen silences."[9]

Amundsen's eyes were variously described as blue or gray. They were warm and genial among friends, calm when facing danger, and cold and piercing in the company of strangers. When Spitsbergen rose on the horizon his eyes surely acquired the kind of light Eva Richards described. "People don't know," he said. "Such beauty...."[10]

Across a choppy sea, a shard of whiteness scraped its jagged edge against an unusually clear and blue sky. The sharp peaks reflected the intense sunlight like the facets of a glittering diamond. It looked as if a star had been struck by a cosmic hammer and a chip of celestial radiance had fallen into the icy waters halfway between Norway and the North Pole. So far as recorded history is concerned, the first humans to be mesmerized by the sight was a Dutch expedition sailing under the leadership of Willem Barents in 1596. Spitsbergen, the name under which Barents's discovery debuted on the world map, is a Dutch word meaning "land of pointy mountains." It is the largest of a group of glacial shards that came to be collectively known as the Spitsbergen Islands. The archipelago was a productive outpost of the international whaling industry in the seventeenth century, until the local waters were fished out. There was no indigenous population; when the whalers moved on, small parties of trappers from Norway and northern Europe moved in. The land of pointy mountains remained largely outside of the world's economy for some two hundred years until coal began to be mined on the island of Spitsbergen around the turn of the twentieth century. The Spitsbergen Islands and a couple of other island groups in the vicinity were awarded to Norway in the diplomatic reshuffling that followed the First World War. All signatories of the peace treaty, the 1920 Treaty of Paris, were granted freedom of access.

The Norwegians called the territory "Svalbard," an old Norse name meaning "land of frozen shores." The modern world has accepted this usage. In 1926, however, English-speaking people commonly confused the issue by continuing to refer to the entire possession as either Spitsbergen or the Spitsbergen Islands. Kings Bay (known today as Ny Ålesund) was a vest-pocket mining town on the west coast of the island of Spitsbergen. It was, relative to Etah, just over thirty miles farther north and could therefore claim the distinction of being the northernmost community of human beings on the planet. Some fifty Norwegians—men, women, and children—lived here year-round. Their business was extracting coal from a mountain named for Count Ferdinand von Zeppelin, the German airship pioneer. Von Zeppelin had visited the island to investigate the possibilities of trans-polar aviation, but suspended the project upon the outbreak of the Great War. He died in 1917. A community of twenty-two wooden houses and a company store nestled at the foot of the mountain named in his honor.

The Arctic islands had at one time been part of a continuous landmass that had fragmented and drifted apart. The topography of the Svalbard Archipelago closely resembles that of the interior of Ellesmere Island: vast ranges of sharply peaked mountains with creased and folded sides. Kings Bay was backdropped by a row of magnificent mountains. Three of them were singled out in the nine-teenth century for the honor of bearing the Norse names for Den-mark, Norway, and Sweden (Dana, Nora, and Svea), and were forever after known as the Tre Kroner or "Three Crowns." The nomenclature is misleading. Actually, there are enough "crowns" piercing the sky for all of the royal heads that remained in Europe. The sun, after six months of hibernation, had emerged on the horizon in March. In late April, the stark countryside still retained its winter pallor. The moun-tains and environs were completely covered with snow and looked like countless white pyramids towering above a white desert. Russell Owen captured a sense of the place—and what might be called a sense of occasion—in one eerily evocative sentence:

> It is silent, calm, majestic, a stronghold of the gods defying the incursions of puny man.[11]

In such a setting would the epic quest for the transpolar flight reach its dramatic climax.

The mining town was laid out like a western frontier town, with buildings on both sides of a main street and telephone poles running straight down the middle of the lane. The snowdrifts reached the roofs of many of the houses; residents had to tunnel through the snow to get in or out. Water was piped down from a lake up in the mountains and then carried by buckets to the houses and stored in barrels. The pipe was heated by means of an electric current to keep it from freezing. The sanitation system was a flock of hundreds of noisy gulls; garbage was piled up in the town dump, and the gulls came and picked it clean. The townspeople nevertheless stayed remarkably healthy; no one ever came down with a cold or flu because it was too cold for germs to thrive. The temperature was ordinarily so low that it was necessary to have a coal-burning stove in every room in the house.

The landscape had been transformed by a construction crew that assembled in November and worked through the months of darkness, using banks of electric lights for illumination. The largest wooden hangar in the world had been built on a stretch of level snow just east of the town, between the mountains and the shore. It was an open-air structure; it didn't have a roof, or a front and back. Only the two side walls had been erected. They were each 350 feet long, one hundred feet high, and stood one hundred feet apart. When the wooden framework was completed, the two sides were draped with green canvas to keep out the wind, and cables were stretched across the top to keep the dirigible from drifting away. The finished structure looked like a magazine rack roughly the size of a prewar apartment house.

Further east, near the shore, a mooring mast towered 110 feet above the snow. A Norwegian flag flew from the pinnacle. The steel mast was anchored in concrete and permafrost, and planted so securely it remains standing today. Then as now it was likely the world's largest sundial. If the workers knew where north was, so long as the sun was out they could tell the time of day from the position of the lengthy shadow. The mast had been raised just four days before the arrival of Amundsen's freighter. The infrastructure remained to be rigged, a system of conduits to enable the dirigible to take on hydrogen, fuel, and water while moored.

A quarter mile due east of the mast stood a large stone monolith. The citizens of Kings Bay had erected the slab to commemorate the "passing" of Amundsen, Ellsworth, and their companions the previous year after having been given up for dead. Amundsen's silhouette was engraved on the slab at about eye level, and his name and those of the flight crews of the Dornier Whales were etched below in the body of the monument. The mast and the "gravestone" overlook the wide bay and the mountains on the opposite shore. In the spring of 1925, the entire bay had been frozen over, and the two flying boats had taken off from the ice. 1926 brought an early thaw. When the *Skaaluren* arrived on April 21, she struck the floes only a mile out from shore and was able to ram her way to within several hundred yards of the wharf, where the ice was packed solid. It was unusually warm, 40°F. Looking over the railing of the ship and across the white slabs and white rubble that extended all the way to the pier, the leaders of the expedition could see, in the distance, the exhilarating sight of the mast and hangar in the foreground of the white pyramids ranging across the horizon. Amundsen smiled. He looked different now from his 1925 self in one respect, having grown what Ellsworth called an "imperial white mustache." The addition made him look like a head of state on holiday. Ellsworth, a shy man, was moved to toss his derby hat in the air and hum, "Give My Regards to Broadway."

Equipment and provisions delivered on a previous supply run were strewn all along the shore, scores of crates, barrels, and sacks piled knee-deep in the snow. This shipment would be augmented by another large cache when the *Skaaluren*'s cargo was unloaded. Amundsen had sailed from Norway with 800 tons of hydrogen in 5,000 gas tanks (enough to inflate the Norge twice over) and twenty tons of gasoline. Before the airship could be summoned from Leningrad, the mast had to be made operational, and the entire stockpile onshore had to be moved one mile inland to the hangar. Uphill. There were sleds to transport the goods, but not enough dogs to pull them. A shaggy team of Norwegian ponies drew one sled, and a tractor towed another, but the machine kept breaking down in the snow. A little railroad ran from the Mt. Zeppelin mine down to the shore to transport coal; the rolling stock consisted of a trolley-sized locomotive and five cars. But the tracks were buried in the snow and would have to be excavated. Until then, the crates had to be man-carried or man-hauled.

Two more Norwegian ships landed within four days of Amundsen and Ellsworth's arrival, the *Hobby*, an icebreaker ferrying more supplies, and the *Heimdal*, a naval vessel. Aboard the latter was an Italian ground crew experienced in airship operations. Also disembarking was a Greenwich Village artist who specialized in polar landscapes. Frank Wilbert Stokes, sixty, had studied at the Pennsylvania Academy of the Fine Arts under the estimable Thomas Eakins; he had accompanied Peary on two Greenland expeditions in the 1890s and had visited Antarctica with a Swedish party at the turn of the century. He would produce a series of paintings based on the events about to transpire at Kings Bay, including two major works: "Return of Commander Byrd and Floyd Bennett from North Pole" and "Departure of Norge for North Pole."

The mission of the *Heimdal* was to assist Amundsen's people in their preparations, maintain law and order on the island during the presence of the two polar expeditions, and stand by for search and rescue in case the Norge ditched at sea on the flight from Russia. While Stokes, a dimunitive man with an inevitable goatee, seated himself on a snowdrift and began sketching, the sailors started in hauling crates off the beach. Other men went to work on the railroad, shoveling through four feet of snow to reach the tracks that ran down to the sea.

Out on the bay the ice began to break up. Two days later, however, the mild weather vanished. It snowed all day and all night on the twenty-seventh, and the snow was followed by a gale. The temperature dropped twenty degrees in six hours; it was down to 20°F on the twenty-eighth and continued to plunge. Roaring, forty-mile-an-hour winds shook the houses, made the canvas sheets billow and thump on the hangar, and brought an end to all outdoor work. The wind drove the ice back into the bay. The *Knut Skaaluren* had departed for Norway with the falling snow, but the two remaining ships, the *Hobby* and the *Heimdal*, had to put out to sea at night to avoid being battered by the swiftly moving floes.

A long and deep trench had finally been dug in the snowdrifts to expose the railroad tracks. Unfortunately, the Evil Spirit of the North caused it to be completely filled in again. On the twenty-ninth, a Thursday, a wireless message was sent to Leningrad informing Nobile that preparations had been delayed. The *Norge* was not expected to leave Russia now before Sunday, the second of May. At King's Bay that Thursday a faint plume of rising smoke from the approaching American steamship could be seen for four hours before the *Chantier* herself rose above the horizon. Sailors, members of the ground crew, and the miners deployed to help them paused from time to time as they shoveled snow or lifted crates, and followed the drift of the plume.

At 2:00 p.m., the *Chantier* finally steamed into view, and for the moment all work ceased. Amundsen, on skis, reportedly watched the smoking object on the horizon from the top of the hill overlooking the bay.[12] Fifteen years earlier, a party of Scott's men were startled at the sight of a ship in the Bay of Whales in West Antarctica. They had read Nansen's book, *Farthest North*, and from the illustrations had recognized it as Nansen's ship, the *Fram*. It was common knowledge that Amundsen had obtained the *Fram* and was on his way to the Antarctic. "Curses loud and deep were heard everywhere," one of the observers wrote.[13]

Below, the *Heimdal* had tied up alongside the dock; she had been coaling since early morning. The temperature had nosedived to minus 4°F at 6:00 a.m., when the circling sun was in the east. The bay was covered with cakes and floes of ice and frozen again in various spots. Amundsen said nothing, his face as impassive as the image of himself engraved in the stone slab. At length, he turned and glided back to the mining compound where he was billeted.

The first person Byrd encountered when he set foot on the snow was Russell Owen of the *New York Times*, who raised a camera, stepped back and asked for "Just one picture." That was the warmest welcome he received. The expressions on the faces of the Norwegians working in the vicinity were as chilly as the climate. A young bench player on the Amundsen-Ellsworth-Nobile Expedition summarized the prevailing mood: "We resent this foreign ship coming here to our own country to snatch the prize which we feel belongs to Captain Amundsen alone. We of his party are loyal to him to the point of worship, and any one of us would lay down his life without question for one of the greatest of all living explorers." The writer, a twenty-seven-year-old aviator, had briefly visited Spitsbergen a year earlier as a member of the Amundsen rescue mission. His name was Bernt Balchen.

The *Chantier* had obtained permission from the captain of the *Heimdal* to tie up just outside of the gunboat as she continued to coal.

Byrd had come ashore with a small party including Bennett; Dr. O'Brien; Doc Kinkade, the Wright Aero engineer; and Leo Peterson, an aircraft mechanic. The ice conditions in the bay had upset Byrd's plans as much as the gunboat. He had expected to be able to take off on skis from a long frozen surface the way Amundsen and Ellsworth had in 1925. To reckon with the early spring, he would have to find a landing field ashore. He also wanted to find Amundsen.

Balchen watched Byrd crunching through the snow; the explorer made a striking impression. "He is in navy uniform, every button of his blue overcoat carefully fastened, the bottoms of his trouser legs stuffed into sturdy buckled galoshes," Balchen wrote. "His face is clean-shaven and very handsome, with small, regular features and a firm mouth. He reminds me at first of a young high-school principal, but there is an unquestioned air of authority as well as competence about him."

Meanwhile, in Balchen's words, the workers "make way in sullen silence." Clipped phrases are muttered in Norwegian as the Americans pass by. Byrd's eyes take in every detail, from the hangar to the mooring mast, "but if he is aware of tension," Balchen observed, "he shows no sign."

Amundsen and Ellsworth felt that they should have the first shot at the transpolar flight.[14] After all, they had organized for 1926 months before Byrd had put an expedition together. They had nothing against Byrd. It wasn't personal; it was, it may be said, strictly business. Their airship adventure was initially budgeted at $300,000. It would wind up costing roughly half a million. Ellsworth had contributed $125,000 of the operating capital; the remainder had been advanced by the Aero Club of Norway. He and Amundsen had assured the Aero Club that the expedition would at least break even by generating successful media products—books, lectures, motion pictures, etc. But Byrd was cutting into their market share. He was competing with them for the public's attention, and attention translates into book sales and box office.

Furthermore, if Byrd was forced down on the Polar Sea, Amundsen, Ellsworth, and Nobile would be morally bound to rescue him. The window of opportunity for Arctic flying was rapidly closing. By late May, the stratus clouds would start to build and fog would obscure the surface. Byrd himself felt it was "highly dangerous" to fly in the region after May 15, due to fog.[15] If the *Norge* had to ascend in search of the *Josephine Ford* and the search wasn't concluded quickly, its transpolar flight would have to be postponed until 1927. Amundsen would have to wait one more year to see the horizons that attracted him like campfire, liquor, and home attracted, respectively, the shivering man, the drunkard, and the exile.

He and Ellsworth were in camp having dinner when Byrd strode through the mining town, looking for them. They connected later and had a meeting in the quarters Amundsen and Ellsworth shared, a small house set slightly back of the main street. Courtesies were exchanged on both sides, and some perfunctory shoptalk. "We are not competitors," Amundsen told Byrd. "We are collaborators. We are partners in this venture together."[16] The atmosphere remained strained.

Byrd then paid a call on the commanding officer of the *Heimdal*, a Captain Tank-Nielsen. Amundsen and Ellsworth accompanied him. Byrd asked the captain when the *Chantier* might have access to the dock to land his airplanes. In four or five days, Tank-Nielsen said, when the coaling would be completed. Byrd had supervised numerous coalings as a junior officer and had probably anticipated the answer before it was given. He firmly and politely requested that the *Heimdal* relinquish the dock at night, after the coaling crew knocked off for the day. Tank-Nielsen refused. The *Heimdal* was much smaller than the *Chantier*, he said, and might incur serious damage if she had to spend another night dodging the ice floes. In any event, the gunboat had to be ready and able to assist the *Norge*; those were Tank-Nielsen's orders. He could not jeopardize his mission to accommodate the Americans.

Byrd's men had located a potential landing strip on the outskirts of town near the Amundsen hangar, a sloping tract of snow about a mile wide and a mile and a half long. Byrd next went to see the director of the Kings Bay Coal Company, a Mr. Smithmeyer, who readily granted permission to use the field. Smithmeyer then announced that the *Chantier* would have to move out from alongside the *Heimdal* to enable a Norwegian whaler to go alongside and coal. At about the same time, the Pathé cameramen attached to the Byrd expedition ran afoul of the local constabulary. A local edict prohibited outsiders from photographing anything on shore within three miles of Kings Bay. This ordinance, enacted to protect the Amundsen media from being scooped, would be relaxed in a few days when Byrd and Amundsen agreed to restrict the rival cameramen to footage of their own separate expeditions.

"They deny us dock, deny movie, make us move out in stream. The Viking valor," Byrd wrote in his diary. That night, with the sun and moon facing one another across the bowl of sky, the *Chantier* lay anchored some 300 yards off Kings Bay. The weather had turned milder again, heralding the approach of summer and rising fog over the Polar Sea. Byrd convened his staff and put an idea on the table, a way of getting the planes ashore. The proposal was based on an expedient adopted at Etah in 1925. Bennett, who had participated in the 1925 operation, thought it was too risky. Noville thought it was too risky. Isaksen, the ice pilot, was opposed.

Byrd was in command. He was by nature a cautious, conservative man. His father-in-law, Boston Brahmin Joseph Blanchard Ames, had always said, "Never buy on a margin," and Byrd had always agreed.[17]

His stock market investments were almost invariably in blue chips, he speculated only occasionally. But he knew when it was time to take a risk.

He figured it was time.

≋ 21 ≋

CROSSING
THE DELAWARE

*These Americans are not to be discouraged by any new
difficulty…. This is the pioneer spirit of America that
I have heard so much about; it is the quality that will
open up the whole Arctic to air commerce some day.*

Bernt Balchen[1]

Two lifeboats were hoisted over the rail of the *Chantier*,
lowered into the water, and lashed together side by side.
Next, two more boats were lowered and lashed together the
same way. One pair of lifeboats was drawn up behind the other. The
two pairs were now yoked together, like a team of four horses
harnessed to pull a stagecoach. The object of this exercise, however,
wasn't to tow anything.

Long planks of wood were then passed over the side of the
Chantier and placed across the gunwales of the joined lifeboats. Men
worked with hammer and nails as thick snowflakes started to fall;
they worked through the night and into the wee hours. When they
were finished, a large raft had been constructed. The wooden platform
was only about six feet long and six feet wide; there was room for a

couple of guys to get in the prow of each of the supporting lifeboats up front and row, and men could sit and row at the stern of each of the two supporting lifeboats in the rear.

While the raft was being built, another team was dispatched to shore in a dinghy that had been equipped with an outboard motor. Their job was to prepare a makeshift landing ramp. With pickaxes, they chopped away at the thick ice that had accumulated along the beach and hewed out an incline that sloped down to the sea. By 4:00 a.m., the raft had been built and 300 yards away the ice ramp had been prepared. The steam winch was swiveled into position over the forward hold of the *Chantier*, and the wingless fuselage of the *Oriole* was raised out of the hold, swung over the side, and lowered onto the raft. The crew had named the yellow biplane the *Richard III*, in honor of Byrd's son; Captain Brennan called it the *Canary Bird*.

Snow continued to descend. It began to sleet, and in the snow and sleet, it became difficult to make out objects more than fifteen feet away. The closest objects were the cakes of ice in Kings Bay, which started to drift with the wind and the tide. Some of those cakes were the size of a pitcher's mound in a major-league ballpark and could crush the raft if they picked up velocity. The *Oriole* was lashed to the platform and the lashings made fast. Robb Oertel was in charge. With rowers in position and Isaksen aboard to find a path through the ice, Oertel gave the order; oars were lowered, and the small plane was ferried across the bay. Early risers among the Norwegian workers and sailors watched with curiosity as the yellow fuselage materialized out of the falling snow. The landing was completed by 6:00 a.m.

The night's work, to Byrd, was something on the order of an experiment or dress rehearsal. The biplane was expendable; if the *Oriole* were lost, the cameramen would be out of luck, but the expedition would proceed. Watching from the rail of the *Chantier* as Oertel and his crew parted the ice floes, Byrd was willing to bet the farm that the *Josephine Ford* could be rafted to shore with equal success.

Working in the cold all night long, the men and their leaders needed rest. The work crews were recalled to the *Chantier*; the ship's company caught a few hours' sleep and was roused at noon. After lunch, the fuselage of the Fokker was raised from the forward hold. Floyd Bennett supervised the operation. Bennett was actually raised *with* the plane. To make sure nothing went wrong, he clung to the nose of the Fokker, when, with a rumble of gears and chains, the aircraft was slowly hauled out of the darkness. Whenever the dangling plane swung too close to the wall of the hold or spun out of alignment with the opening high above, Bennett averted collisions with a swift and timely kick. Meanwhile, he held on for dear life, like movie star Harold Lloyd in one of his daredevil comedies. He was almost crushed several times.

The fuselage was lowered to the raft in a blinding snowstorm. The wind had picked up, blowing drift ice into the bay. The lane Oertel's crew had opened between the ice cakes now began to close. An enormous slab of whiteness with the general contour of a miniature Arctic island came hurtling down on the raft and was repelled with only seconds to spare by the men who had lashed the aircraft securely in place on the wooden platform. The wing of the trimotor had just been raised from the hold and was suspended over the deck, one of the largest airfoils and one of the most gorgeous pieces of woodwork ever brought to the eastern Arctic. Snowflakes settled on the triumphant FOK and KER emblazoned on either end. "If anything slips," Byrd muttered, "the expedition comes to an end right now."[2]

He and Bennett had discussed ferrying the wing and fuselage separately and assembling the Fokker on shore. That option was rejected; the men would have had to build scaffolding in the snow to raise the wing up, and the more the sixty-three-foot airfoil was manhandled, the more chance there was of an accident. The *Josephine Ford* would be assembled at sea. But there were four bolts that held the wing in place on the fuselage. To fasten the bolts, the wing had to be lined up just so, but it was not possible to do this in a stiff wind. The only thing that made sense under the circumstances was to lash the wing to the deck of the *Chantier* and wait for the wind to die down.

The crew had worked straight through the afternoon and evening of Friday, April 30. A twenty-knot wind was blowing when Byrd went to sleep. By morning the entire area between the *Chantier* and shore was covered with ice. There was a slight swell as the tide level gently rose and fell. As a result, the ice was broken into vast jigsaw pieces held loosely in place across the surface of the bay. It looked "as if," Byrd said, "an agile man might walk ashore without getting his feet wet."[3] It was still windy at 6:00 a.m. Two hours later, the air was calm and the ice fairly stationary. "Decided to take chance and put wing on fuselage and get ashore somehow," he wrote in his diary.

> We seem to have either no ice and wind or no wind and ice. The last of course is very dangerous. We may be licked but don't want to be licked waiting around and doing nothing.

The raft was positioned with the nose of the Fokker facing the hull of the *Chantier*. The steam crane, puffing smoke, lowered the wing down over the side of the ship and within half an hour it was bolted in place. The Norwegians meanwhile contacted the *Chantier* by radio and warned that it was foolish to try to land the aircraft through the heavy ice that had accumulated overnight. If the tide ran or the winds rose or a squall suddenly blew up, as often happens in the far North, the floes would be set in motion; the ice would jam up against the raft and not only smash it to pieces but sweep the men aboard it out to sea, and it would be impossible to retrieve them. Whether the warning came from a military or civilian authority is not clear. In any event, the *Hobby*, the Amundsen supply ship, was placed at the disposal of the Byrd expedition. The *Hobby* circled the *Chantier*, to loosen up the ice near the starting point.

Captain Homm, the commanding officer of the *Hobby*, joined Isaksen in the dinghy. With a couple of men standing and rowing, they pressed forward, the two Norwegians using poles to separate the cakes of ice. Byrd stood on the prow of the raft, facing the Fokker and a squad of oarsmen who had arranged themselves on either side of it like galley slaves. The airplane rested on its wheels, its blunt nose towering high over Byrd's head. The wing engines were still in the hold of the *Chantier*, along with the tail assembly. The center engine was in place, but it was covered with canvas and the propeller had not been installed. Some dozen men sat in the lifeboats, below the level of the platform, balancing the oars. Others stood beside Byrd, bearing boat hooks and pickaxes to fend off the ice. They looked more like the two sides of a touch football game than an expedition. Some wore pea jackets, others lumberjack shirts, college sweaters, or overcoats with fur collars. Headgear ranged from sailor hats to navy watch caps to fur-lined hats with fold-down earflaps to colorful wool toppers that would be highly fashionable for tobogganing. Although no two were dressed alike, to a man they shared a common attitude. "They were fighting mad by this time," Byrd said, "ready to carry the plane ashore on their backs. This had become more than an expedition. It was a patriotic American undertaking."[4]

He gave the signal; the rowers began to stroke, and the makeshift pontoon floated out behind the dinghy.

Across Kings Bay, the crew of the *Heimdal* began to gather on deck and many among Amundsen's supply-movers assembled on the beach to follow the progress of the distant flotilla. The Norwegians had bitter knowledge of the violence wreaked when ice, wind, and tide combine. What was wrong with these crazy people from the West? they thought. How many of them have ever seen an iceberg or glacier before? They are overreaching themselves. We told them they were heading for disaster. Quickly word began to spread from the beach all the way up to the mining village that the Americans were coming across.

A dozen icebergs stood between the *Chantier* and shore, blocks of ice five and six feet above the surface of the water, many directly in the path of the raft. Byrd acted as steersman, calling out instructions. He would have to edit himself in the thick of battle. If he called, for example, "Give way port!" at least one of the landlubbers aboard who didn't know port from starboard would wind up rowing *against* the men who understood the command. A third assistant engineer from Washington, D.C., who had never pulled an oar before in his life, energetically rowed backward for almost all of the three hundred yards.

The men with picks and boat hooks shoved the bergs away and fought off the floes grinding against the raft. Meanwhile, Isaksen and Homm had leaped from the dinghy and were hopping from floe to floe to pry open a passage. The ice was still relatively quiescent.

The most furious and ominous moments of life are also moments of heightened awareness. During these experiences we often act, observe ourselves in action, and think about what's going on—all at the same time. While commanding the oarsmen, Richard Byrd's observing self kept thinking of Washington crossing the Delaware. With about a hundred yards to go, he had to steer between two huge icebergs each larger than the raft and plane put together. The three Pathé movie men shouted encouragement. Since for the moment they were not allowed to work on the island, they had erected their tripods on a large ice floe grounded just offshore. Kings Bay residents had swarmed down the hill on skis, and by now a sizable crowd had massed along the beach. "We hold our breath," wrote Bernt Balchen, who stood among them.

"An iceberg is an interesting thing to look at and examine when it is not in your way," Byrd would tell his lecture audiences. When you get close to one, he explained,

> it assumes an air of almost animate malevolence. It moves and the water swishes and hisses up and down its sides. Under the water it is so transparent at times as to be almost invisible, except where the water has melted its surface into a series of cups, the shadowy edges of which form eyes that seem to stare up threateningly.[5]

The raft came close enough to the remaining bergs for Byrd to see all at once the hollows in the substructure of each. They reached the ice ramp just as the floes started to move. Quickly, the men rigged a block and tackle, and in a matter of minutes the Fokker was hauled on shore. The Norwegians were so caught up in the drama that when the plane settled safely in the snow they erupted with a spontaneous cheer. Floyd Bennett, one of the boat-hook men during the crossing, put it this way: "The crew of the *Heimdal* gave us three cheers. We needed them."[6]

The infrastructure of the mooring mast became operational the same day the *Josephine Ford* was landed. Amundsen wired Leningrad, informing Nobile that Spitsbergen was ready to receive the *Norge*. Across the Polar Sea, the Detroit Arctic Expedition was also completing its preparations. Nothing had been heard from Wilkins and Eielson since they departed Fairbanks on April 15. Byrd wrote in his diary on the twenty-eighth, "Got radio message that Wilkins was 13 days overdue. Hope he is o.k." Finally, on the twenty-ninth, the outside world learned that the Australian had been snowbound at Point Barrow and his radio had failed. When word reached the *Chantier*, Byrd wrote, "Got radio that Wilkins is OK at Point Barrow. Hurrah!" The fliers returned safely to Fairbanks on the thirtieth. They had stockpiled enough fuel in the north to support a reconnaissance of the unexplored area.

Three expeditions were now moving towards the starting line. At Kings Bay, the Americans continued running the raft and motor dinghy between the *Chantier* and shore. Three aircraft engines were ferried through the gauntlet of floating ice, two to be installed on the wings of the *Josephine Ford*, one in the nose of the *Richard III*, along with hundreds of gallons of gasoline, scores of cans of motor oil, the rudder of the Fokker, the wings of the *Oriole*, and countless other pieces of heavy equipment. Byrd's navigation instruments came across cradled protectively in the laps of the men entrusted with them. Whenever the pontoon reached the ice ramp, a rope would be slung, in turn, around each crate or gasoline drum; men would grab hold, tug-of-war style, and with a "Heave ho!," yank the container up onto the beach. Then someone else would haul the crate or lug the barrel over to where the planes were being assembled. He would have to plow through snow waist-deep to get there and as often as not ended up toppling into a drift under the sheer weight of the load he carried.

The Fokker had reached shore on the afternoon of May 1. The Byrd party worked all night, straight through to 4:00 a.m. the following morning. They worked with a laughing, boisterous team spirit, the kind of fellow feeling from which a maximum effort flows naturally. Charles F. "Chips" Gould, thirty, a tall, lanky ship's carpenter who would winter over in Antarctica with Byrd, built a shed made of Celotex, an insulating and soundproofing material donated by a Chicago manufacturer. Two gasoline-burning stoves were set up inside the hut. Food was sent over from the *Chantier*, and the expedition cooks started serving hot coffee, sandwiches, and beans. Byrd kept asking the men if they had slept and suggested they get some rest, but no one wanted to quit.

"If they did not smile," wrote Owen of the *Times*, "they would be the toughest looking crowd that ever walked ashore, for they haven't done a thing but work since their arrival." Geisler, the hulking weightlifter who vowed not to shave until the trimotor reached the Pole, stood out among the non-stop Americans not only for his vigor but also for a thick black beard that startled and terrified the children of the mining colony. The example of the Byrd expedition roused the Amundsen-Ellsworth expedition. The Norwegians once more started excavating the railroad tracks out from under mounds of snow. The crew of the *Heimdal*, having finished coaling, came ashore, picked up shovels, and pitched in. The Italian airship men began lugging supplies off the beach.

On the evening of the second, Amundsen and Ellsworth invited Byrd to dinner in the mess hall erected at their camp. Within six or eight weeks, the snow would melt and the Arctic would briefly bloom; at the moment, the only growing things with which the tables could be decorated were onions sprouting in small tumblers of water. Byrd wore his navy blues, Amundsen a wool suit, and Ellsworth a tweed sports jacket. Dr. O'Brien, Cyclone Haines, and Robb Oertel accompanied Byrd. After dinner, the entire group hiked across the snow to the beachfront area where a crew led by Bennett, Kinkaid, and Peterson were working on the various systems of the *Josephine Ford*.

The visitors were shown into the flight cabin. Two rifles and two shotguns were slung in racks on the walls, along with cameras, plates, and reels of film. Ellsworth, who had been studying navigation, was attracted by the sun compass and bubble sextant secured on the wall above the navigator's table. He and Amundsen were less impressed with the survival gear. Amundsen thought Byrd and Bennett's furs were too heavy. Experienced sledgers knew that the greatest risk the ice traveler runs is becoming overheated. ("My most miserable hours in the far north," said Donald B. MacMillan, "have not been encountering low temperatures ... but in the shelter of a tight snow house ... when with shivering body and chattering teeth I attempted sleep with underclothes reeking wet with perspiration.")[7]

Amundsen also felt that the mukluks stored in the *Josephine Ford* were not *warm enough* for a trek across the Polar Sea. He recommended a unique pair of galoshes to wear over the mukluks. These were canvas overshoes lined with sennegrass, a natural insulating material that grows in northern Norway and which the Lapps, the native people of Scandinavia, stuff inside their footgear. Amundsen had two pairs of these overshoes brought down from his camp for Byrd and Bennett.

The most problematic component of the survival outfit was the sledge the aviators would have to pile their provisions on and manhaul across the ice if forced down. Byrd had had it specially built in Alaska; it was lightweight but not durable enough, in Amundsen's estimation, to drag across a series of fifteen-foot pressure ridges.

The chief drawback of a dirigible was its fragility. For this reason, an airship could not be brought out of its hangar when a stiff wind was blowing, particularly a crosswind. When gliding through the hangar door, a sudden gust might force the ship up against the doorframe and fracture the skeletal structure that maintained its cylindrical shape. The *Norge* was scheduled to depart from Gatchina at noon on the second of May, but due to strong winds Nobile postponed the departure to the third. On that day, however, the Leningrad district was struck by a snowstorm and a thirty-mile-an-hour gale. Citizens of the district could not recall such a long winter. The bitter, icy winds lasted through the fourth.

In England, a general strike went into effect at 12:01 a.m. on May 4. When Grettir Algarsson and Frank Worsley heard the chimes at midnight, they knew the economic shutdown meant that it was now impossible for them to get underway. They would have gotten off to such a late start anyway that even had they remained in the race the British expedition had little chance of influencing the outcome.

While the *Norge* waited out the winds, the Byrd Expedition grappled with the problems of cold-weather taxiing and takeoffs. The temperature at Kings Bay was now falling to an overnight low of minus 6°F; the mid-day high ranged from about 14° to 19°F. Dr. O'Brien was now routinely treating members of the ground crew for frostbite. The body parts most commonly affected were hands and feet. Noville was treated for a frostbitten nose. (In Antarctica, in the following decade, an even more sensitive part of Rex's anatomy would be nipped.) Some of Byrd's colleagues in the Navy Department doubted whether the engines would start in these conditions, but the expedition had prepared for zero-degree operations long before it arrived at latitude 78°55′ N. Hoods had been made for each motor from sheets of eight-ounce, fireproof canvas. They basically resembled king-sized versions of Ku Klux Klan headgear and fit snugly around the engines; from the bottom of each hood, a long, narrow duct trailed down within a couple of feet of the ground. The duct was a folded piece of canvas with a twelve-inch diameter. Below the mouth of each duct was placed a gasoline-burning stove. The stoves were fitted with blowtorch jets, but these blowtorches didn't project the flame horizontally like that of a welder's tool. They projected the flame vertically upward. The heated air was carried through the duct and the hoods. It circulated around the engines and warmed the oil tanks and oil lines mounted within the engine nacelles.

The oil was preheated by first clearing snow from a small patch of ground, breaking up wood from the packing crates, and building a fire. Cans of motor oil were arranged in a circle around the fire; each can was turned every few minutes to make sure the entire contents were heated. The oil tanks were filled with warm oil, and the engines easily started fifteen minutes after the blowtorches were ignited. Noville had first experimented with these techniques in 1924, when he had been dispatched to Labrador to assist the army's round-the-world fliers. Unfortunately, neither Byrd nor any of his men had equivalent experience in ski flying.

The Curtiss Company had made the skis (and propellers) for the *Josephine Ford*, but there was no database in the United States to help them determine how large the skis should be. Three sets were made, based more or less on educated guesswork. The largest and strongest set was installed on the Fokker shortly after she was landed on the beach at Kings Bay. So far as anyone knew, no plane the size of the *Josephine Ford* had ever been flown on skis before. The engines were started for the first time on May 3, and the plan was to taxi the trimotor half a mile up the hill and then turn around and take off down the hill for a test flight. The ship had been sitting on the skis for two days; under the weight of the aircraft, the skis had sunk into the loose snow. When Byrd, in the pilot's seat, kicked in the throttle, one ski stuck, and the airplane swerved around in a semicircle. With the motors still running, Mike Brennan and Tom Mulroy bent into the prop wash and freed the problem ski from the snow furrow in which it was embedded by using planks of wood as levers.

Byrd made a couple of sharp turns and began to taxi. An experienced ski pilot will *avoid* sharp turns because this puts more torque on the landing gear than the mechanism is designed to handle. He turned sharply again to start the takeoff run, but the plane stopped short. The right ski had struck a snowdrift and split in two, and the fitting that held the landing gear in place on the right side had been ripped loose of the fuselage. "If no load has cracked ski," Byrd wrote in his diary, "what will full load do?"

To change the skis, the four-ton aircraft had to be jacked up off the snow. The jacks could not be placed on deep snow because they would sink down. The men had to shovel through the snow, then stand empty gasoline drums on the cleared spaces and mount the jacks on the drums. If a stiff wind blew while the airplane was mounted on the jacks, it could have toppled the ship, smashed the wing and ended the expedition. On the fourth, Floyd Bennett took the controls for another attempted test flight. His co-pilot was Marine aviator Alton Parker. Noville and Peterson were in the seatless cabin, clutching the available handholds.

In order to develop lift and fly, an airplane has to build up a certain amount of velocity on the takeoff run. Loose, sticky snow can slow a ski plane down to the point that it fails to reach its climb speed. The snow has to be tamped down to make the surface hard enough to enable the plane to accelerate rapidly enough. This tip was more than likely passed along by Bernt Balchen, who had interested himself in the efforts of the Americans. Balchen was an accomplished skier and ski pilot and had apparently drawn criticism from his own camp for giving aid and comfort to the competition. Byrd had the distinct impression that while Amundsen "professes great friendship," he nevertheless gave Lieutenant Balchen "orders not to come near us again."[8]

Clearing a runway was the next grueling challenge. "When you consider that a man without snowshoes would sink in this snow almost to his hips, you can appreciate what we were up against," said Jon Reed. The implements available were shovels and stomping feet, but the crew was gung ho. While packing down the snow, however, Byrd and his men—the commander had wielded a shovel right alongside his volunteers—had carelessly dumped loads of snow just to the left of the runway. Bennett prepared to apply right rudder to avoid the mound, but when he pushed the throttles forward, the left ski stuck and the plane swerved left instead of right and buried its nose in the snow bank. The left ski, one landing gear strut, and the propeller on the center engine were damaged and had to be replaced.

The third and last set of skis was strengthened before another takeoff was attempted. This pair was over nine feet long and a bit under two feet wide; the ends of each ski were bent upwards at a five-degree angle. One way to reinforce them would have been to sandwich another nine-foot length of bowed wood right on top of each blade. But there were no trees on Spitsbergen and no lumber yards. The expedition was left to its own considerable resources. Long planks of wood about one-third as wide as the new skis were salvaged from the two sets of broken skis. They were placed end to end down the middle of the new skis, reinforcing the center line.

There was one more stockpile of lumber: the oars of the lifeboats. Two pairs of oars were planed down and steamed to the curvature of the skis. They were placed on either side of the column of planks that braced the center. The oars were not as long as the skis, but they effectively reinforced the outer and inner edges.

The center and peripheral supports were bolted solidly in place. The bottom of each ski was then treated with a mixture of pine tar and resin to reduce friction and assure a smoother glide; the solution was burned into the wood with a blowtorch. This was a Norwegian practice recommended by Balchen. Byrd wrote in his diary, "Amundsen got after Balchen again."

At 6:00 p.m. on May 5, a dreary, overcast day, Bennett and Parker resumed their places in the cockpit. Bennett gave her the gun. As Byrd and his men watched with baited breath, the trimotor slid down the slope, picking up momentum. The miners and their families and the Amundsen expedition were having dinner. Hearing the Whirlwind engines develop full power, Amundsen, Ellsworth, and practically all of Kings Bay burst out of doors in time to see the *Josephine Ford* lift off the snow and ascend to the height of the low-lying clouds. "Off at last!" Bennett thought. "What a glorious sensation to be in the air after all that work." He wished "that the ship was loaded and headed for the North Pole."⁹

Nunatuks are mountain peaks that protrude through the surface of a glacier and look like tiny islets in a sea of ice and snow. For an uneventful ninety minutes, the *Josephine Ford* circled out over these picturesque features in the highlands beyond Kings Bay and then looped back over the beach again. Suddenly, a loud and sustained vibration shook the whole plane. Parker, the co-pilot, wanted to land and reached to throttle the engines. Bennett had had a similar experience in his flying career and stopped him. The radio set that had been installed in the cabin was powered by a small generator mounted on the outside of the aircraft near the cockpit. The bolts anchoring the device to the fuselage had torn loose. Bennett glanced through the windshield in time to see part of the generator topple off the fuselage.

The flight continued for another hour without incident. Meanwhile, Byrd kept a close eye on the plane while it buzzed around the sky and waited impatiently for Bennett to reappear whenever he slipped behind the pyramidal peaks. He was particularly apprehensive when Bennett made his landing approach. The volunteers gathered on the edge of the runway, knowing that this was the moment of truth, the first landing of a big transport aircraft on skis. The trimotor descended closer and closer to the surface. Would the skis hold up? Bennett raised the nose, the runners gently caressed the snow and easily supported the weight of the ship as she slid along the hard-packed strip and came to a dignified halt. The ground crew rushed to congratulate the flight crew when they jumped down to the snow. Byrd, who rarely let his feelings show, shook Bennett's hand, smiling openly with undisguised relief.

The *Norge* finally departed Soviet Russia at 9:40 a.m. on May 5, eight hours and twenty minutes before the *Josephine Ford*'s successful test flight. The hangar in which she sat out the storm faced north. A twenty-mile-an-hour headwind was blowing across the field that morning, and a thirty-mile-an-hour headwind was expected on the flight path to her next destination. So long as it was not a crosswind, Nobile decided to start anyway. He had to reach Spitsbergen before the brief window of clear skies over the Polar Sea closed for the season. He flew 700 miles due north over forests blanketed with snow, across frozen rivers and lakes, and on above the tree line to the edge of Europe where northernmost Russia, Finland, and Norway meet. A mooring mast had been prepared for him at Vadsø, Norway, on the tip of a peninsula poking out into the Barents Sea. The *Norge* crossed the Arctic Circle en route to this refueling station. At the moment of crossing, the temperature in the control car was 14°F. The drinking water in the jug passed around among the shivering crew members had turned to ice.

On the sixth of May, George Wilkins and Carl Ben Eielson opened the single-engine of the airplane that had been christened the *Alaskan* and trundled down the dirt runway at Fairbanks. They were using wheels, not skis, and had satisfied themselves that they could defy the experts and put the machine down on snow. Some thirty-five hundred gallons of gasoline had been cached at Point Barrow. On this flight, they would land only to refuel and then take off for the unexplored area of the Polar Sea. As the airplane picked up speed, however, one of the wheels struck a mound of soft earth and the plane flipped halfway over on one side. The occupants were unharmed, but the *Alaskan* was wrecked. Wilkins had one airplane left.

At about 4:00 a.m. on May 7, the *Heimdal* blew a siren to rouse the Amundsen expedition. A radiogram had been received from Nobile; the *Norge* was on her way. The ground crew assembled to receive the airship. It had snowed all night, and the sky remained overcast. Within two hours of the alarm, a dark dot was spotted against the clouds. For a while, it looked as if a child's balloon was approaching the island. Gradually, a large gray football with tail fins magnified out of the sky. A dirigible flies so slowly that observers on the ground could avert their glance for a few moments and, on looking up again, find that the ship was in almost the exact same spot. Sunlight began pushing through the clouds. At length, the *Norge* circled lazily to start her descent. She glided around the natural amphitheater framed by the mountains, and when the sunlight struck her, there was an X-ray effect. Her keel and the rib cage attached to it became visible through the outer envelope. "It was a beautiful airship," said Pete Demas. "We had no doubts that after traveling all the way from Rome to Spitsbergen, that it could not make the transpolar trip."[10]

Some essential maintenance, however, was necessary before she attempted the historic flight. A crankshaft had broken on one of the engines, and the rudder was slightly damaged in transit. A new motor and rudder would be installed before the *Norge* left Kings Bay. Her ballast tanks were intentionally emptied while she was being hauled to the ground—the water and antifreeze solution that had been contained in those tanks drenching the Italians and Norwegians who had thrown themselves on her lowered ropes. Additional fuel would be carried as ballast on the transpolar flight, and it had to be pumped aboard. The gas bags had to be topped off with hydrogen, and all of the survival gear had to be loaded. The airship was safely in her green hangar by 7:00 a.m. but could proceed no further until the overhaul was completed.

Two days had been lost at the outset of her journey, when Nobile was forced to wait for the winds to die down at Rome. Another day or two was consumed by the blizzard that battered Kings Bay on April 28. By the time the Amundsen expedition dug itself out of the snow and completed its preparations, the weather had changed at Leningrad, and the ship was delayed an additional three days. Had any of these delays not occurred, polar history would have been substantially altered.

The test flight of the *Josephine Ford* had confirmed two propositions: First, by virtue of the innovative, cold-weather start-up techniques, the engines would retain their normal operating temperature in flight and the oil would not congeal. Second, the airplane would perform better in the High Arctic than she did in New York. Aircraft are designed to perform in an ocean of air. When the atmospheric conditions change, the performance changes. One of the determining factors is the density of the atmosphere. Cold air is more dense than hot air. The raw, biting air at the edge of the Polar Sea contains more air molecules per cubic foot than the warmer layer of atmosphere over Mineola. Because, in the High Arctic, more molecules of air are pushing against the wing and propeller, more lift is developed, and because more air is available to support combustion, the engines generate more power and the plane can fly further on an equivalent amount of gasoline.

The enhanced performance inspired Byrd to revise his flight plan. The wisdom of advancing a base to Peary Land was beginning to seem questionable. He would have to land and take off repeatedly on a field of snow that had not been packed down by fifty volunteers. If the skis cracked during any of these maneuvers, skilled craftsmen and the facilities of the *Chantier* would not be available to repair the damage. His initial, conservative plan of exploring in small stages would more than likely leave him and Bennett stranded at Cape Morris Jesup. The alternative was to cover as much territory as possible in one long-distance flight. It was roughly 1,630 miles from Kings Bay to Peary Land to the North Pole and back to Spitsbergen. Byrd decided to load up the airplane with as much fuel as she could lift off the snow and attempt to complete the entire loop non-stop. But to win the international competition, he would fly the course in reserve order and head for the Pole first.

On the evening of May 7, Byrd told Amundsen and Ellsworth that he was taking off the next day and flying straight to the Pole. According to Ellsworth, "Amundsen fairly bored him with his eyes as he answered, 'That is all right with us.'"[11] Amundsen's pale eyes could turn as cold as the glaciers and his expression as severe as a northern winter.

He and Ellsworth wished Byrd luck.

Later, Nobile, a small, angular, excitable man in a fascist uniform, surmised what was going on. He rushed in to see Amundsen and told him he could have the *Norge* ready to launch in six hours. The weather was improving at Spitsbergen, but reports from Alaska were as yet unfavorable. Amundsen raised a hand, as if to tell Nobile to relax. "This is not a race," he said. "We will wait for our weather."[12]

On the eighth of May, a Saturday, Wilkins and Major Lanphier departed Fairbanks in the *Detroiter*, their Fokker trimotor, for Point Barrow and the Polar Sea. At 12:30 p.m. that day, Byrd and Bennett sat in the cockpit of the *Josephine Ford*. They were so bundled up they looked twice their normal size. Both wore hooded, knee-length, bell-shaped parkas made of reindeer skin. The skins had a pinto texture with patches of light and dark brown on a cream background. The hoods were augmented with a soft and fluffy wreath of wolf fur which encircled their faces. Under the hoods, they wore leather, fur-lined, military-style flying helmets. Byrd had on polar bear pants, Bennett reindeer. Their knee-high mukluks were made of sealskin soles and reindeer uppers lined with sheepskin. They each had two pairs of gloves available, one made of sealskin and one deerskin. They wore one pair—the other was stored in the back, along with a spare parka, extra mukluks, and Amundsen's canvas ice boots. Pinned to the woolen shirt Byrd wore under his parka was a small coin that had been given him by the Peary family, a lucky charm Admiral Peary had had with him in 1909. In Byrd's left shirt pocket, close to his heart, was the silver dollar that Arthur Hays Sulzberger had given him for luck.

The motors were warmed and idling, the airplane poised at the top of the slope. The sun was shining, and Haines had forecast that fair weather would continue throughout the day. The entire expedition had assembled to watch the takeoff. Bennett, in the left-hand seat, pushed in the throttle. The airplane weighed about 4,000 pounds empty; in addition to the empty weight, she had been stuffed with 6,000 pounds worth of aviators, provisions, and equipment, including enough fuel for at least twenty-three hours of flying. The wings tanks and the extra tanks in the cabin were full, and additional fuel was carried in dozens of five-gallon cans. The total weight was 476 pounds more than the load the Fokker had lifted at Mineola. Bennett wasn't sure she would get off the snow. Byrd doubted whether the skis would sustain the additional weight.

They lumbered along for about the length of a football field before the screaming engines developed full power. Gradually, the ship picked up speed. Beyond the point where the smooth, hard-packed runway ended, a trackless field of loose and powdery snow undulated down to the sea. The airplane was ten miles an hour short of her rotation speed when, up ahead, the hard-pack just about gave way to the rolling mounds. Bennett knew it was no use, the ship would slow down once she got into the soft snow and wind up having to be fished out of King's Bay. He throttled the engines, the plane plunged into the deep drifts and only Bennett's skill and experience prevented her from nosing over before she came to a complete stop.

Byrd and Bennett stared at each other, their faces set back within thick ovals of fur. "She wouldn't do it," Bennett said.[13]

The members of the expedition trotted down the hill. Byrd checked the skis when he stepped from the cabin door; they were intact. He soon found himself looking at fifty crestfallen faces, the breath the men were out of turning to puffs of steam in the cold. The gang had worked day and night to prepare for the takeoff since the arrival of the *Norge*. They had walked the entire length of the runway, up and down, back and forth, arm in arm, to smooth out the snow that had been swished around when the plane took off and landed on its test flight. The stomping crew had been followed by a shovel crew who used the scoop part of their shovels to pat down the remaining lumps. Some of the men had had to roll barrels of gasoline—fifty-five-gallon steel drums—up the hill to be pumped into the Fokker. Noville had supervised the entire loading operation. Haines had sent up weather balloons. Oertel had brought lunches and dinners out to the work site. Meals were eaten on the snow, under the midnight sun, and lack of sleep was just about catching up with the expedition.

"I never saw such a disappointed lot of men," Byrd said.[14] No one was more dejected than big Tom Mulroy. The red-faced chief engineer looked so blue that Byrd smiled just to cheer him up. Mulroy tried to smile back but wasn't up to it. He averted his glance to hide his feelings. Byrd gathered the men together and calmly told them that as they were pioneering, it was almost to be expected that the first attempt to lift off for the Pole would fail. Even when flying under ordinary conditions, he said, two or more takeoff attempts were often needed. He said they would reduce the weight of the load and try again as soon as possible, and asked for volunteers to lengthen the runway. Some of the crew were so exhausted they could hardly remain erect. "All volunteered, to a man, to continue," wrote Pete Demas.

Bennett, meanwhile, found a shovel somewhere and without a word started digging the airplane out of the drift.

The airplane could not be taxied through the soft snow, and it could not be dragged out of the drifts until its weight was reduced. The cans of gasoline were removed and the wing and cabin tanks were drained, the fuel siphoned back into the big steel drums. That brought down the weight of the plane by about two tons. With a block and tackle, the Fokker was hauled a couple of hundred feet onto the hardened runway. From that point, Alton Parker taxied it back up the slope. Once again, volunteers undertook the Sisyphean task of rolling the steel drums uphill for refueling. Another group, meanwhile, in Demas's words,

> started walking up and down the lower part of the soft runway, others are melting snow with the vertical blowtorches and spraying the water over the stamped snow to freeze it into hard slippery ice.[15]

When Byrd and Bennett went through the plane to lighten the load, they found that nearly every member of the expedition had hidden some object in the cabin so as to have a souvenir of the flight: a cigarette lighter, a photograph of somebody's girl friend, someone else's love letters, a navy pennant, a Marine Corps pennant, a jaw's harp, a deck of cards, even one of Konter's ukuleles. By taking these trinkets out and leaving behind some of the five-gallons cans of gasoline and all but the most essential equipment, Bennett estimated that the takeoff weight had been lightened by about 450 pounds.

During the long delay, Amundsen had sent over a sledge that he had one of his men make. The parts were joined together with rawhide; this gave the whole construction a flexible, accordion-like texture that would stand up to rough ice. The Amundsen sledge replaced the rigid, nuts-and-bolts Alaskan model. By about ten o'clock that evening, the *Josephine Ford* once again stood at the top of the slope, her nose pointing down the strip the men had taken to calling "Byrd Boulevard." "The temperature had dropped, the snow was crispy," Demas wrote. "The runway had been lengthened an extra 1,000 feet. It was as far as time permitted."[16]

The mechanical systems had been checked and rechecked. The only question raised was about the human operators. Byrd and Bennett wanted to hop off immediately, but Captain Brennan and Dr. O'Brien insisted that they get some sleep. A compromise was reached. The aviators would go back to the *Chantier* and sleep for four hours. The two fliers started down the runway, heading for the beach where the motorboat was moored. Byrd said to Bennett, "We ought to go while the weather is good." Bennett said, "Then let's go now."[17] They turned around, and Byrd gave orders to warm up the motors.

Bennett lay down on the snow, in his furs, and tried— unsuccessfully—to sleep. Byrd reinspected the extended runway, supervising the men who were leveling out the last few bumps. The first one hundred feet of the strip had been sprinkled with water to form ice, the hardest possible surface for rapid acceleration on skis.

They slipped quietly into the plane at 12:30 a.m. without saying goodbye or shaking anyone's hand. The snow had shaken all the hubris out of them. Doc Kinkade had suggested tying a line around the tail skid and anchoring the plane to one of the rails in the mining company railroad; the plane would not be released until the engines developed full power. Anchored in this way, Bennett opened the throttles. The instruments for the starboard and port engines— temperature, oil pressure, tachometer—were mounted right on the engine nacelles. Those for the center engine were in the cockpit. Crowded together in their reindeer parkas, the aviators divided the work of monitoring each of three sets of dials. The airplane strained to rush forward. The engines roared, the fuselage shook, the three spinning propellers were medallions of blur. This time, Byrd and Bennett had agreed, it was do or die.

Noville stood by the anchor rail. Byrd had wanted to take Rex along on the polar flight, but the weight of an extra man and the survival gear and rations necessary to sustain him in case of a forced landing would add some three hundred pounds to the load already crammed aboard. When the engines were full out, Byrd nodded to Mike Brennan who had taken a position in the line of sight of the cockpit. The skipper relayed the signal to Noville. Rex raised an ax and severed the anchoring rope.

The *Josephine Ford* bolted down the shoveled-out, smoothed-down, and iced-over strip. The aviators could soon feel the wings beginning to carry more and more of the weight of the plane; they knew they were going to get off the snow. Bennett smiled at Byrd the instant they did.

An icy sea glittered on the horizon.

Somehow, Dick Konter had managed to secrete his ukulele back aboard the plane. However far into the unknown they flew, that popular little instrument that captured the fancy of the crew and the spirit of the times would go right along with them.

≡ 22 ≡

THE
GRASSY KNOLL
OF AVIATION I

If Byrd had been a Norwegian there
would have been no controversy!

HOWARD F. MASON
RADIO OPERATOR, DETROIT WILKINS EXPEDITION,
BYRD ANTARCTIC EXPEDITION I[1]

When the *Josephine Ford* returned to Kings Bay late on the afternoon of May 9, Byrd reported that he and Bennett had flown to the North Pole and had confirmed the observations made at 90° north by Admiral Peary in 1909. This was a shorthand way of saying that there was no land in the vicinity of the Pole and no open water. These findings were reconfirmed two days later during the transpolar flight of the *Norge*. Byrd went on to explain that the starboard engine of the Fokker had sprung an oil leak on the outbound leg. They had decided to abort the reconnaissance of Peary Land and head straight back to Kings Bay after attaining the Pole.

From the time he landed right up until the present those claims have been endlessly disputed. In fact, the exact time of the landing and the duration of the flight have themselves been matters of controversy. On May 10, the *New York Times* hit the stands with a headline that read: "BYRD FLIES TO NORTH POLE AND BACK; ROUND TRIP FROM KINGS BAY IN 15 HRS. 51 MIN.; CIRCLES TOP OF THE WORLD SEVERAL TIMES." A front-page article in the same edition gave the departure time as 12:50 a.m. and the return as 4:20 p.m.; total flight time in this case would have been fifteen hours and thirty minutes. An editorial note was inserted in the body of the piece to clarify the discrepancy. It read:

> Some error in the wireless transmission of these figures is possible, according to later dispatches to THE TIMES, which state that the commander's total flying time was 15 hours 51 minutes. This is 21 minutes longer than the elapsed time here indicated. It is, however, possible that the hour 4:20, recorded as marking the commander's return, was the moment at which the returning plane was sighted.

The hours are given in Greenwich time, an international standard used for navigation. The 12:50 departure and 4:20 return were picked up off the newswire by the Associated Press and circulated to numerous papers throughout the United States. In addition to the *Times* correspondents, Owen, and Bird, there were a couple of European pressmen in Kings Bay. The Europeans also clocked the flight at fifteen and a half hours, and this version swept through the continent and the British Isles. "Commander Byrd," said the *Times* of London, "left Spitsbergen at 1:50 AM yesterday and landed back there on his return from the Pole after a flight of 15 1/2 hours."[2] The source was the Oslo correspondent of the *Chicago Tribune*.

Both Spitsbergen and Norway are one time zone ahead of Green-wich. 12:50 a.m. Greenwich time would have been 1:50 a.m. in Oslo and Kings Bay. An interesting question is where the gentlemen of the press were at that hour on May 9. Cesco Tomaselli, a reporter who covered the Byrd and Amundsen expeditions for *Corrière della Sera*, a Milan paper, furnishes a rather startling answer. The ninth was a Sunday. There were no bars or restaurants on Kings Bay, so a large crowd of Italians, Norwegians, and Americans, himself included, said Tomaselli, had gotten together Saturday night in the salon of the *Heimdal*. Except for a skeleton crew aboard the *Chantier*, Byrd and all of his personnel were either working on the runway or flight-prepping the *Josephine Ford*. By his own account, Lincoln Ellsworth was asleep.[3] The only other Americans on the island were the artist Frank Stokes, and Owen and Bird of the *New York Times*.

"It's customary at Norwegian banquets," Tomaselli wrote, "to drink a toast to everyone at the table, and there were forty of us."[4] The rumble of engines occasionally interrupted the merry-making. The old pier, supplanted now by a new dock, but still standing, is to the west of town and perhaps a mile from the area available to Byrd to advance his preparations. The revelers, said Tomaselli, went to the portholes and, looking inland, up the slope, toward the white space between the town and the foot of the mountains, saw that the Fokker was "making another of its numerous attempts to take off." Everyone knew that Byrd had been anxious to get underway since the arrival of the *Norge*. But the carousers "didn't realize that his departure was imminent." Around midnight, "a bunch of audacious Americans" were seen "still trying to level off a runway." Yet, "it didn't seem to us," Tomaselli repeated, "as if the plane was just about to take off."

Milan is in the same time zone as Oslo and Kings Bay. When Tomaselli said "midnight," he knew his readers would understand this to mean midnight their time. "We learned this morning that the Fokker had taken off at 2 AM," he wrote. Whom Tomaselli and his drinking companions relied upon for that information is unknown. His story was filed at 12 noon, local time, on the ninth. At that hour, the Byrd crew was asleep. After the takeoff, Noville, Oertel, Brennan, Mulroy, and all but one of the volunteers had rowed back to the *Chantier* for some shut-eye. Pete Demas was ordered to remain ashore to guard the expedition equipment; as the youngest crewmember, he often drew the worst duty. Demas unfolded a sleeping bag in the Celotex field kitchen and slept from about 7:00 a.m. to 3:30 p.m.

Tomaselli filed a second dispatch at 6:00 p.m. local time. "At 17:25 PM," he said, "the Fokker Trimotor flown by Byrd and Bennett appeared at a high altitude in the limpid sky." Odd Arnesen of the Oslo paper, *Aftenposten*, filed a similar report. Arnesen had the first sighting of the airplane at 5:25 and the landing ten minutes later.[5] Both Tomaselli and Arnesen reported fifteen and a half hours for the flight, as did Owen and Bird in their initial wireless to the *New York Times*.

Captain Brennan also kept track of the flight times and entered them in his log aboard the *Chantier*. Later, at Byrd's request, he prepared a signed statement, which Byrd retained in his files. The skipper declared that he had recorded zero hours, thirty-seven minutes Greenwich for the departure and sixteen hours, thirty-four minutes for the return, or a total air time of fifteen hours, fifty-seven minutes.[6] Demas kept his own record of the event and apparently was thrown by the difference between Greenwich and local time. To further complicate matters, Daylight Savings Time had begun in New York and other parts of the United States on April 25. Due perhaps to the attendant confusion, Demas gives 0030 as the departure hour, 1725 as the moment the plane appeared in the sky overhead, and 1745 for the landing. He somehow managed to be on Greenwich time (and roughly congruent with Brennan) when he clocked the takeoff, and on local time (and in agreement with Arnesen and Tomaselli) when he noted the arrival of the plane in the sky over Kings Bay.

Tomaselli and his colleages apparently were in no condition to do any accurate reporting when Saturday night rolled over into Sunday morning. Bird and Owen eventually realized that they had made a mistake and corrected it to some degree in a later dispatch. The others may not have realized it. The result of one night of serious drinking was the birth of a controversy that has now lasted more than three-quarters of a century. The flight times are controversial because an airplane has to travel at a certain rate of speed to cover a given distance in a stipulated number of hours.

Distances and speeds are reckoned by navigators in nautical miles, which are slightly longer than the statute miles of everyday usage. *Both* units of measurement have variously been employed in the literature of the endless controversy. The distance from King Bay to the North Pole and back, along the route Byrd specified, is approximately 1,335 nautical or 1,535 statute miles. Byrd estimated having reached the Pole at 9:02 a.m. Greenwich time; he said he circled it a few times and started back for Kings Bay at 9:15. The National Geographic Society checked his computations and thought he was off by one minute and had actually attained the Pole at 9:03 a.m. He would therefore have spent either twelve or thirteen minutes circling his destination. For argument's sake, let's average these figures and say that twelve and a half minutes of the flight were spent at the Pole.

If the trip took fifteen hours, thirty minutes, the actual time en route to and from the Pole would have been 15:30 less 00:12.5 or fifteen hours, seventeen and a half minutes. To cover the required distance in this amount of time, Byrd would have had to average 87.3 sea miles or 100.4 land miles per hour. If the flight took fifteen hours, fifty-one minutes, the time en route would have been fifteen hours hours, thirty-eight and a half minutes and an average velocity of 85.4 knots or 98.2 mph would have been required. If fifteen hours, fifty-seven minutes, time en route would have been fifteen hours,

44.5 minutes and his speed would have had to average 84.8 knots or 97.5 mph.

The moment the story broke, the Italian press snickered at the fifteen hour, thirty minute duration. While admitting that such a high-speed flight was technically possible, they were nonetheless dubious that the Americans could have actually accomplished it. In Norway, a couple of leading navigators were even skeptical of Byrd's ability to compute his position; basic information about the instruments he developed may not have been readily available overseas. Amundsen and Ellsworth, however, never expressed any doubt whatsoever about the validity of Byrd's claim. A celebration was held aboard the *Chantier* on the night of the tenth, which Amundsen, Ellsworth, and Nobile attended. According to a report filed by Owen, Byrd briefed his guests on weather conditions at 90° north and gave Ellsworth a chart showing the amount of magnetic variation recorded en route to and at the Pole.[7] Compiling the chart would have been a simple matter of using the sun compass as a check against the magnetic compass. Two and a half weeks later, Byrd gave an interview in which he said he believed he could navigate to the Pole on an overcast day by magnetic compass alone now that he had the variations.[8] He would have had to have been psychotic to provide Ellsworth with this data if it was not authentic.

The *Chantier* sailed back into New York harbor on the evening of June 22 and was met at Quarantine by the *Macom*, a steamer owned and operated by the City of New York. Aboard the latter was a representative of the secretary of the navy, who received the records Byrd kept of the flight of May 9. The Navy Department delivered the documents to the National Geographic Society for review. The Society appointed a committee of experts to examine the records; the members were Hugh G. Mitchell, a senior mathematician at the U.S. Coast and Geodetic Survey; Henry G. Avers, the Coast and Geodetic Survey's chief mathematician of geodesy; and Albert H. Bumstead, chief cartographer of the NGS.

The submission included a nine-page "Navigation Report of Flight to the Pole" and "two charts on which Commander Byrd wrote his observations, made his calculations, and plotted his positions."[9] The flight times Byrd gave in his report were those logged by Mike Brennan: departure at 0037 hours Greenwich time, and return at 1634.

There are two different kinds of speed in aviation: "Airspeed" is the velocity generated by the engines propelling the plane through the sky. This is the speed the plane can develop under its own power. "Ground speed" takes into account the impact of the prevailing wind. A plane traveling at say, eighty knots, encountering a headwind of ten knots pushing against it, will actually be moving ten knots slower than the reading indicated on the instrument panel; it will be making only seventy knots relative to the ground. The same plane would get a ten-knot boost from an equivalent tailwind and would actually be making ninety knots. Ground speed is airspeed minus headwind or plus tailwind.

Byrd reported his ground speed averaged over each of fourteen different hours of the flight. According to this document, the *Josephine Ford* made seventy-seven knots over the ice or 88.5 miles an hour at the beginning of the flight when she was weighed down with fuel, and 94.5 knots (108.6 mph) at the conclusion of the trip when most of the fuel had been consumed. The overall average velocity was 84.85 knots (97.6 mph). These figures dovetail perfectly with the speeds required to complete the course within the fifteen hours and fifty-seven minutes that had elapsed between the Brennan flight times. Byrd was saying, in effect, that he flew to the Pole and back in about sixteen hours with the aid of favorable winds.

Mitchell, Avers, and Bumstead recomputed Byrd's celestial observations, discovered an error of exactly one minute and verified the computations. The documents were returned to the navy on June 29.[10] The in-flight records—the two charts—have not been located by modern researchers and remain missing to this date. The "Navigation Report" survives.

"I have been surprised once or twice to have evidence that there were ill-natured people trying to depreciate your exploit," wrote Arthur R. Hinks, the genteel secretary of the Royal Geographical Society, one of Byrd's many correspondents. This was in December of 1926. "I suppose," he said in his letter, "that what with Peary v. Cook and Amundsen v. Stefansson the newspapers have got it into their heads that any polar man is fair game for a controversy."[11] (Amundsen would not endorse Stefansson's blithe contention that it was always possible for explorers to find enough game to live off the "friendly" Arctic.) The imprimatur of the National Geographic Society ensured the popular acceptance of Byrd's claim and quieted the skeptics, if it didn't entirely silence them.

The controversy remained dormant throughout Byrd's lifetime and was revived shortly after his death in 1957. It reappeared at this late date in the enigmatic person of Bernt Balchen. Balchen made a major career move at Spitsbergen. He switched expeditions, joining the Byrd crew on their homeward voyage to America. As Russell Owen reported in a 1934 memoir, Balchen "had been bitterly criticized and almost ostracized" by his fellow Norwegians for assisting the Americans.[12] He and Owen had become buddies, and Owen interceded with Byrd on the young lieutenant's behalf. Balchen played important roles in two future Byrd ventures and became an international aviation star. In 1958, he produced an exciting memoir, *Come North With Me*, ghosted by humor writer Corey Ford, an early contributor to the *New Yorker*. The book drew such an unfriendly portrait of Byrd and so openly questioned the validity of his North Pole flight that it was withdrawn prior to publication and revised.

The version that actually appeared in the bookstores opens in Kings Bay with the arrival of the Byrd expedition. As the story unfolds, Balchen times the flight of May 9 at fifteen and a half hours. He gives 0037 hours Greenwich time for the departure (same as Brennan) and

1607 for the return, eighteen minutes earlier than the return time reported by the Italian and Norwegian correspondents. That is to say, eighteen minutes before, according to Cesco Tomaselli, the plane "appeared at a high altitude in the limpid sky." Later on, the book reproduces a conversation Balchen supposedly had with Floyd Bennett in the autumn of 1926 when Bennett piloted the *Josephine Ford* on a national tour to promote commercial aviation. Balchen was co-pilot. According to the text, both men agreed that the average airspeed of the plane was "seventy miles an hour." This was undoubtedly a typo; the text should have read seventy *knots* (80.5 mph). Even in nautical miles, "seventy" is a fairly sluggish velocity. In any event, it was left to the reader to work out the implication that an airplane dragging its tail through the sky at this rate could not complete a round trip of some 1,300 nautical or 1,500 statute miles in fifteen and a half hours, at least not without a howling wind on its tail each way.

Balchen was not modest. He and his ghostwriter apparently had no inhibitions about embellishing the role he played in the adventures of Richard Byrd. For example, he takes credit for the idea of using oars to reinforce the skis. Brennan, Noville, and Demas were alive when *Come North* came out; all denied that Balchen had anything to do with the shoring up of the skis, and no contemporaneous account supports his claim.[13] The numerous inaccuracies were neither publicized nor, in many cases, unearthed. The Balchen memoir famously inaugurated a series of revisionist writings about Byrd and the North Pole flight.

In 1960, Gösta H. Liljequist, a Swedish meteorologist, published in an international aviation review a celebrated paper that picked up where the expurgated version of *Come North With Me* left off. Professor Liljequist adopts the Balchen flight times as gospel: departure 0037 hours, return 1607. From a number of sources, he posits the average cruising speed of the *Josephine Ford* as seventy-five knots or 86.25 miles an hour. He does the math and concludes that in fifteen and a half hours, the airplane could "have flown not more than 1,162 nautical miles, bringing it not farther north than 88°36′N."

Liljequist broke new ground by examining historical weather maps. His interpretation of this data was startling. The flight of the *Josephine Ford*, he wrote, took place "in a no-wind atmosphere." The buckling winds that would have been necessary to propel the plane to and from the Pole within the fifteen hour, thirty minute limit were not reported by weather stations on the rim of the Arctic.

The performance of the Fokker trimotor and the weather factor will be examined in the following chapter.

The Balchen-Liljequist argument gained momentum in 1971 when Random House brought out a sensational book, *Oceans, Poles and Airmen: The First Flights over Wide Waters and Desolate Ice.* The author was Jay Montague, a former correspondent for the *New York Herald Tribune, Evening Post,* and *Evening World,* and a former editor of *Newsweek.* Montague, according to fellow New York journalist Charles J. V. Murphy, who knew him "quite well," was "a strange, withdrawn fellow, a reporter steeped in malice" who, for some reason, "detested Byrd."[14] In a lively montage of early aviation, Montague quotes (without attribution) a private conversation between Balchen and Floyd Bennett, during which Bennett confesses that he and Byrd never flew across the Polar Sea at all. "We were just north of Spitsbergen when the commander discovered that oil leak," Bennett reveals.

> He became quite concerned about it and ordered me to fly back to the north coast of Spitsbergen—fifteen or twenty miles away. We flew back and forth for a while and the leak stopped. We discussed the possibility of flying over to East Greenland but he finally ordered me to fly back and forth

and this is what we did till he told me to return to Kings
Bay. We flew back and forth for fourteen hours.

Bennett had died prematurely in 1928. A long and detailed account of
the North Pole flight was published under his byline in an aviation
magazine in 1926. He was interviewed on numerous occasions after
the flight and started a memoir that was completed by his widow.
What he said on these occasions or wrote for publication corroborates
what Byrd said and wrote about the flight. Montague's source for the
confession was presumably Balchen himself. The old aviator was
seventy-two and in failing health when *Oceans* was published. He was
interviewed by the Associated Press at this time and appeared to
endorse everything Montague had written.[15]

Another confession story surfaced in 1979. The reputed confessor
this time was the distinguished geographer, Dr. Isaiah Bowman, director of the American Geographical Society. The person making the
confession was supposedly Richard Byrd. Bowman died in 1949. The
story broke thirty years later when veteran polar explorer Captain
Finn Ronne published his memoirs, *Antarctica My Destiny*. Ronne
first went south in 1933 as a member of the second Byrd Antarctic
Expedition. In the book, he repeats a conversation he claims to have
had with Bowman shortly before the geographer's death. According
to Ronne, Bowman said: "Upon Byrd's return from the Arctic in 1926,
I had doubt that he ever flew over the North Pole. I asked to see his
compilations [sic] and what navigational aids were used to prove that
he had reached 90 degrees north. Byrd always gave evasive answers
and said no one should question his integrity."

Bowman, said Ronne, revealed that he and Byrd had lunch in
Manhattan on a rainy afternoon in 1930. Afterwards, "walking and
talking for almost four hours," Bowman elicited the confession. "I
managed to break down Dicky-Byrd," Ronne has Bowman say. Byrd
admitted "that he had not reached the North Pole, but had missed it

by about 150 miles." Ronne concludes this section of his book with these words:

> According to a staff member of the American Geographical Society, there is a full report on Byrd's alleged flight to the North Pole in the Society's files. However, few have ever seen it, for it is marked "Secret."

This statement is accurate. There is such a report, it has been seen by relatively few people, and it does contain a confession of sorts. On November 24, 1926, writing on a train en route from Buffalo to Boston, in the middle of a lecture tour, Byrd typed up a slightly more descriptive version of the report he submitted to the Navy Department the previous June and sent it off to the A.G.S. In a cover letter to Dr. Bowman, he apologized "for not getting the polar flight figures to you sooner. I had hoped," Byrd said, "before sending them along to work out the sights mathematically at my home, so that I could write a discussion for you,"

> but I have been able to be home only a comparatively few days since my return, and due to the prolonged serious illness of my wife's mother, and, on top of that, a new arrival in the family, I have been unable to get down to any serious work of that nature. I have been travelling around like a "one-night-stand actor."[16]

Helen Byrd was born on October 22, 1926. The explorer continued:

> So despairing of getting the necessary time to work these sights out, and being ashamed to hold up any longer getting our figures to you, I am sending them along forthwith.

Peter Lewis, archivist of the American Geographical Society, confirms that this is the only confession on record.[17] Bowman kept the report confidential because Byrd asked him to. "Do you not think that perhaps it would be better for me to preserve to myself the privilege of giving out the data," Byrd wrote. "Should I not pass on applications from enquirers from certain European countries who have already shown themselves to be ill-wishers; and certain would-be explorers (whom we know) who have declared themselves very much on the other side of the fence. Should I not protect myself from academic discussions with such people ..."

The Balchen and Liljequist arguments, augmented by such stage whispers as the Montague and Ronne revelations, dominated media discussions of the North Pole flight for thirty years. The Montague yarn was finally shot to pieces in 1996, when Dr. Raimund E. Goerler, chief archivist at Ohio State University's Byrd Polar Research Center, opened a box labeled "Artifacts." OSU had acquired Byrd's private papers in 1985, a collection of some 1.5 million letters, reports, records, manuscripts, photographs, and memorabilia. The cataloguing process got underway in the early 1990s, when the Research Center was awarded a federal grant to finance the task. Opening a box of artifacts, Goerler found a worn, black volume about the size of a hardbound, well-illustrated edition of *Treasure Island*.[18] It was a Standard Diary for 1925, the diary Byrd brought to Etah in the summer of that year and used again in the spring of 1926, keeping a journal of the North Pole expedition on pages that had previously been left blank. Sometime during the voyage to Spitsbergen, Byrd transformed the diary into a flight manual, pasting in navigation and conversion tables and some general weather information furnished by William Haines. He had it with him on the *Josephine Ford*.

The roaring noise of the three engines drowned out normal conversation. During the flight, Byrd and Bennett could talk to each other only in the form of written notes. Sixty-one lines of Byrd's penciled dialogue were written in the pages of the diary. Statements such as "20 miles to go to Pole" and "We should be at the Pole now. Make a circle and I will take a picture," prove that the aviators didn't spend fourteen hours circling out of sight of Kings Bay.

The diary also contains two sets of computations that are consistent with the mathematics involved in celestial navigation. Byrd shot the sun with his bubble sextant to get his position at various intervals during the flight. His navigation report lists and interprets ten celestial observations, six made en route to the Pole and four in the vicinity of 90° north. (At the start of the return leg, the sextant broke and no more observations could be taken.) The figures in the diary represent two observations recorded between Kings Bay and the Pole. In accordance with standard procedures, the time of day and observed altitude in each case were corrected for intrinsic errors. The first diary sight was shot some four hours out of Spitsbergen and apparently was discarded; it doesn't appear in the navigation report. The second sight was made six and a half hours out of Kings Bay and was included in the report. However, the solar altitude that appears in the report differs from the corresponding figure in the diary. The calculations made in the diary to process or "reduce" a raw sextant reading were erased in both cases but are still fairly legible.

As might be expected, the erasures became a further point of contention in the on-going controversy. Dennis Rawlins, an astronomer who made a strenuous effort to debunk Robert Peary in a 1973 publication, *Peary at the North Pole: Fact or Fiction?*, examined the diary shortly after its discovery. He concluded that Byrd did the erasing, that the sextant readings he unsuccessfully attempted to rid himself of are authentic, and that the figures the explorer formally presented to the navy and National Geographic Society were largely doctored.

Rawlins interprets the numbers to mean that the *Josephine Ford* was traveling at a slower velocity than Byrd reported. Byrd would therefore have been farther from the Pole than he said he was when the oil leak was detected. At this point, Rawlins suggests, either Byrd conned Bennett into thinking they had reached the Pole, or the aviators evaluated the situation, prudently turned around and headed for home. Rawlins puts the turnaround point within 150 miles of 90° north.

Twenty-eight years elapsed between Byrd's death and the acquisition of the diary by OSU, twenty-eight years during which the suspect figures might have been erased. The "lone gunman" in this case may have been someone who jumped to the same conclusions as Rawlins and sought to protect the explorer. As for the validity of those conclusions, a number of airmen and navigators have looked at the diary sights and have an entirely different perspective on their meaning and significance. One important consideration is an appreciation of the circumstances under which the flight was made. Writing upon the publication of the Byrd diary in 1998, Captain Brian Shoemaker, a former navy aviator and commander of American military operations in Antarctica, crisply put it this way:

> Navigation for aviators is a life or death proposition. Every time we take off and fly over the horizon we stake our life upon our navigational expertise as did Admiral Byrd and Floyd Bennett. We gamble that we can solve our navigational problems and land before we run out of fuel. It is not the academic exercise that this controversy has made it out to be and it does not just involve astronomy. There are other factors involved such as wind drift, torque causing heading creep due to dissimilar thrust of engines, precession of compasses due to engine induced magnetic fields,

increasing airspeed as fuel burns down, etc., while coping with cold, aircraft vibration, turbulence, shifting of fuel and other non-navigational duties. Navigators must figure out where they are, where they want to go and then GO—they have no time to ponder and pontificate about their navigational calculations.[19]

In the pioneer era, navigators had to shift back and forth between dead reckoning and celestial navigation. They had to know what direction they were going in, and to do this they had to, as Shoemaker suggests, constantly correct for wind drift. They also had to know how fast they were going, and this required keeping track of ground speed—the effect of the wind on the velocity of the plane. With this information, they could plot and continually update their dead reckoning position. Every so often, they had to pick up a sextant and shoot the sun. Celestial observation would give them a positional fix, and from those coordinates they would start the dead reckoning all over again.

But how did they know the sextant reading was correct? By looking at the dead reckoning position. If the numbers seemed in keeping with the DR position, fine. If not, the navigator would discard the reading, pick up the sextant and try again. Lieutenant Colonel William E. Molett, a retired air force master navigator and instructor of navigation, and Joseph Portney, a former president of the Institute of Navigation, maintain that the erased readings were figures Byrd didn't use because he realized they were incorrect.

In the second place, it is absolutely necessary to understand how Byrd was *using* celestial navigation. The end result of a celestial observation is a line of position, a straight line you plot on your chart. It could be a diagonal line or it could be vertical or horizontal. It all depends on your position relative to the sun. If you draw an arrow from you to the point on earth the sun is just now directly over, the line of position is always perpendicular to that arrow. A savvy navigator therefore shoots the sun at a time of day when the most useful line of position can be obtained. If you shoot the sun at noon when it is due south of you, the result is a horizontal line. Draw that line on your chart and you have your latitude. If you shoot the sun at dawn when it is due east, the result is a vertical line. Draw this line on your chart and you have your longitude.

Byrd headed north over the ice pack with the sun edging slightly to the right of the nose of his aircraft. During the next twelve hours the celestial body appeared to circle around his starboard wing. As it did so, Byrd could shoot the sun and obtain diagonal or near-vertical lines of position. Those lines, when plotted on his chart, gave him the most important information needed at this stage of the flight. They enabled him to check his course, to ascertain how far east or west he might have drifted from the track he intended to follow due north to the pole. After he had been underway for close to eight hours, the sun had swept past his wing and was slipping toward his tail. He could now obtain lines of position that would be more nearly horizontal. These lines provided the most significant information needed as he approached his destination. They enabled him to check his latitude, to compute the distance remaining to 90° north. This is an elegant application of celestial navigation for high-speed travel on a long-distance flight.

The first sight represented in the diary was shot at 4:39 a.m. Greenwich time, or 5:39 a.m. in the time zone where Byrd was flying. By 6:00 a.m., the sun would have traveled the first ninety degrees of its circuit around the Arctic horizon; it would be due east and off the tip of his starboard wing. A sun sight at this exact moment would yield a vertical line of position, giving Byrd his longitude as well as an accurate course check. At 5:39, he shot the sun early enough to double-check and re-compute his figures. Having decided to discard the reading, he had plenty of time to go back and take another sight at 5:56, just before the sun crossed the wing. He included the 5:56 sight in his report. "This fix," he wrote, "put the true position of the plane about a mile or two to the left of the course."[20]

The second diary sight was taken at 7:07 a.m. Greenwich (8:07 a.m. local). The sun was slightly southeast of the plane. The line of position inclined a bit to the right, but still provided a good course check. "This sight indicated that the plane was about five miles to the left and ahead of the course," Byrd wrote.

These sights were crucial. The computations were probably redone several times on any scrap of paper at hand. Writer-aviator Hardy LeBel—himself a Byrd detractor—described the navigation of the *Josephine Ford* as "a math test given under extremely unpleasant conditions with no way to grade the result."[21] The most plausible interpretation of the diary is not that Byrd manufactured his sights after the flight. Rather, as Dr. Gerald H. Newsom, an OSU astronomer who examined the diary at the behest of the Byrd Polar Research Center, has observed, "it tells use something about Byrd's state during the flight." The diary numbers, in Newsom's view, "indicate confusion and errors." Like a student taking the college boards, the explorer was working under enormous pressure to succeed; he was exhausted and a bit sloppy, but he knew his stuff.

Byrd had attempted to take off at midday, when the sun was directly behind him, and actually took off after midnight, when the sun was directly ahead, because he banked on obtaining longitude sights through the initial phases of the flight. Colonel Molett, the air force navigation instructor, has reviewed the 1926 flight report and pronounced himself "awed by Byrd's careful planning and execution." Molett flew as chief navigator on ninety-one transpolar weather flights in the 1950s, obtaining fixes by celestial means. He considers Byrd "one of the ten best navigators in history," and is convinced that the report is genuine.

⬳ 23 ⬲

THE
GRASSY
KNOLL OF
AVIATION II

If temperature rises, do not expect your aircraft
to have the same performance as it did at
the lower density altitudes of cold weather.

WINTER ADVISORY
FEDERAL AVIATION ADMINISTRATION
ALASKA REGION[1]

R ichard Byrd never completed the manual on aerial navigation that the navy assigned him to write just before he successfully established himself as a polar explorer. That task
was eventually taken up by his friend, Lieutenant Commander Philip
Van Horn Weems. Weems died in 1979 at the age of ninety, and by
the end of his long life he was acclaimed as the greatest navigator of
the twentieth century. He and Byrd had been classmates at Annapolis.
In 1927, while working on one of many textbooks that would become

standard in the field, Weems sent Byrd a synopsis of an innovative technique he had developed for plotting lines of position in celestial navigation. "Dickie," he wrote, "If you see anything in this paper worthwhile I wish you would write the Naval Institute (if only a paragraph), as the method is so new, any good word for it will help me with the book."[2] The debunking of the North Pole flight would eclipse Byrd's reputation as a navigator and aviator both with historians and the general public. But he apparently had a considerable reputation among his peers.

People love excitement, sensation, and controversy. Good ones always develop new twists and tangles. Soon, like an overgrowth of brushwood, the controversy manages to obscure the subject matter. The truth remains hidden under the accretions.

FLIGHT OF THE *JOSEPHINE FORD*
9 May 1926

Approximate Distance
1335 Nautical/1535 Statute Miles

Duration	Time Circling Pole	Time en Route to and from Pole	Average Velocity	
			Nautical MPH	Statute MPH
15 hours 30 minutes	12.5 minutes	15 hours 17.5 minutes	87.3	100.4
15 hours 51 minutes	12.5 minutes	15 hours 38.5 minutes	85.4	98.2
15 hours 57 minutes	12.5 minutes	15 hours 44.5 minutes	84.8	97.5

There are five paths through the underbrush that can usefully be explored:

THE OIL LEAK

This was a serious problem. If all the usable oil drained out of the tank in the starboard nacelle and the flow of lubricant ceased, the engine would fail. Fortunately, the level of oil never fell below a certain critical threshold and the engine continued to function normally for the duration of the flight, but Byrd and Bennett had no way of knowing that this would happen. They had to figure that at any moment the needle on the starboard oil pressure gauge could drop, indicating that oil flow had been depleted. In their published writings both indicated that the leak was detected about seven and a half hours out of Kings Bay, or within one hour of the North Pole. They elected to abort the flight to Peary Land, reducing the miles that remained to be flown by about 30 percent, proceed to the Pole and take their chances coming back on two engines.

Could the airplane have been flown on two engines?

Shortly after Anthony Fokker debuted his trimotor in the Ford Reliability Tour, September 28 through October 4, 1925, he allowed the U.S. Army Air Service to flight test the aircraft at McCook Field in Dayton, Ohio. At Fokker's request, the Army test pilots loaded the plane up with 4,000 pounds of personnel and deadweight. They found that the ship could climb on two engines to 5,000 feet and that they were able to maintain full control in this configuration at that altitude. The *Fokker Bulletin*, an in-house publication, subsequently boasted that, "The rate of climb at sea level of 343 feet per minute indicates that the airplane, with this heavy load, is able to *take off on only two engines*, with perfect safety."[3]

Fokker Trimotor No. 1 had been equipped for the Ford tour with three Wright Whirlwind J-4B engines, the same type of power plant Byrd would install when he bought the airplane roughly three months later and changed her name to *Josephine Ford*.[4] On March 30, 1926, Bennett and Alton Parker loaded the ship with 5,524 pounds (two and a quarter tons of pilots, passengers, gasoline, and oil—and a half ton of sand).[5] They demonstrated that even with an additional three-quarters of a ton over and above the Dayton weight, the airplane could sustain level flight with the center engine and one wing engine.

The trimotor had been loaded with close to 6,000 pounds worth of personnel, fuel, oil, and equipment when she finally lifted off the snow of Kings Bay on May 9. Byrd noted in a series of articles he wrote shortly after the flight that for the first three and a half hours of her northward hop, the airplane consumed fuel at the rate of thirty-two gallons per hour. (32 x 3.5 = 112.) Fuel consumption was thirty gallons per hour for the next four hours. (30 x 4 =120.) By the time the oil leak was discovered, 232 gallons of fuel had been consumed. Fuel weighs six pounds per gallon. (232 x 6 = 1,392.) Figuring in the amount of oil that had been used up or dripped out, the weight of the ship had decreased by over 1,400 pounds in seven and a half hours of flight.

The aircraft, according to the aviators, was flying at an altitude of 2,000 feet. Byrd and Bennett both reported that Bennett momentarily throttled the starboard motor and confirmed that the ship would maintain this altitude on the center and port engines.[6] At that moment, the aircraft would have weighed several hundred pounds more than it did during the Dayton test and several hundred pounds *less* than it did at Mineola.

Would they have been able to get back to Kings Bay on two engines?

When Bennett throttled the starboard engine, Byrd wrote, they found "that not only could we stay aloft but could make a little over

60 miles an hour with the other two motors."[7] Byrd was clear and precise in his navigational report; he specified on the second page of the paper that when he said "miles an hour," he meant nautical miles. He was less careful in his popular writings. Sixty nautical miles an hour and sixty statute miles an hour are two different speeds. The former—sixty knots—is actually faster, equivalent to sixty-nine mph. Let's assume Byrd meant the slower speed, sixty mph, hence a worst-case scenario.

Assume "a little over 60" is 60.5 mph. They had roughly 860 statute miles to fly to reach the Pole and return to base. At 60.5 mph, it would have taken 14.2 hours to get back. In the worse case, would they have had enough gas left? They had started out with 615 gallons of fuel; 232 gallons had been consumed. Three hundred and eighty-three gallons remained after seven and a half hours in the air. At this point in the flight, fuel was being consumed at the rate of thirty gallons per hour, or ten gallons per hour per engine. If they continued burning fuel at the rate of ten gallons per hour over the two remaining engines, they could have stayed in the air for another nineteen hours.

Was it prudent to continue as far as the Pole?

The average weekend aviator would have hightailed it back to Kings Bay at the first drip of leaking oil. But Byrd and Bennett were not weekend aviators. These were the same two airmen who only nine months earlier had encountered extreme turbulence over uncharted mountain ranges in the interior of Ellesmere Island and would have kept trying to penetrate a curtain of rising fog if Donald MacMillan hadn't held them back. They were on another pioneer flight now, with their goal a tantalyzing hour away and the United States Navy and the United States of America waiting to hear how they made out. Their wives and mothers couldn't have held them back.

AIRCRAFT PERFORMANCE

Throughout October and November of 1926, Floyd Bennett piloted the *Josephine Ford* on a tour of some fifty American cities and towns. The flights were sponsored by the Guggenheim Fund for the Promotion of Aeronautics and the U.S. Department of Commerce. Bernt Balchen flew as co-pilot. Officials of both sponsoring agencies participated on various legs of the tour; many were themselves pilots. On at least one occasion, several office-holding aviators were invited by Byrd himself, who was onboard, to enter the cockpit and take a turn at the controls.[8] With one darting glance at the instrument panel, they would have found out the airspeed. Anyone remaining in the flight cabin could have timed the takeoff and departure. They could have picked up an atlas later on and measured the distance flown; if the winds had been negligible that day, they could have calculated the airspeed. Why Byrd would have let outsiders anywhere near the ship, if he had something to hide, is a mystifying question that neither Richard Montague nor any of his successors have paused to entertain. Why he would have let anyone outside the inner circle of Bennett-Noville-Oertel-Parker in the cockpit boggles the logical mind.

If he was not the first airman to reach the Pole, and knew he wasn't, and knew that Amundsen, the pride of Norway, was, why he would have allowed a Norwegian to fly as co-pilot, let alone a member of the Amundsen-Ellsworth-Nobile expedition, is so utterly beyond reason as to be unanswerable without recourse to talk-show psychobabble. Nevertheless, Balchen kept a flight log, and at least two generations of debunkers have read between the numerals in an effort to extract its hidden secrets.

The Balchen log lists sixty-three flights of which fifty-six were undertaken during the Guggenheim tour.[9] He noted velocity in miles per hour. His average airspeed over all sixty-three flights is ninety mph or seventy-eight knots. At first glance, this would appear to indicate that without a stiff and favorable wind, the *Josephine Ford* could not have flown from Spitsbergen to the North Pole and back even within fifteen hours and fifty-seven minutes. But airplanes are not like cars. You can jump in your Toyota today, fill up the tank, drive to the next town, and expect to get the same mileage and arrive at your destination at about the same time as you did yesterday, so long as the traffic flow is equivalent. The engine will deliver the same amount of power. The reason flight engineers exist, however, is that pilots can change the way their aircraft performs. They can choose to fly economically, using a low power setting, getting more miles per gallon, and flying at a relatively low airspeed. Or, they can choose a "best power" configuration, burning more fuel but getting a higher airspeed.

Balchen's engine log shows that most of the time he and Bennett had the Wright Whirlwinds set at 1,400 rpm. Occasionally, they went to 1,450 rpm. They brought the engines up to 1,500 rpm when they needed more altitude to fly over the Rocky Mountains. By contrast, the army test pilots with their 4,000-pound load set the engines at 1,755 rpm. The aircraft made 117 mph, and she made this rate of speed in crosswinds and in rough air.

The Fokker trimotor was built to revolutionize commercial aviation. It was designed to fly economically at airspeeds of from ninety to one hundred mph, with engines running from 1,400 to 1,500 rpm. On 87 percent of the flights in the Balchen log, the throttles were set within the lower half of the economical range. The log does not prove the *Josephine Ford* failed to reach the Pole. It only proves that during the U.S. Tour, Bennett and Balchen were not asking the airplane to work too hard.

The *Josephine Ford* was capable of developing the speeds necessary to reach the Pole within *any* of the reported flight times, *unaided by the wind*, depending on how much power was pulled from the engines. Bennett had learned over Mineola that the motors had to be set at a minimum of 1,375 rpm to maintain level flight with a load of 5,524 pounds. The Wright Whirlwind J-4 series provided maximum power at about 1,800 rpm. The army test pilots had pushed them close to the limit.[10] Byrd and Bennett would not have flown at 1,755 rpm on a fifteen-to-sixteen-hour exploratory haul in the most extreme environment on earth; they would not have babied the engines, but they wouldn't have strained them either. Since they had all the time in the world on May 9 and initially intended to proceed beyond the Pole to Peary Land, they needed to get the maximum number of miles per gallon of fuel. Pilots generally accomplish this by employing a high power setting at the initial stages of a long-distance flight and gradually diminishing power to maintain an optimum airspeed. Byrd's newspaper account of his 1927 transatlantic flight and the flight log of his South Pole hop suggest that he followed this pattern.

The flight log and engine log maintained by Bennett on May 9, 1926, however, are missing.

We do not know how they engineered the North Pole flight. We don't know what engine setting they used or if they changed the setting during cruise. But this is what we do know:

1. Bennett conducted a fuel consumption test in New York with an empty plane and the engines running at 1,475 rpm. If he and Byrd had set the Whirlwinds at 1,475 rpm over the Polar Sea, they would have been pulling 5 percent more power than Bennett and Balchen did on 63 percent of their flights.

2. The Balchen flight log understates the performance of the airplane within the economical range. The lowest airspeeds obtained during a flight of any duration occur at the beginning, when the plane climbs off the ground and up to cruising altitude, and at the end, when the plane glides to a landing. The highest velocity

develops during cruise; airspeed builds up as fuel is consumed and the weight of the plane decreases. On a series of short flights, the pilot takes off, climbs, cruises, lands, and shortly takes off and climbs again, and so on. Each successive takeoff and climb is another low-speed operation. The average airspeed for the series is skewed toward the low-end.

Most of the flights in Balchen's log were about two hours or less and the log even includes some fifteen- and thirty-minute exhibition hops. Only three flights lasted longer than four hours, and the average airspeed over just these three trips is ninety-three mph, three mph better than the overall average.

3. Power output increases at low temperatures. The internal combustion engine feeds on a mixture of fuel and air. The warmer the air, the thinner it is and the less atmosphere the engine has to chew on. The cooler the air, the more dense it is and the more of it is available to support the combustion process.

   Similarly, although fuel is bought and sold by the gallon, its energy content depends on *weight*, not volume, and is measured by the *pound*. The same gallon of gasoline weighs more in cold air because cold air is so much more dense, and the more the fuel weighs, the more energy it yields.

   "As a result," said legendary aviator, Elgen M. Long, the first pilot to fly solo around the world over the North and South Poles, "you get quite phenomenal performance from an airplane in polar regions. The Wright Whirlwind J-4 was a 200 horsepower engine— if Byrd and Bennett had used full power, they would probably have gotten 210 horsepower or 215."[11]

4. There is a close relationship between fuel consumption and airspeed. Fuel is the price the pilot has to pay for speed. The atmospheric conditions in the Arctic are such that the propulsion system works more efficiently. The "currency" is stronger, and the price goes down. The "savings" is a windfall that can be used to "buy" more speed.

5. An aircraft can be equipped with wheels for routine ground operations, floats for water landings, and skis for snow and ice. The different kinds of landing gear affect the aerodynamic profile of the plane in different ways. Floats significantly increase the amount of drag on the ship. A bush plane can lose as much as 11 percent of its airspeed when the wheels come off and the floats are put on. Skis, on the other hand, do not slow a plane up to any appreciable extent. F. Atlee Dodge, an authority on the aerodynamics of ski flying, having been in the aviation business in Alaska for over forty years, said, "If Byrd had great big tires like we have up here, the tires would have been slower than the skis. He probably didn't have big tires, and he may have lost some speed, but it would have been very little. The maximum amount of speed he would have lost would have been 5%."[12]

6. The Wright Corporation designed a special engine cowling for the North Pole flight to reduce the amount of cold Arctic air flowing over the exposed cylinder heads of the radial engines and prevent them from running too cool. This piece of equipment looked something like the lid of a round charcoal broiler, but with a circular hole in the middle; it fit behind the propeller spinner, and, of course, was installed before the propeller blades

were attached. It was not used on the subsequent flights around the United States.

The metal cowling on each of the three Whirlwind engines added an element of streamlining and would have enabled the *Josephine Ford* to make a few more knots over the Polar Sea than she or any other Fokker trimotor would have made with the cylinder heads fully exposed. Admiral Moffet subsequently recommended that the National Advisory Committee for Aeronautics (NACA), a research board, study the use of similar cowling for commercial all-weather operations.[13] By 1929, NACA developed drag-reduction cowling for air-cooled radial engines that became standard, initially, for the Lockheed Vega, increasing the maximum speed of that aircraft from 165 to 190 mph, or 15 percent. Elgen Long suggests that the up-to-five percent of airspeed that the skis might have cost the trimotor would very likely have been offset by the pioneer cold-weather engine cowling and the enhanced performance due to the cold weather itself.

WEATHER

Byrd wrote that "coming up the coast" of Spitsbergen "we had a wind from the right and rear that was setting us out of our course."[14] Some eight or nine hours later, it had shifted one hundred and eighty degrees. Just before reaching the Pole, he reported picking up a headwind. Describing the return leg, he said, "We had a strong wind behind us and were taking advantage of it by flying at various altitudes." The wind, he wrote,

changes both in strength and direction at different altitudes and the aviator can frequently take advantage of this fact to increase his speed over the ground. There was about a twenty mile an hour wind blowing and it was increasing our speed by ten miles an hour. If this wind had been directly behind us as it was at times it would have increased our speed twenty miles an hour.

Is this plausible, a tailwind coming and going?

Dr. Liljequist, the meteorologist who aided the revisionist cause forty years ago, projected an extensive high-pressure system over the Arctic in early May of 1926. Within this system, he identified a particular ridge of high pressure to the east of Byrd's flight path. "This remained stationary from May 8th to May 10th," he said, "and must have been situated north of Spitsbergen, where easterly to southeasterly winds prevailed."[15]

A typical polar weather pattern: an area of high pressure producing a window of good flying conditions. The high-pressure cell also produces swirling winds that flow clockwise around the center of the cell and blow spirally outward. If the ridge sat motionless in the east, the winds would have been quite light by the time they reached the *Josephine Ford*. But how did Liljequist know it "remained stationary"?

Polar meteorology in an age of satellites and computers is hardly infallible. Ronald C. Sheardown, a professional pilot with 19,000 hours of flight time, including 9,000 hours above the Arctic Circle, says, "The reporting stations are just too far apart to give reliable data. Even today, flying from Point Barrow to Spitsbergen, we seldom rely on the forecasts."[16] Sheardown has made eight transpolar flights, the most recent in 2000. Liljequist's conclusions were based on weather observations made in northern Norway in 1926.

"It's not like looking up the temperature high at Los Angeles on December 18, 1917," said navigation consultant Joe Portney.[17] An ex–air force navigator, Portney worked as an engineer and manager of Advanced Programs in the Guidance and Control Systems Division of Litton Systems, Inc., and has written on historic feats of navigation from Columbus to Lindbergh. Portney challenges Liljequist's assumption of a *stationary* high-pressure cell. Generally, high- and low-pressure areas move west to east in the middle latitudes, but their trajectories are chaotic at the high latitudes. If that cell and its swirling winds moved west across Byrd's flight path, something dramatic happens.

The effect would be the same as if, for example, an enormous carousel moved west across the Sheep Meadow in Central Park. If the merry-go-round was spinning clockwise and if you were jogging north to 72nd Street and you hopped on the leading edge of that carousel and hopped off after a couple of seconds, you would find yourself closer to 72nd Street then when you started. On the way back, depending on how fast you and the merry-go-round were travelling, you might find the trailing edge in your path. If you hopped on and off again for a few seconds, you would wind up a bit closer to 66th Street. Similarly, Byrd would have gotten a boost—a tailwind—both ways, a situation that polar aviators Ron Sheardown, Elgen Long, and Colonel William Molett say is not all that uncommon.

How much of a boost could Byrd have gotten? According to his own writings, the wind was light on the outbound leg and not all of it was on his tail. A light wind is considered to be five knots or less. Let's be conservative and give him a tailwind component of 2.5 knots (2.875 mph) en route to the Pole. On the return, he noted a twenty-mile-an-hour wind that was directly on his tail "at times," but generally increased his speed by only ten miles an hour. Again, he may have been reckoning in sea miles or land miles; it remains unclear. We'll choose to err on the conservative side, assume statute miles, a slightly worst-case scenario, and give him a 12.5 mph tailwind component for the homeward leg. This averages out to a 7.7 mph tailwind for the whole flight.

If we adjust for a wind component of this order, the *Josephine Ford* would have had to develop the following airspeeds to complete the trip within the three flight times under consideration:

15 hours 30 minutes	92.7 mph
15 hours 51 minutes	90.5 mph
15 hours 57 minutes	89.8 mph

INSTRUMENT ERROR

Ninety degrees north is a mathematical construct. It doesn't exist in the material sense. Unlike the Grand Canyon or the headwaters of the Amazon, you can't see it and know you're there. The North Pole is a position in a global coordinate system; being "at the Pole" is a calculation based on the use of a number of instruments. Every instrument has a certain amount of error. Richard Byrd reckoned his position with the most sophisticated instruments on the planet on May 9, 1926—sun compass, drift indicator, bubble sextant. But those instruments were primitive compared to modern inertial navigation systems and the Global Positioning System. For example, in September of 1925, the navy tested the bubble sextant in a series of flights off Pearl Harbor.[18] Aviators found that due to the acceleration of the aircraft the bubble tended to lodge itself in an off-level position, and that determining when the sextant was level was a judgment call. As a result, the navigators who participated in the test were off the target by an average of fifteen miles.

Joe Portney worked out an error analysis for each of Byrd's instruments on the North Pole flight. Portney himself made three "first flights" over the Pole, the first flights to reach 90° north using, on each occasion, state-of-the-art inertial navigation systems. Recognizing Byrd's proficiency with the bubble sextant, he generously assigned him a five-mile error on each sight, the same allowance made in 1926 by the experts who verified Byrd's computations for the National Geographic Society. He also tabulated the instrument errors that would have added up each time Byrd calculated his wind drift and ground speed; these errors are cumulative and would have thrown off his dead reckoning.

Portney determined that with 68.3 percent certainty, Byrd would have arrived at least within thirty nautical miles of the Pole, or would have overshot the Pole by no more than thirty nautical miles.[19] But his most probable position would have been a shortfall of either fifteen nautical miles or, according to a second model with slightly different assumptions, twenty-one sea miles. This would not have detracted from his accomplishment because any other navigator using the same or similar instruments, including Amundsen, would have been subject to the same limitations.

The error analysis suggests that either thirty or forty-two nautical miles could be shaved off the distance flown by the *Josephine Ford* on May 9, 1926. Thirty and forty-two nautical miles are equivalent to 34.5 and 48.3 statute miles, respectively. If we reduce the distance in land miles to this extent and assume a 7.7 mph tailwind component, the plane, in this scenario, would have only been required to generate the airspeeds listed below.

	Portney Model 1	Portney Model 2
15 hours 30 minutes	90.4 mph	89.5 mph
15 hours 51 minutes	88.2 mph	87.4 mph
15 hours 57 minutes	87.6 mph	86.7 mph

The way an airplane flies depends on the conditions it encounters. The critical factor is the density of the air at a given time, place, and altitude. Density, in turn, is closely related to temperature. The lower the temperature, the greater the density, the better the performance.

The Guggenheim-Commerce Department tour got underway on October 7, 1926, on the eastern seaboard where the temperature was in the low sixties. There were eleven people, all male, on the inaugural flight from Washington to New York.[20] Considering the weight of eleven men, their baggage, the passenger seats that had to be installed, and perhaps five hours worth of fuel and oil, the plane would have carried a load in excess of 3,000 pounds. This would have been roughly equivalent to the load during the final hour or two of the North Pole flight. According to the Balchen log, the center engine on the Washington-New York run was set at 1,400 rpms, the port and starboard engines at 1,450. The plane made an airspeed of ninety mph, the average for the entire tour. The *Josephine Ford* then flew to the Midwest, where the temperature dropped into the fifties, the far West, and the Pacific coast. In Denver it was seventy-six; in San Francisco, seventy-two; and in Los Angeles and San Diego the mercury rose into the eighties.

Byrd reported a temperature of 14°F on the ground at takeoff on May 9, 8°F en route to the Pole, 0°F at the Pole, and 5°F on the return leg. The Portney analysis suggests that the airplane did not even have to perform as well as it did on the U.S. tour for Byrd and Bennett to have reached the North Pole *within the margin of error of their instruments* and to have returned to Kings Bay in either the fifteen hours, fifty-seven minutes affirmed by Byrd and certified by Captain Brennan or the fifteen hours, fifty-one minutes inscribed in the *New York Times.*

But if, with a favorable wind and extremely advantageous atmospheric conditions, they had pulled just enough power to *match* the average performance of the plane on the Guggenheim tour, they could, within the same margin of error, have easily accomplished the flight twenty-seven minutes earlier than they claimed.

ALTITUDE BAROGRAPH

Every significant flight of the pioneer era was recorded by an onboard altitude barograph, a sealed instrument that, like a barometer, is sensitive to changes in atmospheric pressure. The altimeter of an airplane functions in a similar way; it contains a pressure-sensitive element connected to a calibrated scale. The pressure-sensitive element of a barograph is connected to a timer and to a register on which a mechanical pen produces a long jagged line. The line, resembling a cardiogram, is a record of the altitudes attained by the plane from takeoff to landing.

The purpose of the barograph was to certify that a pilot completing, for example, an endurance flight actually stayed in the air for the amount of time claimed. A smudgy photostatic copy of the barograph record of the North Pole flight was scanned onto a computer at the Ohio State University archives, producing a clear image. The jagged line zigzags across 31.5 pre-printed reference ticks on the barograph form, each representing thirty minutes of real time, or a flight duration of roughly 945 minutes (31.5 x 30) or fifteen hours, forty-five minutes. Three days after the flight, however, the timing mechanism proved to be inaccurate. The meteorologist Bill Haines signed and certified the barograph record on May 12, 1926. In a handwritten note on the form, Haines indicated the "Instrument tested for time [was] found to be erratic, apparently about 15 min [sic] slow in 24 hours, but the error varied."[21]

This is exactly what one would expect to happen: a mechanical instrument exposed to extreme cold became sluggish. The flight actually took longer than the interval represented on the barograph, but how much longer? What does "error varied" mean? Taking into consideration certain checkpoints that occurred during the flight itself, Professor Newsom of OSU believes the error may have been as much as seventeen minutes. If so, adjusting for takeoff and landing roll, and other details, he interprets the barograph record to be commensurate with a total flight time of fifteen hours, fifty-eight minutes (Byrd's time as corrected by the National Geographic Society).[22] If the instrument ran slow by only ten minutes, Newsom determined that the flight would have been completed in fifteen hours, fifty-one minutes (the *New York Times* figures).

Newsom conducted his study in 2001, seventy-five years after Bennett coaxed the trimotor off the snow at Kings Bay. Attention endures like iron and oak. The North Pole controversy is really about the extraordinary amount of attention that had been paid to the quest for the transpolar flight and the amount of attention Richard Byrd received and would continue to receive for the rest of his life. Essentially, it's about people's love of controversy and sensation.

It's not about substantial evidence of duplicity. Because there is none.

≡ 24 ≡

THE BLESSED
SUN

*It is evident that we are hurrying onwards to some excit-
ing knowledge—some never-to-be imparted secret
whose attainment is destruction.*

EDGAR ALLAN POE
"MS. FOUND IN A BOTTLE"

A pproximately fifty (statute) miles out of Kings Bay, Byrd
and Bennett passed the west coast of Danes Island, where
long-lost Andrée had started north in 1897 and Wellman
in 1907 and 1909. The hills were almost completely covered with
snow; from two thousand feet they seemed to roll inland from the
coast like a series of long white mounds or graves. Cakes of ice that
had chipped off the Arctic pack dotted the waters lapping against the
shore.

Danes Island is only about five miles long. Less than two miles
further north, Amsterdam Island appeared, the last known landmass
on their flight path. Amsterdam Island is also about five miles long,
and the northern part of it points like an arrowhead at the North Pole.
As they passed it, Byrd opened his diary and wrote Bennett a note:

"I want to line up the mountain and Amsterdam Island. I will do it from topside. Watch me."

He reached behind him, opened a wooden door and, not having enough leg or elbow room to get up, sort of twisted and squirmed out of the co-pilot's seat. Two dark and bulky containers blocked his way aft, leaving only enough space for the door to swing open. The two extra fuel tanks that had been installed in the flight cabin were each three feet high, two feet wide, two feet deep, and about the shape of mailboxes. They stood facing one another and no more than six and five-eighth inches of daylight separated them. Byrd managed in his furs to squeeze between the tanks. The flight cabin at its roomiest was barely wide enough for a narrow adult to stretch both arms out to the side, and the remaining floor space was barely long enough for a short adult to stretch out on. Almost all of it was crawling with five-gallon cans of fuel—about forty of them. The tapering walls and low ceiling were covered with a white fabric, and it was as bright inside as if an electric light had been turned on. There were rows of windows on either side of the fuselage, with the midnight sun pouring in from the starboard row, making the stout cans glisten against the varnished floorboards. Stepping over them, Byrd brushed past a wireless set on his right and a chart table on his left. He did not hear his soft boot steps—his eardrums reverberated with the thunder of the three Wright Whirlwinds.

A closed wooden door blocked his path further aft. He reached for the handle, opened it, and entered a closet-like space two and a half feet deep and less than five feet wide. Inside, at his left knee was a small toilet bowl. A bulkhead separated this compartment from the emergency rations and survival gear crammed in the storage space in the tail of the plane. A magnetic compass had been mounted in the middle of the bulkhead, at about the level of Byrd's sternum. The instrument was six inches in diameter, the kind used on navy torpedo boats. Here in the aft compartment, the mechanism would not be deflected by metal or electrical phenomena. By virtue of its size, it was expected to be less subject to the strong, downward pull exerted at these latitudes by the horizontal component of the earth's magnetic field than the smaller compasses that had been used on the MacMillan expedition.

At Byrd's forehead was a sun compass that had been installed upside-down on a trap door in the ceiling of the compartment. He opened the trap door and rotated it on its hinge 180 degrees until the sun compass stood right-side up. Hopping on a small platform, he raised his head through the opening and peered out into the windstream. The air was as clear—and as cold—as a crystal of ice, the lay of the receding land visible for about a hundred miles. Byrd had studied the charts and knew that Halduyt's Headland, located just off the point of the Amsterdam arrow, lined up with true north at longitude 11°4′ E. Twenty-five miles south of the Headland, a high mountain on Spitsbergen's Hoel Peninsula lay on the same meridian.

Ten or eleven feet forward, Bennett sat in the cockpit, in the left-hand seat, looking back over his shoulder and over the three-foot fuel tanks. There was a window in the cockpit door, so whether the door was open or closed, he had a clear view of the aft compartment. Byrd waved to the left if he wanted Bennett to steer left, or to the right if he wanted him to steer in the opposite direction. Like a jack-in-the-box, he alternately raised his head topside and scrunched down again, waving left or right until the airplane was aligned with the landmarks and the shadow on the sun compass held steady down the middle of the pointer. The moveable dial on the base of the sun compass was set to "N." The discrepancy between the sun compass and the magnetic instrument told Byrd the amount of variation at this latitude.

The engines had been started when it was midnight in Kings Bay, and the sun, sitting just over the mountains, was perfectly in line with true north. It was now ahead and a few degrees to the right of the *Josephine Ford*, beginning its clockwise march around the rim of a wide bowl of horizon. The aviators had expected to fly a considerable distance over open water, but the drift ice below became more numerous and extensive, and within twenty miles they struck the edge of the Arctic pack. As a boy, Byrd had read an alarming story by Edgar Allan Poe about a traveler who finds himself on a ghost ship pulled relentlessly toward the South Pole. The story has no ending, the ship hurtles toward "stupendous ramparts of ice, towering away into the desolate sky, and looking like the walls of the universe." A young reader, curling up with such a tale, feels a combination of awe and dread perhaps never encountered before and never to be forgotten.

Byrd recalled the story and its associated feelings when the ship reached the polar icefields and the mysterious unknown.[1] Bennett felt the same stirrings of fear and wonder, and what childhood memories it connected with he never revealed. "We did not have much time to let our thoughts wander," he said, "and perhaps it was just as well."[2] To fly an erratic heading was to waste both time and fuel. Both men had to focus their attention on maintaining course and flying as straight a line as possible.

Byrd's job was to constantly detect the drift of the plane. On the starboard side of the flight cabin, a trap door had been cut in the floor between the chart table and the fuel tank just forward of the table. This trap door opened from side to side, and the tube-like drift indicator was mounted above the opening. Byrd would kneel over the instrument, slide the trap door open, and peer into the eyepiece. At virtually the last minute before leaving New York, Robb Oertel had obtained a box of smoke bombs from an outfit that created special effects for the movies. The bombs made dark smoke that would stand out against the snow and present an adequate target for sighting. Byrd found, however, that he could sight with precision on the narrow leads between icefields and the numerous hummocks and pressure ridges. Calibrating the apparent motion of the terrain feature, he could pick up the wind direction and velocity and work out the amount of degrees Bennett had to steer into the wind to correct for drift.

To put Bennett on a corrected course, Byrd had to jump back to the sun compass on the trap door in the ceiling of the toilet. He would readjust the base of the sun compass to the corrected heading. Bennett would constantly look back over his shoulder to pick up Byrd's gestures as to which direction he had to steer to compensate for the crosswind. Byrd would determine via the shadow on the sun compass whether the ship was squared away on the corrected heading and again wave Bennett right or left accordingly. Byrd wrote that he never let three minutes go by without getting the drift. He was a study in perpetual motion. He had to learn how to raise his head up into the windstream without getting frostbitten. The first few times he did it, he felt his cheeks and nose going numb but quickly rubbed the circulation back into them. The first time he opened the trap door in the floor and bent over the drift meter, he took his mittens off and almost froze his hands. He naturally sighted with his right eye; after a while he came down with a touch of snow blindness in that eye due to the white background and had to start sighting with his left.

Bennett at first tended to err to the east. "You are steering too much to the right," Byrd wrote in his diary; he instructed Bennett to set the earth inductor compass on the instrument panel "a few degrees to the left." Sometime later, he wrote, "You are keeping to the right 5° too much." Byrd's frustration surfaced in a strong admonition that followed: "You must not persist in keeping too far to the right." The word *must* was underlined three times.

Bennett soon "settled down" and steered with what Byrd called "astonishing accuracy."[3] Periodically, Bennett either had to use the toilet or wanted to grab a sandwich or just needed a few minutes rest, and Byrd would spell him at the control wheel. During these rest periods, Bennett would calculate fuel consumption, refill the cabin tanks from the five-gallon cans, and throw the empty cans out the entrance door on the port side of the fuselage to get rid of excess weight.

The sun was so low on the horizon it had been anticipated that at certain bearings the wings of the airplane would cast a shadow on the sun compass that had been installed topside. For this reason, Byrd had brought an additional sun compass, one not affixed to any surface. He used it at the window over the chart table, and, when spelling Bennett, he steered with this instrument in his right hand and the round control wheel in his left. He would just turn the wooden wheel slightly to the left or right, making whatever small control adjustments were necessary to hold the shadow steady on the clock mechanism's hour hand.

Both men were fascinated by the bizarre surface extending in every direction some two thousand feet below. The Polar Sea was everywhere covered with snow. At this altitude, it appeared to have a white, stucco-like texture. The rough, raised crisscrossings were pressure ridges, areas where the icefields had jammed together with a terrific force that had left hills of debris piled along the seam. The ice wasn't broken up into as many huge jigsaw pieces as they had expected. Only three times on the outward leg did they fly over open leads where the enormous fields had recently separated. These were long rivers of dark water that zig-zagged laterally across their flight path like flashes of black lightning. Occasionally they noticed a gray streak along the white surface; this was an older lead frozen over with younger, thinner ice. The leads and pressure ridges revealed the processes the human eye could not see: the hidden dynamism of a seemingly static environment.

Every sixty minutes, Byrd brought his sextant to the toilet, opened the trap door, and measured the altitude of the sun as it slowly swung across the starboard wing. Then he went back to the chart table and picked up the Nautical Almanac. The sun is blood brother to the navigator; in it, Byrd had the benefit of a second Floyd Bennett, ever constant and reliable. In the course of an hour, the sun moves precisely another fifteen degrees in its apparent arc around the earth. The Almanac is a log of its journey.

At any time during the day, the sun is directly over a certain point on earth. As the earth rotates, the point the sun is directly over changes. The Almanac gives the coordinates of those points for every day of the year and every minute of the day. Celestial navigation involves using this information and other tables in the Almanac to figure out where you are. The method is first to work out the proximity of a guessed or assumed position to the point the sun happens now to be directly over. You calculate the solar altitude from the point of view of an observer at the assumed position and then basically compare this number with the altitude you obtained with your sextant. A few mathematical rules come into play. Finally, you are entitled to draw a line on your chart—a line of position—representing your proximity to the point on earth the sun is just now directly over.

While doing this type of computation after the seventh hour of flight, Byrd first noticed oil streaming past him outside the flight cabin. The engine nacelles were shaped like dolphins. The window over the chart table framed a close view of the underside of the starboard nacelle. Oil was whizzing out from under its belly. Byrd went forward, jotting a note in his diary for Bennett to read: "The Stb motor has an oil leak." Bennett could see the nose of the nacelle from the cockpit. He went back to the cabin to examine the underside, while Byrd took the wheel. He returned with a grim expression.

Byrd wrote, "Is it a bad leak?"

Bennett wrote, "It is a bad leak and we may lose the motor at any time."[4]

In public, Byrd later tended to make light of or gloss over this incident. He once actually said that he had gotten a "kick" out of it.

But, as he would admit to Fitzhugh Green in private, it was "really a hair-raising moment."⁵ He and Bennett continued to discuss the situation in writing. Bennett reasoned that if they lost the starboard engine and then another engine failed, they would have to land immediately, come what may. So long as all of the motors were running, however, they had the luxury of picking and choosing a place to land. He suggested that they scout out a smooth spot in the stucco, descend, and make repairs. But Byrd remembered the trouble Amundsen and Ellsworth had gotten themselves into when they landed on the ice the year before and suspected that the spots which at two or three thousand feet appeared suitable for a landing were not quite so "smooth" at ground level. They agreed to go for the Pole, accept the probable loss of one engine, and pray that they didn't lose two out of three.

Earlier in the twentieth century, Arthur Hinks of the Royal Geographical Society realized something about the Nautical Almanac that made celestial navigation for polar explorers quick and easy. Before he left Washington, Byrd had gone over this shortcut with engineer George W. Littlehales of the navy's Hydrographic Office. The realization was that the Almanac gives the position of the sun from the point of view of an observer at the North Pole. If the imaginary observer picked up a sextant and measured the altitude of the sun above the horizon, that number would be identical to the figure in the Almanac for the sun's latitude for that instant.

As the flight of the *Josephine Ford* progressed, the sun appeared to move behind the aircraft, that is to say, from east to south. Here is where the Hinks shortcut came into play. Byrd took 90° north for his assumed position. The sun was just now hovering over a point on earth somewhere to the south-southeast of him. He was somewhere between that point and the North Pole. He shot the sun and compared the solar altitude he had just measured with the data in the Almanac.

The difference in degrees and minutes told him the distance that remained between him and the Pole. It did so because one minute of latitude is equivalent to one nautical mile. The distance figures diminished with each observation.

During the eighth hour of flight, Byrd came forward and shook Bennett's hand. He had written: "We should be at the Pole now. Make a circle and I will take a picture. Then I want the sun." He went back to the flight cabin to take a photograph of the polar surface and another series of sun sights. But before he picked up either a camera or a sextant, he saluted Robert Peary.

Byrd had Bennett circle the position he presumed to be the North Pole because he understood the limitations of his instruments. He allowed for the fact that the true Pole might be several miles away from the calibrated Pole, and circled to cover a larger extent of territory. Peary had made a similar allowance with his dog team in 1909.

Byrd realized that he would have the same margin of error on the return leg. They had flown due north on the meridian of longitude that just grazes the northwest coast of Spitsbergen: 11°4′ E. If they tried to fly due south along this meridian and erred several miles to the west, they would not only miss the mark, they would miss Svalbard and wind up ditching in the Greenland Sea when they ran out of fuel. To avoid such an eventuality, Byrd decided to aim for Grey Hook, a mountainous point of land on the northern coast of Spitsbergen. Grey Hook (Grahuken) is located at 15°E longitude. They could err as much as forty miles to the west of this site and still hit the archipelago. If they had been flying on an overcast day, Byrd would have aimed for a point even further east.

After spelling Bennett at the wheel at the start of the homeward leg, Byrd went back to the flight cabin and found his sextant on the floor and the horizon glass, one of the principal sighting elements of the instrument, broken into a myriad pieces. In the excitement of the moment, he had carelessly left the sextant on the chart table, instead of putting it back in its wooden box and securing the box in its protective niche on the shelf above the window. As a result, he would have to find his way back entirely on dead reckoning abetted only by the sun compass, a prospect Bennett found rather unnerving. Bennett was used to dealing with heavy machinery. He understood engines; direction-finding to him was a strange and magical practice. A device he could bounce in the palm of his hand seemed much too small to bear such a huge responsibility.

A navigator understands the relationship between time, the sun, and direction. They were heading south. The low sun was now in front of them and to the left of their flight path, gradually creeping west over the boundless white frontier. It is noon when the sun crosses the meridian of longitude wherever you happen to be, and when it crosses your meridian, it is due south of you. When the sun crosses 0° longitude, the meridian that passes through Greenwich, England, it is exactly noon Greenwich time; the sun is just south of that city and every shadow on the streets of Greenwich points north.

As the sun moved west across the port window at the forward end of the flight cabin and across the left side of Bennett's windshield, it would eventually cross 15°E longitude, the meridian of Grey Hook. From Grey Hook, the sun would have to sweep across fifteen more degrees of arc to reach 0° longitude. Since it takes the sun one hour to travel fifteen degrees, it would cross the horizon at the point they were aiming at precisely one hour before it crossed the Greenwich meridian.

Byrd had two chronometers to keep Greenwich time. At 11:00 a.m. Greenwich, he sprang forward to the cockpit, holding out his diary so Bennett could read this sentence: "Head the plane right at the sun."

He also had two watches and two sun compasses, all four of which were set to local time. The sun compasses had been readjusted for "S." As soon as Bennett pointed the center engine at the sun, Byrd checked one of the sun compasses. The single hour hand pointed to twelve noon, and the shadow extended straight down the length of the hand.

Since the sextant broke, Byrd had been, in his own words, concentrating "on the position of the blessed sun."[6] That was his backup system.

Conditions remained remarkably favorable—a high ceiling, unlimited visibility, a freshening breeze astern, and not a bump in the sky. All they had to do to reach Grey Hook was maintain the magnetic compass heading they were on when Bennett aligned the plane with the sun at 11:00 a.m. Greenwich time and correct for wind drift. Meanwhile, despite the gook leaking out of the starboard engine, the oil pressure gauge, one of three dials on the starboard engine nacelle, continued to remain at normal levels. Both men considered it a miracle that they were still flying on three engines. Not until they landed would they find out what had happened. A rivet had jarred loose on the oil tank within the starboard nacelle. The oil would continue leaking until it fell below that rivet hole, which was about half way down the tank.

"On, on, we went," wrote Byrd. "It seemed forever onward."[7]

There is nothing quite as dreamlike and serene as cruising in an airplane in smooth air. Byrd and Bennett had had little sleep to begin with and had been working more than the equivalent of a full shift since takeoff. As they took their turns at the wheel, the floating sensation, the hypnotic clamor of the engines and the stuffy warmth of the furs lulled them into something of a trancelike state. Byrd dozed off for a moment while piloting and was roused by the louder rumbling when the plane began to dive. Nothing beyond the windshield relieved the monotony.

The frozen sea and its maze of pressure ridges stretched infinitely further than the range of their plane. Its sheer extent was as astonishing as its desolation. "We felt," said Byrd, "no larger than a pin point and as lonely as the tomb, as remote and detached as a star."[8] Said Bennett: "The shadow of our plane moving along on the snow-covered ice below was the only animate thing we saw. We were two lone men, indeed, with no one near but God."[9]

The atmospheric conditions in the Arctic produce a phenomenon known as refraction. Air at the surface of the ice and the air at higher altitudes have a different temperature and different density. The non-uniformity causes light rays to bend so that distant objects that are just below the horizon appear to be sitting right on the horizon. By the time the sun had swung well over to the starboard windows, they saw, perhaps a hundred miles away, what Byrd later described as "a thin streak of white above the pale glitter of the ice."[10]

The waves were breaking towards the shore when they finally reached open water. It takes about an eleven-knot wind to raise whitecaps on the sea. That was the strength of the tailwind propelling them home. They struck the rugged coast about one mile wide of Grey Hook. From two thousand feet, one distant mile on the surface below looks about six inches long. By that much visual distance had Byrd erred. "His sense of direction was positively uncanny," said Bennett.[11]

All that day, a certain conversation was repeated among the members of Roald Amundsen's camp. Someone would look up at the clear and empty sky and wonder how Byrd and Bennett were doing. The veterans of the attempted transpolar flight of the Dornier Wals would think back to their forced landing one year ago. They all knew, as Amundsen himself put it in one of his books, that "So extremely small a thing can cause failure in such a flight."[12]

Someone else would then ask the question that seemed to be on everyone's mind: "What would happen if they don't come back?" The answer, of course, was painfully obvious. The *Norge* would have to rise from its hangar to search for the missing aviators. Meanwhile, the brief season of fair weather would predictably end, and, due to low ceilings and restricted visibility, the transpolar flight would be shelved for twelve months. Everything the Norwegians and Italians had worked to achieve this year and, in Amundsen's case, for a period of ten years, depended on the fate of the Americans. "God grant that they come back safely," Amundsen would solemnly intone.[13]

The conversation started up again at dinner in the camp's mess hall. It was known that the *Chantier* had received a wireless message from the *Josephine Ford* to the effect that the Pole had been reached and the ship was returning with a bad oil leak in one engine. Someone suggested during the soup course that the aviators should be approaching; they were due back around this time. That is, he muttered over his bowl, *if* they were coming back. At that moment, a member of the Italian ground crew burst in, babbling excitedly in English, the lingua franca of the expedition: "She come—a motor!"[14] There were shouts of joy, and a loud clatter reverberated through the hall as the men leaped wildly to their feet, overturning the benches they had been sitting on.

Pete Demas had been policing litter up off the American camp when he heard a rumbling from the north. He scanned the sky until he spotted a dark speck high over the mountains across the bay.

Out on the water, the *Chantier* began tooting its steam whistle, and Pete could see tiny figures swinging over the rail and into the lifeboats. Meanwhile, Norwegians and Italians were streaming toward the landing strip from every structure in sight. When the Fokker circled to land and lined up with the strip, so many of Amundsen's people had massed on the long gutter in the snow that she had to ascend and go around again.

Demas waved the crowd off the runway. The ship finally alighted softly on its skis and came to rest on the exact spot she had taken off from almost sixteen hours earlier. Pete opened the portside door, hopped up on the metal step, and climbed in, followed by Frederick Ramm, a Norwegian correspondent. Byrd stood in the cabin, removing the hood of his parka and one of his fur mittens. Bennett was still in the cockpit, switching off the ignition. Demas extended a hand, "Congratulations on your historic flight." [15]

"What did you say?" said Byrd, shaking hands. "Can't hear you— noise from the engines." [16] Byrd did not realize that the engines had already been shut down. He had completely forgotten to plug up his ears for the flight and was temporarily deaf to any sound other than the roar that still echoed in his eardrums.

Roald Amundsen was running uphill through the deep snow to reach the landing strip, his long legs outdistancing Russell Owen and Lincoln Ellsworth who were just behind him. "Nobody is so happy as I am over this," Amundsen told Owen. "I am so glad!" [17] The old eagle had tears in his eyes. Whether he was thinking of the twenty-nine days of hopeless struggle he and Ellsworth had endured on the ice or the journey he was now free to undertake, or some combination of both, he had shaken off his cool reserve and left it behind in the mess hall with his soup plate.

He pushed aside those of his countrymen who raced up the slope ahead of him and mobbed the aviators when they deplaned. He threw his arms around Byrd's shoulders and with rivers of tears coursing through the lines of his face, pouring over his white mustache and down the sleeves of his tweed jacket, he bent over the smaller man and kissed him on both cheeks. "That is magnificent, wonderful!" he said, trying to summon the proper English words. "I'm so happy!"[18]

PART 4

THE AIRPLANE
OF THE FUTURE

25

DOCTOR
OF LATITUDE
AND LONGITUDE

Hail to the hero of the Arctic dare,
Whose hazard was a lyric of the air,
A radiant writing upon virgin skies,
Toward which the centuries will turn their eyes.

EDWIN MARKHAM[1]

The quest for the transpolar flight was itself part of a larger context. From roughly the end of World War I to the beginning of World War II, Americans became obsessed with expeditions to the ends of the earth. This was, in part, a consequence of what the country had endured. President Woodrow Wilson had mobilized the nation by appealing to its highest instincts, but a new world order had failed to materialize in the aftermath of the "war to end all wars." Warren G. Harding's campaign rhetoric ("America's present need is not heroics but healing; not nostrums but normalcy....") manifested the general disillusionment. In one of the most dramatic mood swings in American history, the public by and large unburdened itself of high-minded principles and notions of duty and sacrifice. People, particularly the young, sought release in madcap music and dance, sexual experimentation and exuberant frivolity. A cycle of giddy consumption coincided with a manic celebration of all things new, strange, unusual, and unheard of.

Meanwhile, hundreds of thousands of square miles of Asia, Africa, and South America, in addition to millions of square miles of the Arctic and Antarctic, remained untrammeled by Europeans. Due to limited information and exposure, the world outside of everyday life and beyond the blue horizon appeared mysterious and dreamlike. In the realm of the imagination, the authority of the storyteller exceeded that of the geographer. Lost cities, lost tribes, prehistoric monsters, wonder drugs—anything seemed possible, and a sensational discovery potentially lurked around the bend of every trail.

Throughout the 1920s and 1930s, a number of extraordinary men and women seized the opportunity to expand the horizons of popular and scientific knowledge. Intrepid explorers emerged from the back of beyond to become major cultural icons in a golden age of high adventure in godforsaken places. In just the period between the Armistice and the flight of the *Josephine Ford*, for example:

Sixty-six-year-old Dr. Henry H. Rusby, dean of the College of Pharmacy of Columbia University, led a party of academics up the uncharted headwaters of the Amazon in search of new medicinal drugs. His sturdy wilderness guide, Gordon MacCreagh, outlasted all of the other members of the expedition and emerged from the jungle after two years with samples of a substance called "caapi." It was rumored to cause people to lose their inhibitions.

Roy Chapman Andrews of the American Museum of Natural History crossed the Gobi Desert three times in search of the fossilized remains of ancient life. A tall, professorial-looking fellow with the heart of a frontiersman, Andrews battled warlords, bandits, and sandstorms, and discovered the richest dinosaur beds on the face of the earth.

Swashbuckling naturalist William Beebe of the New York Zoological Society studied wildlife in headhunter country up river in Borneo and in the line of march of the army ants of British Guiana. In 1925, he sailed to the Galapagos Islands and the Sargasso Sea and pioneered underwater exploration.

Dr. Alexander Hamilton Rice left Miramar, his fabulous estate in Newport, Rhode Island, to chart half a million square miles of Amazon rain forest. He survived a running battle with the Guaribos, considered the most ferocious indigenous tribe in either Venezuela or Brazil, and established a school for would-be explorers in New York, under the auspices of the American Geographical Society.

Martin and Osa Johnson, a cute couple from Kansas who had once been held at spearpoint on the island of Malekula, where the natives were known to dine on human flesh, scored a cinematic triumph with their silent travelogue, *Among the Cannibal Isles of the South Seas*. They switched their base of operations to Africa in 1923 and continued to film consistently sympathetic portraits of exotic people, places and wildlife.

A former American spy, the brilliant, gorgeous Marguerite Harrison joined forces with the future creators of *King Kong*, World War aviator Merian C. Cooper and daredevil cameraman Ernest B. Schoedsack. The trio journeyed to the east with a vaguely conceived idea of finding picturesque nomads somewhere between the Persian Gulf and the Black Sea, and making a documentary film on their migration. They eventually stumbled upon the Bakhtiari, a wild, nomadic tribe of southwest Persia and accompanied them on an epic, forty-six-day trek into the heart of the Zagros Mountains.

The Age of Adventure itself took place within a larger context. The players in this drama lived as we do in a consumer society. The mass media were in place and operated in accordance with a familiar pattern. As always, the media fastened on the personalities and events people were paying attention to and attempted to turn them into products, because those products could be expected to sell and make money. In the twenties, people were paying attention to explorers. Media organizations assiduously processed this attention into money. The leading explorers were offered lucrative contracts to serialize their adventures in newspapers and magazines, write books, appear in newsreels, and go on radio and the lecture circuit. A few explorers, such as Dr. Alexander H. Rice, were independently wealthy. Most were not, and relied on media contracts to finance their expeditions. It was a mutually beneficial arrangement. The polar explorers journeyed to the farthest possible horizons, and tended to receive the most attention and a larger share of the media pie. This was only fitting since they operated on the largest scale, requiring surface ships, aircraft, and a ground crew.

Richard Byrd changed the dynamic in one sense. Like MacMillan, he had the wherewithal to bring a radio station to the High Arctic. Communication between an explorer and the sponsors of the expedition could now continue right out into the field. After Byrd returned to Kings Bay and had a good night's sleep, he dispatched two radiograms from the *Chantier*. One went to his wife, the other to David Lawrence, president of Current News Features. He asked Lawrence:

Will you interpret our successful accomplishing of Pole as fulfilling terms [of] contract. Do not desire to do any further exploration until return States and improve skis for landings, but will go to [Cape Morris] Jesup if necessary to fulfill contract. Answer immediately.[2]

Lawrence, in turn, consulted the two most important papers to which he was syndicating the Byrd story, the *New York Times* and the *St. Louis Post-Dispatch*. A few days later, he sent this terse message to the *Chantier*:

No sales value in further flights.

The *Chantier* weighed anchor seven days later. A flurry of messages continued to be transmitted and received in the ensuing weeks as the steamship left the last of the ice floes in its wake and entered warmer waters:

"Rush first part Commander Byrd story as soon as possible," buzzed F. T. Birchall, managing editor of the *New York Times*.

Companies that had donated fire extinguishers, batteries, and insulating material to the expedition wanted to know if their products were used on the North Pole flight. Mayors, promoters, and leaders of civic associations in five different cities vied to pin Byrd down for a personal appearance. "Can you accept official reception by National Geographic Society, Washington Auditorium, evening, June 23, presidential party present?" asked Gilbert Grosvenor.

Lefkowitz and Pitofsky, furriers, decided that "In honor of Commander Byrd's glorious flight we want to make two beautiful coats for Mrs. Coolidge and Mrs. Byrd. These to be made with the pelts of animals that come from further north [than] any white man had reached. Can you please bring back several fine foxes or other pelts at our expense." A vaudeville agent wanted to know, "What can Bennett do. Query. What salary. Query. Many thanks."

"Rush Byrd's continuation. Make it tonight," hollered Birchall.

As everyone from the furriers to the fire extinguisher people realized, the flight to the Pole—the northern end of the earth—had a far greater impact on the world at large than any other exploit in an era of audacious feats. The last act in the gripping drama was about to take place. On May 9, when Byrd and Bennett flew northward over the Polar Sea, their competition in the Western Arctic remained grounded at Point Barrow due to fog. For three weeks, George Wilkins and Major Thomas Lanphier waited for the fog to lift. It never did. They realized that even if they could gain enough altitude to fly above the mist, the pack ice below would still be concealed by layer upon layer of gray stratus. It would be a waste of fuel under these conditions to hop off in search of undiscovered land. Early in June they sent a wire to their backers in Detroit, informing them that there could be no further flights that season.

But the window of clear weather had remained open in the Eastern Arctic. On the morning of May 11, Roald Amundsen, Lincoln Ellsworth, and Umberto Nobile boarded the control car of the *Norge*. The airship ascended as high as the jagged peaks of the white mountains and glided across Kings Bay, escorted for the first few miles of her journey by the *Josephine Ford*. The *Norge* cruised at an airspeed of roughly fifty miles an hour, a fraction of the average velocity of the Fokker trimotor. Fifteen hours later, at 1:30 a.m. on May 12, Ellsworth's forty-sixth birthday, she reached a spot identified by her instruments as 90° north. Nobile brought the ship down to about 300 feet. All hands doffed their caps as a Norwegian, an Italian, and an American flag were hurled to the surface on sharp-pointed poles. The three flags stood erect in the snow; the dirigible circled over them for a couple of hours and then headed into the unexplored area on the Alaskan and Siberian side of the North Pole.

It had taken the *Norge* almost as long to complete the first leg of the voyage as it had taken the Fokker to cover an equivalent distance and return to Kings Bay. By the next morning, they were only about halfway to Alaska when they ran into fog and heavy winds. Precipitation forms when the atmosphere is moist, and a moist atmosphere in the high latitudes spells another potential danger. Ice began to form on the engines and engine gondolas. Bits and pieces of ice broke off of those surfaces and were batted forward by the propellers. The projectiles tore right through the outer envelope of the airship. The *Norge* became her own target as her propellers were transformed into machine guns spraying a fusillade of ice. The crew had to climb up from the control car into the envelope and patch up the holes in the fabric before the bags of hydrogen gas were punctured and the ship tumbled right out of the hazy sky. Eventually they ran out of patching material and glue. By that time, the fog had thinned, and they caught a glimpse of the Alaskan coast.

Seventy-one hours after embarking from Kings Bay, the *Norge* made a safe landing at Teller, Alaska, a former gold-rush camp that had been reborn as a reindeer preserve. The formerly gleaming and immaculate airship was torn and ragged after having come under a steady bombardment and had to be dismantled. The leader of the expedition, however, was in the pink of condition. Amundsen could now sit back and relax. He had finally found what he was looking for, which was less a thing than a sense of completeness. He had achieved everything he had ever set out to accomplish. He shaved his mustache, making him look ten years younger, and with a carefree spirit assembled his shipmates and announced his retirement. "When I was a young man," he said, "I made up my mind to visit the globe's two Poles and pass through the Northwest and Northeast Passages. Now that these things are done, a new generation may continue."[3]

Both Amundsen and Byrd had successfully united aeronautics and polar exploration. But if Roald Amundsen, like the Arctic itself, was ready to fade into twilight at the end of another glorious season in the sun, Dick Byrd had just emerged as an expedition leader and stood at the dawn of a glittering career. He and Bennett were given a tumul-tuous ticker-tape parade in New York upon their return to the United States. The aviators marched side by side up lower Broadway, as flags

fluttered above the arched entranceways of the Romanesque skyscrapers and ribbons and streamers twisted and glittered in the air. Three
hundred distinguished citizens followed on foot. Hundreds of thousands of spectators overflowed the curbs and burst out from behind
police barricades below a deluge of confetti.

The parade ended at City Hall, where Mayor James J. Walker
presided over a ceremony in the council chamber attended by five
United States senators and five members of the House of the Representatives. Congressman Clifton A. Woodrum of Virginia spoke on
behalf of the congressional delegation. Woodrum represented Byrd's
hometown in the Shenandoah Valley. While he presented a joint resolution passed unanimously by both houses in celebration of the polar
flight, a couple of men dragged in an object the size of a steamer trunk.
It opened up like a steamer trunk, but turned out to be a portable
organ. As prearranged, a musician sat down, hit the foot pedals, and
oodled out a familiar, schmaltzy tune. Woodrum, known as the "Singing Congressman," concluded his presentation by crooning "Carry
Me Back to Old Virginny." He invited everyone to join in the chorus,
and everyone did.

After a luncheon reception at the brownstone palazzo of the
Advertising Club of New York on Park Avenue and 23rd Street, Byrd
and Bennett were given a police escort to Pennsylvania Station, where
they caught the 3:20 to Washington. That evening, before a full house
at the Washington Auditorium, an audience that included two cabinet
members, three sub-cabinet officials, a justice of the Supreme Court,
fifteen senators, fifty congressmen, fourteen generals, ten admirals,
and eighteen representatives of foreign governments, President
Coolidge presented the aviators with gold medals of the National
Geographic Society.

Byrd and Bennett were subsequently honored by the cities of Boston, Massachusetts; Philadelphia, Pennsylvania; and Richmond,
Virginia. They were thunderously greeted in Byrd's hometown of

Winchester, Virginia, and later in the summer Bennett received a hero's welcome in Warrensburg, New York, where he was born and raised, and in the neighboring community of Lake George, where he had lived and worked. The aviators returned to Philadelphia on July 21, when Byrd was presented with a ceremonial sword on which his and Bennett's names had been handsomely engraved. The sword was manufactured by a local firm, and twenty-thousand residents of the Quaker City contributed to a fund to pay for it. The presentation took place outside of Independence Hall on a sweltering day when the temperature soared to a hundred degrees. Byrd said, "If I didn't like Philadelphia and its people so well, I'd almost wish I were at the North Pole on a day like this."[4]

On January 3, 1927, Byrd, Amundsen, and Ellsworth were guests of honor at a dinner hosted by Colonel A. A. Anderson in his magnificent studio in the penthouse of the Beaux Arts building in New York. The *Norge* had embarked on its historic voyage to Alaska two days after the *Josephine Ford* returned to Kings Bay. Before the departure of the dirigible, Byrd gave Amundsen a bubble sextant, sun compass, and drift meter to use on the flight and lent Ellsworth his polar bear pants. They were inducted together as honorary members of the Hunter's Fraternity of America, the organization under whose auspices the Colonel had feted Peary and Amundsen ten years earlier, when the quest for the transpolar flight had officially gotten underway.

Later in the month, Byrd was promoted to commander and Bennett to warrant machinist. Byrd had lobbied for Bennett to be advanced to lieutenant j.g. or at least ensign, but the idea of an enlisted man being raised to the status of a commissioned officer went against the grain of military culture.[5] Instead, Bennett was elevated to the level just above the highest non-commissioned grade and made a warrant officer. At a White House ceremony on February 25, both men received the Congressional Medal of Honor.

Byrd began a lecture tour on June 25 at Carnegie Hall in New York, sharing the stage with Bennett and many of the members of the expedition. He was introduced by Dr. John H. Finley, president of the American Geographical Society, a New York–based institution. Finley bestowed on the explorer a degree created especially for the occasion: "Doctor of Latitude and Longitude." Edwin Markham, author of a world-famous poem, "Man With the Hoe," was on hand to lend the occasion a sense of gravitas. Markham had settled on Staten Island after a peripatetic life. The white-maned scribe waxed eloquent with an epic, fifty-one-line ode commemorating the flight to the Pole as a milestone on the human journey.

The tour would eventually reach seventy-two American cities and extend through the spring of 1927. As Byrd hustled breathlessly from whistle stop to whistle stop, the love affair between hero and public grew. Amateur and professional songwriters composed ditties in his honor. Dime-store poets followed suit with verses ranging from the melodramatic:

> And the groaning glacier lay cowed and still
> And the black sea failed to perform its will
> Palsied and faint was the hand of Death
> And the murderous Arctic held its breath

To the sentimental:

> Some are called, few chosen
> The Lord selected you
> To brave the northern terrors
> and make your dream come true
> How modestly you did it
> A smile, a bow, that's all

You didn't know your greatness
Just answered well the call

To the droll:

Hats off tu dese har navy men
who yumped into deir plane
And sailed away tu no man' land
And back to eart' again

Of course, in a less sensitive and more innocent America, dialect humor was perfectly acceptable. Byrd's praises were also sung by numerous comic voices, including this one:

Yes sah, dat Byrd dun been up Nawth
Ramblin' 'roun dat pole up dah
Stirrin' up dat ice 'n snow
Got no bizness flyin' so fah[6]

"Lecture contracts," Byrd said, after two exhausting months on the circuit, "are among the miserable things an Arctic explorer has to put up with to insure against bankruptcy."[7] Meanwhile, letters poured in from well-wishers and favor-seekers of all ages. "I spend half my nights on the train," he said, "and the rest of the time trying to catch up on correspondence that has accumulated while I have been away." Children studying about the North Pole sent in questions, which Byrd patiently answered. An old shipmate who wanted to open a luncheonette under the boardwalk in Coney Island asked the explorer to use his influence to help him lease a certain lot. "I put it up to you to find out just what I could do," Byrd answered. "It is impossible for me, travelling around as I am, to know just to whom to go to help you out. Unless you tell me just where I can put in a good word I won't know what to do."[8] Marie Peary Stafford, Admiral Peary's daughter, had never been in an airplane and wrote to ask "if I could make my first flight with you, whom I admire more than anyone except Dad."[9] Mrs. Stafford may have had more on her mind than aviation. "Mr. Henry Woodhouse has promised me that he will arrange a flight for me any time I wish," she averred. "But, while that is tremendously sweet of Mr. Woodhouse, I am contrary and *still* not satisfied." Woodhouse was founder and publisher of *Flying* magazine and an acquaintance of Admiral Peary. (This letter apparently went unanswered.)

In addition to keeping up with his lecture engagements and correspondence, Byrd also had to find time for literary endeavors. Naturally, an adoring public wanted to know more about him, and to meet the demand a series of articles began appearing under his by-line in the major magazines, most of which were written by Fitzhugh Green. Although Green still had one foot in the navy, his other foot and much of his energy and imagination was in the publishing business. As executive officer of George Palmer Putnam, Inc., one of his principal duties was to secure writing assignments for Putnam's roster of explorers and to edit, ghost, or re-write the pieces as necessary. Unfortunately for history, Green's approach to non-fiction writing involved a process he called "fictionizing." He told Byrd, "By fictionizing your experiences, that is by putting them in attractive form, we are able to convey the whole narrative to the reader much more gracefully."

One of the pieces that Green fictionized inadvertently damaged Byrd's legacy and reputation. It appeared in the January 1927 issue of the *Ladies Home Journal* and was entitled, "This Hero Business." The snappy title is awfully deceptive, suggesting that the putative author was cynical about his profession. The story, however, was not about the art of making a living as a hero, it was actually about the psychological aspects of being worshipped as one. Besieged by photographers, summoned before the nation's leaders, enjoined to make speeches, Byrd starts to wonder what the adulation and attention really means. Through a series of encounters with ordinary people who seek him out, he realizes that the hero of the moment is a symbolic figure, a person on whom the worshippers project their own hopes and dreams. If someone in the crowd needs to be inspired or reassured in a certain way, or confirmed in some notion, the hero fulfills that need for that person.

It is a wonderful article, despite being entirely a concoction of Fitzhugh Green. But there was a kernel of truth: Green was not fictionizing when he cast a polar aviator in the role of philosophical observer. At that point, he had known Byrd for close to twenty years. Pitching a Byrd proposal to another editor, he described his friend and client as being "of a more or less sensitive nature himself, not to mention the fact," Green added, "that he has specialized somewhat in philosophy."[10] Those were among the more factual words that issued from Fitzhugh Green's typewriter in 1926. By writing "Hero Business" as he did, he exposed a side of Dick Byrd that the explorer himself didn't ordinarily reveal ... with one notable exception.

In the summer of 1926, while Fitzhugh Green was shopping around the "Hero Business" idea, Byrd found some time between speaking dates and drafted an article later polished by Green and published in a magazine called the *World's Work*. "I have put in some philosophy," he told Green, when he sent him the manuscript. "You and Dickey may faint when you see it." Carl C. Dickey was editor of the monthly. The piece came out that fall, in the November issue, and was titled "In Defense of Stunt Flying."

The subject Byrd applied his searching mind to was quite topical in the 1920s. Numerous lives had been lost on the pioneer flights that marked the development of aviation. Ironically, two more people died as the piece went to press. On September 21, 1926, the French aviator Rene Fonck attempted to hop off from Long Island on a non-stop transatlantic flight to Paris. The airplane crashed on take-off and burst into flames; a mechanic and a radio operator, one-half of the flight crew, were killed. Byrd addressed the issue by adopting the method of the holistic thinker: never look at anything in isolation. The meaning is not to be found in the isolated event but in the pattern of which it is a part. Accordingly, he saw each flight as a phase of a learning process, a step in the evolution of a technology that in and of itself would bring the world closer and enable civilization to evolve.

In the original manuscript, he wrote:

> As is true with a great painting, too close a view will show a great number of meaningless dabs of color of different sizes and shapes. But from a distance, those dabs together take on form, meaning and beauty.
>
> So it is with hazardous pioneer flights. May we not suppose that they are happenings, however small, that assist the great procession of the race toward its goal—though the meaning of these movements may be inscrutable? They would have their place in a painting of that procession—a small place that would none the less be a necessary part of the picture.[11]

Fliers of the pioneer era generally tended to see their work as making possible the progress of aviation, and the idea of "progress" was very much in the atmosphere of the times. But the search for meaning and perspective, and a point of view that took in the full sweep of history was fairly unique among the restless spirits who rose to fame in the Age of Adventure. Interestingly, Byrd articulated this vision as a time when he was contemplating perhaps the most hazardous flight of his career.

⫷ 26 ⫸

MUSKETEERS
OF THE AIR

What a trip!

Rodman Wanamaker

The flight of the *Norge* had finally put to rest the myth of a lost continent in the Polar Sea. Byrd, Ellsworth, Wilkins, and their contemporaries nevertheless believed that more islands might yet be discovered in the icefields north of Greenland or Ellesmere Island. One of the projects Byrd had in mind when he returned from Spitsbergen was to pick up where he had left off on the MacMillan expedition and perform an aerial survey of the Polar Sea from bases in the Ellesmere-Greenland region. "This area attracts me greatly," he said, "and so little of it has yet been seen, even by Amundsen and Ellsworth."[1] He was equally attracted, if not more so, by the prospect of surveying the South Polar regions by air. "The South Pole," he felt, "offers, perhaps, the most romantic bit of exploration, because there is a vast unknown continent only the edges of which have been explored." When he ran out of poles to circumnavigate, he imagined he would attempt a record altitude flight and probe the upper layers of the atmosphere.[2] To a celebrated aviator-explorer, the world and the stars were literally wide open.

But while making such pronouncements in print or at public appearances, he privately devoted his attention to the consummation of some unfinished business. In his usual secretive manner, Byrd quietly investigated the possibility of finally making a transatlantic flight. Ocean flying was still a perilous adventure. Since the historic flights of 1919, only three more crossings of the Atlantic had been made by aircraft. The U.S. Army fliers completed their round-the-world flight of 1924 by flying in stages across the North Atlantic by way of Iceland, Greenland, and Labrador. That same year, the best airship engineers in the world, the Germans, completed the ZR-3, a two-and-a-half-million-cubic-foot dirigible earmarked for the U.S. Navy. The ship represented the American share of the war reparations imposed on Germany by the Treaty of Versailles. A German crew made an uneventful, non-stop transatlantic flight in October of 1924 to deliver the dirigible to the Naval Air Station at Lakehurst, New Jersey. The ZR-3 was subsequently renamed the *Los Angeles*. Finally, in January of 1926, Commander Ramon Franco, a Spanish aviator, made the first heavier-than-air crossing of the South Atlantic, flying a seaplane in stages from Europe to South America via the Cape Verde Islands and the Island of Fernando de Noronha, which lies within 300 miles of the coast of Brazil.

Transatlantic flights of a commercial nature were not yet feasible. At least one more spectacular feat would have to be accomplished to demonstrate their feasibility, and this was perhaps the most elusive grail in early aviation. In 1919, Raymond Orteig, the proprietor of two hotel-restaurants in Greenwich Village, offered a prize of $25,000 for the first non-stop flight between New York and Paris. Orteig was born in France on the slopes of the Pyrenees Mountains and had immigrated to the United States at the age of twelve. The prize was initially supposed to remain in effect for five years, but after it had gone unclaimed, Orteig renewed the offer for an additional five years. Within a few days of the flight of the *Josephine Ford*, Orteig had sent a radiogram to the *Chantier*, suggesting that Byrd enter the transatlantic competition. Floyd Bennett was all for the idea.[3]

Fortunately, so was a man worth between seventy-five and one hundred million dollars. Lewis Rodman Wanamaker, sixty-three, was the last surviving son of John Wanamaker, the department-store magnate. Rodman ran the business after his father's death in 1922. The Wanamaker empire consisted of branch stores in New York, Philadelphia, London, and Paris. Rodman lived in a townhouse in downtown Philadelphia and maintained residences in each of the three other cities in which he had retail outlets. He also owned villas in Atlantic City, Newport, and Biarritz, and a country estate outside of Philadelphia. He carried over six million dollars in life insurance and was said to be the most highly insured man in the world. Outside of his business, his main interest was commercial aviation. In 1914, Wanamaker contracted with Glenn Curtiss to build a biplane capable of flying from New York to England by way of the Azores. It was called the *America*, and a British and an American pilot were signed to make the flight. The American aviator was John Towers. The biplane had initially been equipped with two engines; a third was added when it became clear that the ship couldn't lift the required load in its original configuration. The project was aborted when war broke out in Europe, and the British pilot was summoned home.

Eleven years later, the Wanamaker outlet in New York became the first department store to sell airplanes along with furniture, linen and apparel. The single-engine monoplanes produced by the Stout subsidiary of Henry and Edsel Ford went on sale at the store in October of 1925. The retail price was $25,000. Rodman ordered ten planes from the Fords and planned to put some of them to use delivering merchandise to customers wintering in Palm Beach and Miami. When Rodman heard that Byrd returned from Spitsbergen owing thirty thousand dollars in debts incurred over the course of the North Pole expedition, he sent for Byrd and made up some of the deficit himself. He also did Byrd the favor of exhibiting the *Josephine Ford* at his New York and Philadelphia stores in July and August of 1926. Otherwise, Byrd would have had to rent hangar space for the Fokker, which would have been an additional expense. They began discussing a transatlantic flight to Paris almost as soon as they became acquainted.

Nobody did dangerous things more sensibly than Richard Byrd. Byrd's approach to transoceanic aviation in the second half of 1926 was based on two principles. First, he saw no sense in attempting to venture out over the Atlantic Ocean in a single-engine airplane. A single-engine plane was of course smaller and lighter than a multi-engine aircraft. It met less air resistance, operated more efficiently, and for all of these reasons had a longer range. But if you're in the middle of the ocean and your sole engine fails, what do you do? The twin-engine aircraft of the 1920s could not maintain flight on one engine. The only reasonable alternative was a trimotor. As the *Josephine Ford* had demonstrated in her test flights, a plane with three engines could stay aloft if one engine failed, and even if two motors were lost the pilot could lighten his load and remain in the air long enough to spot a steamship and ditch within sight of help.

It was over 3,600 miles from New York to Paris, more than twice the distance from Kings Bay to the North Pole and back. The flight was far beyond the range of the *Josephine Ford*, and no other extant trimotor in the United States had been tested sufficiently enough, in Byrd's opinion, to determine whether it had the requisite capability. The airplane Byrd needed would therefore have to be considered experimental. His second operating principle was that you did not risk your own and other people's lives on a pioneering flight in an experimental plane until it had been properly tested.

His point was driven home when Rene Fonck smashed up. In August of 1926, six weeks before Fonck trundled down the dirt runway of Roosevelt Field in a three-engine transatlantic plane designed by the Russian engineer, Igor Sikorsky, Byrd privately confided his misgivings about the aircraft. He felt the ship had not been given an adequate try-out with a heavy load. "Captain Fonck may make it," he told Wanamaker, "but if he does, it will be in the nature of a very risky stunt."[4] The flight cabin of the Sikorsky plane had been decked out with wood paneling and Spanish leather. It had bulletproof windows and was as luxuriously appointed as a drawing room in Gramercy Park. But one of the landing gear crumpled on the takeoff run; the plane cartwheeled, the fuel ignited like a torch, and two men died. One of the backers of the flight later whispered to Byrd that speed and fuel consumption figures indicated that the plane would never have made it across the ocean.[5]

Byrd wanted to employ what he called "the airplane of the future," a three-engined aircraft that could cross the ocean with passengers, freight and a reasonable margin of safety, and herald an age of regular transatlantic service. Edsel Ford candidly admitted to Byrd that his trimotor couldn't be modified to haul enough fuel for a 4,000-mile flight; moreover, it would cost three times the price of the standard Ford trimotor for Edsel to build a transatlantic plane from scratch. But if the Fords couldn't economically produce the ship of the future, Anthony Fokker could. Byrd had confidence in the standard Fokker trimotor, a tried and true design. Fokker had equipped one of his standard models with an enlarged wing for the Wilkins transpolar flight. He proposed to do the same for a Byrd transatlantic flight. An enlarged wingspan plus the latest model Whirlwind engines, the J-5s, which had 20 percent less fuel consumption than the J-4B's, just might, Byrd thought, do the trick.

Byrd presented the proposal to his prospective backer. He estimated that the total cost of the project, including airplane, engines, hangar, personnel, and equipment, would be within $100,000. He asked Wanamaker for a salary for Floyd Bennett, who could not be expected to receive *paid* leave from the navy (and subsequently did not), and offered his own services without compensation. There was only one hitch: Rodman Wanamaker couldn't stomach Tony Fokker.[6]

Wanamaker had lived in Paris for ten years managing his father's continental outlet. As essayist Joseph Epstein said of another American abroad, author Henry James, he "internationalized" himself, and earned the respect of Parisian society as much for being an art connoisseur as a businessman. When he returned to the United States, he revolutionized the retail industry by showcasing upscale European fashions and home decor. To create the proper atmosphere, he arranged for the finest musicians of his era to give concerts at the Wanamaker stores. Some of the artists performed at these recitals on rare instruments from Rodman's personal collection, which included four Stradivarius violins. Rodman Wanamaker, in short, was a gentleman, and Anthony Fokker was Anthony Fokker.

The flying Dutchman delighted in fast-talking his way into theaters and exhibitions without paying the admission fees he could well afford.[7] He would reach into his pocket, pull out some odd laundry receipt, and say, "Press!" He was boisterous, temperamental, and crude, and habitually complained that he never received enough credit or attention. While Byrd scooted hither and yon across the country in the fall of 1926 fulfilling his lecture commitments, it fell to Floyd Bennett to try to bring Wanamaker and Fokker together. Bennett's impossible task was complicated by the fact that he had to go through Wanamaker's urbane plenipotentiary Grover A. Whalen, the general manager of the New York store. Whalen always wore a homburg hat and a fresh carnation in his lapel, and was famous for his sense of grandeur. In addition to his executive duties, he was also the official greeter of the City of New York. Byrd and Bennett first met Whalen when they were welcomed back from Spitsbergen. Whalen orchestrated the tumult and hoopla, and was busy concocting even more elaborate fanfare for Queen Marie of Romania, due to arrive on the *Leviathan* on October 18.

By November, Wanamaker apparently found the prospect of entering into a contractual relationship with Fokker so distasteful that he gave every impression of backing out of the deal, and Byrd entertained an offer from one of the promoters who had previously stood behind Fonck. But the earnest, low-key Bennett stuck to his course and kept going over the details of the plan with Whalen. On December 30, 1926, Bennett detected a change in the prevailing wind and sent Byrd a telegram that read, "It looks as if Wanamaker is coming around."[8] Wanamaker finally approved the proposal on January 14 and signed the contract a week later. By that time, whatever advantage Byrd might have had by virtue of an early start had been squandered. Numerous entrants on both sides of the Atlantic had revved up plans for a transoceanic flight, and Byrd was once again a major participant in an international competition billed by the media as the most newsworthy event of the year.

1927 was as sensational a year for aviation as it was for Babe Ruth and the New York Yankees. The development of more reliable engines, particularly the air-cooled engine such as the Wright Whirlwind, made possible flights of longer distances than had ever been attempted before. The air-cooled engine eliminated the weight of water, radiator, pipes, and pumps and the various support structures that held the water-cooling system together. More fuel could be carried now, and more fuel of course meant increased range. The first flights from England to India and from Paris to Siberia were undertaken in 1927; neither succeeded. During the first six months of the year, five European aviators set out to replicate the Franco flight of 1926 and cross the South Atlantic in stages. Two made it to South

America; one was forced down at sea; one was forced down on the coast of North Africa and captured by Bedouins; and one disappeared altogether. All of the South Atlantic fliers had hopped off in single-engine airplanes; three out of five amply illustrated Byrd's contention about the inadvisability of embarking on a transoceanic jaunt with a single power plant.

The Pacific Ocean was also challenged in 1927, with several contestants competing for the first successful flight from the west coast of the United States to Hawaii. But the New York to Paris hop generated the most interest, the most coverage and the most excitement of all the record flights that were mounted that year. In February, Byrd quietly brought George Noville into his project as fuel engineer and radio operator. Rex had married Sigrid Matson and relocated to San Francisco, where he acquired a position with Standard Oil of California. He was not a proficient radioman, but at Byrd's suggestion he took a month-long course at the Radio Institute of America. Noville spent five nights a week at the Institute, brushing up on his Morse code.

In March, Byrd summoned Fitzhugh Green to a meeting at the executive offices of the Wanamaker store in lower Manhattan. Green had just faced the biggest crisis of his life. He loved the navy and the sea. But in the early 1920s, when the first of his three children was born, he realized that if he stayed in the service, he would never have a permanent home nor would he be able to support his family in the style to which he and his sophisticated wife aspired. At the same time, he had no business experience whatsoever. He got himself assigned to the Naval War College in Newport, Rhode Island, in 1923 and immediately began casting his eyes further south to the media and financial capital of the nation. In 1924, he succeeded in convincing the navy that it needed a public relations office. The department obligingly installed him in New York to take charge of the operation. For the past three years, he had been simultaneously discharging his duties as propagandist while working his way up in the publishing industry. In early March of 1927, after Green had accumulated four consecutive years of shore duty—an accomplishment on a par with Ruth's sixty home runs—disaster struck. Orders were cut reassigning him to Shanghai.

He dusted off his uniform, took an early train down to Washington, and tried to talk his way out of the Asiatic fleet, but the admirals were unrelenting. Meanwhile, his "volcanic" civilian boss, George Palmer Putnam, erupted with a series of long-distance calls to the switchboard of Green's hotel, insisting that he "get the hell back to New York."⁹ It was impossible to serve two demanding masters. Green decided that he needed a sign from above to show him what to do. While awaiting a visitation, he wandered into the Army-Navy Club for lunch. At the next table, a group of navy men were handicapping the transatlantic race. Dick Byrd was reportedly planning to hop off for France and so was another respected naval aviator, Noel Davis. Both were considered the frontrunners. At the end of February, an obscure airmail pilot named Charles A. Lindbergh had formally entered the competition for the Orteig Prize, but no one gave him much of a chance.

Green snapped his fingers. Someone was bound to make history before the end of spring. If he could pick a winner and secure the book and magazine rights to the story, it would be a publishing coup. He would be able to write his future in bylines forever after. He resigned his commission and took the first train back to George Palmer Putnam, Inc.

The Wanamaker emporium in New York in 1927 comprised two stores occupying the two blocks bordered by 8th and 10th Streets and Broadway and Fourth Avenue. The complex included a 1,500-seat auditorium with the largest concert organ in the metropolitan area. Rodman Wanamaker, like his father, John, considered himself not only an entrepreneur but a citizen of an enlightened republic. Rodman accordingly used his private suite of offices for aesthetic as well as business purposes; the conference rooms were also art galleries where Rodman displayed his latest acquisitions. He had turned sixty-four on February 13, 1927. Green described him as "a tall white-haired gentleman who had one of the most engaging smiles I have ever seen."[10] As Grover Whalen briefed Green on the flight being organized under Byrd's leadership, Wanamaker kept repeating, "What a trip, what a trip!"

"How can I help?" Green asked.

Byrd put a hand on Green's shoulder and asked him if he would be willing to sail to France and act as advance man. Information had to be gathered on landing fields and fight routes over the countryside; contacts had to be established with local officials. The groundwork also had to be prepared in England in case inclement weather forced Byrd to land in London instead of Paris.

Green arrived in Paris on April 12. On that day, while Byrd lectured in Chicago, Bennett and Noville filled out passport applications. They weren't quite sure how to complete the part of the form on which they were required to state the purpose of the prospective journey. Bennett wanted to write, "To see if we can make it." They decided it would be better to say, "For scientific purposes."[11]

At 9:34 on the morning of the twelfth, two stars of early aviation, Bert Acosta and Clarence Chamberlin, took off from Roosevelt Field and started circling over the environs in a single-engine monoplane. Acosta was a big, swaggering, broad-shouldered man with black hair and a black slash of a mustache. Chamberlin was a blond, rail-thin Midwesterner with a self-effacing manner and a down-home smile. They were both in their early thirties, and both had been flight instructors, test pilots, and barnstormers. Chamberlin was so adept with stick and rudder that he had once made a forced landing in the exercise

yard of Eastern Penitentiary in Philadelphia, Pennsylvania, while en route to an air show in Camden, New Jersey. After tinkering with the engine for a while, he hopped over the wall and continued on his way. Acosta had set a speed record of 176 mph and an altitude record of 22,500 feet, accomplishing the latter without oxygen. He could turn barrel rolls so close to the ground that spectators would duck for cover. He was said to be the greatest natural flier of the pioneer era.

The two aviators spelled one another at the wheel of a cabin plane built by Giuseppe M. Bellanca. The aircraft had a unique design feature that enabled it to perform with super efficiency. The struts that branched out on either side of the fuselage not only supported the high wing, but acted just like the wing. They produced lift when the leading edges met the airstream. Acosta and Chamberlin stayed aloft for fifty-one hours, eleven minutes and twenty-five seconds, and when they finally landed on the afternoon of April 14, they had broken the previous endurance record by six hours. "It was just like any other flight," Chamberlin drawled, "except a little longer."[12] The endurance flight was actually a dry run for a more ambitious undertaking. The owner of the plane, a wealthy young man named Charles A. Levine, shortly announced that he had engaged the services of a navigator, airmail pilot Lloyd Bertaud, and that either Acosta or Chamberlin would accompany Bertaud as pilot on a transatlantic flight to Paris. He encouraged both endurance fliers to work on the flight plan and said he would make his selection in due time.

The day after Acosta and Chamberlin landed, Byrd, Bennett, and Noville went down to the Battery to try out an inflatable life raft they intended to take with them on the Atlantic crossing as part of the emergency gear. They were accompanied by a gaggle of reporters and photographers, and hundreds of spectators watched them paddle about in the Hudson River. The media had taken to calling them "The Three Musketeers of the Air." The next day, the trio reassembled at Teterboro Airport in New Jersey to join Anthony Fokker for the first test flight of the airplane he had built to carry the musketeers across the Atlantic. It would be the last time that Dick Byrd, Floyd Bennett, and Rex Noville ever flew together.

Like the *Josephine Ford*, the new *America* had three Wright engines, a forty-nine-foot-long, fabric-covered fuselage and a wooden wing. The wing of the transatlantic plane measured seventy-one feet from tip to tip and was fully eight feet longer than that of the Arctic plane. On each side of the forward part of the fuselage was a sliding door which, when opened, afforded an unobstructed view of the port or starboard engine. A narrow catwalk bridged the gap from this part of the fuselage to the engine nacelles. In case of an oil leak or any other mechanical problem, Bennett would be able to crawl out along the catwalk and work on the wing engines in flight. Cables had been strung parallel to the catwalks and at some height above them. By donning a harness and hooking himself up to the cable, he would be able to traverse the catwalk with a measure of safety.

Bennett had worked with Fokker and his people on adapting their standard trimotor for a 3,600-mile flight. The major issue that had to be resolved was the means of carrying over 1,200 gallons or 7,000 pounds of fuel. The solution was to put the bulk of the fuel—800 gallons—in an enormous tank that sat right over the center of gravity of the plane in roughly the same position as the two extra fuel tanks in the cabin of the *Josephine Ford*. But the 800-gallon tank was four times the size of the mailbox-shaped receptacles installed in the *Ford*. It stood as high as the ceiling of the cabin and was as broad as the cabin was wide, and its weight was essentially borne by the wing spars. Additional fuel tanks were carried in the hollow of the wing and in a smaller container aft of the main tank.

The new configuration had the disadvantage of confining the crew to the section of the fuselage forward of the main tank and blocking access to the section aft. This was partially compensated for by moving the pilot's cockpit a few feet forward, to a point just aft of the center engine. Shifting the pilot and co-pilot forward left room for an additional compartment between the cockpit and the main tank. Here the radio and navigation equipment was installed. A trap door was cut in the floor on the navigator's side for the use of the drift indicator. To take sextant readings, Byrd would have to move forward into the pilot's cockpit, where a ceiling hatch had been provided.

Bennett had designed a switch that enabled him to shut off all three engines at once to prevent the *America* from bursting into flames like the Sikorsky plane if in a pinch they hit the ground hard. He had also helped develop a dump valve that could be operated from the pilot's cockpit. It was anticipated that with a full load the massive weight of the transatlantic plane would impair its ability to fly on less than three engines. In case of engine failure, therefore, a certain amount of fuel could be jettisoned from the main tank to reduce the load to the point where the ship would fly without difficulty on two engines. If they had to ditch, all of the fuel in the main tank could be instantly drained, and the tank could be resealed again for flotation.

Every one of these features, Byrd felt, were experiments that might pave the way for the transoceanic airliner of the future. At about 5:00 p.m. on Saturday, April 16, Tony Fokker took the plane up for the first time to determine if she was airworthy. Bennett was in the co-pilot's seat; Byrd and Noville stood just behind them in the navigation and radio compartment. Fokker flew at only a couple of hundred feet above ground level due to a low ceiling under layers of haze. Some two to three hundred spectators could be seen massed below. Among them stood Marie Byrd. Cora Bennett was sick and confined to bed in the apartment she and Floyd had rented in the Flatbush section of Brooklyn. Sigrid Noville remained at the Manhattan hotel where she and George had booked a room.

The trimotor performed beautifully. After about forty minutes, Fokker prepared to land. As he reduced power, the plane became nose-heavy. The *America* had been designed to lift a relatively large amount of weight, and a great deal of attention had been given to how that weight would be distributed in the plane. But the initial test flight had not been made with a heavy load or a properly balanced load. The wing tanks had been filled with a small amount of fuel and the main tank had been left empty. The tail—the principal storage area of the plane—was also empty. On a long-distance flight, it would have been crammed with provisions, emergency gear, and additional fuel. On April 16, there was no ballast in the tail to counterbalance the weight of the four men in the forward compartments. Fokker had not anticipated any problems.

In order to land, the pilot pulls back on the control wheel, gently raising the nose, as the plane glides down, to allow the ship to settle. By pulling back on the wheel, the aviator manipulates the elevator control. But the weight and balance of an airplane affects the stability of the ship and the effectiveness of the elevator. Fokker described the aerodynamics of the situation in his memoirs. He said that he asked Bennett to crank the elevator trim control to the full nose-up position. Byrd, however, was right about experimental aircraft; no one knew how a multi-engine plane equipped with a seventy-one-foot wing would behave in various configurations. "The combination of large wing, empty tank, and small supply of gas in the wing tanks," said Fokker, "made the speed of landing so slow that the efficiency of the elevator was lower than normal."[13] He and his passengers realized that they could not land safely because the elevator wasn't supplying enough pitch control to hold the nose up and the tail down.

Fokker circled twice above the airfield, but inevitably he had to come down. Floyd Bennett licked his lips. Bennett was as steady in a crisis as any man who ever lived. The lip-licking was the only sign of fear he was known to show, and considering all the dangerous situations he and Byrd had found themselves in since teaming up in 1925, he didn't show it particularly often. But Byrd recognized the mannerism.

His own way of dealing with the tension was to attempt to defuse it. He yelled in Noville's ear, kiddingly, calling Rex's attention to Bennett's quirky habit. Noville didn't respond, his face taut with trepidation. As Fokker dropped down and the dirt runway began to rush up at them, Byrd reached overhead and grabbed hold of one of the steel braces in the skeletal structure of the fuselage. His eyes swept to the airspeed indicator on the instrument panel just to the right of Fokker. The old admonition of Nathan Chase—maintain your flying speed and you'll be all right—had become instinctive. The airplane was making sixty miles an hour when the wheels touched the dirt. Each man expected to die.

In addition to Marie Byrd, the crowd of spectators included Grover Whalen, Doc Kinkade, who had been dispatched to look after the Whirlwind engines, and reporters from all the New York papers. They saw the wheels of the trimotor meet the runway, but as the plane careened along for about 150 feet, the tail kept rising. Suddenly the ship hit a soft spot in the dirt; the nose plunged down, the tail rose up, and the airplane made a stunning somersault, landing on its back with its wheels spinning in the air.

Fokker was disgorged first. By his own account, he was in the left-hand seat at the moment of impact, pulling all the way back on the unresponsive control wheel. There were dual controls for the pilot and co-pilot, and both systems moved in unison; the wheel on the right-hand side consequently moved back against Bennett, pressing him against his seat. As the plane nosed over, the center engine and engine mounting were thrust aft, but instead of being hurtled straight back, the machinery moved diagonally and to the right, crushing Bennett. After the plane had turned over on its back, Fokker fell out of the cockpit, either through the trap door in the ceiling (now below him) or through a rift in the crumpled nose. He landed on his face and except for a few bruises and a spritzing of engine oil was otherwise unhurt.

Byrd found himself alive, upside down and in pain. In the quiet after the noise of the crash, he heard Bennett shout, "Look out for fire."[14] Fokker had already hit the engine cut-off switch Bennett had designed, but the other three had no way of knowing that. Spurred by the memory of what had happened to Fonck and the Sikorsky ship, Noville tore furiously at the fabric sheath and smashed through the confining wall. Emerging into daylight, he collapsed in great pain, holding his stomach. "I felt as if I had been broken in two," he said.[15] Byrd followed, crawling through the hole Rex had made with his bare hands.

When the nose had telescoped inwards, Noville had been thrown against Byrd, and Byrd felt his left arm snap just above the wrist. He had a bump on his head, but the only serious damage was the broken arm. He was described as being "pale and shaken, but able to stand."[16] He sat down on the ground and with his right hand tugged repeatedly on his left until he felt that the broken bones had been realigned. Meanwhile, Marie, Whalen, Kinkade, and a number of mechanics and aviation executives had rushed toward the wreck. The men lifted the plane and extricated Bennett. Marie, it was said, "showed remarkable self-control, standing by her husband and assisting him as best she could."[17]

The designers of the aircraft had placed the oil tank under the pilot and co-pilot's seats. The tank had ruptured during the crash, and when the machine turned over, inverting the position of pilot and tank, the contents had burbled down all over Bennett. Floyd's left leg was apparently broken; his face was badly gashed and drenched with oil and blood. Byrd moved quickly to Bennett's side, bent over him, and identified himself. "I guess I'm done for," Bennett murmured.

"Nonsense," Byrd told him. "You'll be okay."

"I'm all broken up," Bennett gasped. "I can't see, and I have no feeling in my left arm."[18]

Inwardly, Byrd was afraid that Floyd *was* going to die. He pulled out a handkerchief and wiped Bennett's eyes clear of engine oil. The pools of oil had obstructed his vision. Floyd blinked and was able to see again. "I think we both felt encouraged then," Byrd wrote several years later, "but I could see that Bennett was utterly without fear of the end that he thought was near."[19]

"The Three Musketeers of the Air" were taken to nearby Hackensack Hospital. An X-ray showed that Byrd had set his fractured bones perfectly by himself. It was at first thought that Noville had suffered grave internal injuries, but fortunately only some muscle tissue in his abdomen had been torn loose; he was released from the hospital after six days. Bennett had sustained a slight fracture of the right side of his head, which had caused a temporary paralysis of his left arm. His left leg was broken above the knee, and his left lung had been punctured by a broken rib. He was in critical condition for a week, but had the grit and will to pull through. He would remain hospitalized for three months.

According to one unattributed report, Byrd and Fokker had a shouting match in the aftermath of the accident.[20] If so, Byrd had reason to blow his stack. While convalescing, Bennett told Grover Whalen that the mishap could have been avoided *if only* Fokker had let him adjust the trim control.[21]

27

THE ALMOST
IMPOSSIBLE

*They belong to a unique fraternity, these fliers. They are
a little different from other men in their attitude toward
their work. For fliers know that every day they fly death
may lurk behind the next cloud; they all feel that somewhere, some time, they will meet death quickly.
Yet they keep on.*

RUSSELL D. OWEN
"OCEAN FLYING TAKES HEAVY TOLL"[1]

The rivalry supposed by the press to exist between the transatlantic fliers was pure ballyhoo. They all naturally hoped
to be first to reach Paris, but at the same time they were
rooting for the others to succeed, too. Clarence Chamberlin, who
lived in Teterboro, New Jersey, drove over to Hackensack to visit
Byrd at the hospital where he had been held overnight. Byrd went
over the navigation problems of a transoceanic flight with him and
offered to tutor him in the use of the bubble sextant and drift indicator. Noel Davis called the hospital and spoke with Marie. Three
months earlier Davis had written Byrd, saying "I am glad that you

are going ahead with plans for a transatlantic flight. With both of us trying the chances of making this flight an American achievement are doubled, and that is what I am primarily interested in."[2]

They and their fellow aviators also shared a common bond as airmen and pioneers. Every flier represented aviation, and above all they wanted the aerial enterprise to move forward. A record of unvarnished successes was in everyone's favor. But the development of new and untested technology continued to be fraught with peril. Eight days after the crash of the *America*, a reception was held at Curtiss Field for the christening of the Bellanca monoplane, the *Columbia*. Charles Levine, the owner of the plane, appointed his nine-year-old daughter, Eloyse, to do the honors with a bottle of ginger ale. Afterwards, Clarence Chamberlin took Eloyse up for a ride in the plane, along with the fifteen-year-old daughter of one of her father's sponsors. No sooner was Chamberlin airborne than it became apparent to observers on the ground that one of the struts that held the landing gear in place had given way on takeoff. The left wheel was too loose and floppy now to support the weight of the plane.

Another pilot on the field immediately hopped off, flew close to the *Columbia* and by way of signals and gestures informed Chamberlin of the condition of his ship. Chamberlin never flinched. As calmly as if he were buying ice cream cones and asking the girls their favorite flavor, he told them how to brace themselves and directed one of them to move to the tail of the plane for balance. The kids took it all in stride. With their parents watching breathlessly on the field, he then came in with one wing low and made a soft landing on the right wheel. His passengers thanked him for a nice ride.[3]

Two days later, Davis took off from Langley Field, Virginia, on the final test flight of his transatlantic plane, the *American Legion*. Lieutenant Commander Noel Davis, thirty-five, was a craggy-faced genius who had graduated third in his class at the Naval Academy. He was so popular and respected as a midshipman that his classmates wrote in his yearbook entry, "A better balanced man than Noel, or one possessed of as many fine qualities which we admire would be hard to imagine. Five minutes after you meet him he is sure to be your next choice for President."[4] He was born in Utah, had worked as a cowhand, and looked like a short and stocky version of William S. Hart, the star of numerous silent westerns. Davis had supervised the mine-laying operation in the North Sea during the war and the mine-sweeping operation that followed the Armistice. He broadened himself in the postwar years becoming both a naval aviator and a lawyer. He worked his way through Harvard Law School by finding employment as a mining engineer. Like Byrd, Davis was presently a retired officer on active duty; he had been in charge of the aviation division of the Naval Reserves before undertaking preparations for a transatlantic flight. Also like Byrd, he was thorough, energetic, and determined.

Davis had contracted with the Keystone Aircraft Corporation, a Pennsylvania-based manufacturer, for a biplane with a sixty-seven-foot wingspan and three engines. He was backed by a group of businessmen headed by Richard F. Hoyt, the visionary aviation executive who had contributed to the Byrd North Pole expedition. The aircraft was completed on April 9, one week before the *America*, and since that time Davis had been carefully testing it with an ever-increasing load. At 6:20 on the morning of April 26, Davis and his flying partner, fellow Naval aviator Lieutenant Stanton H. Wooster, took off with a maximum load of 17,000 pounds. The *American Legion* was painted yellow and carried her two outboard engines on the lower wing. As she sluggishly gained altitude, Wooster, in the left-hand seat, made a climbing turn to the right to avoid a line of trees. The ship lost airspeed. Wooster apparently looked for a place to land and spotted a marsh. The biplane came down in the wetlands and piled up against the edge of a muddy bank, its tail sticking up in the air, its nose and cockpit submerged in the gook. Davis and Wooster died of suffocation, the third and fourth lives lost in the competition for the Orteig Prize.[5] They had had a dump valve for emergencies such as this; why they didn't immediately drain their fuel tank to lighten the load remains a mystery.

As the press and public began to appreciate the dangers of transoceanic aviation, an even more fundamental question began to be asked: Why do good men risk their lives trying to accomplish the Atlantic flight?

This was Byrd's answer: "They do it," he said, "because they know that some day it will be done."

> Man cannot withstand the lure of the almost impossible. He longs to push back further and further the limitations of his activity, of his life. Call it adventure if you will. I like to call it the unconquerable spirit of man's soul which will not admit defeat.[6]

Bert Acosta was part Spanish and part Irish, and had a bit of Indian in him as well.[7] This rather volatile mixture produced a strapping and darkly handsome caballero whose robust instincts and free spirit were legendary in aviation circles. One night after a few pitchers of needled beer, Acosta and another pilot got into a loud argument over the correct time. They were standing on or near Curtiss Field. "Wait here," Acosta slurred, "and I'll find out." He jumped into an airplane, flew over to Manhattan, located Madison Square, and set his watch by the illuminated clock tower of the Metropolitan Life Insurance building.

Another time, after having thoroughly lubricated himself with about a gallon of bathtub gin, Acosta trained his dark eyes on an ex-World War I fighter pilot named Pierson, who was equally well-oiled. "I could knock you out of the sky with a sack full of oranges," he snapped. Pierson accepted the challenge. They staggered out to the ramp, agreeing to meet at 2,000 feet. When both fliers reached that altitude and Pierson fired the first fruit, Acosta noticed that he had neglected to bring any oranges with him. He proceeded to engage Pierson in a mock dogfight and managed to crowd him out of the sky. Both planes were wrecked as a result, but the principals were unharmed.

The deaths of Davis and Wooster, however, seemed to have jolted Acosta into a period of sober reflection. The Davis and Fonck crashes were both due to excess weight. Weight affects almost every aspect of aircraft performance. A heavily loaded transatlantic plane flew at close to its structural limitations, at the narrow margin between safety and danger. Every pound saved counted. Acosta, a 210-pounder, weighed sixty pounds more than Clarence Chamberlin. He reasoned that *Columbia*'s chances of succeeding where the *American Legion* and the Sikorsky ship had failed were increased with Chamberlin in the pilot's seat and diminished with himself at the wheel. For this reason, at the end of April he withdrew from the project in favor of Chamberlin. His selfless gesture did not go unnoticed.

By that time, Byrd and Wanamaker had decided to go through with their flight. Wanamaker had been willing to table the project pending Floyd Bennett's recovery. He was dissuaded by Bennett himself; having learned how long he would have to remain on the disabled list, Floyd informed Wanamaker that he would prefer to see the flight mounted on schedule.[8] He told Byrd that it was his duty to proceed. "You go on without me," he said.[9] The cockpit of the *America* and its center engine had been smashed up and the steel propeller on that engine was bent, but the wing and outboard engines were unharmed. While Fokker rushed to rebuild the nose of the ship, Byrd solicited recommendations from the army and navy for a gifted pilot-mechanic who could fill Bennett's flight boots. He began negotiating with the co-holder of the endurance championship shortly after Acosta's withdrawal became public.

The ground rules for the Orteig Prize did not specify that the winner had to fly from New York to Paris. The winner had only to fly between those cities, and a westbound, non-stop flight from Paris to New York was equally valid. On the morning of May 8, which dawned gray and overcast in Paris, two rugged and colorful Frenchmen hopped off in a single-engine, open-cockpit biplane on a flight to New York to claim the prize. Charles Eugene Jules Marie Nungesser, thirty-five, had gone to Argentina at the age of about eighteen or nineteen and had ridden the Pampas as a gaucho. He had initially fought in the World War as a cavalryman before becoming an aviator. He had downed forty-five German planes and two Teutonic balloons, and was wounded seventeen times in the process. Shattered bones in his skull, both elbows and a thigh, knee, and foot had been reinforced with platinum plates. He was the only airman in the transatlantic race who could cause his compass to deviate just by looking at it. His co-pilot and navigator, François Coli, was a month shy of his forty-sixth birthday. Coli had enlisted as an infantryman at the outbreak of the war and had received a battlefield commission. When his feet were frostbitten in the winter of 1915–16 and he couldn't continue to fight on the ground, he requested aviation training. He was wounded five times in air duels and lost his right eye. Both Nungesser and Coli had been inducted in the Legion of Honor.

Their aircraft was painted white so that it could be spotted at long distance in case they were forced down at sea and was called *L'Oiseau Blanc*, the "White Bird." Painted on the fuselage was the same symbol that had been emblazoned on Nungesser's fighter plane during the war: a large black heart with a white skull and crossbones in the center and, just above the death's-head, a white coffin tastefully flanked by two white candles. The meaning of the symbol, according to Nungesser, was that "A strong heart doesn't fear a horrible death."[10] As Nungesser and Coli ascended over an open meadow just beyond Le Bourget field, they dropped a set of detachable landing gear, reducing their total load by over 250 pounds. They picked up a predicted tailwind and were last spotted heading west off the southern coast of Ireland.

Just before they drove to the airport, Nungesser had told a reporter that he and Coli expected to come down like a flying boat in New York harbor on the afternoon of Monday, May 9. Thousands of New Yorkers lined the Battery on that afternoon, but the *White Bird* failed to appear and was never seen again. Nungesser and Coli had flown directly in the path of a storm system centered over Newfoundland, and exactly what happened to them remains a mystery to this day.

On May 11, Byrd asked Wanamaker to consider sending the *America* on a rescue flight. The search area—the coast of Newfoundland and Nova Scotia—was terrain Byrd had flown over repeatedly during the war and again with the NCs. "My personal services are at your disposal," he said.[11] His left arm was still in a sling; the bandages were due to come off in about three days. Instead, Wanamaker offered a $25,000 reward for the recovery of Nungesser and Coli alive or dead.

Six lives had now been lost in the transatlantic competition.

To manage the business end of the Paris flight, Rodman Wanamaker had resurrected the America Trans-Oceanic Company, an organization he had incorporated more than a decade earlier when he first dreamed of underwriting a transatlantic hop. Grover Whalen had been brought in to run the operation. According to Whalen, Wanamaker had allocated a million dollars—a whopping sum in 1927—to cover every conceivable expense.[12] The company leased

Roosevelt Field, the airport with the longest runway in the New York metropolitan area, and took over an old wooden hangar erected during the war. Both the runway and hangar were in miserable shape. Fonck had crashed on the same strip in September; Byrd felt that the roughness of the field had been a contributing factor. He had Whalen hire a steamroller to smooth the surface down. The remaining bumps were attacked by a ground crew headed by two veterans of the North Pole expedition, Tom Mulroy and Pete Demas, and augmented by Nels Sorensen of the MacMillan expedition. The ground crew also renovated the hangar. They had needed just one more half day of work to finish painting and roofing the shed when the *America* crashed at Teterboro Airport on April 16. The rebuilt aircraft landed on the reconditioned runway on Thursday, May 12.

Curtiss and Roosevelt Fields were adjacent to one another. Shortly before the *America* arrived, a silver-gray, single-engine monoplane had landed on Curtiss Field, and a tall, slender flier had jumped down. Charles Augustus Lindbergh had raised money in the Midwest to finance an airplane that had been manufactured for him on the west coast. The previous day he had flown from San Diego, California, to St. Louis, Missouri, completing the longest, non-stop solo flight in the United States. He was twenty-five years old with pink cheeks and a bashful smile, and from the moment he had his picture snapped by the New York press, the city fell madly in love with him.

Lindbergh had arranged for hangar space on Curtiss Field, where the *Columbia* was surreptitiously being prepared to hop off, it was said, perhaps by the weekend. After the "Flying Fool" landed, he approached Whalen for permission to use the Roosevelt runway.[13] The tabloids had been scoffing at Lindbergh's chances. Whalen asked him if he couldn't think of a better way to commit suicide, but agreed to let him use the field. The next day Byrd walked over to Lindbergh's hangar and congratulated him on his record flight from San Diego. Byrd astonished Lindbergh by offering to share the Atlantic weather forecasts that were being prepared for him by the U.S. Weather Bureau and reviewed by Roswell F. Barratt, a former navy aerologist who had worked on the flight of the NCs.[14] The reporters on the scene rounded up Chamberlin, and he, Byrd, and Lindbergh were photographed for the morning papers. "What promises to be the most spectacular race ever held—3,600 miles over the open sea to Paris—may start tomorrow morning," screamed the lead line of a page one news story.[15]

But Byrd wasn't racing anybody. He had a brand-new airplane with an outsize wing that had been flown no further than from Teterboro to Mineola. Its range was unknown, and its performance over the open sea could not be predicted. To Byrd aviation was a science, not a stunt; as in the laboratory, knowledge was based on rigorous testing and a painstaking collection of data. If Wanamaker had reached a decision more expeditiously in the fall, Byrd might have easily stayed in the forefront of the pack, even with a near-fatal mishap on the first factory test. But he wasn't going to take chances with other people's lives or his own. He appointed Acosta chief pilot of the *America* and began conducting an extensive series of test flights.

One of the more bizarre aspects of the transatlantic drama was that while bad weather had been forecast over the Atlantic in the middle of May, bad blood developed between the navigator of the *Columbia*, Bertaud, and the man who had engaged his services, Levine. Levine decided to relieve Bertaud of any connection with the flight; the navigator, meanwhile, demanded that his contract be upheld. As a persistent fog finally lifted along the Atlantic coast, the *Columbia* and her able pilot, Clarence Chamberlin, remained temporarily grounded pending a ruling by the Brooklyn Supreme Court.

Before dawn on May 20, Lindbergh's airplane, the *Spirit of St. Louis*, was towed to Roosevelt Field. At sunrise, the lanky, clean-cut young flier stood looking at a propeller that had been planted in the ground at the spot where the Sikorsky plane had gone up in flames eight months earlier and two airmen had lost their lives. Then he walked back to the ramp, where his plane was being fueled. Byrd shook his hand and slapped him on the back. "Good luck to you, old man," he said, "I'll see you in Paris."[16]

The *Spirit of St. Louis*, like the *Columbia*, was a small, fast ship; both were cabin planes about twenty-seven feet long with a forty-six-foot wingspan. The *Spirit* was a one-seater designed for a solo transatlantic flight. To increase fuel capacity the tiny cabin had been moved slightly aft of its standard position, and a 425-gallon fuel tank had been installed right under the wing. The pilot sat directly behind the fuel tank and was consequently deprived of a windshield. Lindbergh had side windows; if he wanted to see where he was going, he had to raise a periscope. In the hollow of the propeller spinner were scrawled the words, "We are all with you," and the signatures of the factory workers who had built the ship.

At 7:52 a.m., Lindbergh began his takeoff run. Byrd watched from the ramp, standing just in front of the *America*. Chamberlin was also on the field. Bert Acosta and Rex Noville, who sat about twelve feet above ground in the cockpit of the trimotor, had the best view. A truck sped alongside the runway, pacing the *Spirit*. Pete Demas was driving; in the back were Lindbergh's mechanics and a bunch of fire extinguishers. The *Spirit* seemed to bounce up and down as Lindbergh made several efforts to get his five thousand pound load off the ground. He was rapidly running out of runway, heading straight for a gully separating Roosevelt Field from Curtiss. The observers understood that Lindbergh was facing a do or die proposition: either ascend or pile up in the gully at full throttle.

His head was bent slightly forward, his eyes glued to the instrument panel, his jaw set. The *Spirit* rose into the air, clearing a tractor at the end of the runway by ten feet and a span of telephone wires by twenty feet.

"God be with him," said Byrd, "I hope he gets there."[17] Then he went back to his hangar and called Bennett to let him know that Lindbergh had just gotten underway. Floyd had been following developments from his hospital bed.

A reception had been scheduled the next day, Saturday, the twenty-first, for the christening of the *America*. The Wanamaker organization had sent people down to the Delaware River to fill a couple of bottles of water at more or less the spot where George Washington had made the historic crossing. Wanamaker's two daughters smashed those bottles over the bow of the trimotor in a ceremony at Roosevelt Field. Byrd's wife, mother, and brothers were among the many distinguished guests. Just before the festivities began, word arrived that Lindbergh had landed at Le Bourget. Byrd pocketed the speech he had written for the occasion and instead praised Lindbergh for having accomplished "one of the greatest individual feats in all history."[18]

Charles Levine now announced that Clarence Chamberlin and a mystery partner would hop off in the *Columbia* for a mystery destination. The Kings County court had dismissed Bertaud's temporary injunction. Levine, thirty, was born in Massachusetts and grew up in Brooklyn. He was short, prematurely bald, and had a scrappy, streetwise sensibility. He had made money in the used car business, married a beauty contest winner, the former Grace S. Nova, the "Belle of Williamsburg," and was currently in the salvage business. His commercial ventures may not have been entirely kosher; he had tried to obtain an airmail contract but the post office, it was said, "objected vigorously."[19] Levine loved fast cars and was crazy about planes. Acosta and Chamberlin had taught him to fly. Aviators called him the "Flying Junkman."

On the evening of the twenty-first, Chamberlin had the *Columbia* towed onto Roosevelt Field for a dawn takeoff, but Grover Whalen refused to let him use the runway. The airplane was subsequently towed back to Curtiss Field. When Byrd learned that Chamberlin had been turned away, he insisted that the runway be available to anyone who wanted to use it. Said Pete Demas: "The battle raged on and Wanamaker himself was forced to take a hand in the situation when Byrd refused to do any more [work] on his own flight plans. The final decision was that the field would be open to anyone as long as they relieved Wanamaker of any form of responsibility."[20]

Exactly two weeks later, after a period of rain, the *Columbia* was poised for takeoff on the Roosevelt runway at the crack of dawn on the fourth of June. She had a high yellow wing over a fuselage the color of a silver bullet. "New York–Paris" had been written in black letters on the fuselage, but on the third, the hyphen and the word "Paris" had been painted out. Chamberlin sat in the pilot's seat, next to an empty right-hand seat. The engine was idling. He looked toward a crowd of well-wishers and sensation-seekers gathered at the edge of the runway and made a beckoning gesture. From out of the shadows, at a trot, came Charles Levine. The Flying Junkman jumped into the co-pilot's seat, Chamberlin kicked in the throttle and the plane roared down the strip. Chamberlin was apparently the only person on the planet who had been let in on the secret. Levine had withheld his intentions not only from the press, but from his own family. Mrs. Levine, the Williamsburg beauty, collapsed into the arms of a policeman as the yellow wings lifted the ship smoothly off the field.[21]

Lindbergh had run into an area of sleet off Newfoundland but generally enjoyed clear weather and favorable winds. Chamberlin and Levine met basically similar conditions over the ocean but encountered rain and fog when they reached Europe. They were aiming for Berlin and got within 110 miles of the city when they ran out of fuel and were forced to land. They took off again after refueling. Their initial hop of some 3,900 miles broke all existing records for a long-distance flight.

During the three weeks between Lindbergh's arrival and his and the Chamberlin/Levine transatlantic flights, Richard Byrd and his team had put a new and larger rudder on the *America*, replaced the center engine and corrected a problem with the landing gear that had caused one testflight to be aborted on takeoff. At Tony Fokker's suggestion, they built a twelve-foot incline at the head of the runway so the trimotor could start her takeoff run going downhill. There were wooden tracks for each wheel, a greased, metal slide for the tail-skid, and guide rails to keep the wheels and tail-skid from jumping the tracks. Big ships with heavy loads require longer runways to develop sufficient velocity to leave the ground. Since it wasn't feasible to bridge the gully between Roosevelt and Curtiss Field and make the runway longer, the incline compensated by making it possible for the trimotor to accelerate more rapidly at the get-go. The effect was comparable, Byrd said, to adding "at least 500 feet to the end of the runway."[22]

During this period, he also continued making what Fokker called, "the most interminable series of test flights it has ever been my grief to witness."[23] Fokker was eager to see another of his airplanes soar to glory and at one point blew up at Byrd because, being greedy for credit and approval, he believed that Byrd was stalling. Bernt Balchen was employed by Fokker as a test pilot at this juncture. "If he don't get going soon," the Dutchman told him, "I myself will buy the plane back and fly it over the ocean, by Gott!"[24] Fokker's impatience was matched by that of the general public. The sporting crowd had made book on the race, and Byrd had been touted as an early favorite. His fan mail began to turn into hate mail as letter-writers castigated him for being left at the switch.

For a sensitive man like Byrd, the reaction was galling. Thousands of spectators had been flocking to Roosevelt Field. The consumer society had generated a demand for heroism and excitement, which Byrd was perfectly willing to satisfy. But he was also a serious technician. His first task was to determine if his aircraft had sufficient range for a transoceanic hop; to do this, he had to find out how much weight the ship could lift. The more weight, the more fuel that could be carried and the greater the range. To cross the ocean, the trimotor had to lift some fourteen thousand pounds. After ferrying the rebuilt *America* to Roosevelt Field, Balchen and another Fokker pilot tested it with loads of 9,600 and 11,410 pounds. The ship was then accepted by the America Trans-Oceanic Company. But it had not yet been demonstrated that she could reach Paris. Accordingly, Byrd, Noville, and Acosta were gradually increasing the takeoff weight by increments of about five hundred pounds of deadweight on each test hop.

Since the incline on which the ship started her takeoff run could not be moved, the runway was essentially a one-way strip. Airplanes take off into the wind; if the wind wasn't aligned just right, the next scheduled test flight would have to be postponed. The reporters who turned out on Roosevelt Field everyday understood this and conveyed the details to their readers. They understood that the aircraft remained grounded on May, 16, 17, and 18, when the wind blew across the runway, because it was dangerous to try to buck a crosswind on takeoff with a heavily-loaded ship. And that for several days after a rainstorm on the twenty-fourth and twenty-fifth, the strip was too muddy for a large ship to develop enough acceleration to get off the ground.

But there were things the newsmen did not understand because they were not aviators, and consequently their readers never knew. When an airplane embarks on a long-distance flight, it carries an enormous amount of fuel. As the flight progresses, fuel is slowly consumed and the plane becomes lighter and lighter. The weight of the aircraft changes during each phase of the flight. When the weight changes, the flying characteristics change. A Fokker trimotor with a seventy-one-foot wingspan was so newfangled it had not undergone rigorous testing for the various stages of a long-range operation.

Byrd conducted thirty-one test flights over a period of four weeks to not only determine the lifting power of the *America* but also the most efficient way of operating that aircraft during each phase of the flight.[25] Some of his data survives.[26] On May 31, for example, his crew loaded the ship with 9,600 pounds and flew back and forth over a certain track. They ran the engines at 1,450, 1,500, 1,550, and 1,650 rpm, and for each different engine setting they noted the airspeed and computed the fuel consumption in gallons per hour, gallons per mile and pounds of fuel per mile. On June 2, they made similar computations with a load of two thousand pounds and the engines set at 1,450 and 1,500 rpm. By making a systematic study of the flight characteristics of the America at different loadings, Byrd was trying to determine an optimum airspeed for each stage of the transatlantic hop as the weight of the plane predictably diminished. His knowledge of optimum airspeeds would enable him to obtain the maximum amount of miles per gallon of fuel. As aviation developed, this technique became central to flight engineering and is known today as cruise control.

Seven years later, Byrd codified his philosophy of exploration in a memo to the field leaders of his second Antarctic expedition. "I have always found it to be the wisest strategy," he said, "to eliminate undue risks to personnel or material in preliminary maneuvers or tactics the failure of which may cause also the failure of the big final objectives [and] failure of the expedition itself. Big risks, however, may be justified [to achieve] the final objectives. All links therefore in the chain leading up to the final objectives must be as foolproof as possible."[27]

After the Lindbergh flight, Harry and Tom Byrd as well as many of Dick's friends suggested that another haul to Paris coming so soon after the triumph of the Lone Eagle could not possibly have the same impact and might not be well received. Dick Byrd was inclined to agree. He discussed the situation with Wanamaker and delicately broached the possibility that the America might instead attempt a first flight to another destination. The transpacific flight from the United States to Hawaii had not yet been accomplished, although several expeditions at that moment were moving close to the starting line. Byrd had turned his eyes to Honolulu, but Wanamaker so closely identified with the French people and culture that he would not countenance a change of flight plans. Byrd felt "honor-bound" to comply with his wishes.[28]

The distinction of the flight in a scientific sense would lie in the data Byrd intended to compile on Atlantic weather patterns. But a Byrd enterprise always combined a certain amount of spectacle along with the science. As Lindbergh boarded an ocean liner to return to the United States, rumors began to circulate that Byrd intended to fly back home after he reached Paris and complete the first non-stop, transatlantic round trip since the R-34 and the first ever in a heavier-than-air machine. Byrd was characteristically circumspect about his plans. No one in the media suspected that he had tentatively outlined a round-the-world flight that would take him in stages from Paris to Moscow and across Bolshevik Russia to Tokyo and Nome.[29]

On June 7, the *America* successfully lifted off the Roosevelt runway with a load of 14,000 pounds. The next day Byrd and Wanamaker met in Philadelphia and both agreed to postpone the departure of the *America* until after Lindbergh's homecoming celebrations. They didn't want to appear to be trying to push the Lone Eagle out of the spotlight.

Lucky Lindy received a tumultuous welcome in Washington on the twelfth and in New York on the thirteenth. There followed two weeks of stormy weather that alternately played havoc in the area between Newfoundland and Ireland, or obstructed the flight path between Newfoundland and New York. While the weather picture remained unsettled, Bernt Balchen was introduced as the mechanic, reserve pilot, and reserve navigator of the *America*. His debut was deferred until after he was persuaded to take out citizenship papers because Wanamaker wanted the flight to be an All-American project. Meanwhile, a lighter set of wheels were installed on the ship, which saved a hundred pounds, and auxiliary fuel lines were run between the gas tanks and the engines as a back-up for the main lines.

Finally, just after midnight on Wednesday, June 29, Dr. James H. Kimball of the U.S. Weather Bureau informed Byrd of a sudden improvement in the forecast. Patches of rain and fog and isolated headwinds would still be encountered, but the flight path across the North Atlantic was for the most part clear. Temporarily. A low-pressure system moving east across the United States was slowly heading for New England.

Several hours later, Byrd stood on the runway with reporter Russell Owen. "It's not all that it might be," he said, looking up at the dark clouds revealed at first light. "But we don't want perfect weather. We're going."

In Owen's words:

> He showed the strain under which he was laboring by his immobile and expressionless face. When Byrd is relaxed he smiles readily and his face is almost boyish, but when the moment of decision in a dangerous enterprise faces him his face becomes set with grim purpose. His voice at such moments is as gentle as a girl's, he rocks back and forth on his toes, but his glance is keen as a rapier.[30]

Every conceivable type of survival gear available in 1927 had been assembled for the flight, including two inflatable life rafts, life preservers, forty pounds of emergency rations, and water, signal flares, a signal kite, and a waterproof emergency radio in addition to the main radio set. Governors Al Smith of New York and Harry Byrd of

Virginia, Mayor Jimmy Walker, and scores of elected officials and local dignitaries had written letters to their counterparts in France. Byrd had been sworn in as an airmail pilot by the Postmaster of New York and entrusted with mailbags containing over two hundred pieces of correspondence. Rodman Wanamaker had somehow located the great-great-grandniece of Betsy Ross as well as pieces of bunting identical to that used to make the original American flag. He had inspired this woman to produce a new flag incorporating the old material. The banner was sealed in a strongbox and vouchsafed to Byrd's keeping along with the mail. Wanamaker wanted the flag to be consecrated at the grave of Lafayette.[31]

Byrd had never completed the entry form for the Orteig Prize. From the beginning, he and Wanamaker had sought to avoid any element of acquisitiveness and commercialism. They had wanted their joint venture to represent the future, to herald an era of international cooperation made possible by the progress of aviation. The airplane they selected to point the way forward perfectly captured the spirit of the enterprise, suggesting advanced technology, structural grace, and idealism.

The *America* was the largest transatlantic plane to take flight in 1927, almost twice the length of the *Columbia* and the *Spirit of St. Louis*, with a 55 percent longer wingspan. A tall adult standing directly in front of her would have to bend backwards and strain a neck muscle to see the leading edge of her high wing. That same observer standing in the shadow of the immense wing would have to jump up to touch her outboard engine nacelles. The fuselage was painted the color of aluminum, a pale, bluish-gray. The name of the ship was printed on both the port and starboard sides in large white, capital letters with red and blue trim. Forward of "AMERICA," in small, dark blue letters was the word "Peace" with a decorative olive branch running through the "e." Aft of the nomenclature, also in small, dark letters, was this official inscription: "U.S. Mail." The tail, on both the port and starboard sides, was adorned with a handsome white star on a dark blue square. The same emblem appeared under each wingtip. The name "Fokker" was not displayed anywhere.

The *America* had been towed to the head of the runway on the evening of June 23 and hauled to the top of the incline with a block and tackle. She was loaded for takeoff, and there she had sat for five days as one scheduled start after another was postponed. The fuel that had been pumped into her tanks for the ocean jaunt weighed more than either the *Spirit of St. Louis* or the *Columbia* fully loaded for a transatlantic flight. The engine oil alone weighed 480 pounds. Her total load with mail, survival gear, a fourth crewmember and additional fuel in five-gallon cans—perhaps 14,700 pounds—easily exceeded the *combined* weight of her predecessors and was almost three times the takeoff weight of either one of the single-engine ships.

"The first three minutes will decide everything," Byrd told his crew, shortly before they took their places. "We shall get off or it's a crash."[32]

At 5:24 a.m., June 29, Noville wrapped his hand around the lever of the dump valve in case it became necessary to abort the takeoff and drop the bulk of the fuel. He sat in the co-pilot's seat, next to Acosta. It was raining lightly. The interior of the *America* had been reconfigured after the crash at Teterboro. A small tunnel seventeen inches high by seventeen inches across enabled crewmembers to have access to the tail of the ship by crawling under one corner of the main fuel tank. They could now distribute their weight as required to keep the tail down during takeoffs and landings. The radio remained in the small compartment between the cockpit and the main tank; the navigation cabin had been shifted to a new compartment just aft of the main tank. Byrd and Balchen braced themselves in this space. They were standing up; the navigator had a small table but no chair,

nor did the radioman have a seat. Additional chairs had been considered excess weight.

As at Spitsbergen, the tail of the trimotor was bound to a post to enable the engines to rev up to full power before getting underway. Tom Mulroy would cut the rope on Acosta's signal. But the tug exerted by the big ship was so powerful that the rope snapped. The trimotor tore down the incline prematurely. In the excitement of the moment, Acosta imagined that the rope had been cut as planned; as the ship hurtled forward, eating up the runway, he had to grapple with the fact that it seemed to be taking an eternity for the needle on the airspeed indicator to reach rotation speed.[33] The decision to abort was his to make. He raised his right hand, alerting Noville to be ready to dump the fuel.

The wobbly, ponderous ship steadied and gained momentum. Big ships with heavy loads require muscle to control. Acosta yanked on the wheel. The ship bounced up then down then up again. The natural inclination of the average pilot would be to try to hold the nose up. Acosta did the opposite; he pushed the wheel slightly forward, lowering the nose, flattening the angle of climb in order to allow the ship to build up airspeed. Within forty-eight seconds of the snapping of the cord, he pulled back ever so slightly on the round wheel and held it in that position, maintaining a flat angle of climb as the ship gained altitude.[34]

After about fifteen or twenty minutes in the air, Acosta relaxed and passed Noville a note. It read: "What a hell of a takeoff that was!"[35]

⚔ 28 ⚔

IN THE HANDS
OF FATE

*I would also like to ask the public to realize that though
we have prepared as carefully as possible we are
to some extent in the hands of fate after we leave.
Ours is a pioneering flight and it cannot be laid
to the door of aviation if we do not win.*

RICHARD E. BYRD
JUNE 29, 1927[1]

The Byrd transatlantic flight was the first moonshot. Throughout the transatlantic spring and summer of 1927, the Radio Corporation of America had collected weather observations transmitted from ocean liners navigating the steamship lanes between Europe and America. Those reports enabled the U.S. Weather Bureau to forecast the weather over the ocean for the benefit of Lindbergh, Chamberlin, and Byrd. Neither Lindbergh nor Chamberlin carried a radio, preferring to lighten their load to any extent possible. The *America* was equipped with a 115-pound, state-of-the-art wireless, in addition to a lightweight, emergency back-up unit. For over a week prior to the takeoff, RCA had broadcast instructions to ships at sea, requesting that all marine radio operators listen for the *America's* signals and report the position of the ship. In case of a forced landing, Byrd and his crew would not simply disappear like Nungesser and Coli, who had also eschewed a radio. The airplane would be tracked along its flight path and rescued by the nearest steamer.

The impact of radio communications, however, went far beyond flight safety. The eight-year-old RCA had formed the first radio network, the National Broadcasting Company, at the end of 1926. By the beginning of 1927, NBC had two flagship stations in New York—WEAF and WJZ—that each fed programs to a separate line-up of local affiliates from coast to coast. RCA had arranged for the shore stations in its net as well as those of the Canadian Marconi Company and the government-owned wireless systems of England and France to receive in-flight transmissions from the *America* and route them back to New York. The messages were exclusively in Morse code. After being decoded in New York, they were simultaneously distributed by the America Trans-Oceanic Company to the press and by the National Broadcasting Company to its affiliates throughout the United States. For the first time, the average citizen was able to follow each stage of a spectacular flight via electronic media.

NBC provided the two branches of its family of stations with saturation coverage. WEAF broadcasted updates every thirty minutes on the hour and half hour. WJZ did likewise, except its reports were aired fifteen minutes before and after the hour. Two independent stations in the New York metropolitan area—WNYC and WOR—competed with the NBC flagships on similar round-the-clock schedules. WOR signed on at 5:30 a.m. on the twenty-ninth, followed by WEAF at 6:45 a.m., WJZ at 9:15 a.m., and WNYC shortly before eleven o'clock. For the rest of the day, New Yorkers could follow the progress of the *America* on four different frequencies.

Floyd Bennett had been booked to supply color commentary for NBC. Bennett had been transferred from Hackensack Hospital to the facility where his treating physician belonged, St. Vincent's Hospital on Seventh Avenue and 11th Street in Manhattan. A transmitter, technicians, two microphones, and a silver-throated announcer named Graham McNamee were installed in his private room. The hook-up, however, failed to work on its initial trial. Like many Americans, Bennett spent the twenty-ninth glued to the loudspeaker of the bulky receiver in his room. At 1:30 p.m., he heard the following relayed from about 3,000 feet over Nova Scotia and read over the air:

> Message for good old Floyd Bennett.
> Tell him we miss him like the dickens.
> Thinking of him.
>
> Byrd[2]

New York was on Daylight Savings Time, a convention that had not yet been adopted by much of the rest of the world. Byrd had turned his watch back an hour to Eastern Standard Time. He had before him on his table in the navigation compartment the same black-bound 1925 diary that he had brought on the MacMillan and North Pole expeditions. "Thought of NC boats flight when passed Halifax," he wrote. The volume was open to entries for "Friday, January 16, 1925" and "Saturday, January 17, 1925," and on those pages he had begun keeping a flight log. Byrd had divided the otherwise blank pages into columns for keeping track of cloud cover, ground speed, airspeed, time, air miles flown, compass heading, wind direction, drift, air temperature, compass variation, and altitude. A duplicate set of flight instruments had been installed for this purpose on the bulkhead separating the navigation compartment from the tail. Byrd stood leaning over the table in a space just about big enough to turn around in. There was a trapdoor in the floor for the drift indicator and one overhead for celestial observations, a sun compass at the window nearest the table, and a thermometer fixed in place outside the window. The latter was another innovation. By monitoring the outside air temperature, Byrd hoped to prevent icing and its attendant dangers. At 12 noon by Byrd's watch, he scrawled the note about the NC flight in a column of the flight log labeled "Remarks." The rugged coastline of Nova Scotia had been visible in the port window for the past three hours. It was 56° at 3,150 feet, and the airplane was making 103 mph over the ground.

The flight log was the bible of the mission. It was intended both for dead reckoning and as a database for future transatlantic fliers, and was just pages removed from Byrd's in-flight dialogue with Floyd Bennett on the North Pole hop and the two computations made in the course of that flight which may or may not have been erased at that point. On a succeeding page, he noted something he saw while sighting for wind drift:

As I looked through our trap door passing north of Halifax a cloud was under us and the shadow of the America on the cloud had a beautiful rainbow around it.

Byrd took this as a propitious omen. So began the most bizarre and mysterious flight of his career. Over the next four hours, clouds began to gather, and the clouds merged and became mist. Newfoundland never appeared below the port wing. The Atlantic Ocean vanished from beneath the starboard wing. Acosta and Balchen, who were taking turns at the wheel, were shortly deprived of a sea horizon to point the nose toward. The windshield and the cabin windows soon disclosed nothing more than the nothingness of the mist itself.

At 5:30 p.m. Eastern time, Byrd wrote: "Thick fog for nearly hour. Can hardly see wingtips. Can't navigate." Another problem bubbled up out of the cauldron-like vapors that concealed land and sea. On two separate occasions, Noville had checked up on the amount of fuel remaining and both times found that the ship had been burning gasoline at the alarming rate of forty-four gallons per hour.[3] A consumption rate of thirty gph or better had been expected. At forty-four gph, the *America* could not possibly reach Europe if the wind blew against the ship and slowed her down.

Byrd had with him a weather map that had been prepared by Dr. Kimball just before takeoff. It showed that as he left Newfoundland he would fly through the southern periphery of a low-pressure system. Winds flow counter-clockwise around a depression. That would give the *America* a westerly wind on her tail as she started across the ocean. The map also showed a high-pressure area nearer the coast of Europe. The aircraft was projected to cross the northern periphery of this system. As winds flow clockwise around a high, Byrd could expect a tailwind toward the completion of the ocean passage so long as the forecast was correct.

Byrd was privy to everything the U.S. Weather Bureau knew about the North Atlantic. Unfortunately, knowledge of Atlantic wind patterns was rather skimpy in 1927. The Weather Bureau nevertheless believed that as you exceed three or four thousand feet, winds get stronger, particularly westerly winds, and that the strongest Westerlies prevail at altitudes of from five to 10,000 feet or higher.[4] It was just supposition, of course. But deep in the clouds with three men's lives on his hands, that was about all Byrd had to bank on: a chart and a theory.

He had felt that reaching an altitude of 3,000 feet with a ship weighing 14,700 pounds "was a remarkable demonstration."[5]

To accomplish that feat, it had been necessary to run the engines at almost full throttle. Now, as the aircraft burned off some of its load, he instructed Acosta to climb as high as was consistent with safety to try to surmount the fog and find the most favorable wind. To reach the higher altitudes, of course, meant that more power had to be pulled from the engines and more power meant that an extra increment of fuel had to be consumed.

"Impossible to navigate," Byrd wrote in his flight log at 6:30 p.m. Eastern time. "Wonder how long this will last." He repeated "Impossible to navigate" at 7:30 and again at 8:30. When they occasionally got over the cloud tops in the remaining daylight, they found themselves looking down on white peaks and valleys that resembled the rugged snowscapes of Spitsbergen and Ellesmere Island. In the darkness, those gauzy shapes and forms were transformed into black masses, relieved only by the flashes in the exhaust pipes of the Whirlwind engines. But the cloud tops rose with them. "Dense fog," Byrd noted at 11:00 p.m. He was about two time zones ahead of New York by now; relative to the immediate locality, that entry was actually written in the wee hours of the morning. At 12:00 a.m. Eastern time, a half hour before dawn over the ocean, he reported: "Dense fog at 6,000 [feet]." Two hours later: "Still fogbound." They were at that point almost 500 miles east of Newfoundland.

"All sense of speed was lost," said George Noville. "We seemed to be suspended in the enveloping mist."[6] Noville tried to get some sleep during the night of June 29–30, curling up on the wooden floor of the navigation compartment. An auxiliary dump valve protruded from the aft side of the main fuel tank. Rex dozed off for about fifteen minutes and dreamed that while twisting and turning he had inadvertently tripped the valve, dropping the bulk of the fuel supply down to the surface of the unseen sea.[7] He awoke with a start and stayed awake for the rest of the trip. Balchen slept for a while on the same floor, and while he twisted and turned one of his feet moved perilously close to the dump lever. Byrd stood over him and watched, and let the Norwegian continue to sleep.

Twenty-five or so five-gallon fuel cans had been stacked up behind the pilot and co-pilot's seats. Once those cans had been emptied and tossed out, the men could move freely forward and aft. Except for Acosta, whose shoulders were too broad to squeeze through the crawlspace running from the radio cabin back to the navigation compartment. Even Noville had difficulty negotiating the passage. Byrd, the slimmest crewmember, started through the tunnel a couple of hours after dawn to take his turn at the wheel and got stuck. He had to wriggle back to the navigation compartment and remove a sweater he had pulled on and then was able to squirm through. It was fifty-four degrees outside at 9,400 feet, and not much warmer in the cockpit. A gust of wind had torn a hole in the fabric sheathing on the pilot's side, letting in the numbing cold.

Air temperature in the damp gloom dropped to fifty-two degrees at 10,000 feet and thirty-six degrees at 11,000. "Dense fog that [we] can't climb out of," Byrd noted at 11,000 feet. "Terribly dangerous." He knew the ship was in the clouds and not above them because water had started to drip into the navigation cabin. Due to the moisture in the surrounding air and the plummeting temperature, ice had begun to form on the aircraft. Ice build-up not only adds to the weight of a plane, it can also change the shape of the wing and diminish the lifting property of the airfoil. Since they could no longer get above the cloud tops, they descended to a warmer strata of air at 9,000 feet. Icing was only one potential hazard. "I sit here wondering if the winds have been with us," Byrd wrote, some twenty-nine hours out of New York, on Thursday, June 30. "If they haven't we don't reach land."

One of the mysteries of the flight occurred in the middle of the night when the ship abruptly lost altitude. Acosta had the wheel. Perhaps the greatest stick-and-rudder man of his era, Acosta, according to Balchen, could not fly by instruments. He lost control in the darkness and fog due to the lack of a physical horizon with which to orient himself, and the airplane plunged into a steep dive. Balchen immediately took over, brought the ship back to a straight-and-level attitude and thereafter handled the wheel whenever visibility was obscured. This story surfaced in print in 1953 in a *Reader's Digest* article about Balchen and was repeated by Balchen in his 1958 memoir.[8] When the magazine article appeared, however, George Noville stated that "Acosta knew more about instrument flying than anyone else in the United States at the time of our flight. To my knowledge," he continued, "Acosta handled the flight 75% of the 42 hours that we were in the air, with an occasional relief by Byrd, Balchen or myself."[9]

Both Balchen and Noville may have forgotten that instrument flying was an embryonic art in 1927 and would be fully developed over the next two years when aviation legend Jimmy Doolittle collaborated on the matter with the Guggenheim Fund for the Promotion of Aeronautics. Doolittle and his team augmented the instrument panel with a new series of devices that simplified blind flying. Journalist Charles J. V. Murphy, who covered the transatlantic competition for the *New York Evening Post*, published a tell-all piece on the flight of the *America* that ran in *Collier's* magazine in the summer of 1928. In Murphy's version, Acosta fell asleep at the wheel just as Byrd momentarily did during the return leg of the North Pole flight.[10] Balchen nudged Acosta awake; Bert quickly scanned the rudimentary instruments before him, and regained control of the plane.

About the night of June 29–30, Balchen, at fifty-nine, included in the original draft of his memoirs the following statement: "Though we had beautiful starlight all last night we have received no estimates of our position from Byrd, and I wonder why he hasn't taken celestial observations."[11] That sentence was edited out of the book. The Balchen excisions were subsequently rescued by Richard Montague and printed in an appendix of his 1971 work, *Oceans, Poles and Airmen*. This was the source of a recent school of opinion questioning Byrd's ability to navigate.

Rex Noville died around the time the Montague book was published, but he gave his own account of the transatlantic flight in two pieces of writing published thirty years apart. Before the *America* left Roosevelt Field in 1927, Noville contracted with the *New York Herald Tribune* for a first-person narrative on the flight. The result was a six-part series produced with the assistance of the *Tribune's* Paris correspondents and carried on the front pages of the editions of July 2–7. In the first and fourth installments, Noville stated repeatedly that Byrd could not take a single astronomical observation for nearly nineteen hours due to impenetrable fog.[12] In the late 1950s, perhaps in rebuttal to the Balchen revelations, Noville wrote a magazine article in which he once again said, "It was impossible to navigate; no chance to shoot the sun, no stars overhead to guide us."[13] He also insisted that during the period of blind flying, "Acosta was at the controls almost constantly."

Floyd Bennett debuted as a broadcast journalist a few minutes after twelve noon, Daylight Savings Time in New York on July 30. He was propped up in his hospital bed with a full-length cast on his left leg and a map spread over his lap. "Good afternoon, radio audience," he said, in a soft voice. "As I cannot be *in* the air, I will have to be satisfied [being] *on* the air."

He continued:

> Commander Byrd and his crew must have had a somewhat
> hectic night, as one of his latest bulletins stated that they

had not sighted either land or water from 4:30 o'clock last night to 6 o'clock this morning. That, of course, means that they must have flown through or above the fog for this whole period, and no one but a flying man can realize just what this means. It is almost impossible to navigate a plane under these conditions and none but the best pilots can do it.[14]

Bennett had been noting on his map the hour and approximate position of the plane each time a new report was received. He was also keeping his own flight log, working out the probable fuel consumption, airspeed, and mileage. Baskets of flowers had to be hauled out of his small room to create space for the radio equipment and personnel, and for a "live audience" consisting of newspaper reporters, nurses, and his wife, Cora. Before relinquishing the microphone to Graham McNamee, the announcer, he assured his listeners that all was well in the skies over the Atlantic Ocean. "We," he said, meaning the *America*, "have a good radio and plenty of fuel."

All of the transatlantic fliers flew a Great Circle course across the ocean. This was due to the recognition that the earth is a sphere, and that by respecting the properties of a sphere, you save miles. A Great Circle is one that spans the circumference of a sphere and also cuts the sphere completely in half. The equator is a Great Circle. The shortest distance between any two points on the surface of a sphere lies on the Great Circle running through those points. The Great Circle course between New York and Paris is therefore a curved line some 3,600 miles long. The next step is to break that curved line down into a large number of segments. Each of those many small segments can be treated as a straight line; they can be plotted on a Mercator projection, and the heading for each segment can be obtained. On a

Great Circle course, the aviator actually flies a succession of compass headings that approximate a curved line.

The man who created the sun compass, Albert H. Bumstead of the National Geographic Society, broke the New York to Paris arc of a Great Circle into thirty-three different segments for Byrd and computed the magnetic and true headings for each of them. Both Lindbergh and Chamberlin had embarked with a similar collection of pre-computed courses. The tricky part of transatlantic navigation in 1927 was determining by how much and in what direction the wind threw you off your course. Lindbergh dealt with this problem by dropping down to the surface of the sea and studying the movement of the waves. Chamberlin's method was equally imprecise and even more idiosyncratic. He spotted an ocean liner and deduced that he was over the steamship lanes. Then he flew low enough to read the name of the ship: the *Mauretania*. He happened to have a copy of the *New York Times* with him. He opened the paper to the shipping news, found the date the *Mauretania* had embarked from Southampton, guessed the amount of knots she was capable of making, and estimated her position and consequently his own.

Byrd's solution was typically visionary and accurate. Since he could not employ the drift indicator in the fog, he relied on his radio. On Thursday morning, Noville established contact with a steamship passing below in the mist. He obtained the latitude and longitude of the ship and a radio bearing from that vessel to the *America*. Byrd plotted the coordinates on his chart and drew a straight line from those coordinates along the indicated bearing. That gave him one line of position. Repeating the process later on with another ocean liner yielded a second line of position. The point where the two lines intersected represented the actual position of the airplane.

Radio bearings from a system of fixed stations would become the dominant method of aerial navigation within two decades. Byrd's radio fixes indicated that the suppositions of the Weather Bureau had been correct: the *America* had at times picked up as much as a thirty-mile-per-hour tailwind during the night. The ship had drifted substantially to the south, which also accorded with the expectations of the meteorologists. Atlantic winds, especially westerlies, were presumed to veer fifteen degrees to twenty degrees to the right.

The intended course of the *America* had been from Newfoundland to southern Ireland, from Ireland to southwest England, and then across the English Channel to Normandy. Byrd took advantage of the southerly drift to plot a direct course for Finistère, the northwest province of France. Communication between navigator and pilots occurred in the form of written messages and via a telephone system that was supposed to enable the crew to hear each other over the noise of the engines. Neither system may have been entirely satisfactory. At one point in the first half of the flight, Byrd wrote in his diary:

> Sometimes have difficult time attracting attention ahead to send radio or change course. Lights don't work so well. Found a long stick and hit Noville on shoe with that.

Byrd's command style was decidedly hands on. In Noville's words:

> He would leave his charts and instruments, crawl forward to the cockpit, listen intently to the engines, check oil pressure, frown at the gasoline gauge, then give us a reassuring pat on the back and return to his navigating.[15]

It had appeared that half the fuel had been exhausted, but Rex eventually discovered that his initial estimates of fuel consumption had been in error. The tail of the aircraft had been slightly weighed down by the emergency gear and provisions; as a result, the fuel gauge had given a false indication of the level of gasoline remaining in the tanks. Floyd Bennett was right. Noville was now able to report that there was enough fuel left to fly all the way to Rome. The aviators were just about halfway across the ocean when holes began to appear in the solid mist, and they had their first glimpse of the sea since the afternoon of the previous day. It was noon in the time zone in which they flew. "Can see water now," Byrd wrote. An hour and a half later, the sun was briefly visible. "Things at last are pleasant," he said. "We had a rough time."

They proceeded to France in broken clouds and sometimes through a clear stratum between a layer of fog above and below. "It was," said Noville, "like being locked in an aerial chamber."[16] The surface of the sea was intermittently visible, but enough so for Byrd to check ground speed and drift, and issue stern injunctions to the pilots to correct a tendency to bear left. One of the messages he sent forward read: "We will never get there unless we keep the ship straight."

The coast of Finistère resembles a mouth jutting open with the city of Brest on the northern lip. They struck the gaping maw on target about twenty miles southwest of Brest at 7:55 p.m. local time. "Now, we think, the dangers are all behind, and a sense of release fills the entire ship," wrote Balchen.

> We cross a line of white breakers, and suddenly green meadows are below us, and farmhouses with red-tiled roofs and smoking chimney pots.[17]

Le Bourget field, just northeast of Paris, was the largest and best airport in the vicinity of the French capital. Airliners hopping across the English Channel to and from London used the field for takeoffs and landings on a daily basis. There was a revolving beacon on one corner of the field visible for over fifty miles on a clear night. Above the white light was a red neon light that could be seen for ten miles.

Additional red lights were mounted on the roofs of the airport buildings and on the tops of obstructions. Together, these lights formed an enormous triangle distinctly visible from the air. On Thursday evening, June 30, as much as ten thousand spectators waited on the field for the arrival of the *America*. Clarence Chamberlin and Charles Levine stood among them. A large detachment of the Garde républicaine (Republican Guard) had been deployed to prevent a recurrence of the mob scene that had engulfed Lindbergh when the *Spirit of St. Louis* landed. The soldiers wore dark blue and red ceremonial uniforms and plumed helmets, and were divided into mounted and foot patrols. The Paris bureau of the *New York Times* sat around a table the office had reserved on the first floor of the restaurant overlooking the runway.

It had rained in Paris every day for the past week, but the clouds had dissipated in the morning. The afternoon had been gorgeous. At around 9:00 p.m. local time, clouds suddenly began to roll in from all directions. They were the blackest clouds Parisians could ever remember having seen. Then it began to rain without let-up. "Serious rain," one observer recalled.[18] Most of the spectators dispersed, but many remained on the field. People opened umbrellas or threw on raincoats which were soon soaked through. Puddles began to fill, transforming the field into a miniature wetlands. *Times* bureau chief Edwin L. James described a phalanx of mounted guardsmen under the sheltering branches of a line of trees, "their plumes looking [like] the saddest sight one could imagine."[19]

Then it began to rain harder. "The weather was so thick," Chamberlin said, he didn't see how Byrd and his crew could possibly land, "unless they could manage to stay in the air and try to get through in the morning."[20]

The crew of the *America* saw the sunset over Brest and for about an hour had decent weather. Noville picked up Le Bourget and asked for a weather advisory. When he decoded the transmission and passed it on, Byrd shook his head. Zero ceiling, zero visibility. Heavy rain. Fog. Strong shifting winds. The weather picture was a mirror image of the conditions Nungesser and Coli had encountered. The *White Bird* had flown into a storm system centered over Newfoundland and Labrador and had vanished. The *America* was flying into a storm system centered almost right over Paris. Byrd could have diverted to another European city. He could have made the first flight, say, to Rome and, in his own words, "set the world on fire."[21] But a Paris landing had been Rodman Wanamaker's dream; it was not in Byrd to be disloyal to the man who had picked up the tab for the flight. He instructed Acosta to fly north along the coasts of Brittany and Normandy to Le Havre and then follow the Seine to the capital. Balchen recommended a more direct route. He had flown in northern France some years previously and thought that by following the Brest-Paris railroad, they could reach Le Bourget before dark, perhaps before the worst of the storm.

According to Balchen, Byrd had come forward and the interchange took place verbally, the men shouting to be heard above the din of the engines. After he made his suggestion, Balchen wrote,

> Commander Byrd turns around to Acosta. "Fly as I've told you," he says.[22]

Balchen was mystified by Byrd's reaction. It was a decision, he said, "which I have never been able to explain since." Actually, it was the most defensible decision Byrd could have made under the circumstances. When Fitzhugh Green went to Paris in April to do advance work for Byrd, he interviewed French pilots and officials and mapped out the best approach to Le Bourget. This was the northern route, the flight path of the London-Paris airlines. The towns along the coast from Cherbourg to Le Havre were said to be illuminated by thick clusters of lights, as were the villages and hamlets along the Seine. Le Havre, moreover, was easily distinguished, Green pointed out, by the "large number of beacons and lighthouses."[23] He included in his report detailed air directions for finding Le Bourget by way of Le Havre.

As they cruised along the coast, they flew into a turbulent darkness, and the lights that should have been apparent could not be discerned. The windows were assailed by rain, the cabin seesawed in the wind. Over the next few hours, the darkness turned inkier. In the heart of the storm, during that period of mounting darkness, something happened to Bert Acosta. Acosta had flown continuously for the first seven hours or so of the flight, "till we got past Nova Scotia," he said, "and the gas cans that blocked the passage to the navigator's cockpit were chucked overboard."[24] Even allowing for an ample assist from Balchen thereafter, he had had little sleep and was exhausted from muscling the big plane over the ocean by the time the *America* struck land.

What transpired is difficult to pin down. Byrd never addressed the issue in public, thereby protecting his personnel, protecting aviation and, to be sure, his own image. Charlie Murphy wrote that Acosta was having great difficulty seeing through the torrential rain and pitch darkness. "In a desperate effort to see," Murphy said,

> he had slid open the window on his left, and a hundred-mile-an-hour wind was howling through it, tearing at his eyes. He would duck his head out the window for a minute or two at a time, hold it there as long as his eyes could stand it, then draw back.

Acosta was offered a pair of goggles, but strangely goggles were of no avail. After two hours of turning his unprotected eyes to the wind and slashing rain, he began to break down. Murphy portrayed a scene in which Byrd stood behind the pilot, peering over Acosta's shoulder at the instrument panel. "You're off your course!" he shouts. "You're flying in a circle."

Murphy continues:

> The pilot turned. His eyes were swollen and red. "I can't see, Dick. I'm going blind," he muttered. His voice carried even above the roar of the motors. His last bit of strength gone, he suddenly toppled from his seat and fell to the floor.

Murphy's revelations first appeared in the July 1928 issue of *Harper's* magazine. One month later his *Collier's* article hit the stands with a blood-and-thunder version of the same tale. Byrd is now holding a large flashlight in his hand. Again, he hollers that Acosta is off course:

> In the unholy glare of the flashlight, Acosta turns, his eyes red and bulging, and cuts the motors. "I'm going back." His voice rises brazenly in the suddenly muted cabin. A different, towering Bert. He whirls back to the controls, the motors burst into a screaming crescendo and the America spurts out, they are soon to learn, toward the sea.

Byrd, in this version, is about to conk Acosta on the head with the flashlight when the pilot passes out. Like Byrd, Noville omitted any reference in his contemporaneous publications to Acosta's problem. Thirty years later, he merely mentioned in passing in his magazine article that Acosta collapsed from exhaustion. In private however, he told a different story: Acosta had been hitting the bottle during the flight, perhaps the real reason he lost control of the ship in the middle of the night.[25] Balchen also spoke confidentially about drinking aboard the *America*, once claiming that he and Byrd were the only sober members of the flight crew.[26]

The effects of alcohol on pilots have been carefully researched. One review cites thirteen detrimental consequences of booze, including constriction of visual field, decreased ability to see under dim illumination, and increased susceptibility to fatigue.[27] When it was all over, Acosta told a reporter:

> "It was flying over France, going around in the sleet and darkness that seemed to make me blind. I wasn't absolutely blind, but I couldn't see anything much."[28]

The storm over northern France on the evening of June 30 was so unusually severe that for once Acosta was unable to glide from bottle to throttle and remain effective. He wound up with a broken right collarbone, which has never been satisfactorily explained. Whether he passed out or panicked and was rendered unconscious, one fact is beyond dispute. When the time came for the inevitable landing, the *America*'s most experienced pilot was unavailable for duty.

"If we hit Finestère after 2,000 miles of almost blind flying," Byrd reasoned, "I thought we certainly ought to be able to reach Paris, a few hundred miles off."[29] When his dead reckoning placed the ship on the outskirts of the capital, a revolving light could be made out on the horizon. Byrd assumed that it was the Le Bourget beacon. He composed a triumphant message for Rodman Wanamaker announcing that the *America* was in sight of her destination, but that message was never transmitted. As the distant sliver swept around, it periodically revealed *water*. "I then realized that I was not looking at an airplane beacon," Byrd said, "but at a lighthouse, and I knew blame well there was no lighthouse anywhere near Paris!"[30]

Balchen had taken over at the controls. His principal steering instrument was an earth inductor compass. Magnetic compasses were used for backup. The latter showed that for some time now, the steering compass had gone completely out of whack. They had spent the past three hours circling back to the coast.

The *America* should have reached Paris at least by 11:00 p.m. or 12:00 a.m. local time. This was dinner hour in New York, between 6:00 and 7:00 p.m. Daylight Savings Time. As the evening wore on and no official word was received from France, Floyd Bennett's expression turned grim. For a time, he sat in a chair between his radio and his bed and rocked silently back and forth. Whenever he heard the name "Byrd" mentioned on the air, he held his hand up, silencing the mob scene in his room and listened, it was said, "with his eyes almost closed."[31]

He climbed back into bed at eight and made his last broadcast at midnight. "I am disappointed that I am not able to announce the safe arrival of the *America*," he said.

> Unconfirmed rumors have reached me of a landing made four miles southwest of Paris, but I do not believe them. Weather conditions, as described to me, are almost hopeless for landing, either by night or by day.[32]

He expressed confidence that his friends were scouring the countryside for a place to land. At one point, he looked up from his notes at his wife, Cora, and said, "I'm sure there is gas enough to last for another hour or possibly two." He signed off by saying, "We can only hope for the best." Bennett had not slept a wink since the takeoff. Before Cora left the hospital at half past twelve, she tried to get him to turn off the radio and rest.

"I've got to get that plane landed," he said.[33]

The earth inductor compass was a flawed instrument that was essentially phased out of use by the early 1930s. When it became clear that it had malfunctioned, Byrd guessed at the position of the plane and plotted a course to Paris. Asked, later, if he reached it, he said, "I don't know exactly. I think so, but I could not be sure."[34] The 984-foot Eiffel Tower had remained illuminated all night as a navigation aide for the *America*. White flares had been shot into the air at Le Bourget periodically from about 10:00 p.m. onward. But neither the tower nor the flares were seen, and hardly anything else.

Flying in daylight, one perceives the beauty of nature. At night, what impresses is the beauty of humanity, the patterns of lights organized across the infinite landscape. Flying at night in the absence of those patterns produces an eerie feeling of being cut off from one's world and one's kind. At one point, the aviators saw a flash off the starboard wing, which they thought was the huge searchlight that had been erected on Mont Valérien, the old fort in the western suburbs of Paris. "We saw it three times from an altitude of 6,000 feet or so and went down to 1,200 feet to try to 'get it,'" Noville said, "but we couldn't see a thing. It was lost, whatever it was."

He continued:

> We were circling in the hope that we might find Paris. We would see a glow in the sky now and then and think it might be Paris. We would go over there and try to 'pick up something,' try to find a chance narrow lane down through the increasing storm and everlasting fog. Then, when we got nearer, we would see nothing at all. The glow always faded and left us in the same inky blackness.[35]

Meanwhile, the fuel reserves were dwindling. For hour after hour, they continued playing a dangerous game of blind man's bluff. Byrd never left the cockpit, Noville said. "His eyes bored into the fog as he directed us—right—left—up—down."

The flight path of the *America* remains another major question mark of the adventure. One of the provincial newspapers covering western France canvassed its readers for reports of an airplane seen or heard on the night of June 30. On the basis of this survey, the editors concluded that the *America* had flown in zigzags across Normandy and hadn't come within eighty miles of Paris. It was suggested that the iron mines at Caen may have caused the earth inductor compass to deviate. The guards at the gates of the palace of Versailles, however, reported hearing and glimpsing an airplane circling overhead after midnight. Versailles is located south of Mont Valèrian and southwest of Paris.

Eventually the exhaustion of the fuel supply had to be reckoned with. By about 1:00 a.m., believing that he was flying over Paris, Byrd concluded that it would not be possible to find a hole in the fog and land at Le Bourget. He wrote the following note, which he handed to Noville:

> It would be extremely dangerous to land on terrain. From our observations France is dotted with little villages and it would be almost impossible to land anywhere without endangering the lives of the people below and probably killing someone. Consequently, we will find the nearest water and land there.[36]

He plotted a course back to the lighthouse they had encountered a couple of hours earlier. That he found it again suggests the *America* had at least reached the vicinity of Paris. One can only navigate from a known position.

For a heavy object traveling at fifty or sixty miles an hour, water can be a deceptively hard and resistant surface. Bernt Balchen had made numerous water landings with floatplanes, but putting an aircraft equipped with wheels down on the choppy sea was something neither he nor his companions nor any pilot known to them had ever done. During the planning for the transatlantic flight, Byrd and Bennett had discussed what might happen if they were forced to ditch and solicited the opinions of other aviators. The consensus was that the ship would nose over and wind up on her back just as she had done at Teterboro in April. This scenario, of course, assumed the pilot could see the water. The *America* was flying at night in conditions of zero or, at best, reduced visibility. Under the circumstances, the most likely possibility was that Balchen would either level off too early or too late. In the first case, he would find himself a hundred or so feet in the air, flying low and slow; before he knew what happened he would stall and plummet to the sea. In the second, he would hit the water nose-first at too rapid a rate of descent. Both cases would result in a terrific crash and fatal or serious injuries to pilot and crew.

George Noville had a red scar across his right shoulder, the result of having been outnumbered and outgunned in a dogfight over Italy during the war. He didn't know how he managed to land, barely remembering having crashed into a house on the way down. Flying in the southwest as recently as January of 1927, he crashed a plane, broke his jaw and nose, and lost a few teeth. He was a fatalist, and his attitude doubtlessly paralleled that of the other members of the flight crew. "It's all written in the book," he said. "If you are going to get it, there is nothing that can stop it. It's written down, that's all."[37]

Between 2:00 and 3:00 a.m. local time, they located the light-house, descended and circled over it. The surrounding area was black, the beams of light rapidly dissolved in the mist. They could tell by the ghostly pulses when they were flying over water, and they could barely distinguish the shoreline. But it was impossible to tell if there was a long, sandy beach below, free of obstruction, or if boats had been drawn up on the sand. The character of the shoreline remained concealed in the darkness. With little more than thirty minutes of fuel left in the tanks, Balchen was instructed to land close enough to shore to swim for it, if necessary, and far enough away to avoid rocks and breakers.

By some sixth sense, he flew out over the sea and aligned the plane parallel with the shoreline. As he was orienting himself, Byrd and Noville crawled back to the navigation compartment to balance the weight of the other crewmembers. In a statement released to the press just before the takeoff, Byrd had written: "Expeditions like wars are won by preparation."[38] One of his precautions had been to take a bunch of flares that were designed to ignite on the surface of the ocean. He had intended to use them as sighting objects for obtaining wind drift at night. The night of June 29–30, however, he was unable to see the ocean through the fog. Afterwards, he had jettisoned some of these flares to reduce the weight of the plane, but had held on to the remainder for just such an emergency as he was now facing. He bent over the trapdoor in the floor of the aft compartment and tossed out one flare, then another and another in as straight a line as possible.

After completing his preliminary pass, Balchen made two ninety-degree turns and flew back in the opposite direction, watching the dots of light lined up on his wingtip. He flew past the flares, executed two more ninety-degree turns, and came around again to begin his final approach. When he banked the plane to make the last turn, the engine on the tilted upward wing sputtered. The remaining fuel in the wing tank was almost below the usable level.

The chart table was screwed into the wall of the aft cabin. Byrd and Noville ripped it from its restraints and tossed it back into the tail of the plane. The table had sharp edges; they didn't want to be thrown against those edges on the impact of the landing. Then they removed the panes from the windows on either side of the compartment and tossed them into the drink to make sure they could get out of the plane in a hurry. Those windows were not designed to slide open. Byrd stood by the rectangular breach in the starboard wall, Noville by the port, in a space about four feet long and five feet wide. "Don't let anyone tell you we are a lot of iron-hearted heroes," Noville said. "We were all scared stiff."[39]

Byrd crossed the narrow wooden floor. There was nothing left but to say "so long." Said Noville:

> He put his arm across my shoulder, smiled, and then gave me a little hug as he shook his head, which seemed to say: 'Well, it's settled' …

Balchen had brought the plane around and began his descent. Noville figured their chances were one in two hundred. He and Byrd resumed their positions, staring out into the darkness. The engines were throttled. Suddenly the only audible sound, Noville said, was "that peculiar whistle like a sick owl that a plane makes when it is gliding."[40]

Balchen couldn't see the water, but he could see the column of burning flares directly in front of him and receding into the blackness. He decided to level off over the nearest dot of light, touch down on the middle one, and judge his height over the water by the third. His instincts were superb, he executed flawlessly; the plane settled with a crash and a bang, the wheels meeting the surface first. As the wheels struck they were shorn right off the fuselage, just as if the water line was as sharp as a razor. The ship sank and hit bottom. For each crewmember, the long glide down through the darkness was followed by an eerie stillness and the sensation of cold, salty water rising above his head.

The aircraft lay nose down and tail up in about ten or fifteen feet of brine. Byrd was quickly out the opening on his side; Noville saw Byrd's feet disappearing through the pane-less window. Rex tumbled forward against the main fuel tank and hurt his knee. He felt for the edge of the window on the port side of the compartment and worked his way out of the plane. Balchen had stayed in his seat until the ship hit bottom and extricated himself with the assistance of Byrd who had dove back down from the surface. The three of them treaded water around the fuselage, calling out for Acosta.

Bert had come back to himself after his breakdown and hunkered down either in the cockpit or radio compartment to brace for the landing. He escaped through one of the sliding windows in the forward part of the ship and swam into the mist, making for shore. Or so he thought. He kept expecting to touch bottom, but never did. (It later occurred to him that he was actually heading straight out across the English Channel.)[41] Looking over his shoulder, he saw three figures clambering onto the wing of the plane. He turned around and splashed back to the wreck. The leading edge of the wing was submerged. Acosta was hoisted up on the trailing edge. Neither he, Balchen nor Noville had worn ear protectors. After suffering temporary deafness on his sixteen-hour flight to the North Pole, Byrd had stuffed up his ears this time around. His hearing was consequently unimpaired, but when he asked each of his men if they were okay, there was no answer. To the other three, the world was like a silent movie without subtitles, all moving mouths and no dialogue.

The scene would have degenerated into lunacy if they had not had a good script to follow. It had been prearranged that if they had to ditch, Noville would fish out the rubber boat from a compartment aft of the navigator's cabin and under the ceiling of the fuselage, where, as expected, it had been preserved high and dry. While the boat was inflated, Byrd checked his crew's arms and legs for broken bones. He himself had received a painful blow over the chest that caused his heart to beat irregularly for some time.[42] He didn't bother to report the injury to the physicians who later examined each of the fliers in Paris. Byrd rescued the strongbox with Wanamaker's sacred flag and part of the mail, and he and his crew piled into the boat and paddled for shore.

Some 200 yards away lay the eastern end of the fifty-mile shoreline of northern Normandy where Allied troops would stage the D-Day landing in the next war. The aviators landed within walking distance of Ver-sur-Mer, a town that in 1944 would find itself situated near the borderline of Gold and Juno Beaches, roughly twelve miles east of Omaha Beach.

Within days of their arrival, Bernt Balchen, an unknown, was given star treatment. He had made a superb landing and was interviewed by staff writers of the *Times* Paris bureau. An account of the flight shortly appeared under his byline on page one of that newspaper. His contemporaneous interview is interesting because he magnified his role in his 1958 memoir, suggesting that he alone made the decision to head to Normandy. Speculation has risen ever since as to the extent to which Byrd actually exerted command. In 1927, however, Balchen was in complete accord with Noville on the nature of the decision-making process. Here is what he had to say in the piece that ran under his byline on July 5 of that year:

> Looking over my shoulder, I could see that Commander Byrd and Lieutenant Noville were exchanging messages. It was a

conference. Commander Byrd finally passed a message to me to land on water as soon as we should come to it.

In New York, on the evening of June 29–30, Balchen was still considered a rookie called up from Hasbrouck Heights. The New York area radio stations had continued to broadcast updates on the flight throughout the night. It was said that more lights were on in Manhattan apartment buildings during the wee hours than anyone ever remembered seeing before. Tenants could look out the windows and spot their neighbors across the court tuning their radio dial, apparently switching from one station to another. WOR scooped its competitors when it announced at 4:40 a.m. that Byrd had landed and was safe. The apartment lights, observers said, all seemed to go out at the very next instant, "as if controlled by one switch."[43] Floyd Bennett received a confirmation from the nerve center of the America Trans-Oceanic Company at Roosevelt Field at about 6:00 a.m. and was finally able to get some sleep. Grover Whalen called Marie Byrd in Boston at around the same time.

After witnessing the takeoff at Mineola, Marie had caught a train for Boston, where she followed the radio bulletins with her children. Katharine Ames Byrd, age three, told that her daddy had landed, said, "Wasn't that lovely of him?" Evelyn Bolling, five, said, "I think that was fine mommie, don't you?"[44] When the full story of the flight came out in the papers, Marie wrote her husband a letter which shortly arrived in France by steamship. "I think you are superhuman Dick, in the way you have come through this," she said. "Only one in a billion could have done as you have done, fighting odds every inch of the way, hitting France and Paris too, and landing safely after that ghastly, heartbreaking flight." It was, she said, "simply superb! There is nothing I have ever heard of that touches it."[45]

She was right, in fact. The flight of the *America* was the most striking demonstration of modern aeronautic techniques in the twenty-four years since the Wright Brothers soared at Kitty Hawk. The aircraft was aloft for forty to forty-two hours. (The time of the landing in the numerous accounts varies wildly, even more so than the figures given for the flight of the *Josephine Ford.*) At an average velocity of about a hundred miles an hour, she had flown a minimum of 4,000 miles. Chamberlin had logged 3,905 miles out of New York in the smaller, faster *Columbia* when he ran out of gas and landed after forty-three to forty-six hours. If the *America* had traveled in a straight line across (and beyond) France, she would have set a new long-distance record despite having encountered abysmal conditions for nearly the entire trip.

This remarkable performance was achieved as a result of intelligent flight planning, efficient flight engineering, proficient piloting, comprehensive weather analysis and accurate navigation by radio bearings. In the absence of any of these elements, the *America* would not have reached France as swiftly, if at all. The most critical aspect of the flight was fuel economy. Byrd had flown long enough to have reached Paris, had circled for several additional hours in the storm, and still had enough fuel left to reach the coast of Normandy. He had that reserve because in various ways he had conserved fuel in the earlier stages. That was the beauty of the operation. He knew how to pick up a strong, favorable wind over the Atlantic, and he was able to fix his position in the fog and make a beeline for France. He had also taken the time and the trouble to learn how to configure the engines so as to obtain the best mileage. The thirty-one test flights saved the expedition. Otherwise, Byrd and his crew might have been forced to descend on land and take their chances splattering down through the murk on a concentration of roofs and steeples.

A decade after his first musings on the theme of engines, oceans, and wings, Richard Byrd delivered a masterpiece undiminished by the loss of his instrument. He, Noville, Balchen, and Acosta were lionized in Paris and given a ticker-tape parade in New York, which they shared with Clarence Chamberlin. Byrd became the first person to be so honored by the City of New York twice, but the lessons of the airplane of the future and the thirty-one test flights were unfortunately lost in the tumult and cheers. The death toll of participants in transoceanic jaunts reached twenty-seven by September of 1927. The overwhelming majority of the victims used single-engine planes. Most failed to take a radio. Few had a dump valve or carried lifeboats or flares. Some had tried to get a big load off the ground without sufficient flight-testing; others lacked adequate navigation training and simply vanished into thin air.

Byrd agonized over these disasters, feeling that the whole point of what he had tried to accomplish had been lost. Eventually he came to terms with the situation. "I am now tranquil and resigned about this matter," he said at the end of the year, "and I have concluded that the blood of these fellows' lives is not on my head. I risked my life to point the way. I cannot do any more. Therefore, finis."[46]

ACKNOWLEDGMENTS

Many thanks are due to the following people for their assistance and generosity in the various phases of production of this book. Circumstances were such that a lengthy period of time passed between its completion and publication. Consequently, some of those listed below are no longer here to receive my thanks. All, however, remain alive in memory, members of my personal Polar Legion. Here they are, the near and the far, the present and the departed. I apologize profusely to anyone whose name was inadvertently left off this list.

Bolling Byrd Clarke; Senator Harry F. Byrd Jr.; Katharine Byrd and Robert Breyer; Leverette S. Byrd; and Robert Byrd Breyer.

Rai Goerler and Laura Kissel of the Ohio State University Archives. Richard W. Peuser and Marjorie Ciarlante of the National Archives. Renee Braden of the National Geographic Society Archives and Records Library Division. Susan Kaplan and Susan Burroughs of Bowdoin College. Gary LaValley and Beverly Lyall of the U.S. Naval Academy's Nimitz Library. Allan Janus and Dan Hagedorn of the National Air and Space Museum. Robert Casey of the Henry Ford Museum and Greenfield Village. Ned Preston of the Federal Aviation Administration. Charles O. Cowing of the Elisha Kent Kane Historical Society.

My aviation and navigation experts: Elgen M. Long, Captain Brian Shoemaker, General Keith R. Greenaway, Joseph N. Portney,

Colonel William E. Molett, Ronald C. Sheadown, F. Atlee Dodge, and Hardy F. LeBel.

Barograph de-coder Dr. Gerald H. Newsom of OSU and polar meteorology authority Dr. Roger Colony of the University of Alaska, Fairbanks.

Authors Jeff Maynard, Richard Sanders Allen, and John H. Bryant.

Floyd Bennett authorities Pat Terrel, Marjorie Swan, Wanda Ross, and Mrs. George Ather.

Naomi Hampel of the Argosy Bookstore, New York, NY.

Mr. and Mrs. Joseph A. Massie Jr. of Winchester, Virginia.

Colonel Theodore A. Petras and Family.

Langdon H. Fulton, whose father roomed with Byrd at the Naval Academy; William M. Reed, whose dad went north with Byrd in 1926; and David Rockefeller whose father helped make the Byrd Arctic Expedition possible.

Arthur O. Sulzberger Jr. of the *New York Times*, heir of the lucky silver dollar.

Captain David Nutt of the American Polar Society, who went north with MacMillan.

For accommodations: Phil Loomis; Trudy, Jim, and the first Susan Russ; and Victor and Carolyn Uhas.

For translation: Frank Balistrieri.

My legal team: Elliot S. Blair and David I. Barrett.

Alex Novak, Maria Ruhl, and the Regnery History crew.

Ms. Julia Lord.

BIBLIOGRAPHY

ARCHIVED COLLECTIONS

Airplane Motor, Fuel Logbook for Fokker VII 3-Motor Josephine Ford, Byrd Arctic Expedition's Round the States Tour. Archives of the Air Force History Support Office. Bolling AFB, D.C.

American Polar Society Collection. The Ohio State University Archives. Columbus, OH.

Annual Register of the U.S. Naval Academy. Richard E. Byrd Midshipman Files. Archives of the U.S. Naval Academy. Annapolis, MD.

Byrd Family Collection. Handley Regional Library Archives. Winchester, VA.

Byrd Papers. The Ohio State University Archives. Columbus, OH.

Edsel Ford Files. Archives of the Henry Ford Museum and Greenfield Village. Dearborn, MI.

E. J. Demas Papers.William Haines Papers. Richard Konter Papers. General Records of the Navy, Secretary of the Navy. Records of the Bureau of Aeronautics. US Shipping Board General Files. Records of the Office of the Judge Advocate General (Navy), Proceedings of Naval and Marine Examining Boards. Records of the Office of Judge Advocate General (Army), General Courts Martial, William Mitchell Case. *Richard E. Byrd vs. Luis de Flores,* Interference No. 44385, U.S. Patent Office, National Archives. Washington, D.C., and College Park, MD.

Eugene F. McDonald Jr. Collection. Donald B. MacMillan Collection. MacMillan Arctic Expedition Scrapbook. Sun Compass File. Archives of the National Geographic Society. Washington, D.C.

Fitzhugh Green Papers. Georgetown University. Washington, D.C.

Richard E. Byrd Collection. Archives of the Virginia Military Institute. Lexington, VA.

Richard E. Byrd Collection. Harvard University Archives. Cambridge, MA.

Robert A. Bartlett Papers. Donald B. MacMillan Papers. Bowdoin College Archives. Bowdoin, ME.

INTERVIEWS AND PERSONAL COMMUNICATIONS WITH AUTHOR

Bolling Byrd Clarke

Brian Shoemaker, captain, USN (Ret.)

David Nutt, captain

David Rockefeller

Elgen Long

F. Atlee Dodge

Gerald H. Newsom, Ph.D.

Hardy F. LeBel

Harry F. Byrd Jr., senator

John H. Bryant

Joseph A. Massie Jr.

Joseph N. Portney

Katharine Byrd Breyer

Keith R. Greenaway, brigadier

Langdon H. Fulton

Leverette S. Byrd

Marie Massie

Ned Preston

Roger Colony, Ph.D.

Ronald C. Sheardown

Theodore A. Petras, colonel

William E. Mollett, lieutenant colonel

PRIVATE COLLECTIONS AND UNPUBLISHED PAPERS

Fokker Bulletin. American Edition. December, 1925. Collection of Elgen M. Long.

Henry Woodhouse Papers. Argosy Bookstore. New York, NY.

LeBel, Hardy F. "*Byrd's Flight to the North Pole: Lingering Questions From the Golden Age of Aerial Exploration,*" Paper presented at the ninth biannual Conference of Historic Aviation Writers. St. Louis, MO. October 24, 1999.

——. "*The Smoking Gun: A[n Explorers] Club Fellow Analyzes Byrd's North Pole Flight.*" Author's collection.

Letters of Richard E. Byrd and Marie Ames (Byrd). 1907–1920. Collection of Leverette S. Byrd.

Mollett, William E. "Yes, Richard E. Byrd Made the North Pole." Author's collection.

Reed, Jonathan Duff. Untitled North Pole Expedition Memoir. Circa 1930. Collection of William M. Reed.

ARTICLES

Acosta, Bert. "The Sky's the Limit." *New York World* (April 15, 22, 29, and May 6, 1928).

Amundsen, Roald. "Amundsen Hopes to Fathom Arctic Mysteries." *New York Times Magazine* (April 4, 1926).

Baker, Marcus. "An Undiscovered Island Off the Northern Coast of Alaska." *National Geographic Magazine* 5 (July 10, 1893): 76–83.

Bennett, Floyd. "Our Flight Over the North Pole." *Aero Digest* (September, 1926): 175–77, 261–63.

Brennan, Michael Captain. "Arma Virumque Cano." *The Rudder Club* (newsletter), September 1945.

Bumstead, Albert H. "The Sun Compass—Why and How." *The Military Engineer* (July–August 1926).

Byrd, Richard E. "The Perils of Arctic Flying." *The World's Work* (May 1926).

Carroll, George. "Wildest of the Early Birds." *The American Mercury* (September 1955).

Clarke, N. R. "Are We Over the Pole?" *Scientific American* 135 (September 1926): 188–89.

"Commander McDonald of Zenith." *Fortune* 31, no. 6 (June 1945): 140–43.

Crowther, Samuel. "Edsel B. Ford." *Saturday Evening Post* (December 25, 1926): 199.

Demas, E. J. "Byrd's North Pole Flight, 9 May 1926." *Polar Record* 18, no. 114 (1976).

Drake, Francis and Katherine. "Bernt Balchen—Viking of the Air." *Reader's Digest* 62 (January 1953): 1211–15.

Duffus, R. L. "Amundsen, At 53, Plans New Quest," *New York Times* (October 18, 1925).

Eaton, H. N. "Aerial Navigation and Navigating Instruments." *Report No. 131, "Aeronautics." Seventh Annual Report of the National Advisory Committee for Aeronautics, 1921*. Washington, D.C.: Government Printing Office, 1923.

Ellsworth, Lincoln. "An Epic of the Polar Air Lanes." *New York Times Magazine* (October 11, 1925).

———. "Ellsworth Tells of His Adventures." *New York Times Magazine* (March 21, 1926).

Goerler, Raimund E. "Archives in Controversy: The Press, the Documentaries and the Byrd Archives." *American Archivist* 62, no. 2 (Fall 1999).

Green, Fitzhugh. "The Mother of Tom, Dick and Harry." *American* (February 1928): 105.

Gregg, Willis Ray. "Meteorology of the North Atlantic and Trans-Atlantic Flight." *Aviation* (August 1, 1927).

Hadden, Jean. "Floyd Bennett: The Untold True Story." *Warrensburgh Historical Quarterly* (Fall 1998).

Harris, Rollin A. "Some Indications of Land in the Vicinity of the North Pole." *National Geographic Magazine* (June 1904): 255–61.

———. "Undiscovered Land in the Arctic Ocean." *American Museum Journal* (February 1913).

Hellman, Geoffrey T. "Geography Unshackled." *New Yorker* (September 25, October 2, and October 9, 1943): 19.

Hunt, A. Leigh. "Rear Admiral Richard E. Byrd: Some Personal Impressions." *Pacific Neighbors* 11, no. 1 (1956).

Liljequist, G. H. "Did the 'Josephine Ford' Reach the North Pole?" *Interavia*, no. 5 (1960).

MacMillan, Donald B. "Account of the 1925 Expedition to Greenland." *National Geographic Magazine.*

———. "The Humorous Side of Arctic Exploration," *The World's Work* 46 (August 1923): 389–96.

Molett, William E. "Due North? Byrd's Disputed Flight to the Pole." *Mercator's World* (March/April 1998).

———. "Examination of Byrd Navigation From the Flight to the North Pole." *Polar Times* 2, no. 8 (Fall–Winter 1996).

Murphy, Charles J. V. "Shall We Fly the Atlantic." *Harper's* 157 (July 1928): 183–94.

———. "The Flight of the America." *Collier's* 82 (August 11, 1928).

Noville, George O. "Cold Weather Engine Starting."*Aero Digest* (December 1926).

———. "High, Wide and Blind." Clipping from an unidentified magazine, circa 1957–1958. Collection of Leverette S. Byrd.

Owen, Russell D. "To the North Pole by Air." *Current History* 24 (August 1926): 678–85.

Portney, Joseph N. "The Polar Flap—Byrd's Flight Confirmed." *Navigation* 20, no. 3 (Fall 1973).

Ramsey, Logan C., and Earle H. Kincaid. "Analysis of Weather Conditions on Recent Transatlantic Flights." *Aero Digest* (October 1927).

Rawlins, Dennis. "Byrd's Heroic 1926 North Pole Failure." *Polar Record* 36, no. 196 (January 2000).

Shoemaker, Brian. Book Reviews. *The Polar Times* 2, no. 11 (Spring–Summer 1998): 21.

Smedley, Doree, and Hollister Noble. "Flying Dutchman." *New Yorker* 6 (February 7, 1931).

Taylor, Robert Lewis. "Captain Among the Synthetics." *New Yorker* 20 (November 11 and November 18, 1944).

Towers, John H. "The Great Hop." *Everybody's Magazine* 41 (November 1919): 9–15.

BOOKS

Adams-Ray, Edward, trans. *Andrée's Story: The Complete Record of His Polar Flight, 1897*. New York: Viking Press, 1930.

Aircraft Year Book. New York: Aeronautical Chamber of Commerce of America, Inc., 1925.

Aircraft Year Book. New York: Aeronautical Chamber of Commerce of America, Inc., 1926.

Allen, Everett S. *Arctic Odyssey: The Life of Rear Admiral Donald B. MacMillan*. New York: Dodd, Mead, 1962.

Althoff, William F. *Sky Ships: A History of the Airship in the United States Navy*. New York: Orion Books, 1990.

Amundsen, Roald. *My Life as an Explorer*. Garden City, NH: Doubleday, Doran, 1928.

Amundsen, Roald, and Lincoln Ellsworth. *First Crossing of the Polar Sea*. New York: George H. Doran, 1927.

————. *Our Polar Flight: The Amundsen-Ellsworth Polar Flight*. New York: Dodd, Mead, 1925.

Anderson, John D. Jr. *The Airplane: A History of Its Technology*. Reston, VA: American Institute of Aeronautics and Astronautics, 2002.

Appel, Joseph H. *The Business Biography of John Wanamaker, Founder and Builder, With Glimpses of Rodman Wanamaker and Thomas B. Wanamaker*. New York: Macmillan, 1930.

Arpee, Edward. *From Frigates to Flat-Tops: The Story of the Life and Achievements of Rear Admiral William Adger Moffett, "The Father of Naval Aviation," October 31, 1869–April 4, 1933*. Published and distributed by the author, 1953.

Balchen, Bernt. *Come North With Me*. New York: E. P. Dutton, 1958.

Bartlett, Robert A. *The Log of Bob Bartlett*. New York: G. P. Putnam's Sons, 1928.

Bennett, Cora L. *Floyd Bennett*. New York: William Farquhar Payson, 1932.

Bryant, John H., and Harold N. Cones. *Dangerous Crossings: The First Modern Polar Expedition, 1925*. Annapolis, MD: Naval Institute Press, 2000.

————. *Zenith Radio: The Early Years 1919–1935*. Atglen, PA: Schiffer, 1997.

————. *The Zenith Trans-Oceanic: The Royalty of Radios*. Atglen, PA: Schiffer, 1995.

Byrd, Richard E. *Skyward*. New York: G. P. Putnam's Sons, 1928.

Collier, Basil. *The Airship: A History*. New York: G. P. Putnam's Sons, 1974.

Collier, Peter, and David Horowitz. *The Fords: An American Epic*. New York: Summit Books, 1987.

Cronow, E. David. *The Cabinet Diaries of Josephus Daniels, 1913–1921*. Lincoln: University of Nebraska Press, 1963.

Daniels, Josephus. *The Wilson Era: Years of Peace, 1910–1917*. Chapel Hill: The University of North Carolina Press, 1944.

Davis, Burke. *The Billy Mitchell Affair*. New York: Random House, 1967.

Doolittle, James H., and Carroll V. Glines. *I Could Never Be So Lucky Again*. New York: Bantam Books, 1991.

Dunbar, Moira, and Keith R. Greenaway. *Arctic Canada From the Air*. Toronto: Defense Research Board, 1956.

Ellsworth, Lincoln. *Beyond Horizons*. Garden City, NY: Doubleday, Doran, 1938.

———. *Search*. New York: Brewer, Warren and Putnam, 1932.

Fishwick, Marshall W. *Virginia: A New Look at the Old Dominion*. New York: Harper & Brothers, 1959.

Fokker, Anthony H. G., and Gould, Bruce. *Flying Dutchman: The Life of Anthony Fokker*. New York: Holt, 1931.

Fosdick, Raymond B. *Chronicle of a Generation: An Autobiography*. New York: Harper & Brothers, 1958.

———. *John D. Rockefeller, Jr.: A Portrait*. New York: Harper & Brothers, 1956.

Goerler, Raimund E., ed. *To the Pole: The Diary and Notebook of Richard E. Byrd, 1925–1927*. Columbus, OH: The Ohio State University Press, 1998.

Green, Fitzhugh. *Dick Byrd-Air Explorer*. New York: G. P. Putnam's Sons, 1928.

———. *ZR Wins*. New York: D. Appleton, 1924.

Greenleaf, William. *From These Beginnings: The Early Philanthropies of Henry and Edsel Ford, 1911–1936*. Detroit: Wayne State University Press, 1964.

Harris, Rollin A. *Arctic Tides*. Washington, D.C.: Government Printing Office, 1911.

Hatch, Alden. *The Byrds of Virginia: An American Dynasty, 1670 to the Present*. New York: Holt, Rinehart and Winston, 1969.

Hegener, Henri. *Fokker—The Man and the Aircraft*. Letchworth, Herts: Harleyford, 1961.

Heinemann, Ronald L. *Harry Byrd of Virginia*. Charlottesville and London: University of Virginia Press, 1996.

Hocking, William E. *Human Nature and Its Remaking*. New Haven: Yale University Press, 1918.

Huntford, Roland. *Scott and Amundsen*. New York: G. P. Putnam's Sons, 1980.

Karsten, Peter. *The Naval Aristocracy: The Golden Age of Annapolis and the Emergence of Modern American Navalism.* New York: Free Press, 1972.

Lindbergh, Charles A. *The Spirit of St. Louis.* New York: Charles Scribner's Sons, 1954.

Loening, Grover. *Amphibian: The Story of the Loening Biplane.* Greenwich, CT: New York Graphic Society, 1973.

The Lucky Bag. U.S. Naval Academy, 1909, 1912, and 1914.

MacMillan, Donald B. *Four Years in the White North.* New York: Harper & Brothers, 1918.

MacMillan, Miriam. *Green Seas and White Ice.* New York: Dodd, Mead, 1948.

McKinlay, William Laird. *Karluk: The Great Untold Story of Arctic Exploration.* New York: St. Martin's Press, 1976.

Montague, Richard. *Oceans, Poles and Airmen: The First Flights over Wide Waters and Desolate Ice.* New York: Random House, 1971.

Morris, Lloyd and Kendall Smith. *Ceiling Unlimited: The Story of American Aviation from Kitty Hawk to Supersonics.* New York: Macmillan, 1953.

Murphy, Charles J. V. *Struggle: The Life and Exploits of Commander Richard E. Byrd.* New York: Frederick A. Stokes, 1928.

Owen, Russell D. *South of the Sun.* New York: The John Day Company, 1934.

Peary, Robert E. *Nearest the Pole: A Narrative of the Polar Expedition of the Peary Arctic Club in the S.S. Roosevelt, 1905–1906.* New York: Doubleday, Page, 1907.

———. *The North Pole: Its Discovery in 1909 Under the Auspices of the Peary Arctic Club.* New York: Frederick A. Stokes, 1910.

———. *Secrets of Polar Travel.* New York: The Century Company, 1917.

Portney, Joseph N. *Portney's Ponderables.* Woodland Hills, CA: Litton Systems, 2000.

Problems of Polar Research: A Series of Papers by Thirty-One Authors. New York: American Geographical Society, 1928.

Putnam, George Palmer. *Wide Margins: A Publisher's Autobiography.* New York: Harcourt, Brace, 1942.

Rawson, Kennett Longley. *A Boy's-Eye View of the Arctic.* New York: Macmillan, 1926.

Reynolds, Clark G. *Admiral John H. Towers: The Struggle for Naval Air Supremacy.* Annapolis, MD: Naval Institute Press, 1991.

Richards, Eva Alvey. *Arctic Mood: A Narrative of Arctic Adventures.* Caldwell, ID: The Caxton Printers, 1949.

Ronne, Finn. *Antarctica My Destiny.* New York: Hastings House, 1979.

Smith, Richard K. *First Across: The U.S. Navy's Transatlantic Flight of 1919.* Annapolis, MD: Naval Institute Press, 1973.

Stefansson, Vilhjalmur. *The Northward Course of Empire.* New York: Macmillan, 1924.

Vaughan, Norman D. and Cecil B. Murphey. *With Byrd at the Bottom of the World.* Harrisburg, PA: Stackpole Books, 1990.

Weems, John Edward. *Peary: The Explorer and the Man.* Boston: Houghton Mifflin, 1967.

Weems, P. V. H. *Air Navigation.* New York: McGraw-Hill, 1943.

Wellman, Walter. *The Aerial Age.* New York: A. B. Keller, 1911.

Weyl, A. R. *Fokker: The Creative Years.* London: Putnam, 1965.

Whalen, Grover A. *Mr. New York: The Autobiography of Grover A. Whalen.* New York: G. P. Putnam's Sons, 1955.

Wilkins, Captain George H. *Flying the Arctic.* New York: G. P. Putnam's Sons, 1928.

Worsley, Frank A. *Under Sail in the Frozen North.* London: Stanley Paul, 1927.

Wright, Monte Duane. *Most Probable Position: A History of Aerial Navigation to 1941.* Lawrence, Kansas: University Press of Kansas, 1972.

NEWSPAPERS AND PERIODICALS

Aero Digest

Aftenposten

Corrière della Sera

Literary Digest

New York Herald Tribune

New York Times

New York World

Washington Post

NOTES

ABBREVIATIONS:

BP   Byrd Papers, Ohio State University Archives

NA   National Archives

NGS Archives of the National Geographic Society

REB Richard E. Byrd

CHAPTER ONE
Early aviation in the Arctic:
Edward Adams-Ray, trans., *Andrée's Story: The Complete Record of His Polar Flight*; William Wellman, *The Aerial Age*.

1. *New York Times*, December 29, 1918.
2. Marcus Baker, "An Undiscovered Island off the Coast of Alaska," *National Geographic Magazine 5* (July 10, 1893).
3. Robert E. Peary, *Nearest the Pole*, 202.
4. Ibid., 207.
5. *New York Times*, May 31, 1925.
6. Rollin A. Harris, *Arctic Tides*, 91.

CHAPTER TWO
1. *New York Times*, January 27, 1924.
2. Alden Hatch, *The Byrds of Virginia*, 255.
3. Skyward Questionnaire (written interviews with REB conducted by Fitzhugh Green for the writing of *Skyward*, circa 1928), BP, folder 4358; *New York Times*, December 26, 1916.
4. Robert E. Peary, *Secrets of Polar Travel*, 312.

5. Statement of Admiral Peary to the Associated Press, December 22, 1916, from the Henry Woodhouse Collection, Argosy Bookstore, Box L-2.

6. *New York Times*, December 20, 1916.

7. Josephus Daniels, secretary of the navy, to the president, March 10, 1916, NA, Records of the Bureau of Aeronautics.

8. *New York Times*, December 23 and 29, 1918.

9. *New York Times*, January 14, 1919; *Flying*, February 1919.

10. Captain Robert A. Bartlett, *The Log of Bob Bartlett*, 19.

11. Roald Amundsen, *My Life As An Explorer*, 107.

12. *New York Times*, April 22, 1924.

13. *New York Times*, January 22, 1924.

CHAPTER THREE
Proposed Byrd 1925 Arctic Expedition:
BP, folder 4235

On Edsel Ford:
Samuel Crowther, "Edsel B. Ford," *Saturday Evening Post*, December 25, 1926; Peter Collier and David Horowitz, *The Fords: An American Epic*.

1. Richard E. Byrd, *To the Pole: The Diary and Notebook of Richard E. Byrd, 1925–1927*, edited by Raimund E. Goerler, 28.

2. Idries Shah, *Reflections*, 69.

3. Thomas J. Sullivan to Charles J. V. Murphy, January 13, 1931, BP, folder 2295.

4. A. Leigh Hunt, "Rear Admiral Richard E. Byrd: Some Personal Impressions," *Pacific Neighbors* 11, no. 1 (1956).

5. Interview with Bolling Byrd Clark, June 25, 1999.

6. Skyward Questionnaire.

7. H. R. W. Miles to REB, October 28, 1926, BP, folder 4279.

8. REB to P. N. L. Bellinger, February 19, 1925, BP, folder 4235.

9. *New York Times*, January 20, 1924.

10. Raymond B. Fosdick, *John D. Rockefeller, Jr.: A Portrait*, 424.

11. John D. Rockefeller Jr. to Edsel Ford, March 24, 1925, BP, folder 4235.

CHAPTER FOUR
On MacMillan:
Everett S. Allen, *Arctic Odyssey: The Life of Rear Admiral Donald B.*

MacMillan; Miriam MacMillan, *Green Seas and White Ice*; Donald B. MacMillan, "The Humorous Side of Arctic Exploration," *The World's Work*, August 1923; various biographical pieces, Donald B. MacMillan papers.

Correspondence, Proposed Byrd Arctic Expedition:
BP, folder 4235

1. Fitzhugh Green to REB, February 8, 1927.
2. Robert E. Peary, *Secrets of Polar Travel*, 52–55.
3. Donald B. MacMillan, *Four Years in the White North*, 80.
4. *New York Times*, October 22, 1975.
5. *Literary Digest*, September 15, 1917, 63.
6. *New York Times*, January 20, 1925.
7. Eugene F. McDonald Jr. to Curtis D. Wilbur, secretary of the navy, February 28, 1925, NA, RG 80, folder 29455-83.
8. *New York Times*, April 11, 1925.
9. REB to the chief of Bureau of Navigation via the chief of Bureau of Aeronautics, "Scientific Exploration by Aircraft in the Polar Regions," March 26, 1925.
10. John H. Bryant and Harold N. Cones, *Dangerous Crossings: The First Modern Polar Expedition*, 1925, March 26, 1925.
11. REB to Paul W. Litchfield, March 13, 1925, BP, folder 4235.
12. REB to Gilbert Grosvenor, March 16, 1925, BP, folder 4235; April 5, 1926, BP, folder 4239.
13. REB to Adam C. Carson, March 31, 1925, BP, folder 4235.
14. *New York Times*, April 12, 1925, IX, 3.
15. *New York Times*, September 28, 1924, VIII, 5.

CHAPTER FIVE

On Ellsworth:
Lincoln Ellsworth, *Beyond Horizons*; Ellsworth, "Ellsworth Tells of His Adventures," *New York Times Magazine*, March 21, 1926; Beekman Pool, "Polar Explorer Lincoln Ellsworth: A New Look," lecture given at the Second Byrd Polar Colloquy, Byrd Polar Research Center, Ohio State University, October 16, 1999.

On McDonald:
"Commander McDonald of Zenith," *Fortune*, June 1945; John H. Bryant and Harold N. Cones, *The Zenith Trans-Oceanic: The Royalty of Radios*; Bryant

and Cones, *Zenith Radio: The Early Years 1919–1935*.

On Algarsson:
New York Times, April 10, 14, and 26, 1926; Frank A. Worsley, *Under Sail in the Frozen North*, 1–4, 13–15, 23, 105.

The Loening Amphibian:
Grover Loening, *Amphibian: The Story of the Loening Biplane*.

Correspondence, proposed Byrd Arctic Expedition:
BP, folder 4235.

Correspondence, MacMillan Arctic Expedition (preparations):
Archives of the National Geographic Society, Donald B. MacMillan Collection, Correspondence of John O. La Gorce.

1. Lincoln Ellsworth, "An Epic of the Polar Air Lanes," *New York Times Magazine*, October 11, 1925, 1.
2. Roald Amundsen to REB, March 1, 1927, BP, folder 4262.
3. *New York Times*, March 31, 1925.
4. REB to Adam C. Carson, March 31, 1925, BP, folder 4235.
5. Peter Karsten, *The Naval Aristocracy: The Golden Age of Annapolis and the Emergence of Modern American Navalism*, xiv, 23–46.
6. W. R. Shoemaker, chief of the Bureau of Navigation, to chief of Naval Operations, March 13, 1925, NA, RG 80, folder 29455-83.
7. Eugene F. McDonald Jr. to Gilbert H. Grosvenor, April 7, 1925, NGS.
8. Agreement between Donald B. MacMillan and Lieutenant Commander REB, U.S. Navy, April 18, 1925, NGS.
9. *New York Times*, April 10, 1925.
10. Bureau of Engineering to commandant, U.S. Navy Yard, Washington, D.C., "Material for Use with Pigeons Being Supplied the Naval Arctic Unit," May 13, 1925, NA, RG 80, folder 29455-83.
11. *New York Times*, May 16, 1925.
12. REB, tribute to Floyd Bennett, May 20, 1928, BP, folder 3493.
13. John O. La Gorce to Donald B. MacMillan, May 8, 1925, NGS.
14. Donald B. MacMillan to Gilbert H. Grosvenor, February 9, 1927, NGS.
15. *New York Times*, May 24, 1925.
16. Ellsworth, *Beyond Horizons*, 130.
17. Albert H. Bumstead to Stanley Mayfield, August 17, 1937, NGS.
18. John O. La Gorce to Gilver H. Grosvenor, June 24, 1925, NGS.

CHAPTER SIX

Note on the MacMillan diaries:

MacMillan kept a diary of the expedition, written in pencil in a large, hardbound volume, hereinafter referred to as "MacMillan Log." After he returned from the North, he reworked the diary into a fluid narrative, which was published as an article in the *National Geographic Magazine*. He also typed up a third version, perhaps intended for posterity. It was something of an annotated edition, with additional editorial comment omitted from the official version. In the following citations, the latter is referred to as "MacMillan annotated diary." All are in the collection of Bowdoin College.

On the Amundsen-Ellsworth adventure:

Roald Amundsen et al., *Our Polar Flight*, 50–75; Lincoln Ellsworth, "An Epic of the Polar Air Lanes," *New York Times Magazine*, October 11, 1925.

On Gilbert H. Grosvenor and the National Geographic Society:

Geoffrey T. Hellman, "Geography Unshackled," *New Yorker*, September 25, October 2, and October 9, 1943.

MacMillan Expedition (embarkation):

Archives of the National Geographic Society; Records of the Bureau of Aeronautics, National Archives, RG 80; Davidoff, MacMillan diaries, Archives of Bowdoin College; Raimon E. Goerler, *To the Pole: The Diary and Notebook of Richard E. Byrd, 1925–1927*; John H. Bryant and Harold N. Cones, *Dangerous Crossings*.

On Floyd Bennett:

Cora Bennett, *Floyd Bennett*; Jean Hadden, "Floyd Bennett: The Untold True Story," *Warrensburgh Historical Society Quarterly*, Fall 1997.

MacMillan Expedition, en route to Etah:

REB, Davidoff, MacMillan diaries; BP folders 4232, 4234, and 4236; Archives of the NGS.

1. Editorial, *New York Times*, June 5, 1925.
2. *New York Times*, June 12, 1925.
3. Frank B. Kellogg to Gilbert H. Grosvenor, June 19, 1925, NGS.
4. Donald B. MacMillan to Curtis D. Wilbur, June 5, 1925, NA, RG 80, folder 29455-83: 10.
5. *New York Times*, June 20, 1925.

6. Donald B. MacMillan, annotated diary, 1925 expedition, 4, Miriam MacMillan Bequest, Box 24, folder 13, Bowdoin College Archives.

7. Donald B. MacMillan to Gilbert H. Grosvenor, May 16, 1925, NGS.

8. Advertisement, *Radio Age*, August 1925, NGS collection.

9. Interview with Dr. Susan A. Kaplan, director of the Peary-MacMillan Arctic Museum and Arctic Studies Center at Bowdoin College.

10. MacMillan, annotated diary, 16.

CHAPTER SEVEN
MacMillan Expedition, en route to Etah:
REB, Davidoff, MacMillan diaries; BP folders 4232, 4234, and 4236; Archives of the NGS.

On Etah:
Kennett L. Rawson, *A Boy's-Eye View of the Arctic*; Fitzhugh Green, *Dick Byrd—Air Explorer*; John Ellingston, "Etah—Capital of New Polar Exploits," *New York Times Magazine*, June 28, 1925.

MacMillan Expedition, arrival at Etah:
REB, MacMillan, Davidoff diaries; BP folders 4234–4242.

1. Donald B. MacMillan, letters from Etah, "The Crocker Land Expedition," *American Museum Journal*, May 1914, 210.

2. Transcript cable from the American minister at Copenhagen to the U.S. Department of State, forwarded to Grosvenor from the State Department on June 13, 1925. The transcript was forwarded by Grosvenor to Donald B. MacMillan under a cover letter dated June 15, 1925, NGS.

3. *New York Times*, July 17, 1925.

4. George Palmer Putnam, "Only Man is Gay in Bleak Greenland," *New York Times Magazine*, October 31, 1926, 19.

5. La Gorce, "Memorandum re eighty tons of coal needed by Perry at Disco," July 23, 1925, NGS.

6. MacMillan, annotated diary, 24.

7. MacMillan log.

8. Kennett L. Rawson, *A Boy's-Eye View of the Arctic*, 90.

9. Quoted in Bennett, 31.

10. Ibid.

11. REB, handwritten note, BP, folder 4231.

12. REB, "The Perils of Arctic Flying," *The World's Work*, May 1926, 72.
13. *New York Times*, August 5, 1925.
14. Davidoff diary, 81.
15. Ibid., 8.

CHAPTER EIGHT
The Sun Compass:
"Inventions New and Interesting," *Scientific American*, November 1924;
Albert H. Bumstead, "The Sun Compass—Why and How," *The Military Engineer*, July–August 1926; Bell Ray Clarke, "Are We Over the Pole?," *Scientific American*, September 1926.

The drift indicator and the earth-inductor compass:
"Aerial Navigation and Navigating Instruments," report no. 131;
"Aeronautics," Seventh Annual Report of the National Advisory Committee for Aeronautics, 1921; REB, "Polar Exploration by Aircraft," Problems of Polar Research, American Geographical Society, Special Publication no. 7.

Flights over Ellesmere Island:
Byrd radiograms to secretary of the navy, BP, folder 4236; REB, "Perils of Arctic Flying," *The World's Work*, May 1926; MacMillan annotated diary; Donald B. MacMillan, "Account of the 1925 expedition to Greenland," manuscript, Bowdoin College Archives, Box 20.

1. Albert H. Bumstead, *The Military Engineer*, 315
2. MacMillan, "Account of the 1925 expedition to Greenland," 13.
3. Byrd to secretary of the navy, August 9, 1925, BP, folder 4236.
4. Donald B. MacMillan to REB, August 10, 1925, BP, folder 4233.
5. REB, *To the Pole*, 36.
6. "OL-1 Amphibian—Performance Tests of," November 4, 1925, NA, RG 80.
7. Soren Thirslund, *Viking Navigation*.
8. Albert H. Bumstead to Stanley Mayfield, August 17, 1937.
9. REB, undated press release, circa October 1925, BP, folder 4257.
10. Ibid.
11. MacMillan, "Account of the 1925 expedition to Greenland," 14.

CHAPTER NINE
Flights over Ellesmere Island:
REB, "Perils of Arctic Flying"; REB, "Perils," uncorrected manuscript, BP, folder 4242; REB, "Flying in the Arctic."

Termination of flights:
REB, *To the Pole*, diary; Davidoff diary, MacMillan annotated diary.

Byrd-MacMillan correspondence, Etah, August 1925:
BP, folders 4232 and 4233.

Radiograms:
Archives of the NGS; Records of the Bureau of Aeronautics, NA; BP, folder 4234. Copies of the deciphered cable from the Navy Department to REB, received August 19, 1925, as well as REB's response composed the same day, were found inserted between the August 18 and 19 pages of the Byrd diary, 1925–1927.

MacMillan on REB:
Memorandum of a conversation between Donald B. MacMillan, George Palmer Putnam, and Fitzhugh Green, April 27, 1926, Fitzhugh Green Papers, Georgetown University, Box 1, folder 16.

1.   MacMillan, annotated diary, 29.
2.   *New York Times*, August 6, 1925.
3.   *New York Times*, August 13, 1925.
4.   MacMillan, annotated diary, 41.
5.   *New York Times*, August 14, 1925; *Halifax Herald*, October 7, 1925.
6.   MacMillan, annotated diary, 45; Bryant and Cones, *Zenith Radio*, 68, 76, 220 note 66.
7.   Donald B. MacMillant to REB, August 17, 1925, BP, folder 4233.
8.   Secretary of the navy to REB, August 18, 1925, NA, M1140 11-99.1, Roll 26.
9.   Donald B. MacMillan to National Geographic Society, August 17, 1925.
10. John O. La Gorce to Albert T. Gould, September 17, 1925, NGS.
11. Eugene J. McDonald Jr. to REB, August 20, 1925, BP, folder 4233.
12. Jacob Gayer, Benjamin Rigg, and Maynard O. Williams to National Geographic Society, August 19, 1925, NGS.
13. La Gorce to MacMillan, August 19, 1925, NGS.
14. Memorandum of a conversation between MacMillan, etc.

15. Affadavit of Harwood Elmes Robert Steele, November 3, 1925, NA.
16. La Gorce to MacMillan, August 20, 1925, NGS; OPNAV to SS *Peary* (message to REB), August 20, 1925, NA.
17. Affadavit of George Patton Mackenzie, November 3, 1925, NA; Affadavit of Lazare Desire Morin, November 3, 1925, NA.

CHAPTER TEN
Windup of the MacMillan Arctic Expedition and its accomplishments: BP, folders 4232–4234, 4243; REB, "Perils of Arctic Flying"; REB, "Flying in the Arctic."

Byrd family history:
Mildred Campbell Whitaker, *Genealogy of the Campbell, Noble, Gorton, Sheltton, Gilmour and Byrd Families*; Alden Hatch, *The Byrds of Virginia*; Garland R. Quarles, *Some Worthy Lives*; Ronald L. Heinemann, *Harry Byrd of Virginia*; Interviews with Senator Harry F. Byrd Jr. and Mr. and Mrs. Joseph A. Massie Jr.

On Eleanor Bolling Byrd:
Fitzhugh Green, "The Mother of Tom, Dick and Harry," *American*, February 1928.

Byrd youth and childhood:
Fitzhugh Green, *Dick Byrd—Air Explorer*; Charles J. V. Murphy, *Struggle*.

Philippine adventures: *Winchester Evening Star*, BP, filder 3875, Accession 19961, folder 8.

1. REB to H. Kelso Teater, November 22, 1926, BP, folder 4318.
2. *New York Times*, July 19, 1925, II.
3. Jesse R. Hildebrand to La Gorce, October 30, 1925, NGS.
4. Louis B. Wright and Marion Tinling, eds., *The Secret Diary of William Byrd of Westover, 1709–1712*, 210–11.
5. Interview with Senator Harry F. Byrd Jr., January 24, 2001.
6. Douglas Southall Freeman to Harry F. Byrd Sr., May 2, 1951, collection of Senator Harry F. Byrd Jr.
7. Interview with Senator Harry F. Byrd Jr.
8. Fitzhugh Green, "The Mother of Tom, Dick and Harry," *American*, February 1928.

9. *Springfield Union/Springfield Republican*, July 18, 1926.
10. *Washington Post*, September 19, 1957.
11. *Baltimore Sun*, May 16, 1926.
12. Ibid.
13. Interview with Mr. and Mrs. Joseph A. Massie Jr., January 25, 2001.
14. Green, "The Mother of Tom, Dick and Harry."
15. REB to Fitzhugh Green, August 24, 1926, BP, folder 1785.
16. Skyward Questionnaire, BP, folder 4358.
17. Ibid.
18. Mrs. Richard E. Byrd (as told to Mildred Johnson), "Byrd's Globe Circling Adventure as Boy of 12 Steeled Him for Life Work, His Mother Reveals," *New York Herald Tribune*, July 2, 1927.
19. *New York Times*, July 4, 1926.
20. Ibid.
21. *Winchester Evening Star*, March 19, 1903, BP, folder 3875.

CHAPTER ELEVEN
Courtship and marriage:
Letters of Richard E. Byrd and Marie Ames, 1907–1920, collection of
Leverette S. Byrd.

1. REB to Mrs. Joseph B. Ames, February 20, 1912, collection of Leverette S. Byrd.
2. "In the Garden of the Old Dominion," published by the City of Winchester, 1900.
3. W. A. Blanchard to Marie A. Byrd, July 3, 1927, BP, folder 4353.
4. *Boston Transcript*, circa April 1930, archives at Virginia Military Institute (VMI).
5. Herman C. Schmidt to Julia Martin, January 31, 1975, archives of VMI.
6. Ibid.
7. *Boston Transcript*, circa April 1930, archives at VMI.
8. Ibid.
9. *Lexington Gazette*, circa July 1927, archives of VMI.
10. REB to Marie Ames, October 12, 1907, collection of Leverette S. Byrd.
11. *The Lucky Bag*, U.S. Naval Academy, 1909.
12. Fitzhugh Green, *Dick Byrd—Air Explorer*, 5–6.
13. REB to Frank Berrien, November 27, 1926, BP, folder 4299.
14. REB to Marie Ames, January 1912, collection of Leverette S. Byrd.

15. *The Lucky Bag*, U.S. Naval Academy, 1912.
16. W. A. Blanchard to Marie A. Byrd, July 3, 1927, BP, folder 4353.
17. Fitness Report, September 25, 1912, to March 31, 1913, Records of the Office of the Judge Advocate General (navy), RG 125, Box 152, NA.
18. REB to Marie Ames, August 26, 1913, collection of Leverette S. Byrd.
19. Medical Record from Promotion, July 8, 1915, Records of the Office of the Judge Advocate General (navy), RG 125, Box 152, NA.
20. REB to Marie Ames, May 26, 1913, collection of Leverette S. Byrd.

CHAPTER TWELVE
Marriage and early military career:
Letters of Richard E. Byrd and Marie A. Byrd, 1907–1920, collection of Leverette S. Byrd; Records of the Office of the Judge Advocate General (navy), RG 125, Box 152 NA; BP, folder 4127.

1. REB to Marie A. Byrd, October 4, 1913, collection of Leverette S. Byrd.
2. Fitness Report, April 24, 1914, to September 28, 1914, Records of the Office of the Judge Advocate General (navy), RG 125, Box 152, NA.
3. Josephus Daniels, *The Wilson Era: Years of Peace, 1910–1917*, 294.
4. REB to Marie Byrd, August 2, 1915, collection of Leverette S. Byrd.
5. Fitness Report, April 1, 1915, to June 4, 1915, Records of the Office of the Judge Advocate General (navy), RG 125, Box 152, NA.
6. Quoted in REB to Marie A. Byrd, April 14, 1915, collection of Leverette S. Byrd.
7. REB to Marie A. Byrd, April 22, 1915, collection of Leverette S. Byrd.
8. Report of Naval Retiring Board, March 2, 1916, Records of the Office of the Judge Advocate General (navy), RG 125, Box 152, NA.
9. *New York Times*, June 18, 1916.
10. Skyward Questionnaire, BP, folder 4358.
11. Ibid.
12. Raymond B. Fosdick, *Chronicles of a Generation*, 163.
13. Fitzhugh Green to Mr. and Mrs. Charles E. Green, February 21, 1926, Georgetown University Archives.
14. General Outline, Commission on Training Camp Activities, BP, folder 4127.
15. REB, undated memorandum, circa June 1917, BP, folder 4127.
16. Interview with Langdon H. Fulton, June 25, 2001.

CHAPTER THIRTEEN

Flight training and early aviation career:
REB Student Flight Log, BP, Accession 19961, folder 12; Skyward
Questionnaire, BP, folder 4358; BP, folders 4126 and 4344; REB, *Skyward*;
Alden Hatch, *The Byrds of Virginia*.

On the flight of the NCs:
John H. Towers, "The Great Hop," *Everybody's Magazine*, November 1919;
Richard K. Smith, *First Across: The U.S. Navy's Transatlantic Flight of 1919*.

On the development of the bubble sextant:
Deposition of REB, August 5, 1920, Luis de Florez vs. Richard E. Byrd Jr.,
Interference no. 44385, BP, folder 8203.

1. REB, *Skyward*, 77.
2. Ibid., 33.
3. *New York Times*, May 13, 1926.
4. Skyward Questionnaire, BP, folder 4358.
5. Ibid.
6. Ibid.
7. REB to Walter Camp, May 13, 1918, BP, folder 4126.
8. Hatch, 260–61.
9. REB to chief of Naval Operations (Aviation), July 9, 1918, BP, folder 4126.
10. Skyward Questionnaire, BP, folder 4358.
11. Heinemann, 22.
12. Skyward Questionnaire, BP, folder 4358.
13. REB to chief of Naval Operations, December 4, 1918, BP, folder 4344.
14. Clark G. Reynolds, *Admiral John H. Towers*, 67.
15. Deposition of REB.
16. Ibid.
17. Holden C. Richardson to REB, September 28, 1927, BP, folder 4344.
18. John H. Towers, "The Great Hop," *Everybody's Magazine*, November 1919.
19. REB, *Skyward*, 88.
20. Smith, *First Across*, 53.
21. *New York Times*, May 16, 1919.

CHAPTER FOURTEEN

The sextant case:
REB vs. Luis de Florez, Interference no. 44385, NA.

On Luis de Florez:
Robert Lewis Taylor, "Captain Among the Synthetics," *New Yorker*, November 11; November 18, 1944.

On the Bureau of Aeronautics and legislative relations:
Skyward Questionnaire; Letters of REB and Marie A. Byrd, collection of Leverette S. Byrd.

On Admiral Moffett:
Edward Arpee, *From Frigates to Flat-Tops: The Story of the Life and Achievements of Rear Admiral William Adger Moffett, "The Father of Naval Aviation."*

Byrd/Moffett correspondence:
BP, folders 161 and 2263.

The R-38 disaster:
Findings of the Court of Inquiry into loss of R-38, BP, folder 161; Report on the Disaster of the R-38 (ZR-2), BP, folder 4126.

1. REB to Lane Lacey, December 20, 1919, BP, folder 300.
2. REB to Walter Hinton, August 14, 1920, BP, folder 8205.
3. REB to Watson E. Coleman, April 2, 1920, BP, folder 8205.
4. REB to W. T. Walker, March 10, 1920, BP, folder 299.
5. REB to J. A. Wilson, August 12, 1919, BP, folder 300.
6. REB to E. O. McConnell, April 10, 1920, BP, folder 299.
7. Josephus Daniels, *The Cabinet Diaries of Josephus Daniels, 1913–1921*, May 17, 1920.
8. Murphy, *Struggle*, 98.
9. REB, statement, May 1920; REB, statement, January 4, 1921, BP, folder 209.
10. Skyward Questionnaire, BP, folder 4358.

11. Franklin D. Roosevelt to Eleanor Roosevelt, October 20, 1919, and October 26, 1919; Franklin D. Roosevelt, *F.D.R.: His Personal Letters, 1905–1928*, edited by Elliott Roosevelt.

12. REB, trans-atlantic flight, May 4, 1921, BP, folder 299.

13. REB, trans-atlantic flight, July 30, 1921, BP, folder 4344.

14. REB to William A. Moffett, August 27, 1921, BP, folder 161.

15. *New York Times*, August 25, 1921.

16. REB to Marie A. Byrd, August 24, 1921, collection of Leverette S. Byrd.

17. REB to William A. Moffett, August 24, 1921, BP, folder 2263.

18. REB to Marie A. Byrd, February 6, 1923, collection of Leverette S. Byrd.

19. Memorandum, J. T. Boone, March 6, 1922, Records of the Office of the Judge Advocate General (navy), RG 125, Box 152, NA.

20. REB to Fitzhugh Green, January 23, 1928, BP, folder 1763.

21. REB, letter fragment, circa 1922, BP, folder 4127.

22. *New York Times*, February 23, 1922.

23. *The Congressional Record*, June 22, 1922, 8049.

24. REB to Marie A. Byrd, February 6, 1923, collection of Leverette S. Byrd.

25. Ibid.

26. Skyward Questionnaire, BP, folder 4358.

27. William A. Moffett to Thomas F. Ryan, February 20, 1922, BP, folder 4126.

28. Fitness Report, February 14–March 31, 1924, Records of the Office of the Judge Advocate General (navy), RG 125, Box 152, NA.

29. REB to Harry F. Byrd, January 28, 1926, BP, folder 34.

30. REB, *Skyward*, 140–41.

CHAPTER FIFTEEN
On Anthony Fokker and the Fokker trimotor:
A. R. Weyl, *Fokker: The Creative Years*; Henri Hegener, *Fokker—The Man and the Aircraft*.

The Ford Reliability Tour:
The Aircraft Yearbook, 1926.

1. MacMillan to National Geographic Society, August 20, 1925, BP, folder 4228.

2. REB, undated press release, circa October 1925, BP, folder 4257.

3. *Lake George Mirror*, July 17, 1926.

4. *New York Times*, October 7, 1925.
5. *New York Times*, October 11, 1925.
6. REB, statement, November 19, 1925, BP, folder 4230.
7. *New York Times*, October 18, 1925.
8. *New York Times*, October 18, 1925.

CHAPTER SIXTEEN

Competing Arctic expeditions, 1926:
New York Times.

William Mitchell on Shenandoah and the MacMillan Arctic Expedition:
Aviation, September 14, 1925.

Court-Martial of William Mitchell:
Records of the Office of the Judge Advocate General (army), General Courts Martial, William Mitchell Case Records, 1925, RG 153, Box 9214-3, NA.

On Sir Hubert Wilkins:
I am indebted to Wilkins biographer Jeff Maynard for the insights expressed in the text.

1. REB to Robert H. Clancy, November 16, 1925, BP, folder 4237.
2. *New York Times*, December 2, 1958.
3. Worsley, *Under Sail in the Frozen North*, 166.
4. *New York Times*, October 14, 1925.
5. *New York Times*, October 1, 1925.
6. Ibid.
7. *New York Times*, October 16, 1925.
8. REB, *Skyward*, 328.
9. REB to A. J. Lepine, undated, circa December 1925, Archives of the Henry Ford Museum and Greenfield Village, Edsel Ford Files, Box 6, File 2.
10. Clinton H. Havill to REB, "Confirmation of telephone call from New York to Naval Air Station, Lakehurst, NJ," December 22, 1925, BP, folder 4293.
11. REB to Gilbert H. Grosvenor, December 28, 1925, BP, folder 4292.
12. Gilbert H. Grosvenor to REB, December 30, 1925, NGS.
13. Captain George H. Wilkins, *Flying the Arctic*, 12.

14. REB to C. D. Morris, North American Newspaper Alliance, January 30, 1926, BP, folder 4257.
15. REB to George H. Wilkins, January 22, 1916, BP, folder 4237.
16. REB to E. N. Gott, Atlantic Aircraft Corporation, January 27, 1926, BP, folder 4292.
17. *New York Times*, May 29, 1926.

CHAPTER SEVENTEEN
Organizing the Byrd Arctic Expedition:
BP, folders 4243–4236, 4251, 4256–4257, 4266, 4269, 4284, 4286, 4289, 4292–4293, 4303, 4320–4327.

Detroit Arctic Expedition and Amundsen-Ellsworth-Nobile Expedition:
George H. Wilkins, *Flying the Arctic*; Lincoln Ellsworth, *Beyond Horizons*; *New York Times*.

On air-cooled radial engines: John D. Anderson Jr., *The Airplane: A History of Its Technology*.

On George Palmer Putnam:
George Palmer Putnam, *Wide Margins*.

1. REB to George O. Noville, March 6, 1926, BP, folder 4284.
2. REB to the secretary of the navy, "Arctic Aviation Expedition," February 4, 1926, NA.
3. George R. Pond to REB, February 3, 1926, BP, folder 4286.
4. Ibid.
5. REB, "Arctic Aviation Expedition."
6. Ibid.
7. REB, *Skyward*, 328.
8. Survey of Chantier, May 21, 1923, Bp, folder 4253.
9. *New York Times*, April 4, 1926.
10. *New York Times*, February 28, 1926.
11. Fitzhugh Green to John Stapler, March 10, 1926, Fitzhugh Green Papers, Georgetown University, box 4, folder 9.
12. Fitzhugh Green to REB, March 8, 1926, BP, folder 1786.
13. *New York Times*, March 31, 1926; and *New York Times*, April 2, 1926.

CHAPTER EIGHTEEN

Byrd Arctic Expedition, departure and personnel:
REB diary; BP, folders 4252, 4271, 4289, and 4290; Skyward Questionnaire; Michael Brennan, "Arma Virumque Cano," *The Rudder Club* newsletter, September 1945, BP, folder 4252; E. J. Demas, "Commander Richard E. Byrd As I Know Him," unpublished manuscript, circa 1928, BP, folder 3892; *New York Times*; *New York Herald Tribune*.

Progress of the Amundsen and Wilkins Expeditions:
New York Times.

1. "Byrd Outlines Plan to Reach the Pole," *New York Times*, March 28, 1926, section ix.
2. REB, "Crusaders," *Saturday Evening Post*, September 22, 1928.
3. *New York Times*, March 16, 1926.
4. Roald Amundsen, "Amundsen Hopes to Fathom Arctic Mysteries," *New York Times*, April 4, 1926, section ix.
5. *Washington Post*, July 12, 1966.
6. *New York Times*, April 16, 1926.

CHAPTER NINETEEN

Byrd Expedition en route:
REB diary; BP, folder 4307; "The S.S. *Chantier's* Cruise to Glory," unpublished manuscript, BP, folder 4002; *New York Times*.

1. Expedition newsletter, 1926, William C. Haines Papers, NA, RG 401 (68).
2. Quoted in Jean Hadden, "Floyd Bennett: The Untold True Story," *Warrensbugh Historical Society Quarterly*, Fall 1998.
3. *Lake George Mirror*, July 17, 1926.
4. *New York Times*, June 25, 1926.
5. Mulroy, "Cruise to Glory."
6. REB, speech, July 9, 1926, BP, folder 4217.
7. George O. Noville to Sigrid Matson, April 10, 1926, BP, folder 4310.
8. REB, Letters of Instruction, BP, folder 4294.
9. REB, "'Doc' Kinkade—The Man Who Put Us Across," *American Magazine*, June 1928.
10. Demas, "Commander Richard E. Byrd ... "

11. Frederick T. Birchall to REB, April 20, 1926, BP, folder 4310.
12. Mulroy, "Cruise to Glory."
13. REB, "Crusaders."
14. REB to Richard E. Byrd, Jr., undated, circa April 23, 1926, BP, folder 4258.
15. REB to Richard E. Byrd, Jr., April 28 1926, BP, accession 19961, box 1, folder 6.
16. Ellsworth, *Beyond Horizons*, 196.
17. REB to Roald Amundsen, April 28, 1926, BP, folder 4307.

CHAPTER TWENTY
On Amundsen:
Roland Huntford, *Scott and Amundsen*.

On Spitsbergen:
John R. Bockstoce, *High Latitude, North Atlantic: 30,000 Miles Through Cold Seas and History*; *New York Times*.

Events at Kings Bay:
REB diary; Floyd Bennett, "Our Flight Over the North Pole," *Aero Digest*, September 1926; Roald Amundsen and Lincoln Ellsworth, *The First Crossing of the Polar Sea*; Lincoln Ellsworth, *Beyond Horizons*; Bernt Balchen, *Come North with Me*.

1. Lincoln Ellsworth, *Beyond Horizons*, 115.
2. *New York Times*, June 14, 1926.
3. R. L. Duffs, "Amundsen, at 53, Plans New Quest," *New York Times*, October 18, 1925.
4. Lincoln Ellsworth, *Search*, 153.
5. *New York Times*, March 4, 1926.
6. *New York Times*, April 22, 1926.
7. Duffus.
8. Roald Amundsen, "Amundsen Hopes to Fathom Arctic Mysteries," *New York Times*, April 4, 1926.
9. Eva Alvey Richards, *Arctic Mood*, 168–69.
10. *New York Times*, April 22, 1926.
11. Russell D. Owen, "To the North Pole by Air," *Current History*, August 1926.
12. Balchen, *Come North*, 17.

13. Huntford, 321.
14. Ellsworth, *Beyond Horizons*, 321.
15. *New York Times*, March 28, 1926.
16. Balchen, 26.
17. Marie A. Byrd to REB, undated, circa 1929–30, BP, folder 64.

CHAPTER TWENTY-ONE
North Pole flight, preparations and takeoff:
REB diary, North Pole manuscript, May 1926, BP, folder 4271, Skyward
Questionnaire, *Skyward*; Floyd Bennett, "Our Flight"; Cora Bennett,
Floyd Bennett; G. O. Noville, "Cold Weather Engine Starting," *Aero Digest*,
December 1926; E. J. Demas, "Byrd's North Pole Flight," unpublished
manuscript, 1975, Archives of the American Polar Society; Bernt Balchen,
Come North with Me; *New York Times*.

1. Balchen, *Come North*, 27.
2. *New York Times*, May 2, 1926.
3. REB, North Pole manuscript, May 1926, BP, folder 4271.
4. *New York Times*, June 26, 1926.
5. *Ibid.*
6. Bennett, *Floyd Bennett*, 69.
7. Donald B. MacMillan, *Four Years in the White North*.
8. Goerler, ed., *To the Pole*, 76.
9. Bennett, "Our Flight."
10. E. J. Demas, "Byrd's North Pole Flight."
11. Ellsworth, *Beyond Horizons*, 204.
12. Ibid., 205.
13. REB, North Pole manuscript.
14. Ibid.
15. E. J. Demas to Charles J. V. Murphy, December 22, 1971, Demas Papers, NA, 401–66, box 14.
16. Ibid.
17. Bennett, "Our Flight."

CHAPTER TWENTY-TWO
On the controversy:
Bernt Balchen, *Come North with Me*; E. J. Demas, "Byrd's North Pole Flight,"
Archiesves of the APS; G. H. Liljequist, "Did the 'Josephine Ford' Reach

the North Pole?," *Interavia*, no. 5, 1960; William E. Mollett, "Examination of Byrd Navigation From the Flight to the North Pole," *The Polar Times* 2, no. 8 (Fall–Winter 1996); Richard Montague, *Oceans, Poles and Airmen*; Analysis of Gerald H. Newsom, Gerald H. Newsom to Raimund E. Goerler, July 7, 1977, Ohio State University Archives; J. N. Portney, "The Polar Flap—Byrd's Flight Confirmed," *Navigation* 20, no. 3 (Fall 1973); Joe Portney, *Portney's Ponderables*; Dennis Rawlins, "Byrd's Heroic 1926 North Pole Failure," *Polar Record* 36, no. 196 (January 2000); Finn Ronne, *Antarctica My Destiny*.

1. Howard F. Mason to E. J. Demas, January 25, 1973, Demas papers, NA, 401–16, box 14.
2. *Times*, May 11, 1926.
3. Ellsworth, *Beyond Horizons*, 204.
4. *Corrière della Sera*, trans. Frank Balistrieri, May 11, 1926.
5. *Aftenposten*, May 10, 1926.
6. Michael J. Brennan to REB, June 10, 1926, BP, folder 4252.
7. *New York Times*, May 12, 1926.
8. *New York Times*, May 28, 1926.
9. "Report of Special Committee … ," Appendix B, Goerler, ed., *To the Pole*, 142.
10. *New York Times*, June 30, 1926.
11. Arthur R. Hinks to REB, December 23, 1926, BP, folder 4274.
12. Russell Owen, *South of the Sun*, 152.
13. Undated statements circa 1958 by Michael J. Brennen, E. J. Demas, and George O. Noville, BP, folder 3997.
14. Charles J. V. Murphy to E. J. Demas, undated, circa August 1974, E. J. Demas Papers, NA.
15. *New York Times*, December 15, 1971; *Washington Star*, December 15, 1971.
16. REB to Isaiah Bowman, November 24, 1926, BP, folder 4352.
17. Peter Lewis to Sheldon Bart, January 2 and 4, 2001.
18. Raimund E. Goerler, "Archives in Controversy: The Press, the Documentaries and the Byrd Archives," *American Archivist* 62, no 2 (Fall 1999).
19. Brian Shoemaker, book review, *Polar Times* 2, no. 11 (Spring–Summer 1998).
20. Appendix B, "Navigational Report of Byrd's Flight to the North Pole, 1926," in Goerler, ed., *To the Pole*, 154.
21. Hardy F. LeBel, "Byrd's Flight to the North Pole: Lingering Questions from the Golden Age of Aerial Exploration," paper presented at the ninth

biannual Conference of Historic Aviation Writers, St. Louis, MO, October 24, 1999.

CHAPTER TWENTY-THREE

1. *Alaska Flying*, September 1987, 14.
2. Handwritten notation by P. V. H. Weems on a copy of "The Line of Position: A Short Accurate Method Using Ogura's Altitude Tables and Rust's Modified Azimuth Diagram," undated manuscript, BP, folder 4351.
3. *Fokker Bulletin*, American edition, December 1925, Collection of Elgen M. Long. Emphasis in original.
4. *Aircraft Year Book*, 1926, 126.
5. "Tests Made at Mineola, Long Island, of Commander Byrd's Trimotor Fokker, Standard Wing, Three Whirlwind Motors," March 29 and 30, 1926, Archives of the Naval Historical Center, Naval Aviation History Branch, Washington Navy Yard, Washington, D.C.
6. Bennet, "Our Flight"; and REB, North Pole manuscript, BP, folder 4271.
7. Ibid.
8. *New York Times*, October 8, 1926.
9. "Airplane Motor, Fuel Logbook for Fokker VII 3-Motor Josephine Ford, Byrd Arctic Expedition's Round the States Tour," Archives of the Air Force History Support Office, Bolling AFB, Washington, D.C.
10. *Fokker Bulletin*.
11. Interview with Elgen M. Long, September 19, 2000.
12. Interview with F. Atlee Dodge, November 28, 2000.
13. John D. Anderson Jr., *The Airplane: A History of Its Technology*, 218–22.
14. REB, North Pole manuscript, BP, folder 4271.
15. Liljequist.
16. Ronald C. Sheardown to Sheldon Bart, November 22, 2000.
17. Joseph N. Portney, "The Polar Flap—Byrd's Flight Confirmed," *Navigation*, Fall 1973.
18. "Navigation of Aircraft," technical note no. 154, September 3, 1925, BP, folder 8202.
19. Joseph N. Portney, *Porntey's Ponderables*, 19–30.
20. *New York Times*, October 8, 1926.
21. The certified document is reproduced in Goerler, ed., *To the Pole*, 158.
22. Gerald H. Newsom to Sheldon Bart, August 28, 2001.

CHAPTER TWENTY-FOUR

Byrd on the North Pole flight:
REB diary, North Pole manuscript, Navigation Report, "Straight to the North Pole!," *New York Times Magazine*, June 20, 1936.

Bennett on the North Pole flight:
Floyd Bennett, "Our Flight"; Cora Bennett, *Floyd Bennett*.

1. REB, "Straight to the North Pole!"
2. Bennett, "Our Flight."
3. REB, "Navigational Report."
4. Bennett, "Our Flight."
5. Skyward Questionnaire, BP, folder 4358.
6. REB, "Straight to the North Pole!"
7. REB, North Pole Manuscript, BP, folder 4271.
8. Ibid.
9. Quoted in Bennett, *Floyd Bennett*, 85.
10. REB, "Straight to the North Pole!"
11. Quoted in Bennett, *Floyd Bennett*, 87.
12. Amundsen and Ellsworth, *The First Crossing of the Polar Sea*, 120.
13. Ibid.
14. Balchen, *Come North with Me*, 44.
15. Demas, "Byrd's North Pole Flight."
16. E. J. Demas to Charles J. V. Murphy, December 22, 1971.
17. *New York Times*, May 11, 1926.
18. Ibid.

CHAPTER TWENTY-FIVE

Byrd/media radiograms:
BP, folder 4307–4309.

North Pole honors and homecoming:
New York Times.

Byrd/Green correspondence:
BP, folders 1785, 4272–4273, and 4358.

1. Edwin Markham, "To the Top of the World," *New York Times*, June 26, 1926.

2. REB to David Lawrence, May 10, 1926, BP, folder 4307.
3. *New York Times*, May 17, 1926.
4. *New York Times*, July 1, 1926.
5. REB to Patrick H. Drewry, December 21, 1926, BP, folder 4259.
6. BP, folder 4259.
7. REB to Harry C. Wilder, September 1, 1926, BP, folder 4328.
8. REB to George Gregory, January 1, 1927, BP, folder 4317.
9. Marie Peary [Stafford] to REB, January 27, 1927, BP, folder 4317.
10. Fitzhugh Green to REB, July 28, 1926, BP, folder 1785.
11. REB, Spectacular Flights manuscript, BP, folder 4328.

CHAPTER TWENTY-SIX

Byrd transatlantic flight planning:
BP, folder 4344; Skyward Questionnaire, BP, folder 4358; Fitzhugh Green,
"The Big Crisis," unpublished manuscript, Fitzhugh Green Papers,
Georgetown University Archives, Box 7, folder 2.

Test flight and crash of the *America*:
REB to chief of the Bureau of Aeronautics, April 28, 1927, NA, Records of the
Bureau of Aeronautics, Box 4076; George O. Noville, "High, Wide and Blind,"
unidentified magazine, circa 1958, collection of Leverette S. Byrd; Skyward
Questionnaire, BP, folder 4358.

1. REB, "Byrd Tells Why Men Explore Polar Regions," *New York Times*,
    June 27, 1926.
2. *New York Times*, February 23, 1927.
3. Raymond Orteig to REB, May 14, 1926, BP, folder 4311.
4. REB to Rodman Wanamaker, August 2, 1926, BP, folder 4327.
5. H. E. Hartney to REB, November 15, 1926, BP, folder 4343.
6. Skyward Questionnaire, BP, folder 4358.
7. Hegener, *Fokker—The Man and the Aircraft*, 109.
8. Floyd Bennett to REB, December 30, 1926, BP, folder 4343.
9. Fitzhugh Green, "The Big Crisis."
10. Ibid.
11. *New York Times*, April 13, 1927.
12. *New York Times*, April 16, 1927.
13. Fokker and Gould, *Flying Dutchman*, 256.
14. Skyward Questionnaire, BP, folder 4358.

15. George O. Noville, "High, Wide and Blind."
16. *New York Herald Tribune*, April 17, 1927.
17. *New York Times*, April 17, 1927.
18. Skyward Questionnaire, BP, folder 4358.
19. REB, statement, circa 1928, BP, folder 3493.
20. Lloyd Morris and Kendall Smith, *Ceiling Unlimited*, 255.
21. Grover A. Whalen, *Mr. New York*, 109–10.

CHAPTER TWENTY-SEVEN
1. *New York Times*, May 1, 1927.
2. Noel Davis to REB, January 7, 1927.
3. *New York Times*, April 25, 1927.
4. *The Lucky Bag*, U.S. Naval Academy, 1914.
5. *New York Times*, April 27, 1927.
6. *New York Times*, May 1, 1927.
7. George Carroll, "Wildest of the Early Birds," *American Mercury*, September 1955.
8. Whalen, 129.
9. REB, statement, circa 1928, BP, folder 3493.
10. *New York Times*, April 21, 1927.
11. REB to Rodman Wanamaker, May 11, 1927, BP, folder 4344.
12. Whalen, 107.
13. Ibid., 110.
14. Charles A. Lindbergh, *The Spirit of St. Louis*, 160.
15. *New York Times*, May 13, 1927.
16. *New York Times*, May 21, 1927.
17. Ibid.
18. REB, statement, May 21, 1927, BP, folder 45344.
19. *New York Times*, June 5, 1927.
20. E. J. Demas, unpublished manuscript, E. J. Demas Papers, RG 401/66, NA.
21. *New York Times* June 5, 1927.
22. REB, *Skyward*, 231.
23. Fokker and Gould, *Flying Dutchman*, 260.
24. Balchen, *Come North*, 94–95.
25. George O. Noville, transatlantic narrative, part V, *New York Herald Tribune*, July 6, 1927.
26. Fuel consumption, May 31 and June 2, 1927, BP, folder 4343.

27. REB to Haines et al., September 15, 1934, BP, folder 5498.
28. REB to Joe Barnum, June 14, 1927.
29. REB to Grover Whalen, June 3, 1927, BP, folder 4344.
30. Russell Owen, "First Ocean Air Liner Off Slowly with a Burden of 17,621 Pounds," *New York Times*, June 30, 1927.
31. Joseph Appel, *The Business Biography of John Wanamaker*, 172, 175.
32. George O. Noville, "Transatlantic Narrative," part VI, *New York Herald Tribune*, July 7, 1927.
33. *New York Times*, July 19, 1927.
34. Owen.
35. Noville.

CHAPTER TWENTY-EIGHT

Flight of the *America*:
REB diary and flight log, Goerler, ed., *To the Pole*; REB transatlantic narrative, *New York Times*, July 2–7, 1927; REB National Geographic manuscript, BP, folder 4348; George O. Noville transatlantic narrative, *New York Herald Tribune*, July 2–7, 1927; Bernt Balchen transatlantic narrative, *New York Times*, July 5, 1927; Charles J. V. Murphy, "Shall We Fly the Atlantic," *Harper's*, July 1928; Charles J. V. Murphy, "The Flight of the America," *Collier's*, August 11, 1928; George O. Noville, "High, Wide and Blind," unidentified magazine, circa 1957–1958, collection of Leverette S. Byrd; Bernt Balchen, *Come North with Me*.

Comparative weather conditions on 1927 transatlantic flights:
Logan C. Ramsey and Earle H. Kinkaid, "Analysis of Weather Conditions on Recent Transatlantic Flights," *Aero Digest*, October 1927.

Development of instrument flying:
James H. "Jimmy" Doolittle, with Carroll V. Glines, *I Could Never Be So Lucky Again*, chapter 6.

1. *New York Times*, June 29, 1927.
2. *New York Times*, July 1, 1927.
3. REB, "Transatlantic Narrative," *New York Times*, part III, July 3, 1927.
4. Willis Ray Gregg, "Meteorology of the North Atlantic and Trans-Atlantic Flight," *Aviation*, August 1, 1927.
5. Byrd.

6. George O. Noville, "High, Wide and Blind," unidentified magazine, circa 1957–58, collection of Leverette S. Byrd.

7. Noville, "Transatlantic Narrative," part V, *New York Herald Tribune*, July 6, 1927.

8. Francis and Katherine Drake, "Bernt Balchen—Viking of the Air," *Reader's Digest*, January 1953.

9. George O. Noville, undated statement, circa 1953, BP, folder 3996.

10. Charles J. V. Murphy, "The Flight of the America," *Collier's*, August 11, 1928.

11. Quoted in Montague, *Oceans, Poles and Airmen*, 291.

12. "Transatlantic Narrative," parts I and IV, *New York Herald Tribune*, July 2 and 5, 1927.

13. Noville, "High, Wide and Blind."

14. *New York Times*, July 1, 1927.

15. Noville, "High, Wide and Blind."

16. "Transatlantic Narrative," part I, *New York Herald Tribune*, July 2, 1927.

17. Balchen, *Come North*, 114.

18. *New York Times*, July 4, 1927.

19. Ibid.

20. *New York Times*, July 19, 1927.

21. REB, *Skyward*, 265.

22. Balchen, *Come North*, 115.

23. Fitzhugh Green, "Memorandum for Commander Byrd," April 15, 1927, BP, folder 1767.

24. *New York Times*, July 19, 1927.

25. Interview with Robert and Katharine Byrd Breyer, May 9, 2001.

26. Norman D. Vaughan with Cecil B. Murphey, *With Byrd at the Bottom of the World*, 88–89.

27. *Private Pilot Manual*, 11-19–11-20.

28. *New York Times*, July 19, 1927.

29. REB, manuscript, *National Geographic*, BP, folder 4348.

30. Eveready Hour, April 10, 1928, BP, folder 4387.

31. *New York Herald Tribune*, July 1, 1927.

32. Ibid.

33. Ibid.

34. *New York Times*, July 19, 1927.

35. Noville, "Transatlantic Narrative," part II, *New York Herald Tribune*, July 3, 1927.

36. Ibid.
37. *New York Herald Tribune*, July 4, 1927.
38. *New York Times*, June 29, 1927.
39. *New York Herald Tribune*, July 4, 1927.
40. Noville, "Transatlantic Narrative," part II, *New York Herald Tribune*, July 3, 1927.
41. Bert Acosta, "The Sky's the Limit," *New York World*, May 6, 1928.
42. Skyward Questionnaire, BP, folder 4358.
43. *New York Times*, July 2, 1927.
44. Marie A. Byrd to REB, letter no. 2, circa July 1927, BP, folder 65.
45. Marie A. Byrd to REB, letter no. 1, circa July 1927, BP, folder 65.
46. Skyward Questionnaire, BP, folder 4358.

INDEX